D1560038

IN SEARCH
OF THE
MOUNT
CLEVELAND
FIVE

Terry G. Kennedy

ISBN: 978-0-9982-5090-8 (sc)
ISBN: 978-0-9982-5091-5 (hc)
ISBN: 978-0-9982-5092-2 (e)

Library of Congress Control Number: 2017905195

publisher name: Bridger Ridge Rewriters Guild
Bozeman, MT 59718
publisher legal name: Terry G. Kennedy

Lulu Publishing Services rev. date: 04/16/2018

Jim Kanzler, 1977. Photo by the author.

Dedication

To my friend, Jim Kanzler.

To my mother and father, Betty and R. Glenn Kennedy.

To Jerry, Hal and Jean Kanzler.

To the memory of the Mount Cleveland Five.

Contents

Acknowledgements

Writing and assembling this book did not happen without the contributions of others. I am very grateful to the following people who offered their expertise to help move this book forward: Steve Jackson, Museum of the Rockies and Montana State University, for preparing the photographs, many of which he took; Kathleen Callahan, Montana State University Library, for the first read-through while the book was five chapters longer; Saryta Rodriguez, Founding Editor of Brave New Publishing, for the great job of editing the manuscript; Pat Callis, Professor of Chemistry at Montana State University, for writing the Foreword; Graham "Gray" Thompson, Professor of Geology Emeritus at the University of Montana and Brian Kennedy (no relation) for reading and making suggestions for the final manuscript.

I want to extend special thanks to Don Anderson, brother of James Anderson, for sharing the photos recovered from the camera that Jim carried on Mount Cleveland; and to the families of Clare Pogreba and Mark Levitan for sharing photographs.

I would like to thank everyone who gave me encouragement to write this book—climbers and non-climbers alike—knowing that the registry would be too long to include everyone on this page. The list would have to start with: Jim Emerson, Barb "The Barbarian" Belt, the late Jim Kanzler, Larry Wilson, the late Carol (Martin) McGrath (Ray Martin's sister), Jamie Kanzler, Lindalee (Kanzler) Cleveland, the late Jean Kanzler, Ed Leritz, Larry Livingood and Dezri Rochin. Thank you to the helpful professionals at Lulu Publishing Services.

I want to express my eternal gratitude to my late mother and father for never discouraging me to follow my path, and to acknowledge my brother, Dan; my sister, Merry Kay; and my daughter, Lindsay.

Most of all, I want to thank my wife and life-partner, Diane Kennedy, for putting up with the drawn-out process of my wandering through the chapter re-writes and telling her the same stories over and over.

Thanks to the rivers and the wind, the rocks, the mountains and the trees.

Foreword

by Pat Callis

My introduction to some of the spirited group of young climbers that would eventually become known as the "Mount Cleveland Five" happened on my first visit to Bozeman in February 1968. I was interviewing for a faculty position at Montana State University, and was treated to an afternoon of skiing at Bridger Bowl. My host, Ed Anacker, informed me that he would be leaving early; when the lifts closed, he advised, I should go to the Ski Patrol room, where a group of climbers would be waiting to give me a ride back to town. The warmth of those young men, their passion for climbing, and their animated and joyous conversation during that ride into town still reverberates in my mind. It was nice to know that if I took the job, there would be knowledgeable and passionate climbers nearby.

Soon after taking the job at MSU, two of the Five—Clare Pogreba and Jerry Kanzler—invited me to join them on a climb in the Humbugs early that fall. We completed a new route, eventually named Gandalf, on the Wedge on which they had been working. During that climb, these new friends informed me that they were the ones who had given me a ride from the ski area the previous February. They also mentioned they were part of a group of climbers known as the Wool Socks Club. When I drove my wife and two-year-old daughter into Bozeman for the first time, I had noticed an alluring fin of rock high above Gallatin Canyon: Spare Rib. A short time after Gandalf, I recruited Jerry's brother, Jim, to join me on the first ascent of Spare Rib. The next spring—on Mother's Day, I am embarrassed to admit, Jerry and I made the first ascent of a route we called Mother's Day.

The following fall, Clare's indomitable spirit and leadership became evident in two ways. He had the awareness and foresight to be the first in the Bozeman-Butte area to purchase a pair of the revolutionary Chouinard rigid-platform, chrome-molly crampons, a tool that became instrumental in the inception and rise of the new sport of water-fall ice climbing. Then, he took us all by surprise when he proudly announced that he had flooded the Montana Tech football stadium grandstand during a period of cold weather, thereby creating a magnificent 45° sheet of ice. He called me, requesting that Peter Lev and I come over to Butte and try it out before it melted.

I had met Peter, an internationally known mountaineer, guide, and avalanche forecaster, in Yosemite on one occasion. I was delighted to find that he was in Bozeman upon my arrival, employed at the University as the Instructor of a novel course called Ski Mountaineering for Engineers. Jim Anderson and Mark Levitan were enrolled in the course—two more of the ill-fated party, who had been linked to the three Wool Socks members through Peter and myself. Peter and I were expected to perform well on this modest sheet of ice, and were definitely nervous; the eyes of the Wool Sox Club collectively watched as we, one at a time, cautiously made our way up, not wanting to make a careless slip in front of our young admirers.

The weather during the autumn of 1969 was an anomaly, and directly responsible for the tragedy that inspired this book—not because it was bad in the usual sense, but because it was good. So good, in fact, that we—Peter, myself, and the "Mount Cleveland Five" felt entitled to make weekly plans for new winter-condition ascents virtually every weekend, well into December. Did we develop a cavalier attitude? Possibly. There was so little snow, and even when we were at higher elevations, we encountered no avalanche conditions.

We accomplished a Thanksgiving vacation ascent of Mt. Wilbur in Glacier Park, and possibly the first winter ascent of the famous Big Couloir of Lone Mountain. Ray Martin—Clare's tall, inseparable friend—drove (with lots of pushing by the rest of us) his beat-up old pickup to the top of Andesite Mountain, where we bivouacked in the abandoned fire lookout seventy feet above the ground. Lone and Andesite Mountains were to become the Big Sky Ski Area a few years later. Just before Christmas, Jerry and I were in the Tetons with Peter and internationally known alpinist, George Lowe.

I will never forget Clare Pogreba's beaming face standing at my doorstep in bright morning sunshine the day after Christmas 1969, as I handed him my climbing skins, having decided not to join them on Mount Cleveland in order to spend time with my family and rest following the strenuous adventure the preceding week in the Tetons. We joked that the skins would never be put on the skis because so little snow had fallen.

I was not too worried, because Clare had hinted that they probably would not attempt the north face; they just wanted to hang out near it. I understood the strong desire to do this, having had this kind of relationship with the east face of Mount Index, near Seattle. This is a kind of savoring of anticipated adventure well before one is ready to make a serious effort.

Nevertheless, I recall my parting words were to beware of avalanches. It was more of a fatherly thing to say than an informed bit of advice from an experienced mountaineer. Having moved from the West Coast barely a year before, I knew nothing of the immense danger signaled by a few inches of powdery snow lying innocently at the base of a high peak. Even Peter and Jim, who were earning their livings protecting the public from avalanche danger, seemed unconcerned.

There are as many "reasons" given for why people climb mountains and crags as there are climbers. In the late 1960s two prerequisites were a love of being outdoors, close to nature, and love of athletic activity somewhat more intense than hiking. Beyond these, what takes a person into serious mountaineering is nearly always quite personal. In the case of the author, it was ironically a tragic mountaineering accident involving these five young Montana climbers, who were barely older than Terry was at the time. Terry was drawn irreversibly into the mystic of mountaineering that lies deep in the soul of all true climbers. He embarked on a life that was in many respects similar to that of most climbers, but with a unique focus: to complete the dream of his young friend and his comrades, as a kind of living monument to the five who perished.

When Terry appeared on my doorstep one day, on his first trip to the Tetons, before enrolling at Montana State University in June of 1973, I had no inkling of the quest that burned at his core. Over several years, we became good friends and climbed together frequently. I became increasingly impressed with his climbing skills and savvy. Somewhere along the line, family and profession pulled me away from the extreme alpinism that had been an occasional—but important—part of my life during the previous decade, and I saw Terry take my place as the companion of Jim Kanzler. Terry completed his long journey to the North face of Mount Cleveland, fittingly with Jim, the Wool Sox brother/comrade who had been so greatly scarred by the loss of those who died there.

This book is the story of that journey, filled with poignant passages relating to the tragedy. But it is also a chronicle of the often-hilarious antics of the Dirty Sox Club, the semi-underground association of climbers, which succeeded the original Wool Sox Club.

Patrik Callis
Professor of Chemistry
Montana State University
Bozeman, Montana
September 27, 2014

Preface

—Writing about one's self and one's friends comes with risks—just like climbing. I have accepted most and walked away from a few. —

Two days after Christmas in 1969, five young, forward-thinking mountain climbers set out to climb Mount Cleveland, the highest peak in Glacier National Park. Their interest was the previously unclimbed north face, a project that had been in the works for several years. It had to be confronted during the winter, for some reason. Perhaps, it was the influence of the conquest of a *directissima* on the Eiger's north face during the winter of 1966, when American alpinist John Harlin was killed. The Mount Cleveland Five arranged boat transportation from the Canadian end of Waterton Lake to the American end, just ahead of ice-over to begin their journey. They were never seen alive again.

The Mount Cleveland tragedy will remain one of most enigmatic mountaineering accidents in the United States. It was not unlike the disappearance of the Edmond Fitzgerald into the stormy waters of Lake Superior five years later. In both cases, no one returned to tell what had happened.

We know that the Mount Cleveland Five were caught in an avalanche on the west face of the mountain after placing a base camp under the north face, confounding the search effort. Tangible evidence remained hidden for five days into the search—and then only a few items were discovered scattered over the 3,000-foot-long avalanche path before the next wave of winter storms moved into the region and the search had to be abandoned until the following June. Circumstances suggested that the fatal mishap occurred on December 29—but we don't know for sure. The bodies were recovered seven months later.

McKay Jenkins wrote about the search and recovery mission of the

Mount Cleveland Five in *The White Death: Tragedy and Heroism in an Avalanche Zone*, (Anchor Books, 2000). *In Search of the Mount Cleveland Five* picks up the saga just after the search begins and chronicles the next 22 years in the shadow of Mount Cleveland, most of it with Jim Kanzler, a brother and climbing partner of the missing five.

In Search of the Mount Cleveland Five is not intended to be a thorough history of climbing in Montana. I will leave that for someone else to write. This is simply a book that I have been writing for a long time, which began as a collection of climbing stories, and then morphed into a larger tale through the common thread of the Mount Cleveland tragedy.

If there was such a thing as a "golden age" of technical alpine climbing in Montana, then it began with the likes of Clare Pogreba, Ray Martin, Jerry Kanzler, Jim Anderson and Mark Levitan—all college students who were raised in Montana, ages 18-22, who died on Mount Cleveland. Their contemporaries were an expanding close-knit group emerging throughout Montana in the 1960s and 1970s.

Montana climbers in those days were by and large self-taught. There were influences from other well-known climbing figures in this country such as Royal Robbins, Yvon Chouinard, Tom Frost, Chuck Pratt, Layton Kor, Fred Beckey and others; and famous European climbers such as Joe Brown, Tom Patey, Maurice Herzog, Hermann Buhl, Don Whillans, Dougal Haston and Reinhold Messner to name a few.

In 1968, two years before the Mount Cleveland tragedy, there came a handful of "older climbers" in their later twenties and early thirties who arrived at the universities in Montana with PhDs, bound for professorships. The influences of Pat Callis (MSU) and Gray Thompson (UM) came from opposite coasts, and not only taught Chemistry and Geology respectively, but lent their climbing expertise to the upstarts. There was also Peter Lev who was a professional guide in the Tetons and taught a winter mountaineering class at MSU the year leading up to the tragedy. I came onto the scene a few years later, tumbling over the wake and into the slipstream.

Were the Montana climbers on the national forefront of climbing in the 1970s? Not exactly. It could be said that Montana, as an arena for climbing and those who engaged the pursuit, were about ten years behind the other climbing hubs in the country. The golden age of Yosemite climbing began in the late 1950s and continued through the 1960s. Colorado's golden age of climbing occurred over a similar time line.

The development of high-level alpinism and the successful pioneering of significant routes in the Big Sky Country began to take place in the early 1970s.

Three years after the Mount Cleveland tragedy—almost to the day—20-year-old Brian Leo and 18-year-old Doug McCarty made a bold winter climb of the north face of Granite Peak (12,799 feet), Montana's highest mountain, influenced by the audacity of other young climbers taking on Mount Cleveland's big face in the winter.

Leo and McCarty were engulfed by a fast moving Arctic storm as they neared the top and the pair literally climbed for their lives, bivouacking without sleeping bags on the summit on New Year's Eve, 1972. The storm lasted all night and into the next day. They had only a simple nylon shell to crawl into and a bag of lemon drops with which to endure 15 hours of shivering, pitch-black, raging torture as McCarty's feet froze solid.

Six thousand feet below, at a small hydroelectric station from where the long, two-day approach to the base of the mountain started, the temperature that night was said to have been 25 degrees below zero Fahrenheit with the wind exceeding 40 m.p.h.

Leo and McCarty lived only by great survival instinct. After they down climbed off of the upper mountain, they were assisted back to civilization for three days by other members of their party who had attempted the standard east ridge route and turned back in the storm.

McCarty miraculously kept every black toe—thanks to physician and mountaineer Warren Bowman, MD of Billings, who partnered with Chad Chadwick on a direct line on Granite Peak's north face in July 1971. It is hard to imagine that Brian Leo, who led the steep snow-plastered rock to the summit ridge in horrendous conditions as McCarty's eyes lids froze open, had no frost bite in spite of wearing steel-shanked single boots all night. To this day, the first winter ascent of the north face of Granite Peak has to be considered the greatest mountaineering epic without a death to have occurred within the borders of Montana.

Callis, Thompson, Leo, Hank Abrons and Chadwick climbed the southwest face of Upper Doublet in the Beartooth Mountains during the summer of 1972. This was thought to be the first grade VI route in Montana. McCarty and David Vaughn made contributions on previous attempts. Jim Emerson and Craig Zaspel added a second route on Upper Doublet in 1975.

Chadwick and Jim Kanzler placed the first route on Silver Pillar, a 1,000-foot-high rock cylinder in the Beartooths in 1973, with a bivouac in hammocks. Leo and I added the second route in 1975, after a fall and near double fatality detailed in Chapter Ten, "Bombs Away, Sir".

Gray Thompson had already pioneered the steep, avalanche-swept American Direct route on the 10,000-foot-high south face of Denali in 1967, before moving to Montana. He, Dave Seidman, Denny Ebrel, and Roman

Laba were trapped high on the face for 13 days in Sears and Roebuck tents while one of the deadliest storms in mountaineering history killed seven other mountaineers elsewhere on the mountain. The Dartmouth-Harvard team persevered and reached the summit. Gray continued a career of notable first ascents and repeats around the world.

Pat Callis recorded first ascents in Yosemite and the Canadian Rockies, and first winter ascents in the Cascades of Washington and Oregon. He was a key figure in developing frozen waterfall climbing in Hyalite Canyon near Bozeman, refining some of the techniques. Peter Lev pioneered routes in the Tetons and was a member of several expeditions to the Himalayas. Callis and I climbed the first route on the southeast face of East Kahiltna Peak in 1993 (a satellite peak to Denali), a year after the conclusion of *In Search of the Mount Cleveland Five*.

Washington, California, Colorado, and the east coast had greater numbers of talented, ambitious climbers who succeeded on more noteworthy rock climbs and technical alpine routes during the 1960s and 1970s. Word got back to Montana that a group of leading Colorado climbers described Montana as "the backwater of American alpinism."

The colorful epithet reached Jim Kanzler and me as we were making our bids for the overlooked faces in Glacier, with our eyes cast even further north. We joked about it.

"Hey, do you wanna take the ol' canoe up the slough this weekend?" Jim smirked one day." "I've got my eye on another line in the (Gallatin) Canyon."

"Okay, maybe we oughta take a paddle this time," I replied.

"Yeah well, I thought we probably oughta take two."

Montana really didn't paddle its way to the national alpine forefront until Jack Tackle succeeded on his mammoth route up The Isis Face (which he named after the Egyptian Goddess) to the south buttress of Denali with Dave Stutzman in 1982. They elected not to climb the remaining 4,000 feet to the summit. Jack continued a long career of first ascents in Alaska and Asia. It came as a brutal shock when Dave was killed in an avalanche while alpine skiing at Big Sky, Montana, the following winter, where he was a member of the professional ski patrol.

Alex Lowe burst upon the scene in the early 1980s—inexhaustible and talented beyond measure; raised in Missoula, educated in Bozeman. He pushed the standards above the clouds—not just in Montana, but also in the mountains around the world. His climbing achievements have become a legacy for climbers and alpinists of my generation and those to follow. *In Search of the Mount Cleveland Five* is what happened before that.

Introduction

There was a time, when I was very young, when I thought all kids grew up with a creek or a river to explore and mountains to climb within view of their houses—where they could flash mirrors back to their mothers, who watched through binoculars from their front yards. At an early age, my father instilled in me the rudiments of good judgment as I explored the Flathead River bottom near Columbia Falls in northwest Montana—sometimes with neighborhood pals, or my younger brother, Dan, or my dog, Jack.

For a while, I thought I still had a chance to be a Big League baseball player— even though I sat on the bench through most of my Little League days.

I had no idea that the older kids, who I looked up to as role models, would die before they grew up and had families of their own.

By age 15, I understood that life could end tragically at any time and, if there was a grail out there, it was time to start looking for it.

For the better part of five decades, I thought the most important thing I could do was to climb: rocks, mountains or ice—whatever was in season. The mountains of Glacier National Park lay just beyond the Flathead River and the mountains that rimmed the Flathead Valley. I found my way into Glacier's mountains as a teenager, knowing that most of the steeper faces were still unclimbed.

I held the notion that if my climbing partners and I were careful—and lucky—we would climb together until we were old men, barely able to ascend a hill, but we would still endeavor a hike with enthusiasm, because we loved climbing and each other's company so much. By the time I was in my later fifties, it was apparent that life wasn't necessarily going to turn out that way, either.

One autumn day in 2010, Jim Kanzler, my most influential climbing partner, who grew up in Columbia Falls, Montana, a couple of blocks from where I did, called me at my home in Bozeman, Montana, from Jackson

Hole, Wyoming. He asked me if I had finished the book yet. No, I told him, but I was getting close.

"You've been writing it for about ten years now," he pointed out.

"Actually, more like 40," I conceded.

"Well, don't wait too long...." Was Jim foreshadowing? After his father's suicide and the loss of his brother, I had always worried that he might follow the same route. I felt a sense of urgency—an urgency about which I could do nothing.

My wife, Diane, and I invited Jim to Bozeman for Christmas that year, and I was overjoyed when he accepted. By the time he arrived on Christmas Eve, Diane was in the fourth day of a nasty viral illness and I was coming down with it. The three of us drank coffee and ate the Christmas cookies Diane had made. I then persuaded Jim not to stay with us, since he was sure to get sick, too. He left with a peculiar look of disappointment I had never observed on his face before, and he spent that night with his mother, now in assisted-living not far from Bozeman. It was the last time I saw him.

Four months later, on April 18, 2011, I was at my keyboard writing when my cell phone rang. It was Dougal McCarty, one of our colorful climbing partners.

"Kennedy..." his voice halted.

"Yeah?"

"Kanzler shot himself."

"Oh-h, No-o!" I tried to persuade myself that I misunderstood what Dougal had just said.

"Is he...is he...dead?"

"Yeah..."

Jim Kanzler's younger brother, Jerry, was named after a soldier who was killed in the battle of Okinawa during World War II. Jerry was a cheerful, extraordinarily talented, upstart climber with an otherworldly presence, not easily forgotten. He once told his mother that the north face of Mount Cleveland silently beckoned to him. He referred to mountains in the feminine the way sailors refer to their vessels.

Jim and Jerry Kanzler became instrumental in a push to be the first climbers to tackle the largest rock face in Glacier National Park— thought to be the highest in the contiguous United States— while they were still teenagers. Jim certainly would have been with them, but he had just taken a job as a professional ski patrolman at Bridger Bowl, just outside Bozeman, where he and his young wife had a one-year-old son. He needed to work, so he bowed out of the ill-fated expedition at the last minute.

In Search of the Mount Cleveland Five is a true story that takes place between 1970 and 1992, beginning with the Mount Cleveland tragedy and charges forward through a journey inspired and troubled by an avalanche that never receded from the rear view mirror. I was the compulsive one, on a mission, and Jim Kanzler kept me off balance with spontaneity and an air of triviality toward life's endeavors.

We climbed the north faces of Mount Cleveland and Mount Siyeh and other firsts in Glacier and southwestern Montana together. Between us, we climbed routes in Yosemite, the Tetons, the Canadian Rockies and Alaska, complete with mishaps and close calls that could have gone either way.

Jim had long careers as a mountain guide in the Tetons and as a professional ski patrolman at Bridger Bowl, Big Sky and Jackson Hole. He was the first Director of the Ski Patrol in Big Sky, mapping Lone Mountain's terrain and developing avalanche control strategies the year before the ski area opened. At Jackson Hole, he became the lead Avalanche Hazard Forecaster for the resort and the Bridger Teton National Forest.

I had short careers as a climbing ranger and a mountain guide. I was hired as Glacier Park Seasonal Ranger from 1981-83 and worked under Bob Frauson, a veteran of combat in World War II, who orchestrated the Mount Cleveland search and recovery mission in 1970. The lionized Hudson Bay District Ranger was Jim Kanzler's and my nemesis for a time. A couple of years later, I became a climbing ranger in Rocky Mountain National Park and made a patrol up The Diamond (face) of Longs Peak with Billy Westbay, who had been one of the greats of Yosemite climbing in the 1970s. I gave up considering a career with the Park Service and instead took a job with the Colorado Mountain School as a guide and climbing instructor in the autumn of 1985. I co-guided an expedition to Mount Logan, the highest peak in Canada, in the Yukon Territory; but the wages I made were bread line and I was nearly homeless. The climbing lifestyle did not lend itself to a career of public school teaching; nor did it prepare me for marriage while I was still in my twenties. I eventually went to physical therapy school.

The saga ends in the Alaska Range on East Kahiltna Peak connected to Denali, with a third generation of Kanzler— Jim's son, Jamie— on an unstable snowpack and history on the verge of repeating itself.

In Search of the Mount Cleveland Five is a coming-of-age story of mountain climbing and how those devoted to this passion revere those who have gone before them, striving to be like their predecessors—catching glimpses of themselves along the way.

Jerry Kanzler en route to Mount Cleveland.
Photo courtesy of Lindalee Cleveland.

Jim Anderson, age 16, on the summit
of Mount Cleveland, 1967.
Photo courtesy of Don Anderson.

Mark Levitan from his 1969-70
Bridger Bowl season ski pass.
Photo courtesy of Robert Levitan.

Ray Martin, circa 1969.
Photo courtesy of Lindalee Cleveland.

Clare Pogreba, 1969. Photo courtesy
of Janet (Pogreba) Long.

CHAPTER I

The Mount Cleveland Five

January 4, 1970

The lugs of the dual tires on the old diesel bus made a buzzing sound against the pavement. I sat next to a window near the front of the team bus, a row behind the coaches. I preferred to sit alone to contemplate the Montana countryside as it passed by. Most of the other boys on the wrestling team entertained themselves with a poker game at the back of the bus returning from a three-day road trip that began the day after New Year's.

The bus groaned up a steep grade on U.S. Highway 93 to the top of a hill 30 miles north of Missoula, on the Flathead Indian Reservation. It then rolled east toward the Mission Mountains, rising 6,000 feet above the Mission Valley. The sky had become a gray shroud obscuring the range, forming a line of demarcation just above the valley floor and casting a sense of gloom. I rested my head against the seat and stared out of the window, disappointed that I couldn't see the mountains.

The bus leaned into a sweeping 90-degree curve at St. Ignatius and rumbled north toward Flathead Lake, Columbia Falls and the mountains of Glacier National Park. We entered a snowstorm and the monotonous drone morphed into a soft hum as the highway became snow-packed.

My life was about to change direction, too. What was happening behind the veil at that moment, in the mountain chain a little further north, would define me for years to come.

Home was an hour away.

I grew up in the small town of Columbia Falls in northwest Montana, the son of a World War II veteran. My paternal grandfather was a veteran of the First World War and worked long shifts seven days a week in the copper-smelting mill in Anaconda, Montana, during the Great Depression.

My maternal great-grandfather drove cattle from Texas to Montana, earning the nickname Tex Terry.

I was a boy with many heroes—the most revered of whom were local high school basketball players. During the 1964-65 boy's high school basketball season, the Columbia Falls Wildcats ended the 56 game win streak of the largest high school in the state—Missoula Sentinel—in the Columbia Falls gym. The whole town cheered madly. The Wildcats went on to lose the state tournament finals by just one point. Ralph Johnson was named "Montana Big 31" Coach of the Year. The Johnsons lived two houses away. Ralph's sons and my younger brother, Dan, were pals.

After the snow melted away and the yellow bells and shooting stars had blossomed in May, Dan and I and the rest of the neighborhood boys took to the empty field beyond our house and emulated Mickey Mantle, Roger Maris, Willie Mays, Juan Marichal and Sandy Kofax. Teams were chosen, uniforms were made from white T-shirts, and a makeshift backstop was erected.

A good day was defined by a run scored in Little League or a brook trout caught in nearby Crystal Creek. An exciting day might include a snow cave dug in a drift in the backyard, or the reenactment of D-Day on the shore of the Flathead River—a short hike from home, through the river bottom, with the neighborhood platoon advancing swiftly along the gravel bar, toy weapons blazing. We proudly wore the stripes and ribbons our fathers earned in World War II and our mothers had sewn to the sleeves of homemade battle uniforms. A great day was a 12-pound bull trout hooked and landed on the same gravel bar after a sleep-out in a backyard.

I wanted to be on the high school basketball team and make that driving lay-up with seconds on the clock, or swish the long set shot from the corner. I wanted to ride on the Columbia Falls fire truck, celebrating success at the state tournament.

My father was five-foot-four and my mother was an even five-feet tall. I weighed 86 pounds and was five-foot-one when I started high school in 1968. I held out hopes for a growth spurt that never came. I was not a particularly fast sprinter nor a good jumper nor a great shot. I was cut early in basketball tryouts in October. My dreams of being like my childhood heroes were dashed. That was on a Friday.

The next morning, I went hunting with my best friend, Jack. I took my single-shot 20-gauge shotgun and we walked down to the Flathead River. Jack was a Collie mix with a full, white cape. As usual, we didn't bag anything; but it didn't matter. Just being by the river, experiencing the power of all that water flowing by from the mountains of Glacier National

Park and the Bob Marshall Wilderness, captivated me. I sat on the bank listening to the subtle sound the river made with one hand on my shotgun and the other kept warm in Jack's thick mane. The whispered "awe" of the river and the quiet anticipation that a duck might fly by in range were more engaging than a noisy gym with the bumping and shoving of basketball, anyway.

I picked a slab of cottonwood bark out of the shifting, water-rounded rocks. It was dry and weathered, having traveled down the river from some place far upstream. I felt the stringy, papery inner surface and the gnarled texture of the outer surface— like the back of a crocodile. I imagined an ancient tablet with inscriptions of a strange alphabet on it. I stood up and flung it as far into the river as I could. The slab skipped once, making a meager splash and leaving no ripples, the current being much too swift. The tablet was quickly ushered away, bobbing and twisting. It turned with the river into the next bend and disappeared in less than a minute into choppy ripples. With it went frustration and disappointment. I needed a new dream. Being a Daniel Boone or a John Colter seemed all right to me.

At home in Columbia Falls, after the wrestling road trip, I gave my mom and dad the details of my matches.

"You see," my mother, Betty, said, "you can do it! Your dad and I knew you could…." Then her face drew long.

"You know," she went on, "there are some young men lost in Glacier Park."

"Oh? I hope they find them, " I said, my mind shifting from wondering how I might win a school letter.

"One of them is Jerry Kanzler." There was concern in her voice.

"Jerry Kanzler?" Jerry had been in my sister, Merry Kay's class, and she had had a crush on Jerry. He had been the Den Chief in the Cub Scouts den I belonged to until the Kanzler family moved away a few years ago. Jerry Kanzler stood up for me on a number of occasions, when my stature made me a convenient subject for teasing. I liked the guy.

Jerry was a role model. He interacted well with younger kids and was polite to adults. He was energetic, always wanting to do something. He was tall—or at least, he seemed tall. He had thick black hair and radiant brown eyes. He always seemed happy. Jerry had a brother, Jim, who was three years older. They were the first kids in Columbia Falls to cut their hair like the Beatles. My sister told me privately that she had danced with Jerry at a school dance.

"Jerry and four other boys are lost on the highest mountain in Glacier Park. They were trying to climb a side of a mountain that had never been climbed before. The rangers haven't been able to find them."

"Oh heck, Mom, he'll find his way out. Jerry Kanzler was the best Boy Scout I ever knew. Jeez, he's a mountain climber. He'll know what to do."

"Terry," she paused. "They have been missing for four days."

A sharp pain twanged through my gut. Four days! That was a long time. It was cold out. It was below zero. Snowing.

The end of the 1960s and the beginning of the 1970s was a transition time in American mountaineering. The Golden Age of Yosemite climbing was in its twilight, with routes established on all of "The Valley's" big walls.

Certain climbers focused their attention on the higher alpine realms with snow, ice and rock with different challenges. Alpine climbing required different strategies and tactics.

While the world's largest mountains in Asia and Alaska were being climbed, via the most logical routes, to their summits, a multitude of steep, unclimbed faces remained in the Rocky Mountains. This included the generally larger-scale Canadian Rockies and the smaller-scale Rocky Mountains of the United States. Attention shifted to these objectively dangerous prizes by savvy alpinists from Canada and their southern counterparts, who slipped in on the harvest of first ascents on previously unclimbed faces.

One area with a concentration of steep, unclimbed faces in the contiguous 48 states was hiding in plain view. The mountains of Glacier National Park boasted precipitous faces ranging from 2,000 to 4,000 feet in relief. Some looked as though they might belong in the panoramas further north.

The bigger and steeper north and east faces typically were left unchallenged. The east face of Mount Gould and the north face of Mount Cleveland were two enigmas to the mountaineers and scramblers in Glacier—and talking points in the early editions of *A Climber's Guide to Glacier National Park* by J. Gordon Edwards.

The domain of the steep northern aspect of the double pyramid of Mount Cleveland lies secluded—fewer than five miles south of the Canadian border. With a relief of 4,000 feet, the north face of Mount

Cleveland may be the highest precipitous face in the contiguous 48 states. Montana's big *nordwand* can only be seen from a few locations in the deep, heavily timbered Waterton Valley. It is most readily observed from Canada—and only if one travels south, by boat or by trail, from the northern end of Waterton Lake proper in Canada's Waterton Lakes National Park toward the head of the lake in Glacier National Park, Montana. The north face of Mount Cleveland rears up three miles from the inlet.

It is hard to believe that the entire north face of Mount Cleveland had not been climbed by the end of the 1960s. After all, the north face of the Grand Teton had been climbed (to within a few difficult pitches of the top) in 1936. The complete face was first scaled in 1949, with some aid, and free climbed in 1953. Even the north face of the Eiger in Switzerland was climbed in 1938.

It must have been the dubious reputation of rotten rock that kept America's best alpine climbers disinterested in Glacier Park's highest mountain. The north face was a trophy waiting for the right climbers to come along. Jim and Jerry Kanzler were keenly aware of this, even during their schoolboy years in Columbia Falls. So was their father, Hal.

"Jim is up there, looking for Jerry," my father, R. Glenn, added, joining the conversation in the kitchen. "Jim is with the rangers and a couple of older men who are experienced mountain climbers. They haven't been able to find them." My parents sure seemed to know a lot about what was going on. "Let's turn on the radio," Dad continued, "there might be some more news."

On the kitchen table was the morning newspaper, the *Missoulian*. The front headline read, "Hunt for Climbers to Resume Today." Each morning brought a new headline and the familiar roll call:

> Missing on Mount Cleveland, 10,448 feet, the highest peak in Glacier National Park, are Clare Pogreba, 22 and Ray Martin, 22, both of Butte; Jerry Kanzler, 18, of Bozeman, formerly of Butte and Columbia Falls; Mark Levitan, 20, of Helena; and Jim Anderson, 18, of Bigfork. The five left Waterton, Alberta, Canada on December 27, [1969] and have not been seen since.

A few days after I returned from my wrestling trip, the local weekly newspaper—the *Hungry Horse News*—arrived. The headline read, "Mountain Holds Climber Mystery." The *Hungry Horse News* was the pride of Columbia Falls and the Flathead Valley. It had a loyal readership in Montana and throughout the country. Mel Ruder was the owner-editor of the weekly publication, who wrote the stories and took irreproachable photographs. No one could capture a scene or assemble the subjects like Mel, with his Speed Graphic camera and the blinding magnesium flash bulbs he carried in the pockets of his trench coat as he clomped around in the rubber overshoes he wore six months of the year.

Mel Ruder lived across an undeveloped city park from the Kanzlers. Mel knew Hal and Jean Kanzler and their two sons. He had written of Kanzler outdoor exploits and published some of Hal Kanzler's photographs in the *Hungry Horse News* in the past.

Hal Kanzler had been an officer in the Marine Corps and had fought in the Battle of Okinawa, the bloodiest battle in the Pacific. People in Columbia Falls understood that Hal had seen men die, and many considered him a brave and heroic figure. Hal had vowed before many of his friends in the community to live his life fully, for the sake of those who never came back.

"Jim will find Jerry," I tried to assure my parents, though I knew nothing about what had been developing for days while I was on the wrestling trip. "Jim will find Jerry and they will make their way out of the mountains."

I tried to imagine Mount Cleveland, up there somewhere in Glacier Park. I wasn't sure exactly where it was; but that was soon to be rectified. Outside, the weather continued, cold and snowy. I tried to imagine an exuberant Jerry Kanzler, with a serious Jim Kanzler placing an arm around his younger brother—happy, but reprimanding Jerry for causing such concern. I could see the two of them walking out of the mountains to hot chocolate and worried "den mothers."

The January 7, 1970 issue of the *Hungry Horse News* had the headline, "Search for Missing Climbers Continues". Inside the paper was a heartfelt remembrance of Jerry Kanzler and a solemn tribute to Jerry's mountaineering partner on Mount Cleveland: 18-year-old Jim Anderson, who lived in Big Fork, Montana, on Flathead Lake—25 miles from Columbia Falls.

Jim and Jerry Kanzler lived three blocks from where I grew up. Jerry was three years older than I was, and Jim was three years older than Jerry.

Some of Jim and Jerry's high school classmates were the stars on the celebrated basketball team.

Neither Jim nor Jerry played team sports, but they were no less athletic. They excelled in skiing and mountaineering. The basketball players and the mountaineers were all friends in the small community.

Glacier National Park has been a beacon to mountaineers since the 1920s that favored scrambling on talus and scree through cliffs that appeared improbable from a distance. The sedimentary rock carried a stigma of being rotten and untrustworthy over the decades and technical climbers shied away. Such endeavors, it was understood, were better suited for the Tetons. Nearly every peak in Glacier still had an unclimbed face in the 1960s. Youth and ambition, however, would not sit still for long.

Hal Kanzler worked as an engineer on the Hungry Horse Dam project. As the 564-foot-high structure neared completion in 1953, he was hired as a manager with the newly built Anaconda Aluminum Company plant in Columbia Falls.

The hard-driven outdoorsman hunted birds and big game. Hal shot a Montana bighorn ram in 1960, which made the Boone and Crocket record book, with his 12-year-old son, Jim, spotting the quarry. Hal was instrumental in developing what became the Hunter's Safety Program in Montana.

Jean Kanzler (Jim and Jerry's mother) was the initial inspiration in the family's learning to ski. The family skied on the black wooden Head Standard skis with cable bindings and the low-cut leather boots of the day on Big Mountain (now called Whitefish Mountain Resort), within view of Columbia Falls. Hal preferred to lash sealskin climbers to his skis and ascend peaks and ridges away from the lifts and his boys followed.

Hal taught himself the rudiments of climbing from Geoffrey Winthrop Young's *Mountain Craft* (1920) and engaged his cohorts. They climbed mountains in Glacier National Park and the Mission Mountains between Flathead Lake and Missoula. He made detailed maps of an area called the Pot Hole Lakes, in the southeast corner of the Flathead Valley, and made an even more detailed contour map of the Mission Mountains. He contributed stories and photos to *Field and Stream* and other outdoor periodicals.

In 1963 Hal Kanzler and his sons tackled the fearsome Mount St. Nicholas in southern Glacier Park. St. Nick had a reputation among

Glacier Park mountaineers as steep, scary and the most difficult peak to summit, averaging about one ascent per year in those days. Jim was 15—the same age I was when the Mount Cleveland search unfolded. Jerry was 12. The Kanzlers wore industrial hard hats for protection from rockfall, courtesy of Anaconda Aluminum. Hal led the way, hammering in Swiss and Austrian soft iron pitons as they went. Jim belayed with a 120-foot, seven-sixteenths-inch-diameter Goldline rope. They rappelled on the descent. Hal reported he woke up in the middle of the night before the ascent in a cold sweat, worried about Jim and Jerry's safety. They persevered and climbed the mountain. From the summit, Jim and Jerry used a mirror to exchange signals with their mother, who waited patiently for the ascent on a highway outside Glacier Park, miles away.

Hal Kanzler and his sons had earned a reputation. To some, they were bold adventurers and wowed other outdoor people with their prowess, stories and slide shows. To many ordinary people, Hal was reckless and foolish to subject his sons to such dangers. This was the image climbers of the day had to put up with; truth be known, the more tarnished the image, the prouder the heart. To me, the Kanzlers were heroes, beyond the hometown basketball team.

Heroes often suffer and die tragically. With little advanced notice, Hal Kanzler was transferred from Columbia Falls to the Anaconda Company Division of Copper Mining in Butte, Montana, in 1965. On January 21, 1967, in the basement of the new family home, Hal Kanzler loaded his .44 Special revolver, he carried in grizzly bear country, put the muzzle to his chest and shot himself.

Jim heard the shot and responded. He would never be the same. Jean and Hal had had a fight the night before. Jerry, then 15, hitchhiked a hundred miles early that morning to downhill ski at Bridger Bowl, near Bozeman to escape the fray. Jim, then 18, had to drive to the ski area and bring Jerry home.

Less than three years later, Jerry was missing.

Eighteen-year-old Jim Anderson was on Mount Cleveland in December 1969. His brother, Bud Anderson, was 25 and already a civilian pilot. The two brothers had climbed the west face of Mount Cleveland the summer before. Bud flew from Kalispell to Mount Cleveland in a single-engine airplane on December 31, 1969, to check the location of the five climbers. When he flew past the west face, he saw distinct signs of a recent avalanche. He banked the plane hard left and looped around for another look. He saw tracks leading into the slide path—and this disturbed him. He made another pass. This time, he thought he saw tracks leading out of the top of the slide, but he wasn't sure. Bud flew on. Far beneath him, he saw the base camp below the north face—the primary interest of the expedition—and was somewhat relieved. He was unable to see any activity from 4,000 feet above. No one in the party made himself visible or waved in acknowledgment.

On January 2, 1970, Bud and a third brother, 16 year-old Don Anderson, drove from Kalispell to Waterton Townsite and went by boat to the head of eight-mile-long Waterton Lake back into Montana. This was to be the day the five climbers were due out. Canadian Warden Jack Christiansen and boat owner Alf Baker went with them in anticipation of meeting the expedition for their return to civilization. Baker had transported the climbers to the end of the lake on December 27. Six days later, no one had returned. Bud, Don and Jack Christiansen followed old ski tracks leading toward the mountain and found the Mount Cleveland Five's skis, cached for the lack of snow, a mile and a half from the lake. There was no sign of recent activity. They returned and notified Glacier National Park authorities. A full-scale search began.

Jim Kanzler, Dr. Patrik Callis (Montana State University chemistry professor and expert climber), MSU winter mountaineering instructor and Exum Mountain Guide Peter Lev, and climber Barry Frost mobilized in Bozeman. They began the 400-mile drive to Waterton Lake in Alberta on January 3, in blowing snow and icy road conditions, having been summoned by the park authorities. The four Bozeman climbers were "the people to notify in case of an emergency." The back-up team spent the night at the St. Mary Ranger Station compound at the east entrance to Glacier, and were briefed by District Ranger Bob Frauson.

The five younger climbers had stopped at the Hudson Bay District Ranger Station the week before, en route to Mount Cleveland. They had discussed their itinerary with Frauson, a six-foot-four, barrel-chested, former soldier of the Army's elite Tenth Mountain Division. He had been in the midst of combat and carnage on Riva Ridge in Italy during World War II. Frauson had been the same age during the war as the young mountain climbers who stood before him. He had a perceived sense of duty as he tried to dissuade the climbers from going into battle on the big mountain, citing the dangers of winter weather and avalanches. Frauson was a soft-spoken man who communicated with simplicity and pragmatism. He rarely engaged in small talk and moved straight to a point. He carried a strong undercurrent of authority that drew one's respect.

Frauson was old school. He clearly did not like the idea of a winter climb and called for a shake down, inspecting the young mountain warriors' gear. He had a few concerns, but allowed them to pass his inspection. The five climbers already had three attempts on alpine peaks between them in full winter conditions—before Christmas that year. They had been successful on two— including Mount Wilbur in Glacier that Thanksgiving, which was in Bob Frauson's district.

The original intention of Clare Pogreba, Jim and Jerry Kanzler and Ray Martin was to climb the north face of Mount Cleveland. Jim Kanzler then landed a job as a professional ski patrolman at Bridger Bowl, and was unable to participate in the expedition. Jim was a 21-year-old father by then, struggling to support his wife and year-old son, and the ski season was already in full swing.

There will always be debate as to whether the Mount Cleveland Five made a concession with Frauson that day to not attempt the north face on that trip, but to try the easier west face as a consolation. Mount Cleveland's beckon was strong. Ranger Frauson's influence did not prevail. The aspirations of young men on the heels of the unknown were not to be forsaken.

The search got underway. There was unique cooperation between the national parks of Canada and the U.S. The missing climbers were most likely in the U.S. but the only logical point from which to coordinate the mission was on Canadian soil.

Bob Frauson was in charge of coordinating personnel and resources from the Waterton Townsite at the Alberta end of the lake. He had not wanted the Bozeman backup team to be actively involved. Frauson was concerned about having the brother of one of the missing on the mountain. He argued that a family member could jeopardize the operation should there be a sudden development—such as finding bodies. Frauson had been through similar circumstances in the war.

Ranger Willie Colony was in charge of the field operation at the Montana end of the lake. Colony agreed with Frauson's premise; however, he cited that the Bozeman group's superior mountaineering skills had to be utilized. It was Colony's decision.

The Bozeman-Butte climbing connection was a small, cohesive group. Jim Kanzler was a key figure in the younger climbing contingency, lending a more reserved and calculating approach to climbing projects. Professor Callis was 32 and Peter Lev was 29. Both had been climbing since their early teens and had big mountain and winter climbing experience between them. Lev, Callis, the Kanzler brothers, Clare Pogreba, and Ray Martin had climbed together frequently. Callis and Lev served as mentors for the highly motivated younger climbers. The group pioneered many Montana routes in just a few years.

Jim Kanzler and the Bozeman team were eager to get on the mountain and arrived at the foot of Waterton Lake in Alberta, Canada on January 4. They were shuttled by boat to the south end of the lake to the backcountry Goat Haunt Ranger Station, which had been boarded up for the winter but was quickly re-commissioned as the field base for the search.

Before dawn the next morning, January 5, Jim Kanzler, accompanied by the two older climbers, set out to find his younger brother, Clare and Ray. Jim Anderson and Mark Levitan had made friends with Jerry Kanzler that autumn, when they met in Peter Lev's winter mountaineering class and joined the Mount Cleveland expedition after its inception. The plan was for Anderson and Levitan to support the other three should they try the north face. The Glacier Park Rangers and the highly trained alpine rescue specialists brought into the search from Banff and Jasper National Parks in Canada and Grand Teton National Park in the U.S. focused the search in the base camp area and lower north face of Mount Cleveland. Barry Frost was posted as an observer on Goat Haunt Mountain north of Mount Cleveland to glass the north face.

The Bozeman civilian adjunct was assigned to climb the west face. This was likely a compromise between rangers Colony and Frauson to sequester the Bozeman team away from the north face, where Frauson felt the greater likelihood of finding distressed climbers—or bodies—existed. The Mount Cleveland Five's base camp was, after all, located at the base of the north face. On January 5 and 6, 1970, the Bozeman trio functioned as a unit within the broader search schematic on Mount Cleveland. Ranger Colony's plan was for Lev, Callis and Kanzler to go light and search quickly as high up the face as they could that day and return to the bottom. In the meantime, tents and other overnight gear would be either flown or carried on foot to the base of the west face to establish a camp.

"Peter Lev and I really didn't like the idea," Dr. Callis said many years later. "If we were going to cover that much terrain in winter, we didn't want to have to rely upon others like that because of the many variables in the search, such as the helicopter's dependency upon minute to minute conditions to fly or getting support personnel with the right supplies to the right location with limited hours of daylight. We insisted we go self sufficient to spend the night on the west face, if need be."

Willie Colony had little choice but to defer to Lev and Callis's mountaineering experience. The team carried a stove, sleeping bags, and a #10D grain scoop. They approached the west face on foot and began to ascend. They climbed and searched until the end of the day, but found no sign of the five. They dug a snow cave and spent a long night crammed inside.

The next morning, they descended. It was the sixth day of the search and Dr. Callis made the key discovery: A rucksack on the surface of a previous avalanche slide path that had involved most of the northern bowl of the west face. It was in the avalanche Bud Anderson had seen.

As a 15-year-old boy, I hung on every word from the local radio and television stations at home. I conferred with the assistant wrestling coach, Larry Wilson, as practice resumed after the road trip on the bus. His tenor was grim. "Wil," as students and wrestlers called him, had been Jim and Jerry's eighth grade history teacher. Wil held Hal Kanzler in high esteem. He had befriended the Kanzler brothers when family life turned turbulent.

At the moment when Dr. Callis lifted the partially buried pack from the snow mid way down the avalanche path and radioed in the find, everyone on the search effort suddenly understood why they were unable to find any of the missing climbers. The mission was no longer a rescue. It became a search for bodies.

The *Missoulian* was delivered to my parents' door. Each day a new headline appeared. Together, they read like lines of a tragic poem:

> Five Climbers Overdue in Glacier Peak Ascent (1-3-70)
> Hunt for Climbers to Resume Today (1-4)
> Hunt for Climbers Continues (1-5)
> Crews Fearful Climbers Fell (1-6)
> Packsack Found No Trace of Five (1-7)
> Searchers Believe Five Young Climbers Dead (1-8)
> Search Operations Abandoned for Five Young Mountaineers (1-10)

Hope for the five young mountain climbers dissipated like the dust cloud of the avalanche and bereavement set in like the debris in the run-out zone. Days turned to weeks. The weather and avalanche conditions deteriorated on Mount Cleveland, and the search was called off. Jerry Kanzler and the Mount Cleveland Five would not return. The January 16, 1970 issue of the *Hungry Horse News* could offer no solace: "Mountain to Reveal Mystery in July".

Why such a big face? Why in winter? These were the questions asked repeatedly by the residents of Columbia Falls and the Flathead Valley and the people who followed the saga in Montana and elsewhere. "They were too young." "Those boys were inexperienced." "There should have been someone more experienced with them." These were the only conclusions of readers and rescuers alike. Few supported, much less understood, the pursuit of such endeavors.

Jean Kanzler had a different point of view. She was quoted in the *Daily Interlake*, published in Kalispell. "Those were young men up there. They died doing their thing..." Her stoic words sounded philosophical and accepting; but her life was forever turned upside down, shattered like a fallen vase, the pieces never recovered. She would go on to live a life of grief and bitterness, isolation and derangement.

My father grew up during the Depression of the 1930s, in the shadow and effluent of the Anaconda Mining and Smelting Company in Anaconda, Montana. He was the second child of five boys and one girl. His older brother died the summer after his junior year of appendicitis and his sister died of rubella at age one.

R. Glenn was drafted into the Army soon after the attack on Pearl Harbor. An officer asked if anyone in his group of inductees could read a detailed map. R. Glenn raised his hand and proved it so. That landed him in the Regional Intelligence Operations section of the First Calvary Division, where he became a Master Sergeant. Dad claimed he was never in combat; however, he and thousands of soldiers had climbed over the edges of transport ships into smaller landing craft in Yokohama Harbor in preparation to invade Japan just days before the dropping of the atom bombs that ended the war.

R. Glenn became the Scoutmaster for one of the two Cub Scout troops in Columbia Falls in 1962. I learned more directly from my father than I did from Cub Scouts. I followed my dad on hunting trips before I was school aged. R. Glenn felt it was his duty to teach his sons safe gun handling and good hunting practices at an early age. When I reached the first grade, he let me carry his .22 rifle, which was taller than I was, on big game hunts before I was legally old enough to do so, "...just in case we get into the grouse."

By the fourth grade, I was allowed to explore the Flathead River bottom alone, after Dad and I toured the river area together. Certain guidelines were drawn, and I never disobeyed them. I spent hours along the river, accompanied by Jack.

On a hot day in June in 1964, with the Flathead River in flood stage, Dad, Dan, Jack and I scrambled up Teakettle Mountain behind the aluminum plant near Columbia Falls. Standing on top was a moment of triumph; but it took everything R. Glenn and his boys had to endure the dense brush thickets, loose scree, hot temperatures and dehydration. I declared I would never do that again.

The discomforts were soon forgotten. Mountains stretching from Canada through Glacier Park, the Great Bear Wilderness and into the Bob Marshal Wilderness left the more lasting impression. There had been a feeling of accomplishment—I had done something Jerry Kanzler had done.

I lost interest in scouting after R. Glenn turned the title over to another man, after Dad was elected to the school board. Not long after the Teakettle Mountain adventure, I explained to my father that I had outgrown Cub Scouts and did not want to go into the Boy Scouts. This was hard for me to do; I thought it would hurt his feelings. My father had achieved Eagle Scout—the highest rank—along with his older brother, George, who had since died.

I discovered at an early age that I was not a group guy. What I wanted from experiences of being outside and challenging myself did not require a social network or peer acceptance. I expected my dropping out of Scouts would disappoint my father; but he never discouraged my decision.

The Mount Cleveland tragedy, on the other hand, brought me front and center. Who would fill the void left by the Mount Cleveland Five and shoulder the load—the passion that is mountain climbing? Who would carry the torch? What about Hal and all those soldiers who did not come home? It seemed to me that Jim and Jerry had decided to live more fully for Hal after his death, which meant pushing the envelope of mountaineering, tackling even bigger mountain faces than even Hal would attempt. What would Jim do now? Who would be his partner? What would become of Jean? Would Jim take on a vengeance with Mount Cleveland? The questions kept turning like a vinyl record on a turntable.

It bewildered me to think that the legendary tale of the Kanzler family would come to such a tragic end. It dawned on me that there might not be a more noble pursuit than to climb mountains. I had already gotten a taste of it. By then, I had hiked the long, strenuous trail to summit Columbia Mountain, overlooking Columbia Falls.

Some say that if you stare into a mirror long enough, you will go insane. Others say you will see your soul. I noticed that if I stared into my own pupils, I could not see my eyes move. I could peer into the black, light-absorbing portals directly and see them fixed; but it was impossible to see the motion of my eyes turning away.

Looking into my own eyes in a mirror, up close, I could feel my truth. "This is me. This is who I am." There was no turning away. Holding my gaze, less than a week after the search was called off, I made a promise to myself. I would pick up the torch Jerry and the Mount Cleveland Five had carried and find whatever it was those guys were seeking.

"I will climb the north face of Mount Cleveland with Jim Kanzler, no matter what it takes. The Kanzler legend will live on." Perhaps, I stared too long; perhaps, I did become crazy. Maybe I just saw the craziness that was already there.

My gravitation to the north face of Mount Cleveland was irresistible. I had created my own call to duty. I vowed to climb the north face of Mount Cleveland by the time I was 22—the same age as Clare Pogreba and Ray Martin at the time of the avalanche. I would show the doubters and naysayers that "The Mount Cleveland Five" were not too young or inexperienced. I could hear an echo of the Mount Cleveland Five and I was determined to go in search of it.

The basketball players took their places back in the trophy cases, with the yellowing pages of the *Hungry Horse News*, in the foyer outside of the high school gym. Wrestling faded to a distant second. I was to become a mountain climber. I was going to teach myself how.

So, I headed for the only reference book I could think of—the encyclopedia—on the family room bookshelf.

"There's no entry for climbing or mountain climbing," I complained to my dad.

"Try looking under mountaineering," he suggested.

I flipped through the pages. Wow, there it was: a whole new world! The entry was written by a guy named Sir Edmund Hillary, who was one of the two climbers to first climb the highest mountain in the world. This was great stuff! Best of all were the photos of ropes, nailed boots, ice axes, crampons, pitons and snap-links.

"...So that is how the rope gets attached to the pitons!"

There was a mountain climber with a rope wrapped around his body going down a cliff. He was wearing pants that looked like a baseball uniform, with the long socks...and keen-looking boots with cleats (tricouni nails)! There was a photo of the Matterhorn, steep and forbidding. I imagined Jim and Jerry Kanzler climbing the most imposing face on the famous mountain when they got older, had fate not taken such a tragic twist.

The next day, when no one else was home, I dismantled the yellow polypropylene rope my dad had set up for a clothesline, grabbed the encyclopedia and headed to the box elder tree in the back yard. I climbed 15 feet up and, following the picture, wrapped the rope around my body and made my first rappel. I understood why the climber in the picture had extra patches on one shoulder and on the crotch of his knickers. I made my first Dulfersitz body rappel that day.

In the high school library, under "mountaineering," was High in the Thin Cold Air, written by that same Sir Edmund Hillary and Desmond Doig. My mountaineering mania set me adrift into a fantasy world. I saw myself up there, plodding away on some high, snowy peak. The door swung wide open. Destiny waited, just past the threshold. I never felt so free.

My determination to climb the north face of Mount Cleveland was a secret I shared with few as I covertly transformed myself into a mountain climber. Yet, kids would come up to me and ask, "Hey, Kennedy, when are you going to climb the north face of Mount Cleveland?"

Sometimes I felt taunted, but I just blew them off. "Just wait and see," I would answer silently. "You are going to read about it one day."

For most of those kids who grew up in the Flathead Valley during the Mount Cleveland Five tragedy, Mount Cleveland was one mountain that stood out vividly in their memories. Everyone knew the names Teakettle and Columbia Mountains. Some recognized the name Mount Everest. Most knew that somewhere in Glacier Park was Mount Cleveland, the highest mountain in that part of Montana, on which five guys got killed. The kids at school just assumed the north face of Mount Cleveland was where I was headed. As it was, they were right; and I have to admit, there were times when I actually liked the attention. Every time someone brought up Mount Cleveland, it drove me a little harder.

Jack, Dan Kennedy, age 9, and a ten-pound bull trout he caught
in the Flathead River, June 1967. Photo by Mel Ruder.

Cub Scout meeting in the Kanzler back yard, circa 1963.
Jim Kanzler is in full Boy Scout uniform standing on the far left. The author is on the
right waving with Eddie Woster on the far right kneeling. Photo by Jean Kanzler.

The north face of Mount Cleveland in similar conditions
to December 1969. Photo by the author.

On the summit of Mount Henkel, Glacier Park,
May 1965. Left to right: Jerry Kanzler, Jim Kanzler and
Jim Emerson. Photo courtesy of Jim Emerson.

On the summit of Citadel Spire, Glacier Park during the first ascent,
August 1967. Left to right: Clare Pogreba, Jim Kanzler, and Ray Martin
with Jerry Kanzler in front. The north face of Mountain Cleveland
lurks in the background. Photo courtesy Jamie Kanzler.

CHAPTER 2

Packing the Torch

As the days of the January 1970 search came and went, hope for the Mount Cleveland Five faded. I discussed Jerry Kanzler with my Cub Scout friends Eddie Woster and Roger Newman. Eddie lived next door and Roger lived across the alley from Jim and Jerry. Eddie and Roger's fathers had managerial positions at the aluminum plant. None of us had ever known kids who had died before. We tried to comprehend that Jerry's life had ended as the community of Columbia Falls lapsed into grieving for Jean Kanzler's second loss. The Flathead Valley mourned Jerry Kanzler and Jim Anderson. I began a life journey of fashioning myself into a mountain climber. The north face of Mount Cleveland loomed large.

"We need to carry on for Jerry," I proposed one day. "I think we should carry his torch, climb mountains and keep his spirit alive." This was the first time I allowed myself to speak my ambitions out loud, rather than working on them in secret. Eddie and Roger agreed; but neither seemed to know what this would entail.

Eddie was athletic and good at any sport that didn't make his hands and feet cold. He liked an occasional hike in the summer. He climbed Teakettle Mountain with Jerry, Roger and Roger's older sister, Leslie, in 1963. In June 1965, Eddie, Roger and I hiked the grueling five miles of trail with 4,000-foot elevation gain to the summit of Columbia Mountain, across the river from Teakettle Mountain.

As we reached the top, the thick cloud cover lowered, socking-in the mountain; and it began to rain. We signed our names on the note pad in a coffee can (a mountaineering tradition) as we huddled beneath a single poncho, and headed back down the mountain to the trailhead, soaked to the bone and on the verge of hypothermia.

Eddie became a standout track athlete. He would rather high jump or pole vault than stand on top of a cliff. Columbia Mountain was okay; but clinging to exposed rock and dangling from ropes was not his bag.

Roger, on the other hand, was not as keen on scholastic sports. He and I had spent time together in Dad's basement shop making our own fishing lures and duck decoys, earning credit for Cub Scout badges. Roger loved getting off the beaten path. Between his grief for Jerry and his own adventuresome spirit, Roger felt ready to begin.

"I think it is time to start climbing the mountains in Glacier," I told Roger. I swore him to secrecy about my destiny with the north face of Mount Cleveland.

We took the same clothesline rope and headed for a dirt bluff on a bank above an old channel of the Flathead River. We looped the rope around a tree near the edge. The ends of the rope just made the bottom. We wore gloves, two pairs of jeans and an extra sweatshirt for padding against the harsh friction of the rope and I showed Roger the infamous Dulfersitz body rappel. Lowering myself down a vertical 20-foot drop was exhilarating.

"Hey, how are we going to get the rope down?" Roger asked.

"Here, I'll show ya." I pulled one end of the clothesline down and the other end traveled up the dirt cliff, flipped around the tree and dropped into a pile at our feet.

"Oh-h, slick," Roger said, "just like dental floss."

In one of the newspaper follow-up articles in the aftermath of the Mount Cleveland search, I learned there was a book with descriptions of mountain climbing routes to reach the summits of the peaks in Glacier National Park by J. Gordon Edwards, called *A Climber's Guide to Glacier National Park*. I pestered my parents for a copy, and it showed up with another book, *Basic Mountaineering*, on my 16th birthday in March of 1970. Inside the book cover of Edwards's guide were the following words from my brother:

> To: Terry
> From: Danny
>
> "Though this is the book you really wanted, *Basic Mountaineering* has to be mastered first."

Dan later admitted that Dad had made him write those words, but Dan thought it was a good idea. I turned the pages to Mount Cleveland before reading the birthday card. There, on page 75 (in the 1966 edition), were the tantalizing words:

> "It [Mount Cleveland] will certainly also be ascended directly up the north face someday, although that would be a hazardous and arduous route."

Did J. Gordon Edwards have any idea what prophecy he had unleashed upon a young generation of mountain climbers of the small towns of Montana? I flipped to Mount St. Nicholas page 131:

> "This peak is considered the most difficult and dangerous [standard route to a summit] in the park..."

I had my work cut out for me. Mount St. Nicholas would be a touchstone for evaluating my progress toward Mount Cleveland's north face. St. Nick became a priority. I set my sights on climbing it in two years.

I called Roger the evening after my birthday. We picked out a laundry list of ten peaks that did not require ropes and planned to climb them all over the upcoming summer.

A week later, Dad and I drove 45 minutes from Columbia Falls to look at Mount St. Nicholas from U.S. Highway No. 2. The pointed mountain looked just like the Matterhorn in the encyclopedia. I gawked through a cheap telescope as if looking at the Moon, far away and mysterious.

Hal Kanzler led his sons up Mount St. Nicholas in 1963. They were the only mountaineers from Columbia Falls who had climbed it. The Kanzlers were like space explorers who had been where no one else had. I wanted to be like that. I made the hour-long drive dozens of times just to look at St. Nick before I was ready to climb it.

I deduced that the west face of the sharp peak was unclimbed. It was only half as high as the north face of Mount Cleveland; but it was a worthy prize. Dad and I took a rubber raft across the Middle Fork of the Flathead River and hiked up to a shoulder of a lower mountain just for a better view of St. Nick's west face. I took black and white photos to study the face; with an old camera someone gave me that always scratched the film. One night I dreamed there was a man who lived inside Mount St. Nicholas and made weather observations. Another night, I dreamed of people in white robes casually climbing and descending Mount St. Nicholas, on some journey.

The Columbia Falls high school band raised funds to go to Europe for a two-week tour in April of 1970. Roger was a decent trumpet player; I was last-chair trombone. The trip turned out to be a breakneck bus ride in the rain. I was bummed because the tour did not get close to the Matterhorn. Multitudes of mind-boggling mountains flew by the windows. I imagined myself high on those cliffs with Jim Kanzler.

I bought my first mountaineering boots, a pair of Raichles, in a mountain shop in Lucerne as the winter snow accumulated on Mount Cleveland, back in Montana. I waited weeks before applying Sno-seal to the golden-brown split-grain leather, to keep the handsome look and texture as long I could, before it was necessary to waterproof them, which would darken the leather and make the boots look old.

Roger ordered a pair of Raichles from an REI catalogue one of Hal Kanzler's mountaineering partners had lent him. Soon Roger and I had our own copies of the catalog, which would play a significant role in learning to climb. I began to piece the ideas of technical climbing together looking at the equipment, along with *Basic Mountaineering*. There were many pieces of gear I needed and wanted, and I would have to use my own money to get them. Mowing lawns in the summer and shoveling sidewalks in the winter yielded paltry earnings for such an expensive sport; as a result, gear accumulation was slow. I could not afford both an ice axe and crampons, so I ordered the ice axe first.

Ice axes had straight picks when I started mountaineering and long, straight shafts made from hickory. The one I ordered from the REI catalogue was a beauty! I remember curling my fingers around the pick, thumb under the adze, and holding the shaft across my body in the self-arrest position. I was a warrior with his first bow.

Toward the end of April 1970, there was still a considerable amount of snow on Teakettle Mountain. The days were warm, but the nights still dropped below freezing. The snow was too soft to make a climb during the day enjoyable; I opted to go at night, when the snow set up hard. On April 21, I waited until 10 p.m. while a full moon climbed into the sky. I did not have a headlamp yet, but I decided I would not need one in the moonlight.

The climb was a tough sell to R. Glenn and Betty because that was a Tuesday— a school night. I explained the importance of the cold temperatures and the moonlight, and all they could do was sigh. As you can imagine, neither one was terribly enthusiastic about driving me to my takeoff point three miles away. They were even less enthusiastic about coming to pick me up in the wee hours of the morning. So I finagled the keys to the '52 Ford four-door, the primary family car at the time. I drove myself to a place just north of the aluminum plant, where I set out on foot. I did not have a driver's license yet; but I knew how to drive the three-on-the-column stick shift, and Dad was okay with it.

I scrambled up the side of Teakettle almost half way before I got into the snow. It was time to put my homemade crampons to the test. I had constructed my own set of spikes in my dad's wood shop using roofing nails, Masonite wood, washers, and lots of glue. I strapped the prickly fabrication to my Raichles with giant rubber bands cut from tire inner tubes. I had to take one step from the scree to the snow. The "point" below the big toe bent 45 degrees when it hit a piece of rock. Uh-oh. I needed one more step to get to the snow, so I very carefully placed the left foot onto dirt. It was the most delicate move on mixed terrain I had made up to that point in my mountain climbing career. Once established on the 30-degree angle crunchy snow, I could feel the bite of the roofing nails. At last I felt like a mountaineer, with the staccato steps, the crunch of hard snow under the crampons, the ice axe held in the right position, and the spike embedding securely.

Well sir, 100 feet up the slope I began to notice the bite of the ol' spikes did not have quite the same feel as they did at first.

"Maybe they were clogging up with snow," I thought.

I lifted one boot to have a look and, to my chagrin, noted that the roofing nails were beginning to bend every which way. Some were completely folded over. A few still maintained vertical. I accepted that my design had flaws; but I would worry about them later. I had a mountain to climb.

After another 100 feet, I took another look at my crampons. Oh, my! All the nails were now crimped over. Not only were some chewed out of the Masonite and had washers missing, but also the Masonite was beginning to show signs of material degradation—like cornflakes in a bowl of milk when breakfast has ended long ago. By the time I stomped off of the snow and into a mixture of brush and scree, I only had the rear half of the right crampon intact. The inner tube rubber bands held tough. I committed what was left of my invention to the mountain and continued to the next snow patch. I discovered I could climb just about as well without crampons, anyway.

The only sounds I could hear were the shifting of scree, the swipe of brush against my clothes, and my own breathing. The moon, peering around the south ridge of the mountain, cast shadows of towering skeletons of ancient larch and Douglas firs—casualties of a raging forest fire that had started from a sawmill between Columbia Falls and Whitefish in 1929. The inferno burned Teakettle Mountain to bedrock before turning up the North Fork of the Flathead River drainage and into Glacier National Park. The devastation—and, later, the pollution from the aluminum plant—prevented Teakettle Mountain from full regeneration, giving Teakettle the appearance of a higher mountain. Climbing in the eerie moonlight was like traveling through the landscape of a strange planet.

I reached the top around 2 a.m. My own shadow stretched out on the snow. I didn't know it at the time, but it was now Jim Kanzler's birthday. To the northeast were Lake McDonald and the panorama of Glacier National Park's mountains. Mount Cleveland lurked behind Longfellow Peak, 41 miles away. The bodies of Jerry Kanzler and the Mount Cleveland Five were still up there, frozen in the avalanche debris.

The aluminum plant sprawled along the base of Teakettle, 3,000 feet below. I could faintly hear the hum of the electrical rectifying yard and the drone of big fork trucks carrying molten aluminum from the *potlines* to the furnaces; and the bursts of jackhammers breaking the crusts of ore so it could mix into the molten aluminum, brewing in bus-sized cauldrons. I got whiffs of the acrid fumes from the process—the same smell that came home on my father's work clothes.

Beyond the plant was the Flathead River. It was too dark to make out our house, but I could see the Frazers' on the bank above the river bottom with the old pair of binoculars I carried. I could see the city park across the street from the former Kanzler home. A few lights dotted the gravel streets. Most of the inhabitants were now sleeping, except for those who were pulling graveyard duty at the plant.

On the summit of Teakettle Mountain, next to wind-scoured sheds housing electronic equipment that broadcast television to the Flathead Valley, a young warrior announced himself to the sky. He faced the direction of Mount Cleveland and chanted his decree to carry the torch and climb the north face of Glacier Park's highest peak with the brother of one of the fallen.

I paid tribute to the seven-foot-high stone ghost of a cairn Jim Kanzler and some of his buddies had built the year he and Jerry climbed Mount St. Nicholas with their father.

I was home sometime after 5 a.m. and fell asleep on the couch. I went to school that day more tired than usual, but with the personal satisfaction of knowing where I was headed in life.

"Hey, Kennedy, when are you going to climb the north face of Mount Cleveland?"

Six weeks later, on July 3, 1970, we had a hand-me-down Ford Galaxie 500 from my grandfather. I was at the wheel, and Mom was in the passenger seat. We drove to Roger Newman's house across town. By then, I had a driver's license. Roger was waiting in the driveway, under the early morning sun, with his new rucksack. "Good morning, Mrs. Kennedy. Hi, Terry."

"Good morning, Roger. Here, you sit in the front. I'll sit in the back."

"Oh, no, Mrs. Kennedy. I'll sit in the back."

"No, I think you and Terry should both sit up front. That way you two can discuss your plans and see the mountains better," Mom insisted.

We drove to West Glacier and entered the park. It was the first time I had driven the car to Logan Pass. I eased the big car around McDonald Lake and up the deep mountain valley. Roger and I gawked at the mountains.

I had ridden up Going-to-the-Sun Road through Glacier Park once or twice a year as a child, mostly in the old '52 Ford, often as an outing to entertain a grandparent. For me, the narrow, winding road meant getting carsick. Until 1970, I hated the trips into Glacier. Not only did I not look forward to getting car sick, but also as a young outdoorsman, I was irked that you could not hunt in the park. What good was that?

My attitude toward Glacier changed. On that day, Roger and I would climb our first mountain in Glacier. The mountains seemed to come alive.

In May, Bob Frauson and the Park Service had renewed the search and recovery effort on Mount Cleveland. Since the search was called off on January 8, the Park Service had made flights over Mount Cleveland a couple times during the winter to check on the status of the snow pack. On May 23, Rangers Jerry DeSanto and Larry Feser made a foot reconnaissance to the base of the west face. At the end of the avalanche run-out zone was Jim Anderson's camera. The cover was found 300 yards up slope. The carrying strap was broken but the camera itself was—remarkably—intact. The film was developed and showed The Cleveland Five high on the west face. Two days later, DeSanto and Feser climbed higher on the west face and found other articles, including half of a broken hickory ice axe shaft. In June, patrols continued when conditions permitted. Most of the grieving people of the Flathead Valley and in Montana hoped the rangers could recover the bodies and bring the young mountain climbers home. Mark Levitan's father thought it would be most appropriate to let his son and buddies stay buried, with Mount Cleveland serving as their eternal tombstone.

That June, I had finished my sophomore year of high school and had upgraded from mowing lawns to moving irrigation pipes and bucking hay bales at a farm near Kalispell with another guy on the wrestling team. My earnings were primarily for college, a necessity I understood. Formal education notwithstanding, the money I made was more urgently needed for mountaineering gear. The farmer gave us a three-day Fourth of July weekend off. Going-to-the-Sun Road had been cleared of snow and was open for travel. Roger and I had hung in the wings long enough.

On June 29, 1970, DeSanto and Feser, along with three other park rangers, made a predawn start to climb high onto the west face, thinking the snow melt would be sufficient for the mountain to start giving up bodies. At 9 a.m., the search party had ascended along the lower avalanche run-out zone and negotiated the first rock band not far from a waterfall coming over the 35-foot high cliff. They moved to the stream to rehydrate as it emerged from the lower edge of the middle snowfield on the face.

As Jack Christiansen bent over to fill his water bottle, he was greeted by a telltale odor coming from beneath the snow, in the cavern formed by the stream and the outside air. Hanging upside-down from the ceiling 30 feet away was the body of Ray Martin. The mystery of the Mount Cleveland Five's location was, at last, solved.

Pilot Jim Kruger and his helicopter had been on standby for the Park Service. Kruger was radioed and the recovery mission fell into full swing. Ray Martin and Jim Anderson were recovered that day. Different ropes tied to them ran up slope into much deeper snow. Four more days of exhausting trench shoveling ensued to find the other three.

Roger and I had selected Mount Oberlin at Logan Pass as our first mountain in Glacier because it was "the shortest and easiest climb in the park," according to J. Gordon Edwards. Oberlin was the logical mountain to start with, I figured. As the big car cruised past the switch back on "'Sun Road," Mount Oberlin came into view. I had to bite back. Roger's eyes became wide, too. The northeast face of Mount Oberlin was a 1,500-foot precipice. I had to remind myself that Roger and I were going to do the southeast slope, which was completely out of view.

"Which one is Mount Oberlin?" Mom asked.

"That one," Roger and I pointed out through the front windshield simultaneously, with some measure of bravado. Mom leaned forward from the back seat. Her nose was a little scrunched up to hold her glasses in an optimal position before her eyes.

"Oh, O-h-h," she began to exclaim before plunking back into the seat. "Oh, oh-h…I don't know if I want you two boys going up there. It looks so steep. I thought you said it would be just like Teakettle. Oh, o-h-h, I don't think you should be going up there."

"It's OK, Mom," I tried to assure her. "The way we are going up is on the other side. It isn't steep at all, like we've talked about before—really. It might even be easier than Tea Kettle."

"Oh-h, but oh-h-h you might fall off the top. You'd go all the way to the bottom. You'd just be a little grease spot. Oh, please don't go all the way to the top! I don't want to have something happen to you like what happened to Jerry Kanzler and the other boys. Please, please don't go all the way to the top!"

"Mom. Jeez. We will be OK. I promise."

The coincidence of the recovery of the Mount Cleveland Five and my first mountaineering endeavor in Glacier with Roger was more than my poor mother could handle. Betty was a nervous person by nature.

I sped the car up a little. I wanted to get us to Logan Pass quickly so Mom could see we were going to climb a very gentle slope, and she could be at ease. Unfortunately, as we got closer to Logan Pass, we got closer to the daunting northeast face of the otherwise insignificant mountain. The menacing cliffs seemed to watch us as we traveled along the opposite side of the deep drainage of Logan Creek. Mom had transformed from her usual little happy chipmunk self into someone who had taken a swig out of a Tabasco Sauce bottle and was just realizing it was hot. By the time we pulled into the parking lot, she was squirming around in the backseat, tormented with worry.

If keeping my mother in one piece wasn't enough, we still had to get past the seasonal ranger on duty at Logan Pass Visitor Center. I think the guy took one look at us and sirens went off in his head. He lectured us with the obvious intent of dissuading us from climbing Glacier's easiest mountain. It was equally obvious that he had been well schooled by the Park Service. He kept referring to the poor quality of rock in Glacier and how it should not be climbed. He did a reasonable job at intimidating us; but, by God, I was not going to let some flatlander with an accent from the southern part of the country get in the way of my mission. If he was an authority on mountaineering in Glacier, then why wasn't he on Mount Cleveland as part of the search and recovery team?

"Come on, Roger, let's get going." I said. We started to walk away from the parking lot, in the direction of Mount Oberlin. From that particular angle, the route didn't look like much of a climb at all. It was just a scree slope with a few scrub fir thickets and patches of snow that could be avoided. We shouldered our brand new Sacs Millet packs. I had a red one, Roger a blue one.

The seasonal ranger knew he had not succeeded in turning us back. He followed us a few steps so as to have the last word.

"Remember, it's not the fall that kills you—it's the sudden stop."

I felt my face starting to flush. I was beginning to imagine myself shooting a wrestling takedown on the guy and putting a little road grit into that neatly pressed uniform of his. We kept walking. Was this the way it was going to be every time we were to check out with the rangers?

At the same hour Roger and I headed over to Mount Oberlin, Bob Frauson was on the west face of Mount Cleveland. The team had recovered Ray Martin and Jim Anderson a few days before by cutting Martin loose from the ceiling of the snow cavern and digging down to Anderson, whose boots could be seen protruding from the ceiling of the snowfield a little further uphill. The others were encased in snow that was morphing into ice. The whole recovery process was complicated, dangerous, exhausting and most unpleasant.

When Roger and I reached the summit of Mount Oberlin an hour and a half later, I was surprised to find others already there. That never happened on Teakettle or Columbia. I was disappointed. I thought mountain climbing was a solitary thing one might share only with one's carefully chosen climbing partner or partners. We made friends with the couple who had come to Glacier Park from the Seattle area on a Fourth of July vacation to scramble up a few peaks outside of the Cascades. The two were delighted this was our first Glacier summit also.

Phil Stern was a manager with Boeing and the current president of the Tacoma branch of the Seattle Mountaineers. Charlotte Ekman was Phil's fiancee and worked for Boeing as well. They had been mountaineers for many years and instantly took Roger and me under their wing. We enjoyed the view together. Mount Gould swept upward from the McDonald Creek Valley across Going-to-the-Sun Road. The Highline Trail traversed below the Garden Wall and Mount Gould. We asked Phil and Charlotte's advice on our plan to scramble the west face of Gould the next day. It looked inviting, a staircase of short cliffs. Mount Gould was 2,300 feet higher in elevation than Columbia and much more mountain than Teakettle or Oberlin.

By July 1970, I was already familiar with Glacier's mountains through books—especially the pictures. I could not wait to peer down the unclimbed east face of Mount Gould. I figured Roger's and my climb of Mount Gould would be the true beginning of the pursuit of serious mountaineering. The four of us read the route description to the top from the Edward's guidebook Phil had packed. Phil and Charlotte assured Roger and me that we would have no problem if we searched for the easiest way. Before they left the summit to Roger and me, they invited us to their car camp at Rising Sun Campground about ten miles east of Logan Pass. I agreed to ask my mom.

There was no mistaking Mount Cleveland 16 miles to the north. We could see her broad shoulders. At that very hour, Mark Levitan, Clare Pogreba and Jerry Kanzler were extricated from the snow of Mount Cleveland. It was finally over.

The bodies were secured to the struts of Jim Kruger's helicopter and flown to a landing zone next to the highway near Chief Mountain on the eastern boundary of the park where the coroner was waiting. One of Hal Kanzler's mountaineering partners and photography buffs, George Ostrom, identified Jerry Kanzler's body. Jerry's remains were placed in a sleeping bag and George placed a peace medallion around Jerry's neck, as Jean Kanzler had requested. Jerry's body was placed in a simple handcrafted coffin made by a family friend and local cabinetmaker. George Ostrom then fastened the lid tight with screws, and the parcel was loaded into the back of his pickup truck.

"Jean wanted to see Jerry one last time," George Ostrom told me many years later. "Those boys were very badly broken, and they had been in the snow and ice a long time. This wasn't something a mother should see. I told Jean, I just could not open Jerry's coffin back up. She understood."

I did not want to stay long on the summit, since Betty was waiting in the visitor center parking lot on the pass. Our Raichles held sure on the descent. I wanted to climb every mountain in my new world, especially by their steepest faces.

Anyone who knew Betty knew she had extraordinary social skills. As Roger and I strode proudly into the parking lot, there she was chatting away with Phil and Charlotte like they had known one another for years. They already had made plans for a get together the following evening at Phil and Charlotte's campsite after Roger and I returned from Mount Gould. The Kennedy group had not planned to camp, so we had to return to Columbia Falls that afternoon. My dad had the Fourth of July off and could join us the next day.

We started down the pass for West Glacier. Roger and I gave Mom our account of Mount Oberlin and even more enthusiastically discussed our plans for Gould the next morning. She enjoyed every detail as I drove carefully down the steep, winding road. When there came a two-second lull in the conversation, Betty turned serious.

"Just want to let you two boys know I overheard they got the last three climbers off Mount Cleveland. I talked with the ranger (probably the same one that hassled us, I thought) and he said it was true. All the bodies are now off the mountain."

There was silence. No one spoke for at least a minute. I looked over at Mom. She had tears rolling down her cheeks. My eyes welled with tears, too, and I tried not to let them fall. Roger was silent in the back seat.

I regained enough composure to speak in a relatively normal voice.

"It's O.K., Mom. Tomorrow, Roger and I will climb Mount Gould for Jerry and the other guys."

George Ostrom was traveling over Going-to-the-Sun Road and Logan Pass—at that same hour—with the body of Jerry Kanzler. Jerry was the last of the five off the mountain. The coroner had already examined the bodies of the five, and George had already sealed Jerry's pine coffin.

Jerry was laid to rest in Glacier Memorial Cemetery that evening, next to his father, as the sun approached the western edge of the Flathead Valley. Only a handful of local people knew of the plans for interment. The Episcopal Church's soprano soloist sang "Climb Every Mountain", from *The Sound of Music* (1965). From Jerry's grave, one can look to the Northeast and see the 10,000-foot Mount Jackson framed between Teakettle and Columbia Mountains. Jerry had climbed Mount Jackson when he was ten. His mother stood over his grave. A flower wreath in the shape of a peace sign was laid on top. She spoke these words:

I thank my God that he allowed me to bear this child into the world. I thank my God for 18 wonderful, living years. It was a joy to be Jer's mother, to watch him develop and mature, to live each moment with an intensity especially his. Well do I remember the days after Hal's death when Jer and Jim talked about the future, about how we would do things and what we would find from life. I watched Jer catch another kind of spark after his father's death and watched the way he savored each moment of his life. Today I can say I am so very proud to be his mother and to wish him God bless on his final journey to the horizon he loved so well. This was his life, his love. Therefore it is my life of my love.

She turned to the small group of friends who had gathered with her at the cemetery. There were tears in everyone's eyes except Jean's, so the story goes. Her final words were: "Please leave here in Christian joy. Jerry would have wanted us to be happy."

The next morning was the Fourth of July. My parents dropped the two young mountain climbers off at Logan Pass and, after the "be careful" pep-talk, they drove down to St. Mary for a little sightseeing of their own and returned seven hours later to pick us up.

Roger and I churned our way up shifting gullies of scree and climbed a dozen short cliff bands. Sometimes we avoided the easiest way because making moves on the rock was so much fun. I was mountain climbing at last. The cliffs ended and a mound of scree led to a cairn.

I peered over the edge of an abyss just beyond the cairn. "Oh my God." I inched my way forward in a crouch and then on hands and knees so I could see as much of the wall below me as I could and not just air. I started getting that weak sphincter feeling and backed off. "Wow, wouldn't it be neat to climb something like that?" We were quite pleased with ourselves from our vantage point among a sea of peaks.

"We've got to climb the north face of Mount Cleveland for Jerry," I proclaimed.

I cannot recall Roger's reply. I don't think he was so sure; but I knew my day was coming.

The aroma of alpine fir etched itself into my memory that day. Whenever I am in the mountains and smell them, I am reminded of the day Roger and I hiked the Highline Trail and scrambled up the west face of Mount Gould and the day the Mount Cleveland Five were recovered from the snow.

That evening, the two teenage mountaineers and my parents visited Phil and Charlotte in Rising Sun campground. The adults sipped cocktails and discussed beginning climbers.

"The first three years of technical climbing are the most vulnerable," Phil pointed out. "Young climbers are acquiring many skills and are often overconfident. This period is critical, and the boys will have to be especially careful; but they will get much enjoyment from this."

Roger and I were invited to Tacoma, Washington the following year for some training with the mountaineers and a climb of Mount St. Helens. I was psyched.

So began my journey to the north face of Mount Cleveland. I scrambled to the summits of ten Glacier Park Mountains that summer, most with Roger. Dan, who was 12, when all this got started, had just finished the seventh grade. He wanted to join me, but R. Glenn decided Dan was not quite old enough and had to wait until he was 13.

So Dan focused on baseball that first summer of the mountaineering campaign, but was still chomping at the bit when his birthday rolled around in August. I started Dan out with the mighty Mount Oberlin, at Dad's request. Then it was open season.

I decided we should work on technical climbing skills. Dan got his knee stuck in a crack in Bad Rock Canyon, where the river courses between Teakettle and Columbia Mountains. I had to leave him stuck for two hours while I enlisted two friends to reach over the edge of a 30-foot cliff and reach a hand down to Dan; as they did so, I climbed to him from underneath and pushed up on the foot of his stuck leg. The ordeal soured Dan on crack climbing.

I felt even more responsible for Dan after the stuck-knee incident and began carrying my 3/8" x 120-foot Goldline rope on scrambling routes that might have a cliff over ten feet high. Besides, it felt cool to be packing a rope, and always good to practice the hip belay in different situations.

Dan and I saved our best mountain adventure for the end of the season, before school started. We went for the easy route up the south side of Mount Siyeh, one of the six esteemed 10,000 footers in Glacier. We were especially excited because we knew the north face of the mountain was a sheer drop of several thousand feet to Cracker Lake—and had never been climbed. If you were daring, however, you could crawl up to the edge from the summit and look down the abyss.

It was a cold, windy day and we wore all of our extra clothing to stay warm. When we got to the summit ridge, strong gusts sometimes made us take awkward steps. It was becoming difficult to communicate, so we stayed very close to each other. As we neared the summit, we became more and more aware of the drop on the other side. I was afraid the wind would blow one of us over the edge.

"Dan!" I shouted next to his ear. "We're going to stop right here and rope up."

"OK!"

We tucked behind a rock and I got the Goldline uncoiled. Then we tied bowlines around our waists and I led to the summit cairn, as Dan executed unanchored sitting hip belays.

"Yuh think we oughta try tuh have a look over the edge?" Dan asked, leaning his head toward mine.

"Yeah. I think so. We are gonna havta be careful. We'll take turns belaying each other. Don't stand up near the edge. Crawl on your belly. I'll go first." Dan nodded. I crawled to the edge and looked over, digging my fingers into the talus with white knuckles as I inched forward and my face peered into what seemed like another galaxy, in another time. The wind tore at my hood.

"Mother of God in Heaven!" I muttered. I backed away before I pissed my pants, and returned. We traded places.

"Be careful! Don't lean too far over!" I ordered.

"Don't worry! I won't!" Dan headed out from the belay in a crouch, the wind flipping the tail of his jacket. Then he got down into his crawl. He didn't seem to be as squeamish approaching the edge. He was always more the daredevil, the gutsier of the two of us. He took a long look at the edge, his face looking straight down. He was making me nervous.

"That's enough," I hollered. "Come back!"

He didn't hear me.

"Dan! That's enough!"

He still didn't hear me.

I gave a good yank on the rope to get his attention and a wave for him to come back. He returned in a scampering crouch.

"Man, that's incredible!"

"I am going to climb that face someday," I informed him. Dan nodded and looked toward the edge again. He nodded again before turning back to me.

"I think you better climb St. Nick first. This thing looks like it would be even harder."

"Don't worry, I will. And a whole bunch of others." Dan kept nodding. He never doubted me. He just assumed I would do it.

"Let's get outta here."

The following April, Phil and Charlotte sent a present, just six weeks before I was to arrive in the Seattle area for my first mountaineering road trip. It was a copy of the fourth printing of the first edition of *Mountaineering: The Freedom of the Hills*. Inside the cover, Phil and Charlotte had written:

> This is the book of mountaineering! It is the bible and only out of date on the technical rock and ice! All other data applies! Page 264 is for you to live by—you follow those rules, and you'll love the mountains as much at 65 as at 20. We plan to do much with you this summer. Have your Mom and Dad write to us and we'll get to know each other better. AND HAVE THEM REMEMBER—MOUNTAINEERING HAS RISK!
>
> 7 April 1971
> From Philip Stern & Charlotte Ekman

In June of 1971, I climbed St. Helens with a group of some 30 or 40 Tacoma Mountaineers, none of whom I knew. On the summit rim, I overheard a conversation of older academic types: "...of all the Cascade volcanoes

St. Helens is likely to be the first one to erupt. It's possible it could even happen in our life time..."

Perhaps more prophetic words were never spoken. Just nine years later, on May 18, 1980, Mount St. Helens made her famous cataclysmic eruption. That day, I was climbing a new route on a buttress in Gallatin Canyon south of Bozeman. I carried a hand drill and hammer for a section that was devoid of cracks for gear protection. I drilled two bolts but I needed three. I down climbed and lowered off. My partners and I planned to come back the next day and finish the route.

When we returned to Bozeman, we learned Mount St. Helens had erupted big time. Southern Montana received substantial fallout, and authorities advised the public not to drive because the ash and dust might damage vehicle engines—or, possibly, lungs. The following week, I returned and finished the route. It was necessary to blow ash off the holds for better grip, and I named the route "Ashes of Stone".

The northeast corner of the Flathead Valley, 2010: Columbia Falls, the Flathead River, Teakettle Mountain on the left (with the aluminum plant below it) and Columbia Mountain right. The prominent mountains of Glacier in the background are: Mount Stimson, center, and Mount St. Nicholas, right; Mount Siyeh and Mount Cleveland are out of view to the left. Photo by GravityShots.com.

The author, left, and Roger Newman, right, at Logan Pass in Glacier Park, July 3, 1970, with Mount Oberlin in the background. Photo by Betty Kennedy.

Dan Kennedy, age 13, peers over the north face of Mount Siyeh, August 1970. Photo by the author.

CHAPTER 3

The Long Way Home

Early August 1995

I closed the door of my Ford Escort with my knee, not wanting to disturb the peacefulness of the morning, and started up the trail, adjusting the straps on my pack. I crossed a gurgling stream on a foot bridge made of parallel barked logs, slick with dew; then churned up a short grade, eroded from a previous thunderstorm, exposing coarse granules of granite and dust. I lengthened one step to avoid stepping on a wood beetle and flushed a grasshopper.

Moose Creek turned and tumbled through the boulders, willows and riparian tufts, the rush of water blending into a chord of a hundred soft voices. Skittish cutthroat trout thrived in every pool. The aroma of pitch, decaying conifer needles and decomposing trees mixed together was familiar as I walked on, into the consortium.

Over 25 years had passed since the Mount Cleveland Five disappeared into the snows of Mount Cleveland—a time span longer than any of the young explorers had been alive. I was on a weeklong vacation from my position as a staff physical therapist with a small hospital in Cottage Grove, Oregon, hurrying back to Montana to spend time with Mom and Dad, who still lived in Columbia Falls.

By 1995, I was dating a woman, Carol Copley, a medical social worker from Eugene. She was already an avid hiker when I met her in a coffee shop in 1991 next to (then) Sacred Heart Hospital in Eugene, where we both worked at the time. She had just ambitiously coaxed her nine-year-old son to within a few hundred feet of the 10,358-foot summit of South Sister Peak in the Oregon Cascades.

I cleverly seized upon the opportunity for a first date and offered to return to the volcano with her and take care of unfinished business. She bit...and we made the summit. Carol and I spent nine years together mountaineering, rock climbing and going to concerts; plus after-school sports and floating the McKenzie and Willamette Rivers with my daughter, Lindsay, and Carol's two children.

I had been married previously for 5 1/2 years and divorced in 1984, after I returned to Montana from climbing Denali in Alaska. Lindsay was 14 years old in 1995. She had taken up rock climbing with me for a few years (sometimes with Carol and me), and then moved on to pursue her talents as an artist.

I took the long way home.

My usual route from Oregon would have exited Interstate Highway 90 at St. Regis, east of the Idaho-Montana border, and wandered north to Flathead Lake and on to Columbia Falls. This time, I kept driving to Missoula and another two hours to the junction of Interstate 15, just west of Butte, where I turned south toward Dillon. Nestled among the rolling hills and ridges were the Humbug Spires.

The Humbug Spires are part of the igneous intrusion of rock known as the Boulder Batholith, which appears on the surface as boulders and eroded hoodoos of varying quality. Jim and Jerry Kanzler had spotted the Spires from a distance one day, while exploring not long after moving to Butte in 1965. With their new friends, Clare Pogreba and Ray Martin, and a small cadre of other climbing partners, the era of rock climbing in the Humbug Spires began.

I turned off of Interstate 15, onto a dirt road, and drove to the public access of the Spires. I arrived just before sunset and rolled out a sleeping bag under the stars. The next morning, I brewed coffee on my MSR stove and set out before the sun extended a greeting into the creek bottom. The Douglas firs and the lodgepole pine were becoming increasingly gnarled from the elevation and years of arbor toil, with sustenance derived from the air and the deteriorating granite-like quartz monzonite—plus the remains of their own discarded body parts. It had to be a rigorous existence.

The "menk, menk, menk," of red-breasted nuthatches and the peeping of the chickadees maintained a constant presence, as if the birds were keeping track of me as I strode along.

The sun had been up for an hour, and I felt the morning slipping away. My plan was to cover the public trail quickly, then continue cross-country.

Elk and moose trails would lead to a destination among a group of rock formations I privately called the Inner Sanctum.

Seeing other people along the way would detract from my experience. Feeling connected with the natural world was all that mattered that day. Being connected meant being without distractions. The connection I sought could only be accomplished by being alone. A-lone. Being the only one. Separate, isolated, unique. All one. Alone and all one with the enchantment of the Humbug Spires. Every day with the Humbugs is unique. It's a land of magic.

The cars and trucks on I-15 were folded away on the other side of a ridge of boulders and eroding outcrops, firs, lodgepoles, sage and mountain mahogany. The morning commercial flight from Butte to Salt Lake had just flown by overhead. The evening return flight was a half-turn of the Earth away. Not a soul was around as far as I knew.

I stopped and placed one foot on a log to tighten a shoelace. I was almost to the place where the creek turned east and disappeared into a steep, twisting ravine of jumbled boulders and deadfall. The subdued rush of midsummer flow around the boulders filled a vessel in my attention. As I turned my head to better drink it in, the sound of the warming breeze wafted through a small stand of ancient firs and drifted into my awareness. I recognized the familiar tone of "aw-w-e".

I was consumed. Fully awake, acutely aware. Alone. Al-one. *All one* in my world.

"Nothing matters," I said out loud. "Nothing in this world matters."

Jim Kanzler told me one time. "I just walked around school in Columbia Falls one day and said to every one I encountered 'nothing matters'. I'm sure everyone thought I was weird."

Jim Kanzler was the most interesting human being I have ever known. For weeks he could be depressed, sulking and sarcastic. Then one day he would be bubbling with energy, highly motivated, complimentary to everyone—and could climb like a chipmunk.

Jim Kanzler's epiphany, *nothing matters*, became his tagline. It stuck with me.

I pondered "nothing matters" as I sat on the trail leading into the Humbug Spires. No thing matters. Matter comes from no thing. Matter was not a thing. No thing is made of matter.

Matter is energy—Albert Einstein.

Nothing matters—Jim Kanzler.

I leaned into the log and drew a deep breath. I held it for a second or two, and then expelled it slowly through my lips—like blowing through a straw. As my heart rate slowed, so did time.

I had first visited the Humbug Spires in 1972, the summer after I graduated from high school. I was 18—the same age as Jerry Kanzler when he made his *last* trip to the Humbugs; the autumn he started college and the only quarter he would live to attend.

Before graduation, I began mountaineering with Carl Sanders, a man ten years older than me, and the most graceful skier I had ever seen. He and I climbed the regular route on Mount St. Nicholas that summer. I wore a new pair of mountaineering boots and developed open heel blisters so painful that I tried crawling and walking backwards on the long hike out.

Carl told me that Jim Emerson had returned home from the Navy and was back in Columbia Falls, hot to pursue technical climbing. Jim was a pal of the Kanzler brothers and his father, Bob Emerson, had been a mountaineering partner of Hal's. The two fathers climbed the west face of Mount Cleveland in 1961, with two other mountaineers from the Flathead Valley.

I knocked on Jim Emerson's door and when he opened it, I took a step back. "Whoa." I had never met a hippie before. I knew that many of the Yosemite climbers of the day had long hair—but Yosemite was like Disneyland to me and the climbers I read about were only partly real. The breakaway from the mainstream status quo to a liberated lifestyle was novel and refreshing.

I was intrigued with Jim Emerson at first glance. He had a full beard and round wire-rimmed glasses. He looked like John Lennon. Within an hour, we had plans to climb on the rotten sedimentary rock of the Flathead Valley for training. We developed a list of unclimbed faces to do in Glacier, plus some of the classics in the Tetons. Emerson strengthened my resolve to start climbing where Jerry and his Butte companions had left off. Emerson and I wanted to learn how to climb cracks—something far different from the stratified holds of sedimentary rock; but finding the Humbug Spires went to the top of the agenda.

In 1972, I doubt if anyone in Columbia Falls knew where or what the Humbug Spires were, much less had ever walked into them. The area was not on the Montana highway maps yet; I suppose this was because the Humbugs were not a designated "Wilderness Study Area" yet.

There was no Bureau of Land Management (BLM) hiking trail into the area. There was no trailhead parking lot with an outhouse or display case with maps and brochures. There were no cars from out of state whose occupants had come to visit the playground where Pogreba, Martin, and the Kanzler brothers had taught themselves how to climb cracks. There were no battery-powered drills back then or climbers eager to string lines of bolts into the weathered stone so they could climb anywhere they wished and not accept the consequences of falling off. Not yet. All that would change in the 1980s.

By August of 1972, a group of "social degenerates," a label that climbers of the era accepted and were proud of, left the Kalispell area in a two-vehicle caravan and struck out to find the Humbug Spires. In a VW hatchback were Roy and Shirley Harrison and their two boys, a toddler and a preschooler. Shirley Harrison, formerly Shirley Anderson, was the sister of Jim Anderson of the Mount Cleveland Five. Roy had been a Big Sky Conference wrestling champion in his weight class at the University of Montana, which certainly earned him my respect. He was also the best climber among us at that time.

Another ski bum and climber, Gary Benson, rode with the Harrison family. Gary was an intellectual and a comedian who worked with Roy for Anderson Masonry in Bigfork and Kalispell. The other vehicle was Jim Emerson's VW microbus. The group piled most of the camping and climbing gear into the underpowered hippie van. I rode along with the counterculture champion and one-time sailor in the U.S. Navy who would one day be affectionately known as Emer-fucking-son: The one and only.

We had a copy of Montana's Humbug Spires, an article written by Jim Kanzler and published in the March 1967 issue of *Summit* magazine, to follow Kanzler's description of finding the obscure location. Jim was 18 years old himself when he wrote the article, at the urging of his father. In just over a year's time since living in Columbia Falls, Jim and Jerry Kanzler climbed four of the Cascades' high peaks in five days (along with Jim Emerson), moved to a new location, discovered the Humbug Spires for rock climbing with their new friends, and wrote an article about their find. Hal Kanzler would not live to see the article in print.

Jim Kanzler's lead-in description of the Humbug Spires was superbly ironic. "Resting atop of the Continental Divide in southwestern Montana, in view of U.S. Highway 91 [later becoming Interstate 15], and overlooking the valley of the Big Hole River is an unimpressive mountain called Humbug."

The key to finding the Humbug Spires on the 1972 road trip was to locate the appropriate gate—"with a horse skull on a fence post"—along miles and miles of barbed wire fence. Apparently, the horse skull had fallen from its mooring when our little convoy arrived in the (then) desolate sagebrush flat south of Butte. We drove back and forth until we were certain we had the right gate, and then followed a two-rut road toward the higher timbered hills. Fortunately, it hadn't rained within the past several days, if it had, we might not have negotiated the deep ruts.

One of Ray Martin's closest friends and fellow Humbug climber, Ed Leritz, told me many years later the Butte climbing contingency was upset with Jim Kanzler writing the article about the Humbug Spires in *Summit* magazine. "It was just human nature—none of us wanted Jim to publish an article on the Humbug Spires," Ed explained. "Why would anyone want to invite the whole world into our little utopia? None of us would give Jim any specific information—in fact, we shunned him for a while. But Jim Kanzler was a great guy and one of the leaders of the group, and our disdain for his article didn't last long. I don't think many climbers, if any, came to the Humbugs because of the article."

Well, there were at least seven. The 1972 Columbia Falls caravan arrived at the Humbug cabin in mid-August. We wandered around the strange rock formations for several days; tried to climb a few routes but always found them harder than they looked and retreated. Our hands were bloodied from jamming them into the cracks of extremely coarse rock, trying to discover the technique. Roy led us up a 30-foot long hand crack the rest of us struggled with; but we wound up consuming more wine than we did granite.

My enchantment with the Humbug Spires started before I set eyes on them. After Hal shot himself, "Wil" (the wrestling coach) contacted Jim and Jerry. Jean Kanzler planned to move her two teenaged sons from their brick home in Butte, where Jim graduated from high school, to a mobile home in Bozeman just two weeks after the family tragedy. The idea was that Jerry could finish high school there and enroll at Montana State University in the autumn of 1969. In Jean Kanzler's grief and haste, she planned to throw out Hal's personal photo collection, which included volumes of black-and-white prints and negatives and color slides taken by Jim and Jerry on their rock climbing adventures near Butte. Wil, fortunately, was able to convince Jean to entrust the collection to him.

After wrestling season in 1970, perhaps due to my new pursuit of climbing, Wil entrusted me to look through the Kanzler photos. I spent hours at Wil's house, sometimes with Dan tagging along, immersing myself in the Kanzler and Humbug lore. I was privileged with the Kanzler mountaineering adventures in Glacier Park and the Mission Mountains, including slides of the Kanzler 1963 Mount St. Nicholas ascent and the first few years of Humbug Spire climbing with Clare Pogreba, Ray Martin, Ed Leritz and others.

At a nondescript— dare I say unimpressive—location, in August 1995, 30 years after the Kanzler brothers found the Humbugs, I left the BLM trail and tip-toed on exposed rock and logs so I would not disturb the ground and leave a visible trail of my own. I had been this way before, and I was careful not to leave clues to the sanctuary of the "Inner Sanctum."

Soon I was on a familiar game trail. An hour's walk brought me into a draw with aspens and a moist forest floor. The terrain merged into grass and widened at the head of a small, secluded glen. One section was marshy with an open pool of brackish water. There was a beaver dam that had not existed the last time I was through. I took this for a good omen and relaxed a bit. I was entering the familiar ground of an old homestead.

I approached the remnants of what had been a small barn or shed in 1976. It had only been large enough to shelter one or two animals or store mining tools. Almost 20 years had slipped by, and the edifice was no longer standing. Aspen samplings had interwoven with the collapsed logs.

Clear water trickled from a pipe propped up by two rocks and into an old enameled basin nearly full of submerged rock granules and forest debris. This was an important water source—an oasis, since Moose Creek was now far away. The source was tucked away to the north in a myriad of boulders and trees. An old four-legged bathtub lay on its side nearby. Perhaps, tired prospectors had bathed in it. Just to be on the safe side, I took out my water filter and pumped two liters.

A short distance beyond was the terminus of that "two rut road" leading down from the final timbered ridge into the glen from the west. By the looks of it, there hadn't been anyone here for weeks, perhaps months.

On one side of the open area, where the grass had been trampled down earlier in the summer, were a series of hewn stone steps leading to the faint remnants of the Humbug cabin. The outline of its base was barely discernible.

The old homestead belonged to a family in Butte and passed down through generations. In the 1960s, the property owners allowed an open door arrangement where people could come and go, using the cabin. As you can imagine, this policy always hung in the balance. This worked because relatively few people were aware of the cabin. It served as the rendezvous point for the rock climbers from Butte in the 1960s and by the

1970s the sphere expanded to include other proud, self-proclaimed "social degenerates" from Bozeman and Missoula.

The Humbug cabin had been the destination for a party or a sojourn in the Humbug Spires. The log structure had been constructed with hand tools, muscle and sweat. She had been a simple one-room dwelling originally with an annex off of its west end added later, serving as an extra bedroom. There had been a porch the full length of the front. Inside were two worn sofas, obviously from a more modern era, a wooden table and a set of chairs that might have been 1930s vintage. The cabin could accommodate four comfortably, six or eight if necessary.

Tents were pitched outside if more sleeping space was required. The pride of the cabin had been the old Monarch wood-burning stove, complete with oven and bread warmer. It kept the cabin warm in the evenings and mornings and offered an option for preparing hot meals.

An important element of Humbug lore was the logbook kept on a clipboard with loose pages where details of an outing were chronicled or words of witticism were expressed. Jim Kanzler kept a separate written collection of climbing routes. His journal was lent to other climbers so new information could be added. Eventually, no one could remember who had it last.

Then, in April 1976, the stove was missing. The owners, naturally, thought climbers had stolen it. The climbers insisted upon their innocence. The owners acquitted the climbers of blame. A few weeks later, one climber, a little more degenerate than the others made a show of good will to prevent anything else from being stolen that would require a vehicle. He acquired a certain quantity of dynamite and blew up a log bridge over a dry wash gully. He also dropped a small outcrop of rock onto the two-rut road to prevent vehicle access. For a time, cabin visitors had to walk in.

Then one evening, during peak climbing season, when a group of us were wandering back to the cabin after a day of cragging, a pair of sheriff's deputies arrived in a four-wheel drive vehicle and questioned us about the demolition. Who had done it? No one knew. At least, no one was saying. That was all that became of it. Activity returned to normal but the stove would always be missed. Vehicular travel to the cabin was restored with a few detours.

A stay at the cabin included an unwritten code that you left it in as good of condition or better than you found it. Frequent occupants tried to leave something like a pot or a pan, a candle, a broom, or a mousetrap for the next visitors. The theft of the stove bummed everyone out. Staying there was a privilege and a tradition. Two years later the cabin was gone. Burned to the ground.

I paid a silent tribute to an era gone by, and headed up a wooded ravine. In the early 1970s it was easy to see the bottom of the ravine had been excavated and stones laid in place to create a narrow roadway, most likely part of a prospector's operation. At the close of the twentieth century, I had to look harder to see the man-made structure. Cheers for Mother Nature, who could return earth to Earth.

An elk and moose trail continued beyond. Two ravens croaked at one another as they flew overhead, destined to wherever the breezes and their whims were taking them. A light dust stirred under foot and covered my shoes. The dew had evaporated. A few fluffy clouds were beginning to materialize. As I worked to maintain my pace with the steepening grade, I felt the sweat on my temples. I might have welcomed this as a good workout and kept pushing; but I reminded myself there was no need to hurry. I was now a long way from the BLM trail and would meet no one. I would miss the whole point if I continued to hurry.

I had arrived in my sacred place. I took stock for a minute to let my breathing and heart rate drop. I was not packing the full complement of rock climbing hardware, just climbing shoes and a chalk bag. All I needed to do was be there.

I arrived in a small corner of the world seldom visited. I drew in a few deep breaths and slowly exhaled through pursed lips. All was well. All-oneness returned. I sat on the ground, leaned against my pack and gazed at the branches of the lodgepole pines above me and let my awareness unfold from the sweet sound of quiet. From 30 feet above came the hush of a light breeze coursing through all those pine needles. The undulating "a-w-w-w-e" became ambient like the sound of a distant waterfall. The tone varied with the ebb and flow of the current of the air. When the breeze strengthened, the tone rose to a slightly higher pitch. As the breeze softened, the pitch lowered.

How many pine needles were within a hundred feet of me? Millions? Billions? I was consumed by the sum of individual tone variations of each needle.

Then came another subtle disturbance in the air. A "pdrrrt, pdrrrt, pdrrrt," like short bursts of a cat purring. Then a small bluish gray bird looking as though he had no neck landed on a thin branch ten feet away—red-breasted nuthatch. His underside was the color of a robin's. He had a black and white striped face with a bill like the tip of a pen that turned upward. He couldn't sit still, rapidly maneuvering around the tree taking small insects off of the bark. Sometimes he was right side up, sometimes upside down, jumping to the next branch with a quick "pdrrrt". Then came the nasal "menk, menk, menk" and more wing sounds. Four more miniature acrobats emerged out of nowhere, flitting about on the sparse branches of the lodgepoles. They moved to the tree next to me about three feet from my face. I turned my head as slowly as I could, watching the nuthatches move down the trunk headfirst as easily as they did right side up. Even calling to each other in proximity, their voices seemed distant. I remembered the call of a mysterious bird when I was a boy hunting grouse with my dad. It was years before I knew whom the voice belonged to.

A minute more and they indeed sounded far away. Then I could no longer hear them at all.

"This is middle of nowhere," I thought to myself, "just where I want to be."

"But," another part of me said, "You are now here."

"Now here?"

"There is no such place as nowhere...because there is always a place called *now-here*.

"Oh."

I closed my eyes and observed further, tuning my attention to a single engine airplane flying by miles away. Ordinarily, I might have disdained the invasive distraction of a vehicle in such a circumstance. But the airplane held something peculiar for me. The monotonous drone gave me a strange melancholy feeling not unlike the feeling I got hearing the breeze in the conifers. One sound was natural, pristine and purifying, the other unnatural and polluting. Yet both shared a common characteristic—a chant that seemed to change time and space.

Sometimes a distant airplane makes me feel like I have been abandoned; part of me wants to go with it. This time, sitting undisturbed in the middle of the Humbug Spires with the airplane moving toward the Highland Mountains to the southeast, the receding pitch of the engine made me feel even more remote—closing an invisible curtain as it drifted further away, leaving me with an expanding wilderness.

When I was sure I no longer heard the airplane, there was still a background tone—something left behind. Perhaps the frequency of the airplane's vibrational disturbance was in harmony with another underlying tone.

One day, I was skiing across a frozen lake in the Canadian Rockies with Jim Emerson. It was a rare calm, sunny afternoon as we returned from an ice climb. We stopped, looking at the extraordinary scenery of high mountains above us, loaded with snow. The air had become perfectly still. We stood there silently, each lost in the moment. I heard Emerson mutter as if to no one, "It is so quiet you can hear the Earth hum."

I shifted my butt on the ground while the sun moved through the trees and the waving shadows played on my face. I tried to focus on the space between pine needles, but all I could think about was my full bladder. Mother nature was calling, not giving out secrets. I had to answer. I stood up and brushed off the rock granules and pine needles, returned some nitrogen to the soil and moseyed on.

I approached familiar rock formations and greeted them in my mind. The earliest Humbug climbers named the first of two distinctive boulders along the trail *de Gaulle*, because the rock had a profile of former French president Charles de Gaulle, who had an unmistakable nose. The bouldering attention in the '60s and '70s at this location went to a slightly smaller rock just behind de Gaulle. This one was 15 feet high on its shorter uphill side. It was called *Egg Cup Rock* because it was shaped just like an egg and sat on a pedestal. It had only one route. In the '60s, the first Humbug climbers, still all teenagers who called themselves the Wool Socks Club, made repeated attempts on Egg Cup Rock. It had been a tradition among them to see who would be first to stand on top. As they hiked up the same game trail I was following en route to larger rock formations just beyond, they would drop their packs here, get into their best climbing shoes and continue with a little bouldering session. Ropes and hardware stayed in the packs.

By the end of the decade, only one among them had succeeded in standing on top of Egg Cup Rock: Clare Pogreba. Clare was Mr. Ambition, according to Jim Kanzler, and a great schemer.

Clare was the shortest climber of the group, at five-foot-three in mountain boots. He figured a way to reach around the egg and mantle up where his six-foot-seven pal, Ray Martin, and the others came up short.

A new problem emerged: How to get down. It was too far for a rational person to jump.

"In the end," Jim Kanzler told me, "Clare reached out to a branch of the closest tree with a hand shake grip and leaped into the tree and down climbed the trunk."

Jerry Kanzler, who had one of the highest scores at the high school state gymnastics meet in the fall of 1968, didn't make Egg Cup Rock. Nor did Jim. Clare's lone success the summer of 1969 remained for a number of years.

Then, in the spring of 1973, I had connected with Jim Kanzler, a surviving member of the original Humbug Spires climbers, and found myself joining a new group of guys at the Humbugs who called themselves the Dirty Sox Club. As we hiked along, we came to Egg Cup Rock. The packs came off, the tight toe-curling smooth-sole E.B. climbing shoes went on, the fingers got chalked, and we all had a go at Egg Cup Rock. No one made it until suddenly, a burly, rough-cut character with wild, curly dark hair and gray spacey eyes, called Dougal McCarty, was suddenly standing on top.

A round of applause went up for Dougal. Kanzler, with an extra charge of energy, went to the boulder and in ten seconds was on top himself. More applause. Kanzler used the Pogreba grab-and-leap technique. I was among the others who gave it a number of attempts. As the rest of the group began to shoulder their packs, I was still at it. As the others proceeded up the game trail, Kanzler hung back to give me the mandatory "spot" for my last attempt.

"A little further to the right, reach as far as you can," he said encouraged, "you've almost got it."

The tips of my fingers began to just feel the edge of the little depression. It wasn't much but the coarseness of the rock allowed some purchase. I spider walked my fingers desperately forward trying to gain more of the dish. When I realized I had all I was going to get, I gathered all the strength and will I could muster and powered up, realizing I might pop off in the next split second.

I didn't.

I stood up on Egg Cup Rock, proud as can be—not so much because I'd conquered the boulder as because I had joined my heroes: Clare Pogreba, Jim Kanzler and the wild man, Dougal McCarty. In that moment, I realized I was a step closer to the north face of Mount Cleveland.

I pondered the leap into the tree. No one else noticed I had just climbed Egg Cup Rock. Their attention had turned to the roped climbs that lay ahead as they hiked up the hill through the woods. Even Kanzler had left me to figure out the rest. By the time I jumped into the tree and changed shoes and had my pack on, the others were gone. The climb remains a fine memory.

Twenty-two years later, I was a man over 40, meandering through the Humbugs, scouting routes I might like to try in the future when I had a partner for *trad rock climbing*. Just ahead were: the *Wall,* the *Nose,* the *Mustache*, the *Thumb*, the *Fingers*, and *Rook Rock*. The *Wedge* was a few of miles further, tucked behind a couple of ridges. I thought how simple the names were. Elsewhere around the country from the Schwangunks of New York to Yosemite Valley in California names varied from lavish to grotesque to vulgar. In a cluster of gritty outcrops secluded in meandering hills and ravines in Montana there had been innocence. The pioneers were emerging schoolboys searching for adventure, camaraderie and *themselves*, making plans for big mountains and gothic faces of snow, rock and ice.

After February 1967, on all the journeys to the Humbugs, the Tetons and Glacier Park, the young guild of climbers had to be carrying the weight of Hal Kanzler's suicide. Somehow, they just kept climbing. None of the names of the rocks or the routes seemed to reflect the tragedy, but surely some of the innocence was lost.

Jean Kanzler told me years later that Clare and Ray were very caring. They helped with moving to Bozeman. Jim told me Clare drove the truck like a racecar driver along the Jefferson River and windy Montana Highway 2 past the Lewis and Clark Caverns in the days before Interstate 90 existed. "Clare told me he wouldn't live to be 30. He was right. He didn't even come close."

The rock formations I passed all had routes from the boys of the 1960s. I had come along in the early '70s as part of the next generation and joined a new contingency of young climbers from Bozeman. I climbed many of the old routes and added new routes of my own. I wandered among the craggy outcrops, trying to remember those I had climbed and those I had not.

Something struck me as remarkable. Signs of human activity were absent. The place seemed forgotten. Other than The Wedge with its BLM trail, the place was undisturbed. There was no erosion left by climbers at the base of popular climbing rocks. The only soil disturbances were from wild animal tracks and erosion from past rains.

I had returned to the playground of my youth. The proximity of familiar rocks, trees and ridges triggered a mildly distorted memory. The Humbugs have a way of distorting perception. Rock formations seemed closer together and smaller than I remembered them. I strayed into an era gone by, left to wander through my own past. Time and space perception began to change further. I had a perception of Pogreba, Martin and Jerry Kanzler. I felt left behind to revel in their abandon.

One day during a Cub Scout den meeting not long after R. Glenn, Dan, Jack and I made our little excursion up Teakettle Mountain in 1964, Jerry Kanzler came up to me and said, "I am proud of you climbing Teakettle." His dark eyes seemed to twinkle as a smile etched across his face.

I guess that's all it took; just a few simple encouraging words from such an unusual guy.

With no one else to keep me in the present I might just as well have walked onto the holodeck of the Starship Enterprise of *Star Trek: The Next Generation* and commanded, "Computer! Load Humbug Spires May 10, 1969. Merge past and present."

I continued among the deep clefts, nooks and crannies. The Humbug Spires were eroding. Some walls were like Swiss cheese with holes and pockets, undercut at their bases. Some flakes of rock I could pry from the wall with my hands or rub two together and cause them to disintegrate. They were decaying. Some formations loomed macabre, like the boney remains of extinct creatures—bigger than dinosaurs.

I sat down in a scoop formed by a huge exposed root of an ancient Douglas fir at the base of the Nose. The grandfather (or would that be the Grandmother?) tree had thick gnarled bark and yellow lichen growing on its north side.

"Computer! One liter of water—air temperature."

I had sat there 20 years before belaying my most steady climbing partner of the mid 1970s, Steve Jackson, as he took the second lead of a two-pitch crack climb up the center of the Nose. Clare, Ray, Jim, Jerry and the others of the old group had likely sat there too.

I focused on the air moving through the branches of the old tree and drifted away. Then and now became the same. I felt heaviness inside me and became uneasy. I considered walking away, but my arms and legs would not move. I felt a need to hide, but I didn't know what from. I thought about grabbing my pack and heading back to Moose Creek, then driving to Columbia Falls, to escape the strange feeling. I couldn't make myself leave. I wanted to brush the feelings off like sparks from a campfire, but I forced them down with the defiance of drinking a shot of whiskey. I could have pulled the moment out by the roots and thrown it in a heap; instead, I planted it in my water bottle to see what might bloom.

What I really wanted was a vision. I resigned myself to sit there and experience whatever it was I would experience. I convinced myself that nothing could harm me because "nothing mattered." I persuaded myself to be the warrior, unafraid.

I could hear the familiar sounds of rock climbing—the belay signals shouted, the jangling of pitons hanging from a gear sling of one-inch tied webbing carried around the neck-and-shoulder. I could hear the ringing of pitons driven with a simple rock hammer. I could smell the burned gunpowder odor of pulverized rock when pitons were beaten sideways and taken out. I recognized the conversation of young men in their teens and early twenties and their laughter—the product of exuberance and uneasiness at having done something risky. I searched the features of the rock wall above me hoping I might find the route Jerry named Revolution Number Nine after the psychedelic John Lennon song. Jerry had climbed the new route with Ed Leritz the summer before Mount Cleveland. It was supposed to be hard for the day. The exact location and details had been lost with Jim's route journal. I could see Jerry up there in the corduroy knickers and colorful knicker socks and a Scottish wool tam. I could make out his thick, black, shoulder length hair wafting in the breeze, his square jaw grimace at the crux move, pushing the climbing to a new level. I wanted to hear his exuberance just like in Cub Scouts. Jim once told me Jerry came back that day after climbing Revolution Number Nine with Ed in his usual excitement. Jerry suggested he and Jim go back and do the climb together. They didn't get the opportunity.

I have always envisioned Jerry Kanzler a study of talent and enthusiasm. I knew he had an uncommon presence, which I had seen—yet I never saw him climb.

Merry Kay got married just out of high school in 1969. She gave birth to her first daughter as news broke about Jerry Kanzler missing on Mount Cleveland. Kay told me she wept for days for the loss of her one-time childhood sweetheart.

Billowing cumulus clouds had been steadily growing and gray bellies were showing by noon. If I was to do any climbing myself, I had better get to it soon before the clouds matured to thunderheads. I stood up and walked back to the Wall.

The Wall is a nearly symmetrical pyramid with a crease up the middle when viewed straight on from the south. Its face is steeper than the Great Pyramid of Giza and almost as high. The overall angle lays back enough so most of the routes are moderate in difficulty as they meander up the features.

Like most rock formations, there are places where very difficult routes could be contrived. None of the Humbug climbers I had climbed with would consider rappelling down the Wall and plastering the elegant contours of rock with permanent bolts. What would be the point just to claim authorship or conquest of an artificial route? By 1995, I don't think there was a single bolt on the Wall.

I laced up an old pair of high-topped smooth-soled climbing shoes. My plan was to solo (unroped) up the "Center Route" for a little game of concentration on a route I had soloed several times before.

I unzipped the lid on my pack and fished around for my Croakie. Crap! It wasn't in there! What to do? I didn't want to climb if there was a chance my glasses would come off. I was as blind as a bat without them and I had already one tense, hairball experience with losing a lens when free-soloing years before.

The problem was solved with a shoelace from one of my sneakers. I lashed my glasses to my head.

I put my game face on and took slow, deep breaths. My heart was already racing a little with the anticipation of being high off the ground. I focused to get "into a groove" or a rhythm to allow myself to be smooth and deliberate. I buckled a chalk bag to my waist, took my watch off and sunk it deep into a pocket.

I made my way to the base of the rock and the initial crack, resembling a rain gutter, inset into the rock. I focused on maintaining my breathing rhythm.

"If I get too jittery or become unconfident, I can always climb back down this," I told myself. I hadn't done many climbs in the previous months, though I felt I was in reasonable shape. I didn't know just how I was going to feel once I got off of the ground without a rope. Belayed climbing with a partner would have been saner, but I didn't have one. So I chose a climb a number of clicks easier than I would have ordinarily chosen with a partner and a rope.

I climbed ten, twenty, forty feet. I felt good. I shut the proverbial trap door beneath my feet, blocking the view below.

Humbug "granite" is like the coarsest grit of sandpaper one can find. It scuffed the skin white on the back of my hands. One goal was to not draw blood—scraping my hands indicated a lack of finesse. Rock granules adhered to the modern sticky rubber soles so I repeatedly had to brush them off on the opposite pant cuff. My energy level was high and I was intoxicated with the joy of moving well over stone.

On top of the Wall, I still had to be careful. Hundreds of feet dropped off on three sides. I sat on the hard, bumpy stone. The clouds were beginning to tower.

I could see spires and crags of the Humbug in every direction. Anything much higher than the trees had a name: *Baldy*, the *Bullet*, the *Brothers*, the *Crown*, *Little Dome*, Rook Rock, *Poge*, *Arch Rock*, *The Bird*, *Hobgoblin* and *Sun Dog*. Way back in there was the top of the *Wedge*, the big daddy of the Humbugs tucked deep into the hills. The BLM trail goes right to the bottom of it. Since then, The Wedge has become a destination for climbers. It's not enough to have wilderness. How can there be a wilderness without a trail, or a parking lot and a reader board? How can there be a climbing area without a published guidebook? Those who walk to The Wedge on the Moose Creek trail will never know what it was like to set out cross country for The Wedge by dead reckoning, packs bulging with ropes and gear, sometimes getting lost.

Even Pat Callis—the man Pogreba, Martin and the Kanzler brothers called "Gandalf"—got disoriented trying to find his way back to the cabin from The Wedge in fading light. Pat recounted the story from time to time throughout the years.

"I had to admit to myself I was lost," he would say shaking his head and grinning. "So I dropped my pack and waited until morning to figure things out. When it got light I realized I was only 300 yards from the cabin."

I started to lose my climbing rush and morphed back into sober thought gazing into the menagerie that stretched out before me. I became reflective and brooding. Often in the Humbugs I felt connected to the era gone by. The past and the present became very close together as though separated by a thin transparent film of no-thing. I was still the observer.

The proverbial holodeck program played on. "Computer! Fast-forward to September 13, 1969."

Clare Pogreba, Ray Martin and Jerry Kanzler were marching through the gap between the Nose and the Thumb. Perhaps the trio was returning from a climb on the *Finger* or The Crown. Their knuckles were barked from the abrasive rock. Jerry carried an English Karrimor rucksack made of rusty-orange canvas and leather. He had a red Mammut Perlon rope in a mountaineer-coil looped around his shoulders, the same rope he and Ray would be tied into when they were recovered on the west face of

Mount Cleveland. The pack would be recovered with one shoulder strap completely avulsed and missing.

The three young climbers drew their attention to the steep wall of The Thumb above them as Clare pointed upward. They stood there a moment gawking at the route that Jim, Rick Hooven (a climber from California) and I climbed in 1979 called the "Hangnail". They took turns reaching upward, jamming their fingers into the thin crack. Jerry made the first few moves in his mountaineering boots then reversed them easily. They studied the rock for another minute then began running and plunge stepping down the loose granular footing of the corridor, heading in my direction.

I rose to my feet from my semi reclined position unsure of what decade I was in. Then and now, here and there seemed the same. I may have been on top of the Wall an hour or more but it felt like one long paradoxical moment: all-one in the middle of now-here.

Clare, Ray and Jerry followed the game trail that veered along the base of the Wall just below me, headed back to the cabin. They were chatting and cajoling one another. There would be a campfire beyond the flat stone steps of the cabin that evening with stories and laughter. Discussion of the north face of Mount Cleveland would carry them into the night and on toward destiny three and a half months later.

"Perhaps this is your opportunity," I heard a part of me say. "Why don't you call out to those guys, what could be the harm? Hell, there is no one else around."

The next thing I realized I was shouting, "Jerry Kanzler...Ray Martin...Clare Pogreba...over here!" My voice rang off of the Nose and the Mustache and I could hear the echo of the last syllable. I half expected the three young guys to stop at my voice, but they kept walking. I repeated their names. They stopped and at first I thought they heard me, but they just turned toward each other, apparently Pogreba, who was in the lead, was clarifying a point to the other two.

"Up here," I yelled down, "I'm up here." They continued and I lost sight of them below the Wall.

"Jerry—Kanzler! Ray! Pogreba! I just want you to know that I've been carrying on for you guys. Jim and I climbed the north face of Mount Cleveland...and Siyeh. We haven't forgotten you."

The sky grew dark and the air got cold. I had that giddy feeling again. I sensed Jerry Kanzler was right in front of me, though I could not see him. The hair on my neck stood straight out and I felt tingly. Should I offer a greeting or something?

There was a tap on my shoulder! Before I could turn around, there was a loud clap of thunder. I nearly stumbled off of the top as I turned around, expecting to see a ghost. Whoa! A thunderhead was bearing down on me with virga streaking out of the bottom. A lightning strike hit Fleecer Mountain, a couple miles to the west.

"I'd better get out of here!" I had forgotten all about watching the weather. The hail began to fall sporadically like tiny meteorites bouncing off of the rock. I scrambled off of the other side of the Wall as fast as I could. "Computer! End program—now!" I left the other part of me on the summit, nothing more than a smile.

I made my way around the west wing of the Wall, down low angle slabs slippery with lichen and shifty granules of granite. I scurried around to the front side without incident...or so I thought. I had just beaten the thunderstorm's fly-by. The thundercloud did little more than rumble a few times before drifting off to the northeast in the general direction of Butte but it had successfully chased me off of the top.

I slowed to a walk along the base, feeling more grounded, you might say. With the weather threat over for the time being, I decided to look for the first route I did on The Wall with Jim Emerson in the spring of 1973— a route Jim and Lindalee Kanzler climbed first in 1969.

As I scrambled past three old Douglas firs, my eye caught a glimpse of a small metallic cube with a hole and a strap through it, right at my feet. Baffled, I bent over and picked it up. I knew what it was—a piece of 1960s climbing gear—an artificial chock (or nut) manufactured in England. It was one of the first commercial models of climbing chocks available in the United States. I had owned a couple Clog chocks of different sizes that I had randomly acquired during my first year or two of climbing. These pieces of gear were obsolete by the time I started leading significant rock climbs because designs had improved quickly.

The chock I found was approximately 3/4 of an inch per side and strung with half- inch, army green webbing. It was crudely melted at the cut ends to prevent the nylon edge from fraying. It was not quite long enough to be carried around the neck-and-shoulder, but long enough to be carried around just the neck.

The webbing certainly didn't look new. A rodent had gnawed a small spot on one edge. The consistency of the webbing was soft and supple, suggesting minimal UV damage. Any webbing left in the elements since the end of the 1960s would have been sun-bleached, stiff and friable. If the chock and webbing had been lying on the duff all those years it would have been buried in a year's time under the surface of accumulating needle shed from the trees; or rodents would have long since dispatched of the nylon fabric or even carted the object away.

Adhered on the underside of the chock, which is normally not in contact with the rock, was a clue to who may have lost this piece of equipment. Two small squares of colored tape were intact—one of blue and one of red plastic marking tape—the color code mark of whoever had lost the chock.

Again, the tingle sensation ran up my spine as I realized the implication. "This cannot be here! Not fifty feet from the rock! Not lying on top of the duff!" I looked up into the venerable old firs— like the trees knew the answer. I held the artifact in my hand as if it were a sparrow.

"By 1969," Jim Kanzler told me about a year later, when I showed him the chockstone, "We were using a mixture of pitons and nuts in the Humbugs. The nuts were a hodgepodge of chocks—mostly from Great Britain. We didn't have full sets of chocks in a wide range." (That didn't come about until Yvon Chouinard made his first sets of Stoppers and Hexentrics in 1972.) "What we had in 1968 and 1969 we carried around our necks or over our shoulders on long slings—like this one." He picked up the antiquated piece of gear and rolled it in his fingers as he examined it. Then he added, "I remember buying a quantity of half-inch military webbing in Butte just after we moved there in 1965."

I knew Jim color-coded his gear red and yellow when we first started climbing together. He later switched to stamping his initials onto his climbing hardware. He did not remember the color code Jerry used on his gear. However, if Jim used two colors, it made sense that Jerry would have as well. Ray Martin's sister, Carol McGrath, once gave me a piton belonging to Ray. It was stamped "RM." No colored tape was on it.

After the Mount Cleveland Five were given up for dead, six soft iron pitons and an early REI aluminum oval carabiner attached to a sling of one-inch webbing were recovered from the base camp. The sling had green and light blue tape on it; the carabiner had two separate marks of light blue. Jim was quite sure the equipment belonged to Clare Pogreba. Perhaps Clare had initially marked his gear with light blue. As the camaraderie of climbers grew, he may have added a second color to his color code so that more combinations were possible within the group. Apparently, the Butte contingent all had two-color combinations— or stamped their initials into the hardware.

I folded the sling over the chockstone with reverence and placed it in the lid of my pack. The relic quickly took on totemic status. I left the Wall area, retracing my steps past the old cabin site and down the elk trail, alone—I think. By the time I reached the BLM trail and Moose Creek, I had about a seven-minute mile going. I jumped in my car and drove another five hours to Columbia Falls.

Fourteen years later, in 2009, while I was writing this book, another revealing discovery was made. Bill Dockins and Tom Kalakay had just published the third edition of *Bozeman Rock Climbs*. The book devoted much attention to the historical progression of southern Montana rock climbing. Therein was a full-page photo taken by Pat Callis in 1969 of Jim Kanzler, in knickers, making the second ascent of the "Mother's Day" route in Gallatin Canyon. (Pat and Jerry Kanzler had made the first ascent a week earlier.) There on Jim's swami belt (dangling almost to his knees), was that chockstone on half-inch webbing, placing the mysterious Clog anchor on the Kanzler hardware rack in 1969. There is no doubt that Jim and Jerry would pool their gear for climbs, whether or not they were both on a given climb together or not. Since Jim color-coded his gear with yellow and red, then the blue and red chock had to be Jerry's. The question remains—how did the chockstone find its way onto the duff in good condition in 1995.

The Humbug cabin, August 1972. Left to right:
Jim Emerson, Shirley Anderson (Jim Anderson's sister),
Roy Harrison and their two sons. Photo by the author.

The author 1979. Kennedy collection.

The author leading the first ascent of the "Hangnail" on The Thumb:
"…a route for the next generation." May 1979. Kennedy collection.

CHAPTER 4

Meet the Dirty Sox Club

Jim Kanzler and I exchanged letters after the summer of 1972, the first year that I climbed in the Humbugs. The topic of ice climbing came up. It was becoming a pursuit in its own right, and climbers were now seeking frozen waterfalls in addition to granite spires and cliffs. This was made possible by a change in the ice axe design by Yvon Chouinard, who designed a pick that curved downward. This allowed the climber to place the pick into vertical ice and have it stay in place. The shaft of the ice axe functioned as a handhold. I had many questions for Jim about gear and procedure.

Around Christmas of that year, Jim Emerson discovered a small, frozen waterfall a short distance above his parents' house at the base of Columbia Mountain that spilled over a mossy, 15-foot ledge. The stream appeared frozen in space and time. We set up a top rope.

Emerson had a pair of SMC twelve-point hinged crampons with front points and a beautiful Simond Super D straight-picked ice axe he bought in Switzerland while in the Navy—possibly the same year I bought my Raichle boots in Lucerne while playing last-chair trombone in the high school band. The Simond Super D bore many Himalayan climbers to the summits of the highest peaks in the world.

I sported a pair of ten-point snow-slogger crampons, which lacked front points. I had trudged up Mount St. Helens with them the year before, and Mount Rainier earlier that year with the Tacoma Branch of the (Seattle) Mountaineers. More impressive was my brand-new Chouinard-Frost Piolet: the state-of-the-art ice axe with the curved pick and a 70 centimeter laminated bamboo shaft. Kanzler had strongly advised that I get one, and gave me a small discount because he could buy them on a professional account. Thus, I retired my straight-picked ice axe at age 18, after three years of service.

Emerson and I laid siege to the 15 feet of vertical, welded icicles. Many aspects of ice climbing became evident that day; for instance, if you didn't have front points or a curved pick ice axe, you couldn't get off the ground.

Even if I twisted my ankles around or dropped my heels low enough so I could get one or two vertical crampon points biting into the ice with my butt sticking out, I couldn't stabilize myself enough to place the high-tech ice axe into the vertical ice. My attempts to gain a secure crampon placement resulted in my flailing on the end of the rope.

Emerson got both feet off the ground and onto the ice at the same time, with his crampon front points; but only briefly. The Super D pick would not stay in the ice long enough to let him advance a single foot higher before it would pop out and he would flop around like a carp on the end of a fishing line. I ducked and dodged to avoid being bowled over or impaled by the pointed instruments.

Since Emerson had front points, I gave him the Chouinard-Frost axe. The goal became simply to "get one man to the top," just like on those Himalayan expeditions. Every time he tried to place the Chouinard-Frost, the Simond popped out and the wrecking ball dance started over again.

Emerson had the most powerful and barbaric ice axe swing of anyone I ever knew. That distinction still persists—a stark contrast for a self-styled peace-loving hippie. As Emerson bludgeoned his way up, debris flew in every direction while columns of ice fell like the walls of Dresden during an Allied bombing raid. Eventually, Emerson belly-crawled over the top, with me yarding tension on the rope as hard as I could. It was difficult to tell who had worked harder: the climber or the belayer.

"Fucking-A, man, this ice climbing is really strenuous," Emerson conceded.

"It seems like it's going to be harder than rock climbing—and more dangerous, with all the falls and sharp things," I added.

"Yeah. Well, I think it will help a lot to have the ice hammer with a curved pick so you have two curved tools that stick," Emerson correctly figured. To my chagrin, I didn't make it up the climb in my ten-point crampons, no matter how much tension Emerson gave me.

That evening, I called Kanzler. He ordered a pair of Chouinard twelve-point adjustable platform crampons with synthetic straps and a Chouinard Alpine Hammer, to be shipped to Columbia Falls. I didn't care how much of my college savings it took. If I was going to be able to climb ice at all, I needed the full battle armament; that's all there was to it.

In early February of 1973, Kanzler wrote me a letter:

> ...the big news here is that a couple of [my climbing partners] from Bozeman climbed the north face of Granite Peak over the Christmas break. Their names are Brian

Leo and Doug McCarty. They are just out of high school. They were forced to bivouac on the summit in a blizzard and McCarty got severe frostbite on both feet. He just got out of the hospital in Billings...

Wow! I had seen a photo of the north face of Granite Peak in a *Missoulian* Sunday sports feature article. It was steep, and would be technically difficult...and no doubt a very serious endeavor in winter! Big faces in winter—it can be done! Leo and McCarty had done it—and they were in that 18-22-age bracket! Perhaps the idea of climbing the north face of Mount Cleveland in the winter wasn't as farfetched as other "experienced" and armchair mountaineers had proclaimed. Even though the north face of Mount Cleveland was twice as high as the north face of Granite Peak, the same kinds of problems existed in winter on both mountains.

Who were these guys who had succeeded at such a big undertaking? They were my age and climbing with Jim Kanzler!

I was determined to climb with those guys. I became more excited than ever to enroll at MSU in Bozeman the following autumn.

In the same letter, Jim suggested I meet him in Bozeman and climb Green Gully together. I was ecstatic. I had a month to prepare.

"When you use these tools, the procedure is pretty much the same as rock climbing," Jim explained on the telephone. "You belay the same way. Instead of pitons and nuts, you chop a little starting hole with your alpine hammer pick, then take these (Salewa) tubular ice screws and crank them in with the hammer pick. This ice protection is much more solid than with the old pound-in ice pitons or 'coat hanger' ice screws that are nearly worthless. Pat Callis and I only took six ice screws when we made the first ascent of Green Gully. You don't have to carry such a wide variety of anchors as in rock climbing."

Jim didn't own a new Chouinard-Frost ice axe. When the word was out about the new design, before the tools were first available, Kanzler took his straight-picked axe and heated the pick to red-hot on the gas stove in his mobile home. He laid the heated pick over a rock and reshaped the pick into a droop with his rock hammer. He filed in deeper teeth and cut the hickory shaft back to 60 centimeters.

There were old-style European ice hammers already in production, and they had teeth; but their picks were also straight. Kanzler modified the hammer pick in the same fashion and made the first ascent of Green Gully with Callis.

"My modifications of the obsolete tools worked about as well as Pat's new models," Kanzler told me years later. The truth was: Jim couldn't afford the new models with a wife and son to support on ski patrolman's wages.

Kanzler was an expert at thriving in poverty. He led dozens of ice climbs with his modified old gear. Jim Emerson modified his Simond Super D the same way, following Kanzler's instructions, and never did get a Chouinard-Frost Piolet. In a later era, Emerson upgraded to "reverse-drooped" tools.

I assembled my new crampons as soon as they arrived and admired the curves and angles. The hickory handle of the Alpine Hammer fit the hand well and felt as solid as stone—and just as heavy. The menacing pick looked like a medieval battle weapon. "By God, that ought to stick into the ice!" I told myself reassuringly.

It did—often too well.

The Chouinard-Frost ice axe held the most intrigue. The long pick with the graceful arch was a thing of beauty. I put my face up close to examine it, like one might a flower. I ran my hands over the angular adze and the arc of the pick, and viewed it end-on. I swung the tool through space, moving it about like a boy might play with a model airplane. The laminated bamboo shaft seemed as strong as steel. I attached a sling of webbing through the carabiner hole in the head of the ice axe and measured out a loop through which the gloved hand could be inserted. Jim had told me to do this. Dr. Callis had figured out that one got a better grip on the end of the shaft with this, and the hand could rest better just after blows and not fatigue the arms so much. It was a tool modification that caught on worldwide.

I rubbed linseed oil into the wooden handles, at R. Glenn's suggestion, and I was all set.

I took a day off from work at the plant and drove the '54 Chevrolet to Bozeman. It gradually became my car. I met Jim Kanzler early in the morning on St. Patrick's Day at the Western Cafe on Main Street in Bozeman, then continued east to Livingston and followed the Yellowstone River south to small the community of Pine Creek. Jim pointed out the small house where Richard Brautigan, author of *Trout Fishing in America*, had once lived.

We turned off River Road, through a cattle pasture and up a steep, boulder-strewn hill into the Absaroka Mountains. The four-door sedan pushed snow with its bumper for the last two miles to the Pine Creek trailhead.

Jim made sure I understood how to place the picks of the axe and alpine hammer, could kick in the front points of the crampons, and knew to drop my heels to set the first vertical points and stabilize the boot. We climbed Blue Gully first, and Jim let me lead the short second pitch.

We rappelled off and traversed to the longer and steeper Green Gully. Jim led both pitches with our 150-foot rope, and we traversed off to the right through trees and cliffs and descended. Kanzler noted it was the first time both climbs had been done in one day, though they are now done together routinely.

It was well after dark when we returned to the Chevy. The first section of road required driving back uphill. Plowing snow with the bumper on the way in had not been a problem; but the torque of the rear wheels on the heavy car dug deeper into the snow on the initial grade, and we got horribly stuck. Kanzler and I shoveled trenches for each tire over fifty yards in at least two places. We yanked logs and branches out of the snow and placed them under jacked-up tires. We broke one of the two tire chains after mounting them on the rear wheel drivers, which in turn beat a hole in the muffler. This brought on a duet of cussing and laughter.

It was midnight before we were free.

"I am in deep shit!" Kanzler lamented. "Lindalee didn't want me to go climbing today, anyway..." He insisted on driving on the final attempt. After all, he'd done this before.

"I'll rock it a few times, and you push. On the third rock going forward, jump on the back for extra traction. Once I get going, we won't stop until we get to the place where it goes downhill again."

Kanzler jumped in and cranked the three-speed shifting lever on the steering column up and down like a drum major in a parade. His mountain boots had the three pedals going like a Clydesdale riding a bicycle. On three, he took off like a bat out of Hell.

My legs churned. At the last possible moment, I belly-flopped onto the trunk with one knee on the rear bumper as snow jetted out from the back tires. My arms flailed, with nothing to grasp initially. Kanzler gunned the engine and the Chevy fishtailed madly, sounding more like a locomotive with the hole in the muffler. I got one foot, then the other onto the bumper and made a desperate lunge for back of the roof rack with a gloved hand and hung on for dear life.

Four cleats held the rack to the seams of the roof, tightened with webbing. I could feel the whole thing shift as I maintained my grip. If those cleats had come loose, things would have gotten ugly in a hurry.

As the rear of the car slipped left, my body swung right, my feet slipping off of the eroded chrome bumper. When the rampaging auto slid right, my body whipped left—back and forth, like a salmon swimming up the rapids. At one point, I considered jumping off for fear we might run off the steep bank on the right; but it was too late. We were going so fast that I thought I would probably cartwheel and break my neck. Kanzler hit second, and the ride smoothed out some. The trees were rushing by with terrifying speed.

I stole a glance through the back window. Kanzler was steering and counter-steering wildly. His hands were up near his cheeks, gripping the big steering wheel, with elbows held close to his body. His head craned over the dash, face nearly to the windshield to better see the track in the headlights as the wipers flipped back and forth, full blast.

Now and then we'd hit a drift or a dip and the snow would stream up over the hood, obscuring Kanzler's vision and blasting me in the face, obliterating my glasses.

"Su-su-slow down, Kanzler. Please!" I huffed. There was no way he could hear me. The snow and windblast choked out my breath, so I prayed, "Just keep those cleats on, Jesus!"

We charged into the night. Had I fallen off, Kanzler would have sped on without me. Finally, we topped the grade and pulled out of the timber. Kanzler let up on the gas. I unpacked the snow from behind my glasses. My face was freezing. Kanzler got out.

"Sorry man, I almost forgot you were back there; you O.K.?"

"Yeah, I guess. Wow! That was some kind of driving!"

"Yeah, well, this car is great," he replied. "It drives like a tank."

From that day forward, my grandfather's Chevy was often referred to as the Tank.

"Now let's get the hell outta here and to a pay phone. I gotta call Lindalee or my ass is grass. I hope she hasn't called the sheriff to come find us."

At the Pine Creek store, three miles below in the Paradise Valley, the pay phone was in working order. We fumbled for dimes. I could hear one side of the conversation from inside of the car.

"She's pretty upset with me," Jim Kanzler explained, soccer-kicking a clod of snow before getting back into the car. "Now she has to wake up Jamie and take him with her to drive an hour from Big Sky to Bozeman to get me. I told her we'd be in Bozeman about six. Lord, God Almighty, I should have never let you drive all the way down to the campground. We should have walked. It's my fault. I thought I had learned that lesson before, but apparently not."

Except for the hole in the muffler and the heater blasting away, it was a pretty quiet drive back to Bozeman. I had no experience with wives or children—or girlfriends, for that matter. I could find no words of comfort to offer my older friend. I will never forget the musty smell of wet wool and the earthy scent of linseed oil as we rumbled along.

Six weeks later, I got a phone call from Jim:

"A bunch of us from the Bozeman area are going to the Humbug Spires next weekend. I thought you might like to go," he offered. Jim was the first director of the professional ski patrol at Montana's newest ski resort, in Big Sky, which promised to be bigger and more pompous than anything else in Montana.

"Brian Leo and Dougal McCarty will be there. Dougal is recovering from his frostbite, but he can climb in loose boots now..."

I could hardly believe it. Kanzler had called me to go climbing in the Humbugs—the sacred rocks Jim and Jerry, Clare and Ray had pioneered and on which they had cut their teeth. I was honored and overjoyed. My dream of becoming a climbing partner of Jim Kanzler's was coming true.

When would I pop the north face of Mount Cleveland question to him? Certainly, I wasn't ready yet. I still had a long way to go; but things were happening. Now I was not only going to have another chance to climb with Jim but I would also meet Brian and Dougal. If I became climbing partners with these guys as well, I would most certainly accelerate the development of my technical abilities and gain the ever-important experience.

All roads led to Mount Cleveland.

Of course I would go.

There wasn't time to get an extra day off from work, so I had to make the 250-mile journey on a two-day weekend. I loaded up the Tank and left after work on Friday, May 11, 1973. I drove for four and a half hours to Anaconda and spent the night with shirttail relatives. That put me within an hour of the Humbug Spires.

I was on the road again by sun-up. I turned off of the highway onto the two-rut road, and the Chevy jostled along through the sagebrush and on to the Humbug cabin. When I arrived, there was smoke coming out of the chimney pipe; seven climbers were in various stages of fixing breakfast. Some were cooking on an antique Monarch wood stove and others were on the porch, standing around a sputtering backpack stove with a dented pot sitting on it.

"Hey, Terry, glad you could make it," Kanzler called from the door of the cabin as I bailed out of the Chevy and followed him inside.

"Hey, man. What's happening, Kennedy?"

"Emerson! I heard you might be here."

"Hey, I wouldn't pass up a chance to go climbing with a bunch of degenerates like these guys." Emerson belted out. He had moved to Bozeman from Columbia Falls two days after Big Mountain had finished its ski season.

"Yeah, Kanzler took me up Gallatin Tower last week. That was the toughest rock climb I ever did. Awesome rock—it's so much better than anything in the Flathead, man."

"Yeah, it's pretty good," Kanzler chimed in, then proceeded to introduce me to the rest of the group. "This is Brian Leo—I call him Breo..."

A guy no more than an inch taller than myself stepped forward. "Hi, I'm Brian," he grunted, "Nice tuh meet yuh."

"It's nice to meet you, I'm Terry Kennedy," I nodded. I had just walked onto the baseball diamond with a bunch of Big Leaguers. The players were all clad in old, baggy clothes, with elbows and knees shredded from the coarse Humbug rock. They smelled like campfire smoke.

I extended my hand to Brian. His hands were thick and calloused. His baggy cotton pants and long-sleeved T-shirt hid his muscular shoulders and torso. Brian's shoulder-length brown hair and long handlebar mustache might have passed him as a gun fighter a century earlier. He spoke slowly and deliberately, and his pale blue eyes had a habit of fixing in one position when he spoke.

"I've heard a lot about you..." I began; but my sentence was cut short by a big guy who walked up on the conversation. He had a mat of tangled Afro hair, the likes of which I had never seen. He had the appearance of a pirate who had been at sea for many months.

"...Actually, it's Mister Leo," he corrected Kanzler, then burst into a laugh that began with a gulp of air one might expect someone to take as they were immersed into cold water.

"Well," the big guy continued, as he recycled his breath, "you can call him Brian—or Late for Breakfast if you like—but most of us call him Sir. He is the greatest climber in the world" (making a reference to Brian Leo's heroic performance on the winter ascent of Granite Peak three and a half months earlier).

"Oh, yes," Jim continued, "This is the incomparable Doug McCarty. The one and only."

"Hey man," he said, thrusting a hand toward me the size of a 1914 infielder's glove. I went for a traditional handshake, but Dougal slipped in for a thumb clasp—popular among hippies. I think it was the first time I had ever shaken hands that way.

"You can call me Dougal; most of these dirt-bags do. It's after Dougal Haston—you know, the famous British climber who climbed the south face of Annapurna and the west face of Everest?"

"I know, I've read about Dougal Haston," I replied. "It's nice to meetchu... Dougal."

McCarty's magnum fingers had the ability to bend backwards at the knuckles, giving them a talon-like appearance. He gestured with his hands as he spoke, like a 210-pound hawk changing the lug nuts on a tire rim.

"We're the Dirty Sox Club," he continued with a straight face that lasted about two seconds. "Basically, I'm the one who put the dirt into the Dirty Sox Club." Then he launched into unusual two-stroke laughter again.

Normally, one doesn't activate one's vocal cords when inhaling; but Dougal McCarty was one of a kind, and he did. When he laughed—which was often—his vocal cords rattled as if breathing in from the wrong end of a goose call. It was bewildering, if not (at first) concerning. I thought he was having a fatal asthma attack, or something had lodged in his throat. A vision flashed through my mind of chest thrusts, the Heimlich or, God forbid, mouth-to-mouth. There was partially chewed bagel goo stuck to his teeth; it wasn't long before I was as used to it as the others were.

When the son of a son of a Scotsman's lungs were filled, McCarty bore down into a forceful down-stroke, making a dry Heh-Heh-Heh sound— as if he were trying to start a Cessna, but the airplane was either out of fuel or the magneto had been disconnected. Then the cycle would repeat with an even bigger gulp of air through the goose call and increased determination to crank the pistons.

By the third cycle, Kanzler began laughing himself, and everyone else followed, having forgotten what was so funny in the first place. The cabin shook from hysterics over Dougal's bizarre respiratory spectacle. Once the phenomenon got started, it was hard to stop. Abdominal fatigue gradually took over, and the Dirty Sox Club began drying its faces on its tattered sleeves. Someone walked out onto the porch and expelled a loogie.

Lord knows I had never before been in such company.

"Well, it's nice to meet you, too," Dougal said cordially, once homeostasis was restored. "I hear you are becoming quite a climber yourself."

Whoa! I was not expecting an accolade—not from one of the two guys who had just survived the most harrowing winter climb done up to that time (and perhaps to this day) in Montana.

"Maybe we will get a chance to climb together," McCarty continued, grinning down at me. He was six feet tall, and I was five-foot-six. His widely spaced upper teeth hung down like a set of daggers. His upper right incisor had been broken off diagonally by a ski tip, after leaping off of a cornice. His face was dotted with pimples and sparse whiskers.

I searched for evidence of horns, but didn't see any.

"Uh, thanks," I replied, "I'd really like that."

At the other side of the cabin room were three physics graduate students. They were sticking together. Brian Leo knew them.

Kanzler, Leo and McCarty were firming up plans to climb a route on The Finger: a prominent spire among a group of formations on a ridge tucked a half-mile behind the cabin. I would have liked to join them, since nothing in the world would have been better than climbing with Jim Kanzler and some of his contemporaries. They were discussing a route "5.9 or 5.10." I was hoping I would be invited to join them on one hand; but I did not want to try something too hard and have to take tension on the rope on the other, so I did not pry. There were the aces and the physicists; and then there was Emerson and me. Emerson had done many rock scrambling routes on the mountains in Glacier, as well as snow and glacier climbs on the big volcanoes in the Oregon and Washington Cascades with his father and the Kanzlers during his Columbia Falls days; but neither Emerson nor I had the opportunity to develop our technical rock climbing skills like the Kanzlers (and their partners) already had in Butte and Bozeman due to the availability of granite rock. Emerson had only known Leo and McCarty for a matter of weeks, and had just become acquainted with the cerebral bunch. He and I were a pair of jacks on the discard pile that day.

"I know a route you and Emerson ought to go do," Kanzler suggested, seeing his old climbing buddy and me on the sidelines. "It's something Lindalee and I did on the Wall a few years ago. Why don't you hike up there with Dougal, Breo and I and I'll show you where it starts?"

Then he said to me, "Maybe tomorrow, you and I can do something together."

Emerson and I took several hours to do three 5.6 or 5.7 pitches on the Wall. I was as proud as punch. We sat triumphantly on the top and scrambled off the back. By then, it was late afternoon.

We could hear the voices of the others between the Nose and the Thumb, just east of the Wall. The other two groups had finished their routes, and Kanzler was engaging everyone in a bouldering session. Kanzler powered his way up an outcrop with an overhanging fist crack ten feet high, making it on his first try. Leo followed and made it on his second or third try. McCarty gave it an effort; but his recovering, frostbitten feet were not up to the torque necessary to stay in the crack. The three top-echelon climbers had their hands wrapped with tape.

"Does the tape help?" I asked. It was kind of a dumb question.

"Yeah, oh—yeah," Kanzler replied. "You would completely shred your hands in this rock if you didn't."

I could see what he meant. The backs of my own hands were scraped and sore, and several knuckles were nicked and bloody from the much-easier route Emerson and I had done.

"Well-I, it's a pretty good ide-a," Brian Leo surmised.

"Kennedy, if you don't tape your hands when you climb in the Humbugs, your hands will just be raw meat after two days of climbing," Dougal explained.

I could barely get both feet off the ground, limited by the pain from bare hands.

"Let's go over there," Kanzler pointed to a 30-foot-high slab next to the Thumb. It was less than vertical, but appeared smooth—except for small inlays of thin ledges. Kanzler climbed it with little difficulty. If he had fallen off near the top, he would have been hurt—even with McCarty spotting him. Next, Leo climbed it, looking solid. McCarty did the sequence with Kanzler coaching him and everyone else guarding the bottom of the slab. I suspected that if McCarty fell from near the top, he would knock us all over like bowling pins and we would be hurt worse than he would.

I found I could do the lower moves, but there was no way I was going to let myself that far off the ground. A few years later, it didn't seem like such a big deal.

When we had had our fill of the slab, Kanzler walked below the overhanging wall of the Thumb and pointed upward. "Take a look at this!"

"Hole-y fer-menting cheeses," McCarty gasped, "look at that!"

"Yeah, there's a route for the next generation," Kanzler declared.

"Looks pretty har-rd," Leo assessed.

"Oh-my-God, Kanzler, could you do something like that?" The narrow crack started offset from the scooped-out lower wall, then widened to one inch and turned left for a body length behind a roof, emerging fist-width and angling straight up vertical rock to the top—75 feet above us.

"Well, they're doing cracks like this in Yosemite. I don't know..." he pondered. Then he walked up to the lower crack, jammed his fingertips into it, turned his body sideways and leaned back. This twisted his fingers into a tighter jamming configuration. Kanzler pasted his smooth-soled EBs against the wall, walking them upward as his arms locked into extension. When his feet were high enough, he pulled himself upward, bending his elbows, his biceps straining hard.

He moved his feet up further, then quickly pulled his top hand from the crack and shot it upward and back into the crack higher, jamming his fingertips again. He removed his lower fingers and quickly began stuffing them into the narrow crack below the top hand. "Getting a nut in the crack is going to be very difficult," he said, grunting through clenched teeth. He reversed the sequence and climbed down, with McCarty and Leo spotting him, and jumped the last few feet. His fingers were white with chalk and dotted red at the knuckles.

"I think it will go," he said, catching his breath. "It's going to be very tough. Maybe someday, when I'm rested and feeling strong, I'll give it a try."

Emerson and the three physicists had observed the action. Emerson looked at the daunting crack. "Fucking-A, man. I think it would even be hard to do [with] aid climbing [tactics]."

"That's about the only way I could get up it," Dougal declared. He took a quick inhale that briefly fluttered the reed, but that was it. The daunting route was no laughing matter.

We took turns jamming our fingers into the lower crack. No one else was able to move his feet up or advance his hands. Even with my smaller hands, I could barely get my fingers in beyond the first joints. It was torturous—like squeezing your fingers behind the hinges of a door textured with broken glass and then having someone slowly close it.

We called it a day once everyone had had a chance to assess the menacing crack. Kanzler and I would return six years later—and climb it free (unaided). The group filed through the hills towards the cabin, and we soaked our knuckles in the spring water just beyond it.

I awoke early the next morning excited to have a chance to climb with Kanzler in the Humbugs. No one else was stirring yet. I dressed quietly and went outside. The sun was just starting to highlight Forgotten Spire, west of the cabin. There was frost on the grass and the unburned firewood. Jim's tent was pitched just beyond the fire ring. The orange tent was one of the first self-supporting tents available at the time. It was made by Sears and Roebuck and endorsed by Ted Williams, the Hall of Fame baseball player.

As I approached his tent, I realized Jim wasn't there.

Puzzled, I returned to the cabin and my pack and took out my Svea 123 and Sig Tourister pot set-up to boil water on the cabin porch. While the stove sputtered on, I brought out the clipboard and paper that served as a logbook for activities at the Humbug cabin. I flipped through several years of entries and came upon these:

Sat. May 10, 1969

We're loading to go and can barely fit everything on the V.W. [bug]. On the way up the car rack fell off when we hit a bump in the road. Jim made us all walk the last two miles...Jim and I climbed a dihedral & W. ridge crack system on [The] Wall & a scary 60' aid crack on East Zingy near Hobgoblin. Jim did a first on Whisky Flask [a] crack 5.8 (5.9) near Zingy. Jer and Ed [Leritz] did a new route on the Nose—named it Revolution Number 9. [We] hiked up Forgotten Spire Rock last night just at dusk and gloried in the beauty of the Humbugs—Lindalee Kanzler.

[P.S.] Jim, Ed, & Jer did a new first ascent on The Bird near Hobgoblin [—Jim]

Fri. May 16, 1969

...Stopped at 'Palanteer' [Palantir] (boulder) and did a new route just left of the crack. Now there are three routes on that face... —Jerry

May 17, 1969 [early a.m.]

...It's a little rainy this morning, but it's starting to clear. We will be heading toward Sundog & Hobgoblin today to look for a really difficult climb. —Jim

May 17, 1969, 9:00 p.m.

Today Jerry & I climbed the south face of Sundog. We named the route Mother Hawk. It took six hours of very strenuous free climbing and direct aid. We started at 9:20 a.m. and finished at 3:00 p.m. The route makes a fairly direct line just left of the hawk's nest. Up to that ceiling required many 5.8 moves in a row & just below where the aid starts there is a 5.9 move with poor protection. The ceiling is definitely A3 & probably A4...[more route description of the four pitches]. After that climb we were very tired. We ate some lunch and practiced some difficult friction climbing at the base of Sundog. Then we went over & did an old route on Hobgoblin which had [a] strenuous squeeze chimney—after that we had no energy and left & came back to the cabin... —Jim

Jerry, Jim and Lindalee had been coming to the Humbugs from Bozeman almost every weekend since they moved to Bozeman—a few weeks after Hal died, in January of 1967. Although routes were being done on a frequent basis in Gallatin Canyon, twenty-five miles from Bozeman, the frequency of the Kanzlers' cabin visits spoke of their strong connection to the Humbug Spires, which required a drive of one hundred twenty miles each way—on two-lane highways, in those days.

One by one, the other guys arose and began their morning routines. A few minutes later, there were boot steps outside. I walked out of the cabin just as Jim tromped back to his tent. His gait was quick and self-assured. He had on his down parka and wore Eiger Darbalay mountain boots, the top hooks unlaced.

"Hey, good morning, Terry," he looked up and greeted me.

"Good morning, Jim."

"I found what I think we should climb today," he told me. His voice was deep and brimmed with confidence. "It's something I think you would enjoy, and not far from the cabin." He pointed to an open area just beyond the cabin. "Let's go over there; you can see part of it." We walked toward the split-log, mud-chinked outhouse seventy-five yards away, on the side of a hill.

"There it is. See the second crack to the left of the highest point? That's a very neat jam crack, and I don't think it's ever been done before. The one on the right is harder and is cut away at the bottom. It would need a bolt or two, and aid."

Jim Kanzler was asking me to climb a new route in the sacred Humbug Spires with him. No doubt Jerry Kanzler, Clare Pogreba and Ray Martin had seen the feature on this spire before, from where we were standing. The thought of climbing that route probably had occurred to them, as well; but there were so many rock formations and potential natural lines. There were nooks and crannies everywhere. There was so much exploring to do.

"Jeez, that would be great, Jim. I'd really like to give it a try. You don't think it will be too hard for me, do you?"

"Oh, I doubt it. I don't think it will go harder than 5.8. I'll lead it. Let's see if McCarty wants to go with us. His feet were really bothering him in a 5.9 jam crack yesterday. This might be a little easier on him. Breo is going to do something with his physics buddies, and Emerson was going to go with them."

"All right! Let's do it!"

"Oh...you see that rounded dome-like spire over there, to the right?"

"Yeah."

"That one is called Poge. One day, Clare Pogreba was off exploring, waiting for Ray to arrive at the cabin, while Jerry and I were climbing on the Nose or the Mustache or something. When we got back to the cabin later in the day, here was Poge [Clare's nickname] badly scraped up and bleeding from his bare legs and elbows and forearms. He had gone in to check out that spire and actually soloed the long ridge you see there— and down-climbed the same way.

When he got closer to the bottom, he decided to take a shortcut across a friction slab and lost it and slid down it. He looked like hamburger when he got back. He was too sore to climb with Ray that day. So we thought naming the spire after him was appropriate."

In my mind, I could see those guys cruising about the Humbug Spires, climbing and exploring and enjoying each other. I always had the impression that there was a very tight bond between that foursome—Jim, Jerry, Clare and Ray—and they, in turn, had a special connection to the Humbug Spires. It was hard to imagine that Clare, Ray and Jerry would no longer be running around the enchanted hills. Perhaps, they still were.

"How did you and Jerry ever hook up with Clare and Ray?"

"Well, when we moved from Columbia Falls to Butte during the summer of 1965, Jerry and I were pretty excited to be living in a new place that had all kinds of granite around—more granite than we had ever seen before, put together."

"I'll bet—having lived in the Flathead, with nothing but rotten sedimentary rock to climb on."

"We set out looking at all the possibilities right away. We saw this particularly high formation near Pipestone Pass and checked it out. It was amazing to us, all these vertical cracks. There was nothing like this in Glacier or the Missions Mountains. We'd never done pure crack climbing before."

"So, did you climb it right away?"

"Actually, I think we had to return home and get our gear together, and I think it was probably the next day or something before we made it back; but we returned with our Goldline ropes and soft-iron pitons and started climbing easy routes and teaching ourselves how to climb cracks. We called this rock 'Our Tower.'"

"Did Hal climb with you?"

"No, not so much. My father didn't think this rock climbing stuff was real mountain climbing. He just called it 'rock gymnastics.' He was old school. Climbing to summits of peaks was where it was at, for him; but he'd explore with us sometimes. Looking back, his new job with the company seemed to drain him. He grew more and more unhappy and depressed, and sometimes he was hard to be around...

Anyway, Jer and I found this beautiful crack that was challenging for us at the time. It was the perfect size for ¾-inch ring-angle pitons. So we took all that we had, six or eight of them, and fixed them in place so we could come out every day after school and lead the route without having to bang in the pins every time. Our plan was to practice this pitch over and over again, until we got really good at it. Then we came out one day and the pitons were gone."

"No way! Gone? Like somebody had taken them?"

"Right. That meant there had to be other climbers around. I couldn't believe that someone had taken them."

"What did Jerry think?"

"I think he was more interested in meeting these other climbers. I just wanted to get our pitons back. So we got home and I started calling around and found out there was a climbing club at Montana Tech. So I went charging up there and asked around and someone said go talk to this guy, Clare Pogreba. So I found him in this chemistry lab."

"You mean you just barged into this lab during class?"

"Yeah—well, basically. It wasn't exactly a class. There were just some students in there, fiddling around. Anyway, I found Clare Pogreba—and he was this very short guy— and I demanded to know why he took our pitons."

"It sounds like you were kinda spoiling for a fight."

"Well, no—not really. I just wanted my gear back. Pogreba was pretty cool. He said he and his friend Ray Martin had found them and thought they were abandoned by someone else, and figured they would just collect the bootie and add to their own gear. He said they thought they knew all the climbers around—probably wasn't more than a dozen in their club— and the pitons had been there from climbers who were no longer in the area. Anyway, Clare was happy to give them back, which he promised to do the next day. We shook hands and, before I left, we made plans to go climbing the next day or so. Clare brought his buddy, Ray Martin, who was six-seven or something. Instantly, we became friends, and we all went out to Pipestone and went climbing."

"That's neat."

"Yeah, it was," Kanzler said, with little emotion other than a shrug. He looked down and kicked a pinecone out of a tire rut. "Now, they are all dead. Come on, let's get some breakfast first, and I'll see if McCarty wants to go."

A short time later, I followed Kanzler and McCarty up a steep hill, hiking on the coarse surface of duff and the abrasive granules of decomposed granite. The air was rich with smells of pitch and decaying pine needles. Another cold winter was over, summer was coming and I was coming of age.

The granite fin was suddenly before us. I watched Kanzler size up the routes.

"How's this look, Dougal?"

"Looks great, man. The start looks hard. We might have to climb that tree a ways and then get on the rock," the big guy said, shrugging with an inquisitive look on his face.

"That's what Fred Beckey would do," Kanzler said supportively.

"Fred Beckey! You guys know Fred Beckey?" I interjected. They were talking about a very famous climber. I was impressed.

"Everybody knows Fred," Dougal said with a little draw on the reed of the goose call and a short press on the starter switch of the malfunctioning airplane, constituting a chuckle.

"As in Beckey's Bible, right?" I asked, referring to The Climber's Guide to the North Cascades.

"The Dean of American Mountaineering," Kanzler said with emphasis. "Fred is famous for climbing trees to avoid aid."

"Or lassoing rock horns," Dougal added, pointing upward. "I think we should climb the tree and step over to that dish."

"The question is: Is it still free climbing?"

"I think Fred would say so. He'd call it a 5.7 stemming move." (McCarty chuckle.)

Kanzler took the rack of hardware and carefully ascended several thin branches on the tree. It wasn't that the lower part of the rock looked particularly difficult; the issue was that the tree was growing right up against the rock and prevented one from being able to climb the lower holds without damaging it. Jim stepped over onto the rock with an old pair of shredded PAs—a smooth-soled climbing shoe that preceded the more popular shoe of the day, the EB. Jim liked the old pair because it was stiffer and more comfortable in wider jam cracks and held up better in the Humbugs' extremely abrasive stone. He wanted to save his EBs for harder routes. McCarty wore well-used Robbins' Shoes; he couldn't yet tolerate the tight fit of the smooth-soled rock shoes, due to his frostbite several months earlier. I had on a pair of off-brand *klettershoes* I had bought from REI, which were quite stiff and had thin, Vibram soles.

"You should get a pair of EBs," Kanzler suggested.

"They are the best," Dougal added. "Every climb you do will be easier."

"I can get a pair for you," Kanzler offered. "Before you go, give me a foot tracing and twenty-five bucks, and I'll mail you a pair."

Kanzler led the route. I went second, and Dougal "cleaned the route." I didn't have much trouble; Kanzler called it 5.8.

The three of us stood on top, admiring the view in our knickers and long socks.

"What should we call this route?" Kanzler asked.

"How about *Moon Shadow*," I answered, "because of the full moon last night— and I really like the Cat Stevens song."

"I like that."

The three of us began singing, "I'm being followed by a moon shadow. Moon shadow, moon shadow..."

When we returned to our packs at the bottom of the climb, I asked, "So how did the Dirty Sox Club get its name?"

"That's kind of a long story..." Dougal took a draw on the goose call reed and glanced over at Kanzler.

"It used to be called The Wool Socks Club," Jim pointed out. "I guess Jerry, Ray, Clare, some of the other guys and I were just sitting around the cabin after climbing one evening and decided we should call ourselves the Wool Socks Club, since you always wore wool socks in the mountains."

"But it became the Dirty Sox at Jim and Lindalee's trailer in Bozeman two years ago—just before they moved to Big Sky." Dougal explained, looking over at Jim as we headed back to the cabin. "A friend of mine, Davy Vaughan, was with me—he helped make the name stick. I'm not sure how we got on the subject, but you mentioned this 'club' of just a few close guys and I said how neat it would be to be a member of it. I asked you if I could join."

"And I said 'sure,'" Kanzler confirmed.

"Right...and then Lindalee cuts in and said that she didn't think there should be a Wool Socks Club anymore since most of the members were dead...something like, 'It wouldn't be the same without them, and the name should be retired.'"

"Right," Jim agreed.

"Then Lindalee gives me this strange look..." McCarty jammed down on the starter switch and the prop started turning, followed by a hard draw on the goose call. Kanzler broke into a grin.

"Lindalee gives me this strange look and says, 'Why don't you call it the Dirty Sox Club?'" McCarty broke into a full-blown fit of laughter. "I had just finished changing the oil in my V.W. bug (inhale through the reed) and my clothes—not just my socks—were (inhale) pretty fucking filth-y." McCarty was gulping air like a drowning man.

Kanzler folded his arms across his ribs and began to double over with laughter. It was every man for himself. Dougal was leaning against a tree to prepare himself for the next shock wave. I just stood there dumbfounded by the unfolding spectacle.

"'Dirty Sox Club'—wow—that's, that's uh— perfect!" I said.

"Then you and I and Davy started laughing," Dougal reminded Jim. The next wave hit.

"It was so funny," Kanzler added, almost unintelligibly. "Lindalee was trying to be cynical...not amusing. I thought she was upset...because...you were sitting on her couch with such dirty clothes."

"I know, I know," (reed followed by magneto). "We were...(reed) we were laughing...as hard are we are now (magneto—reed). Everyone was laughing..."

"Except Lindalee..."

"She didn't think it was funny..." (reed—magneto).

Kanzler was losing it. He dropped to the ground and rolled around with his sides heaving, moaning "ha-ha-ha, ho-ho-ho."

Frankly, I didn't see what was so funny in the first place—except watching McCarty grasping at branches on a young Douglas fir (how fitting) and Kanzler on the verge of a seizure. I was laughing so hard that tears rolled down my cheeks.

McCarty managed a brief hiatus. "She got pissed off at us and walked out..." Then he launched into another series and he lost his legs, lapsing into full dependency on the sapling.

"Lindalee thought we were all laughing at her," Kanzler said on behalf of his wife and former Columbia Falls High School cheerleader, "but we weren't...we were just laughing at Dougal. Dirty Sox Club," he attempted to explain, "she had nailed it perfectly."

McCarty was too much for the young tree. The first branch snapped and the second one avulsed from the trunk, ripping a strip of bark nearly to the ground. Dougal fought his way to his knees and sucked in another breath, determined to continue the story. "'You dirty bastard,'(reed)...she said." McCarty started laughing so hard that I thought he might start heaving up breakfast or bile.

"Stop, please, stop, McCarty," Kanzler pleaded. He was rolling on the ground from side to side. There were pine needles, fir cones and little granules of granite all over him. He looked like an ice cream bar rolled in chopped nuts. I was on my knees, glasses in one hand, wiping tears with the sleeve of the other.

McCarty reached down deep—if not for more oxygen, then for sheer determination to get to the climax of the story. "'You're a bunch of dirty bastards,' she said." With the focused concentration of an Olympic high jumper, he continued, "then she slipped on some ice on the porch as she walked out the door."

We simultaneously leaped into a new height of belly rolls.

"But she held onto the handle (monster draw on the goose call reed) of the screen door...and never hit the deck..." McCarty drew so hard on the reed that I was sure he would implode his vocal cords right out of his larynx. Instead, he started to cough. He recovered enough to continue, "I looked up and...and saw the door swing open with her hanging on..." (more coughing—expectorating, this time).

"She is very strong, you know," Kanzler pointed out, struggling to all fours.

Indeed, she was. Lindalee had been a cheerleader in the mid 1960s, during the same time Columbia Falls produced its sensational basketball teams that had so captivated me as a boy. The cheerleaders were equally sensational. Even fifth grade boys, like myself, were fascinated by the cheerleaders—Lindalee not the least of them. Because there were no sanctioned scholastic sports for girls in those days, the best female athletes became cheerleaders. Others, like my sister, were on the drill team.

Jim did not participate in high school sports. He was an outdoor athlete, though that term was not used back then. Jim and Lindalee were casual friends at school in Columbia Falls and never really dated, per se. However, there was a spark of interest. In the 1965 Columbia High School Annual, Jim Kanzler wrote more than a half page in Lindalee's copy following their junior year, the summer the Kanzlers moved to Butte.

"...I gained very much through our discussions—we should carry on with them...I'm sure going to do lots of climbing this summer. We should go on a hike together. Your ['re] the only girl who can really hike, that I know personally." –Jim Kanzler

The romance didn't occur until the summer of 1966, after the Kanzlers had moved to Butte and Jim finished his senior year and Jerry his freshman year at Butte High. That summer, Jim went to work on a field crew in Glacier Park and Lindalee got a job as a waitress at Eddie's Cafe in Apgar (West Glacier). There, the two reacquainted. They got married in Jackson Hole two years later.

Lindalee climbed Exum Ridge on the Grand Teton and with Jim in 1968—while she was four months pregnant with their son. She climbed only sporadically while Jamie was little. By 1973, she had accompanied Jim and Dr. Callis on their forays to the Canadian Rockies, ultimately in pursuit of the Emperor Face of Mount Robson. Jamie stayed with his grandma and grandpa in Columbia Falls for a couple of weeks each summer. During the 1973 trip to Canada, Lindalee was sidelined with pneumonia while Jim and Dr. Callis did the Y-couloir on Andromeda.

In 1974, Lindalee and Jim climbed the Enclosure Couloir on the Grand Teton in blue ice conditions before heading to Canada.

"She just flew up it." Jim once told me. "She led some of the pitches."

Shortly thereafter, they returned to the Columbia Ice Fields, where Jim and Lindalee met up with Dr. Callis and the three of them climbed the north face of Athabasca as a warm-up before they made their epic attempt of the first ascent of the Emperor Face. The following year, in 1975, Jim and Lindalee climbed the Northwest Shoulder Direct on Andromeda in the Ice Fields area before meeting Callis. Indeed, Lindalee proved to be a worthy mountaineer and loved ice routes.

Lindalee would look every bit as athletic in her 60s as in her 20s. She might well have had the attributes to be world class—at climbing or some other sport. Not only was she strong; she also always impressed me with her single-minded determination, pragmatism and perception.

"So, what happened?" I asked from my position on the forest floor. I would have expected Lindalee to come flying back into the mobile home after the slip on the porch, sending the fur flying.

Kanzler and McCarty were silent.

"Well," Kanzler continued; his tone had changed. "She said, 'It's not funny. Those guys are dead.' She was crying. Really, we were all just laughing at Dougal's bizarre laugh, not at her. That poor woman."

Kanzler got up and started to brush himself off. McCarty crawled to a sturdier tree and slowly got to his feet. I knelt there a moment, staring at the ground. I understood Lindalee better. She had been mourning the Mount Cleveland Five the whole time. I felt like crying, too; but realized I had already been through most of the lunacy. No one said anything further. It was a warm spring day, and the sun was high in the sky. Chickadees sang and flitted about in the lodgepole pines overhead. An isolated patch of shooting stars was making its way through the soil on the edge of a boggy oasis below the cabin.

A voice was heard from far below.

"It's Emerson. He's down by the cabin," I reported. "Listen."

"Doo-gull? Is-that-you-up-ther-e?"

McCarty, fully sober, drew a normal breath and bellowed, "Yeah-h!"

The question came ringing through the hills. "What's-so-fun-ny?"

We started back toward the cabin, having survived the ordeal.

"I'm going to the Tetons this summer, then starting college at MSU this fall," I said to Dougal, the change of subject welcomed.

"Really? I know a guy in Bozeman you should meet. His name is Steve Jackson. He's a year younger than me, and has been climbing for a year or so. He is going into Film and T.V. Good guy. He is in the Dirty Sox Club, too. The two of you would hit it off."

I returned to my job at the Anaconda Aluminum plant the next day. I would never be the same. That weekend in the Humbugs had been transformative. The one-time Cub Scout dropout, sandlot center fielder and district science fair grand prize winner was now an initiate of the Dirty Sox Club.

The doors just kept opening, and the whole world was unfolding before me. I was now a climbing partner of Jim Kanzler's and this new camaraderie of friends. Mount Cleveland was emerging on the horizon like the full moon.

Brian "Breo" Leo and Doug "Dougal" McCarty, circa 1977. Photo by the author.

Brian Leo unloads the Tank, circa 1975. Photo by the author.

Lindalee Kanzler leading the Enclosure Ice Couloir on
the Grand Teton, 1974. Photo by Jim Kanzler.

CHAPTER 5

On to the Tetons

I drove the Tank up Story Street in Bozeman until I came to Dell Place: a gravel street four houses long, with chuckholes full of water and out of synch with the Bozeman street grid. It was the third week of June 1973.

I came to the second house on the left. It was not what I had expected. The small house was dilapidated, with gray shingle siding, some of which was in the process of falling off. It had a small, enclosed, narrow porch with a screen door skew to the frame. Could this really be where Dr. Callis, the chemistry professor, lived? Perhaps I had the wrong street. I checked the directions again. No— this was it.

I turned the Tank around, driving part way into muddy tire ruts that led to a neighbor's garage at the end of the lane, and parked just short of the ramshackle house. I was nervous. If this was Dr. Callis's house, then I was about to meet the most important mountain climber— next to Jim Kanzler— I might ever know. I had no idea what I was going to say. Maybe I should have prepared some lines; but it was too late. I walked up to the screen door, trying to pump myself up with last minute confidence. I hesitated, not sure if I should knock on the floppy screen door or walk through the porch and knock on the door inside. If I did have the wrong house, then whoever did live there might take exception to my trespassing through his or her porch. The door rattled and slapped, so I pressed it against the frame.

I was a young man who had just left home to seek his fortune. I had the roof rack on the 54 Chevy with a tarp covering a few items. The "grub box" my dad had built out of thin plywood and painted a pale green occupied the trunk. The front panel could be opened and lowered on hinges that locked into a small table space. It had been an important utility for the Kennedy family during our camping trips over the years gone by.

"Son," Dad had said, "I think you should take the grub box to the Tetons with you. It will come in handy. You can keep all your food and utensils in it and pull over anywhere and cook with the Coleman stove when you need a meal."

The grub box did not fit well into the climber image. It was hick, and I was 19 and transformed, as you will recall. I had climbed with some of Montana's elite. Jim Kanzler had sat in a belay seat all night, 2,000 feet up El Capitan. McCarty and Leo had bivouacked in a raging blizzard with no tent or sleeping bags on Montana's highest mountain. The Dirty Sox Club carried their belongings in their packs and, when they did cook, it was with backpack stoves placed on a rock or a bumper. None of those guys had grub boxes.

My dad was making an offering; he knew when I left for the Tetons, I was leaving home. When September rolled around, I would be starting college at Montana State University in Bozeman, where he had earned his degree, and who knew where life would lead after that? I accepted the grub box as a gift, a connection to the family and my childhood.

The first stop of my journey would be to meet with the mentor of the Mount Cleveland Five, who had climbed with the likes of Warren Harding, Fred Beckey, George Lowe and Willie Unsoeld. I felt it would be wise to get his advice about climbing in the Tetons—and I wanted to see this mysterious person who Jerry Kanzler had spent so much time with prior to the Mount Cleveland tragedy, who had searched for the Mount Cleveland Five and made the first find in the avalanche debris on the mountain's west face. I wanted to meet the one they called Gandalf, the wizard.

"He is an amazing man," Jim Kanzler had said.

I think what I wanted most of all was his blessing. With it, I would have a straight path to the north face of Mount Cleveland. It was a bold leap for me to introduce myself to Dr. Callis.

The Tank sat a few feet away with the grub box, stocked with peanut butter, raspberry jam, a loaf of bread, instant coffee for a month and four cans of sardines. There was a rustling just inside the house, and the main door opened.

"It's him," I exclaimed to myself.

A slim, lanky man with thick, shoulder-length coal-black hair and a long, straight beard slipped through the inside door. He had a narrow, lined face with sunken cheeks, a pointed nose, and dark eyes with a faraway look. He moved like a cat.

"Please. Come in." His voice was smooth and accommodating, like the leather of three-year-old pair of Raichles. He reached out his hand and I shook his long, tendinous fingers that were neither calloused (as if he had been climbing on a daily basis) nor soft (like one might expect from a man of science who spent most of the day at a desk or chalkboard, or mixing concoctions in beakers and test tubes).

"I was expecting you, but not sure just when you would be arriving." He turned and I followed through the doors and a tidy living room with a mixture of mismatched furniture. Two toddlers, a boy and a girl, took a look at me from behind their mother, Gayle, and galloped away.

There was another man sitting in the kitchen, at a wooden table painted with off-white enamel. He was tall and lean, and wore jeans and a pair of green, striped Adidas. There was a vague familiarity I could not place. He set his cup of coffee down as we entered.

"I'd like you to meet Peter Lev," Dr. Callis said once we were inside. I realized I was standing in the presence of both mentors of the Mount Cleveland Five. Peter Lev taught a class in winter mountaineering at MSU. Jim Anderson, Mark Levitan and Jerry Kanzler were three of his students. Of course Peter, Jim Kanzler and Dr. Callis had searched for them. I might as well have been standing before Mickey Mantle and Roger Maris during the 1961 season. I was awestruck.

"Uh, oh, hello, Mr. Lev. I, uh, I'm very glad to meet you."

"Hello, Terry," he said with a warm smile, and stood. "You are a friend of Jim Kanzler's?" I shook his hand. It was much larger than my own, and felt like the hand of someone who had spent a lot of time working with tools or stone. His face was deeply tanned.

"Uh yeah, well, I've been climbing with Jim a couple of times. Uh, we climbed in the Humbugs and uh—he and I did Blue and Green Gully together last March. I led the second pitch of Blue..."

"Oh yeah, I think Jim mentioned something about a new young climber he'd been out with who was going to come through on his way to the Tetons. That must be you. Well, great!" I was not sure if Jim had said anything about the likes of me, or if Peter Lev was just trying to make me feel good, which he did.

"I'm going to try to climb the north..." I cut myself off. Perhaps it wasn't a good idea to just blurt out my plan to climb the north face of the Grand Teton that summer, since I hadn't climbed anything on that scale yet. I did not want to look foolish in front of Callis and Lev. "I'm just on my way to the Tetons for the summer. I'd like to do something on the Grand." There, that sounded better.

"Would you like to have a cup of coffee?" Dr. Callis offered.

"Oh, yes, please." To think I was drinking coffee with Dr. Callis and Peter Lev! This was going to be like playing catch with the Yankee outfield. My mind was flashing with questions, trying to sort out the ones that would not make me appear too naive. I just wanted to catch each ball cleanly and make good throws.

It would be stupid to start in on Mount Cleveland. The tragedy was only three years past, and I had only known Peter Lev and Dr. Callis for two and a half minutes! I didn't need to be gauche.

Dr. Callis had the effect of slowing conversations down. His personal ambiance was intriguing; still, there was a barrier I perceived, perhaps of my own construct that commanded a certain respect when approached.

Peter Lev was reminiscent of a varsity athlete. He had an energy around him, poised to spring into action. Of the two enigmatic strangers whose midst I found myself in, it was Peter Lev whom I felt more comfortable initiating conversation with at that time.

"I have heard that you have climbed in the Himalayas, Mr. Lev."

"Please, just call me Peter." He stole a quick glance at Dr. Callis. "That's right. I just got back from Dhaulagiri in Nepal, about six weeks ago." The American Expedition had tried to make the first ascent of the southeast ridge, but had to turn its attention to making the third ascent of the northeast spur instead.

"Wow, what was that like?"

"There were some big storms and some bad avalanches. Our team made the summit, but another storm up high prevented me from getting to the summit personally."

"Shoot, that must have been really disappointing."

"Well, that's the way it goes on big mountains like that."

"Didn't you and Jim Kanzler climb the northwest face of Half Dome and Quarter Dome?" Of course, I knew he had. Jim Kanzler had told me about them already.

"Well, yes, we did those two climbs." Peter Lev glanced over at Dr. Callis again. The chemistry professor was slouched in a kitchen chair; his feet perched on the first rung of a kitchen step stool. He cradled his coffee cup, smiling softly.

I could see Peter really didn't want to expound on his personal achievements. Then he engaged me.

"What were you planning to do in the Tetons?"

"Well, just about anything," I said, trying to act subdued; but my fervor boiled out from under the lid of the pot and went hissing onto the proverbial Coleman stove. "The north face of the Grand Teton," I blurted. Oh-h, stu-pid—jeez.

Peter Lev's eyebrows rose about half an inch; he welded his eyes on Dr. Callis this time. I glanced at Gandalf. I suppose both Peter and I were expecting a little magic. The wizard's head was cocked slightly to one side as he stroked his beard, staring at a leg of the table. I felt my face flush. I had bobbled an easy fly. "Dang it Kennedy, that was stupid!" I scolded myself mentally. "Stu-u-pid!"

What else was there? I mean the north face of Mount Cleveland was quite a bit higher than the north face of the Grand Teton. Didn't it make sense to climb the North face of the Grand Teton first, before taking on Cleveland? I could feel the stirring uneasiness. I knew I had better justify myself.

"Uh, well, not right away, I mean, someday—later in the summer—you know. I probably need to get a little more experience first, " I explained, trying to temper what was blabbering out of my mouth as soon as it was assembling in my brain. "You know, I was thinking more like August—late August."

The Exum Mountain Guide/Himalayan climber and the wizard became silent. I thought I could hear a strange sound coming from nowhere in particular, like the sound of two tall trees rubbing against each other in the wind. Thinking back, it was probably Peter Lev and Pat Callis groaning. What might have passed as a simple pause in the conversation was becoming an awkward lag in the flow of reason.

"Have you guys ever done the north face?" There, that made sense—shift the conversation to the experience of the sages of mountaineering.

As a matter of fact, both Peter and Dr. Callis had climbed the North face of the Grand Teton... each more than once. Of course, that really got me revved up.

"Wow, what was it like?" It was a good move. Within seconds, Dr. Callis and Peter were comparing notes. They were relating things like: "The bergschrund wasn't too bad that year...we were too early and had a lot of rock fall... did you bivouac on the first ledge... we had to use crampons up high...the pendulum pitch was wet the second time we did it...oh, really it was dry both times I was there...we had three guys and made the summit just before dark..." This was great!

Two weeks before the fateful Mount Cleveland expedition, Jerry Kanzler, Clare Pogreba and Ray Martin pioneered the route up Big Couloir on Lone Mountain with Lev and Callis: a straightforward, one-tool snow climb that became a must for extreme skiers at Big Sky. Pogreba and Levitan, Jim Anderson, Jim Kanzler and Dr. Callis climbed the east face of Heavy Shield (Mount Wilbur) over Thanksgiving of 1969, in full winter conditions.

"Didn't Jerry go with you guys to try to climb the Grand Teton in winter, just after Mount Wilbur, just before Christmas—you know—just before

Cleveland?" There was silence. Neither Dr. Callis nor Peter Lev responded. Callis stared out the window at a spruce tree and Peter looked out the archway of the small kitchen-dining room, perhaps hoping Gayle might be there and he could divert the conversation. I really wanted to know about Jerry's life one month before the Mount Cleveland tragedy.

"I heard you almost got hit by an avalanche." A few more seconds passed with silence. By now everyone was uncomfortable—especially me. It was like we were all trapped in separate boxes. Dr. Callis finally spoke holding his gaze outside the window.

"Well...Jerry and I were with Peter and George Lowe—"

"George Lowe! You were climbing with George Lowe—the George Lowe?"

I recognized the name, George Lowe, as having already made the first epic winter ascent of the north face of the Grand Teton, the year before. (George would go on to be one of the preeminent alpinists in the U.S. making first ascents up terrifying faces.) Now, I really wanted to hear about what happened in the Tetons. Jerry Kanzler had gone climbing with George Lowe?

"Well...Jerry and I went in to try the Chouinard Chimney on Mount Owen and Peter and George were going to try the East Ridge of the Grand Teton."

"But you didn't make it and had to turn back, right?"

"Yeah, it snowed about a foot," Callis continued. "Jerry and I broke trail over to Mount Owen, but decided the route would be too difficult after the snow, so we came back."

"What about the avalanche?" I asked again. Pat sat up in his chair.

Peter laced his fingers behind his head, slouching back into this chair and looked at the ceiling.

"Well, there was an avalanche that came off the Grand. George and Peter may have gotten it started as they were coming back down. It came pretty close but it missed us."

"That must have been scary!"

"Yeah, it was kinda."

About ten years later, long after Pat and I had become good friends and climbing partners, he told me more of the story.

"Jerry and I went back to our camp. We had already dug a snow cave the day before, because the storm was pretty bad, and we got better protection in the snow cave. Peter and George had climbed for quite a while before they thought they should bail. Jerry and I were hanging out in the cave waiting for them."

"So, when did the avalanche hit?"

"It's funny, I just happened to be looking out the door of the cave and one moment I could see normal day light outside and the next it looked like it was suddenly just dumping snow, and I thought, 'that's odd, I thought it was done snowing.' Then all of a sudden it was dark outside—couldn't see anything—there was snow in the entrance of the cave."

"Uh-oh!"

"Yeah-right! I said, 'Oh shit, we've just been buried!' But it wasn't too bad. Jerry and I dug our selves out rather easily. Fortunately, we were in the very edge of one side of the debris and it wasn't too deep."

"Man, you're just lucky you weren't in the middle."

"Yeah. Actually...there were two avalanches. The second one didn't hit us—we just got some of the windblast. It actually knocked Jerry down."

Another 30 years went by. During a gathering at the Grand Teton Climbers' Ranch in July 2011, I had a chance to talk with Lindalee. I was writing this book and I wanted to know more about Jerry.

"He was absolutely fearless," Lindalee said. She took a step back, away from the picnic table. Her voice became impassioned. "I never knew anybody like him."

"Did he ever say anything about the trip to the Tetons just before those guys left for Mount Cleveland?" I asked. She seemed to have anticipated my question.

"Jerry told Jim and me all about it, when he got back. He said he and Pat dug out of the snow cave after the first avalanche. They were standing around for a while thinking how lucky they were and they heard another *thump* and Pat said, 'Jerry, get back in the cave! Quick! Here comes another one!'"

"What happened?"

"Jerry said Pat was right next to the entrance and dove in expecting Jerry to be right behind him; but Jerry was a ways from the entrance. Jerry said, 'I looked up and could see the cloud billowing toward us and I thought, wow that sure is cool!'"

"R-really?"

"Yeah, then Jerry said, 'I figured I'd better get into the cave but it was too late. The windblast lifted me up and blew me 50 feet back down the slope and rushed by.'"

"God, that's amazing!"

Lindalee paused for a moment. She turned her head slightly and her eyes narrowed. "Then Jerry blew my mind." Her voice was now sharp—as if she would like to have been scolding Jerry—maybe for denying the rest of us the privilege of knowing what he might have become during the rest of his life, had he lived. "He said, 'I wasn't even afraid.'"

What little interaction that I actually had with Jerry Kanzler, created an impression I carried with me for all those years. It still does. I imagined him standing there with the avalanche boiling down on him, almost curious and unafraid. I suppose, that much did not surprise me. But what Lindalee said next did.

"I got an overwhelming feeling about the Mount Cleveland climb." Tears welled up in her eyes. "I knew he was going to die up there!"

I felt another rush of Lindalee's energy—not unlike the windblast that knocked Jerry down the slope. I stood there spellbound and speechless as she added, "I think he did too."

"You know, a good route to do in the Tetons is the Durrance Ridge on Symmetry Spire," Peter suggested, taking a last swig of coffee.

"Oh, that would be a good route to do," Dr. Callis quickly agreed. They both knew the Durrance route on Symmetry Spire was easy. It was multiple pitches, but if you had trouble it would not be too hard to get down.

Peter stood up and said, "I gotta get going, Pat. I'll get back to you later." Callis saw Lev to the door and returned.

"That was great, mister—I mean, Doctor…I mean, do you prefer to be called Doctor…?"

"Oh please—just call me Pat."

Before I parted company with Gandalf, I managed a few route details of the Grand Teton.

"You know, the North Ridge of the Grand is considered the better route. When you are ready to do a big route on the Grand, that might be the one to do."

I had not considered the north ridge before. I had thought north faces were where it was at... that is, until Jim Kanzler told me in a letter that summer that Jerry climbed the North Ridge in 1968, when he was 17, with another teenager, Dick Weaver, from Bozeman.

The two months at the American Alpine Club's Climber's Ranch, with its bunkhouse and cooking pavilion, seemed to go by slowly. I managed to find a few others looking for climbing partners and I did Owen-Spalding route on the Grand with a kid younger than me and some popular rock climbs in the side canyons and minor peaks with other climbers who needed a partner also. I felt I was just biding my time. It was not my style to go up to other climbers and invite myself on one of their outings.

I was lying on a bunk in the middle of the afternoon, reading Vardis Fisher's *Mountain Man*—the novel that inspired the movie *Jeremiah Johnson*, with Robert Redford—when I heard a VW van pull into the Climbers' Ranch. That was not unusual, because there were a lot of VW microbuses around; but I knew the voice that soon followed:

"Wow, man, that sounds pretty far out. I'll throw my shit inside and get back to ya. Later, man."

I headed out to greet him, and we nearly collided at the door.

"Emerson!" He looked like ol' Liver-Eatin' himself.

"Kennedy! Hey man, what's happenin'?'"

"Not much. I didn't know if you'd be coming for sure."

"Fuckin'-a, man. Dougal McCarty and I first had to finish this shit job, tearing down a grain elevator, before I could split. It was awful. We got our socks extremely dirty. The rest of us, too—you been climbing any?"

"Well, not much, really. I'm going to Devil's Tower in a few days, and I'll be back in about a week."

"Well, let's you and I go do something before you go."

"What do ya wanna do?"

"Everybody says to do something on Symmetry Spire for a warm up. You done anything on it?"

"Durrance Ridge. It's a good climb to do," I went on, trying to sound like Pat Callis and Peter Lev. "It's seven pitches, but not very hard...a good one to do to get a feel of the Tetons."

"You wanna do it again?"

"No, but I will." So we did.

"What do you think of, uh, maybe...doing the north face?" I winced as I asked him.

"Oh man, I don't want to do the north face. It's supposed to be a pile of shit. There's a lot of rock fall on it. You could get fuckin' killed up there, man. I've heard the north ridge is a much better route. I wouldn't mind doing that."

Pat Callis, circa 1980. Photo by the author.

CHAPTER 6

Emerson Leads the Way

The most common way to climb the North Ridge route of the Grand Teton in the 1960s and early 1970s was to bivouac on top of the "Grandstand," a prominent shoulder of the north ridge that juts out, away from the north face—and, at 12,700 feet, is higher in elevation than most of the summits of the other peaks. Emerson and I dutifully roped up on the Teton Glacier, using ice axes and crampons. We crossed the bergschrund and picked our way up the ledges and ramps to the top of the Grandstand. We arrived late in the afternoon, with a towering black cloud approaching from the west, which we could not see as we ascended. Suddenly there were strong gusts of wind. The first thunder and lightning hammered us within minutes. We backed down to a wide ledge 50 feet below the crest. It was the best we could do without a full retreat in the storm.

The storm bore down on us: first rain, then sleet, then hail and lightning that came from everywhere. I have been in nasty thunderstorms over the years, where the flash and crash occurred simultaneously. Each one seems like the worst storm you have ever been in. This one knocked the power out in Jackson Hole for four hours.

After the worst of it passed, we killed a couple of hours melting hailstones with my SVEA stove, which barely stayed lit. We slowly filled our water bottles. I am not sure what we would have done for water otherwise. We stuffed our feet into our rucksacks and sat on the two climbing ropes we carried. When Emerson was not snoring, he was smoking cigarettes inside the hood of his cagoule, looking like a smoldering grim reaper with a red, glowing eye.

It was a long night, but I was psyched. I was a real mountain climber, by God, bivouacked high in the Tetons. I figured if Emerson and I could get up this route, the north face of Mount Cleveland would not be too far out of reach.

The next morning, there was still hail-slush on the ledge. "What do you think, Emerson—wanna keep goin'?" We had come 6,000 feet off of the valley floor, and it would be a shame to give up our position. The technical climbing of the last 1,000 feet would be extra difficult with the wet and cold. The clouds were still drifting on and off the mountain. We were young, energetic, and full of piss and vinegar. We wanted to tuck a big route on the Grand Teton under our belts.

"Fuckin'-a man," Emerson responded without giving it further thought, "let's climb this pile of shit!" So we packed it up, tied in and had at it.

I got the Chockstone Pitch. My fingers were numb as I thrashed my way around the bulging block of granite, wedged into the chimney. My rucksack, with crampons and ice axe attached to the outside, scraped and hooked the sidewalls, threatening to rip open or yank me into oblivion. I was exhausted, thinking about joining a religion, when I desperately threw a knee over the top of the stubborn barrier.

"If that was 5.7," I huffed and puffed, "I'll be an uncle's monkey."

Emerson crawled up the next long pitch like a snail up a tombstone. I stood belaying and shivering with plenty of time to look over the tops of the other peaks and beyond Mount Moran. I thought of Jerry Kanzler climbing this route while he was still in high school. Jim and Jerry Kanzler were self-taught climbers. Some of the basics were probably worked out with Hal in the early days, but Hal's two sons left him quickly behind during the two years in Butte, while their father struggled with corporate life. Envisioning 17-year-old Jerry with a rack of pitons and mountain boots, similar to what I was wearing, leading over the Chockstone Pitch with his 17-year-old partner, Dick Weaver, was an inspiration. I was already 19.

Jim Kanzler once told me that he and Jerry drove to the Tetons from Butte to climb an obscure peak called Yosemite Point. They thought that because of the name, the rock would be just like the granite in Yosemite, where they were planning to climb when they saved up enough money. Jim fell off of the hardest pitch, which had not been free-climbed yet. Jerry caught Jim with the rope but Jim was rattled, so the Kanzler brothers traded ends of the rope, and Jerry led through the crux.

"My little brother was a better climber," Jim told me without a hint of rivalry. "He was really good and, basically, fearless."

Emerson and I took all day to finish the North Ridge to the summit. I imagined Jerry Kanzler touching each of the same holds. I was literally following his footsteps.

We slid down the famous rappel to the Upper Saddle of the Grand, as it grew dark, using the now outdated six carabiner brake system and the 11 mm and 9mm rope we had dragged all the way up the mountain (a feat in itself as both ropes were wet). No way did we want to bivouac again high on the mountain; so we kept going down.

Neither one of our headlamps were functioning, which was typical. For some reason, in those days, big fat D-batteries, feet of wire and a pocketful of spare bulbs did not guarantee there would be light when you needed it. We reached the Lower Saddle between the Grand Teton and the Middle Teton S.O.L. The openness of the sky allowed us to see well enough to skid our way down the snowfield, but we were on our hands and knees patting the ground trying to feel the trail beyond the Boulder Field in the trees.

"This is crazy, Emerson. We should just crash here and wait 'til morning."

"Man, we can't bivvy here. One of these trees could blow over on us."

"The wind isn't blowing, Emerson."

"But it might later on."

"Oh come on Emerson, we froze our butts off last night and could have gotten welded to the stone, and now you are worried about a one in 900 million chance that a tree will fall on us in the next few hours..."

"I don't want to stay here, man," he insisted, "it's too dangerous." I was too tired to argue logic and there was no sense in dividing the party.

"O.K. Maybe if we hurry we can make it down before Dornan's (bar and cafe) closes and we can get a beer and a hamburger."

"Wow man, that sounds great! What time is it?"

My watch had hands that glowed in the dark. "Uh, it looks like 11:40."

"We'd better hurry. The bars close at two." (So we thought.) With that, Emerson turned around and took off in a run. He made it about five or six steps when he tripped and stumbled headlong off of the trail.

"Are you O.K.? Where are you?" I could not see him, but I could hear him thrashing and cussing on the steep slope below the trail.

"Yeah, blankety, blankety, blank. I skinned my shin pretty blankety-blanking bad."

"Emerson, take it easy, man! I think we'll make if we just walk fast."

The former sailor and the Cub Scout dropout—the Dirty Sox contingency from Columbia Falls—were "butt-draggin' wasted" by the time they stumbled to Emerson's hippie van in the Lupine Meadow trailhead.

We desperately wanted hot food and beer. Emerson throttled the microbus and we roared and rattled along the washboard road to the highway, then fixed our eyes on the beacon that marked Dornan's, just a few more miles away. I looked at my watch.

"We'll just make it, Emerson. Hurry!" We were ready to sink our teeth into a couple of grease-dripping gristle biscuits, oozing with cheese and ketchup, slake our gullets and numb our tired, aching shoulders with foaming barley squeezins.

The parking lot was empty; the bar was dark. I was in shock, and lapsed into mental illness. Emerson broke into a verbal tirade. "What's wrong with these dirty rotten...so-and-sos?" We yipped and barked like a couple of coyotes as if at the last white buffalo hunter headed over the prairie. We were too tired and dehydrated to carry on very long. That is what I have always loved about Jim Emerson. I could be myself around him, and he around me. If only with the language, we brought the worst out in each other, which made us the best of friends.

Life was always colorful around Jim Emerson and Jim Kanzler. The James Gang. The name would live on.

"To hell with these Wyoming blanking, redneck blankety blankers. The bars are still open in Montana. Come on, Kennedy, let's drive back over the river to Moose and see if there is some-blanking-thing open over-blanking-there."

There wasn't. We pulled into the only gas station and pooled what change we had—enough for one can of pop and a candy bar out of a vending machine: our celebratory dinner after tackling the mighty North Ridge.

It was almost time for breakfast.

Jim Emerson, January 1975. Emerson collection.

CHAPTER 7

Jackson

On September 19, 1973, I arrived at Montana State University, in Bozeman. Mom and Dad helped move me into my dorm room in Langford Hall. I had driven the family car through an early snowstorm that dropped a foot of snow between Missoula and Bozeman that year. My parents visited an aunt and uncle in town and returned home the next day with the big yellow Ford. My old '54 Chevy stayed in Columbia Falls my freshman year.

I walked across West College Street to Joe's Parkway, a small grocery store, to grab a snack and check out the surrounding neighborhood. Being around all the noise of excited college kids drove me nuts. The snow on the lawns I passed was melting as I strolled up the sidewalk between Langford and Culbertson Halls, wondering what college life would bring. My top priority, at the moment, was to hook up with the climbers in Bozeman.

Jim Kanzler was in Big Sky, 40-some miles away. He was the first Director of the Ski Patrol, and was busy preparing for the first season of commercial lift skiing at the new resort. Jim Emerson had been established in Bozeman for six months, and was already climbing with Kanzler, Leo, McCarty and Craig Zaspel (Dr. Z) on Montana granite. I was ready to join them and start preparing for the north face of Mount Cleveland.

Coming toward me was a tall kid about my age, dressed in a plaid shirt, ambling along with hands in his pockets. He wore a strange sheepskin hat sewn together with leather lace, making him look like a six-foot-three-inch blond Mongolian nomad. His thick blond hair reached past his shoulders, emerging from under his headdress like a horse's mane, with a slight curl at the ends. There was something familiar about him. I could not help staring at the hat, not sure if I thought it was silly or if I admired the creativity of what had to be a carefully handcrafted vesture.

My staring caught his attention. The stranger returned an inquisitive glance as we neared. We made room on the sidewalk for each other to pass and locked eyes. I began to feel uneasy gawking at the lanky guy, hoping he wasn't offended.

"Hi. Uh, I like your hat," I stammered.

He stopped, looking down at me and smiled warmly. His teeth displayed like piano keys as he shrugged his shoulders, hands remaining in his pockets. "Huh? Oh, thanks," he replied. He seemed bashful, like me.

"I know this guy," I said to myself. I felt obligated to strike up a conversation. I had climbing on the brain. I always did. Without further thought, I blurted out the one thing I wanted to know most.

"Uh, are you—by any chance—a climber?"

"Wow, how did you know?" The tall guy's grin broadened further and he turned square to me. His right hand came out of its pocket and slid the piece off of his head. "I made this in Explorer Scouts a couple years ago," he offered, maneuvering it for me to see more easily. "You must be a climber, too."

"Uh, yes, I am."

In the 1960s and 70s, being a climber somehow set one apart; or at least, I thought it did. Climbers were like an ethnic minority, a subculture. Climbing was not a mainstream activity back then; it was a way of life for a few diehards. It still is, in many ways. Repeated exposure to climbing (especially through television) and the public's appetite for watching thrilling and daring events—especially those that could lead to catastrophe—began to change all of that. Climbers of the Baby Boomer generation began to have children, and many of them learned to climb. First were the how-to books and videos, then more guide services. Many climbers became self-styled rock climbing instructors to make a buck and help support their habit. I would become one of those 15 years later— when I ran out of job options.

In the 1970s, climbing was the fabric of one's soul...or at least an essential thread woven into it. It was invigorating to meet others who shared this way of life. Because there were so few climbers in the early 70s, it was a unique happenstance to meet one just walking down a sidewalk.

I liked this guy with the unique hat at once. What were the chances that the first guy I would talk to in Bozeman would be a climber? Probably not very good—not like they would be 30 years later. Given that this new acquaintance was a climber, what was the probability that he would be someone of whom I'd heard? Probably quite high. In the small climbing community, everybody knew, or knew of, everyone else who was a serious climber. Light bulb!

"Hey, are you by chance Steve Jackson?"

The tall guy laughed softly as he placed his monumental headgear back in place, making him look closer to six-ten. "How did you know that?"

"Well..." I started to explain; but the tall guy continued.

"May I ask you something? Are you, by chance, Terry Kennedy?"

We both broke into uninhibited laughter. Our hands shot out simultaneously and clasped with a vigorous handshake.

"Yeah. How did you know that?"

"This guy I know, Dougal McCarty, told me about you. He said you were coming to MSU and said you were a climber and I should look you up."

"That's weird. I met Dougal in the Humbugs, last May," I said, all inhibitions melting away quickly. "He said I should look you up. I did a climb with Dougal and Jim Kanzler. Man, Dougal McCarty has the strangest laugh."

"Oh, tell me about it," Steve Jackson said, tilting his head back. Together, we laughed out loud, lapsing into full knee slapping as we heard Dougal's laughter in our minds. "I spent several nights with Dougal this summer in the Spanish Peaks with my friends, Dave Catlin and Scott Travis. They were in my Explorer Scout troop."

"Well hey, let's go climbing," I suggested. There was no point wasting any time getting started.

"O.K. When can you go?"

"Anytime."

"How about tomorrow?"

So began a three-year journey full of adventures—and misadventures— leading to the north face of Mount Cleveland. I think that Steve and I, as a pair, were similar to Ray Martin and Clare Pogreba.

The next morning, Steve came by my dorm room and we walked out to his faded green VW Bug. We drove up Hyalite Canyon to an outcrop of granite-like gneiss known to climbers simply as Practice Rock.

"Why don't you try this one?" Steve pointed to a deep, finger-width crack with crisp edges and square, angular footholds. "I did this one recently, so you can lead it if you like."

We set our packs down and sorted through our gear. We both had new straight-sided Chouinard Stoppers on shoulder-length knotted Perlon slings.

"Be sure your knots are good and tight," Steve advised with an uneasy chuckle. "I was up here with Scott Travis trying a route around the other side of the rock called The Fiver last spring. It was one of my first leads on my new gear. The climbing was pretty hard and the route was wet with dirt and moss. Anyway, I got up there near the top and my foot slipped off of a wet hold and I took a big leader fall."

"Really!"

"Yeah—it was quite a zipper. The knots on my sling rope weren't tight enough, and I pulled the knots through on the first two pieces of protection. I almost hit the ground," Jackson continued nervously. I stood there, incredulous and bug-eyed, listening to my new friend's story and wondering if I should be climbing with this guy or not.

Phil Stern's words were playing in my head. "The first three years as a climber are the most dangerous. That's when you think you know enough and are willing to try just about anything. That's the time you will make most of your mistakes. Most climbing fatalities happen to climbers in those first three years." I became astutely aware that Steve Jackson and I were both in our first three years of technical climbing.

"Holy shit," I exclaimed, "did Scott Travis catch the fall?"

"Yeah, he caught the fall; but, when I stopped, I was upside-down, looking right at his knee caps."

"You're kidding! You would have been killed if you hit head-first."

"Well, I did...kinda."

"What!"

"Of course I had my eyes closed, and I wasn't sure why I was falling so far; but I heard and felt this little 'tick' on my helmet. Scott said I just barely hit the ground with my head. But with the stretch in the rope retracting some, when I opened my eyes, my head was two feet off the ground." I was speechless. "It was a good thing Scott was tied in with a back anchor," Jackson added, "or I wouldn't be here. You still wanna lead?"

"Uh, well, I guess." I took a look at our gear and singled out all my pieces. The tails on my knots were substantially longer than Steve's, and they seemed tight; but I gave them all a yank with my teeth, just to make sure.

Later that day, I hung and bounced on all of my slings to snug them up even more tightly. From that day forward, I always preferred to use my own gear. I led the "5.6 Crack," which is closer to 5.8, promising myself not to fall. Jerry had done several of the first ascents at Practice Rock. I knew I was following the footsteps of Jerry Kanzler.

Steve Jackson and I did several routes on Practice Rock that day, without falls or other mishaps. We bonded and began climbing together at every opportunity.

I dropped by Pat's office and lab in Gaines Hall periodically, relating the climbing plans I had and showing him photos of unclimbed faces in Glacier Park. He never seemed to mind being interrupted. As our conversations grew more candid, I began to swing the conversations around to the Mount Cleveland tragedy. I wanted to know every detail.

One day, I sat on the edge of one chair and Pat slouched in another with his feet crossed and propped up on a desk littered with papers and a coffee mug.

"How did you find the pack?" My elbows were on my knees as I leaned forward, one hand massaging the fingers of the other.

Ever the teacher, the professor listened closely to each word of a question and pondered them before he answered. "Well," he began, "Peter, Jim and I were descending after we concluded it was pointless to go on, and after we realized how dangerous a slope we were on and that it might slide again at some point. We were on old avalanche debris—but it didn't look like much." Pat's eyes narrowed and he stared at a wall on which hung glassware and gadgets, but his focus was far away. "We were heading down and off to the right where we had climbed through a break in a cliff band the day before. Peter and Jim were a little ahead of me and my eye caught something out in the slope a hundred feet or so off to my left. There was something just protruding through the rough texture of snow that just didn't look right, so I veered over to it. There was just a little part of something sticking out—a bit of fabric. I dislodged it—it was a pack! My heart just sank."

I knew the story but I hadn't heard Pat tell it. I sat silent for a moment. Pat stood up and walked to a window and gazed out at the mountains to the south. Then I asked the question that for three and a half years had dogged me and—no matter what the answer—would hound me for another 20.

"If you had been there with those guys, would it have turned out differently?" I stared at the floor, letting the moments of silence ring.

I had no idea how he could answer such a question. It was impossible to know. It was an absurd question; but it was one that I just had to toss out into the ether. Pat stood motionless at the window for what seemed like a minute. As always, he took any question seriously—even absurd ones. He turned around and looked right at me and said softly. "You know, it probably...would...have...turned out the same."

His answer blew me off my feet. I left Gaines Hall, drifting down the stairs like a raven 20 feet off of the snow and ledges of Mount Cleveland.

The west face of Mount St. Nicholas was to be a stepping-stone to the north face of Mount Cleveland. I had already climbed the Northeast Ridge route that Hal and his sons had climbed in years past. The west face remained unclimbed. I piqued Steve Jackson's interest in it right away.

During Christmas break, 1973, Steve and I found ourselves a full day's trudge up steep-timbered mountain slopes above the Middle Fork of the Flathead River, grunting and cursing our way— with huge packs full of climbing gear—including an 11 mm and a 9mm rope; tents and sleeping bags—thrashing along on downhill skis with skins and steel shanked Galibier boots lashed into unreliable cable bindings. I was 19; Steve was 18.

Why was it that every mountain face I saw, unclimbed or otherwise, had to be attempted in the winter? It was ridiculous. It all harkened back to the Mount Cleveland Five.

From what I gather, Clare Pogreba (nicknamed "CEP" or "Poge" by his climbing buddies) got Jim, Jerry and Ray excited about climbing the north face Mount Cleveland—in the winter. The north face of the Eiger had just been climbed in the winter, and John Harlin lost his life during the project. There seemed to be some connection there.

A plan was hatched to climb Mount Wilbur in Glacier under winter conditions as a warm up for Cleveland's big face. There was a winter climb up Lone Mountain by Callis, Lev, Jerry, Martin and CEP. Then, there was Callis and Jerry Kanzler, Lev and George Lowe in the Tetons in December—all before Cleveland, between mid-November and mid-December in 1969.

With an hour of daylight remaining, a shoulder strap on my frame pack broke and Steve and I threw down our loads and pitched a Ted Williams endorsed (yes, the baseball player) Sears and Roebuck tent in the brush. That night, we lay in total darkness and listened to three freight trains churning up the highline route of the Burlington Northern Railroad toward Marias Pass on the Continental Divide, with four additional locomotives pushing from the rear. We could hear them from 20 miles away. One would fade toward the pass and another would start from far way. They rumbled all night. It seemed like ages.

The stark beauty of the rime-plastered cliffs of St. Nick stunned us the next morning. I jerry-rigged my pack and we went down without even getting to the mountain. That was probably a good thing.

Steve Jackson on the summit of Mount St. Nicholas, September 1974.
Photo by the author.

CHAPTER 8

The Seventy-Centimeter Fall

A month later, in January (1974), Pat Callis agreed to go ice climbing with Steve and me. We were ecstatic and felt privileged: a couple of rookies taking the field with the all-pro.

"I saw an ice formation from Palisade Falls looking up into the Flanders Creek drainage," the wiry, bearded climbing paragon told us. "I'd like to go in there and have a look at it."

We couldn't see the ice formation until we were right below it. Looking up was rather daunting.

In the early to mid-70s in Montana, ice climbs were rated "easy," "not too bad," "pretty steep," "very steep" and "dead vertical." Ice that spilled over roofs or was otherwise dead vertical might as well have been a moon of Pluto for most of the Dirty Sox at that time. We would look at such formations and oooh and ahhh at them for five or ten seconds then turn our attention toward formations that might be a potential climb. Eventually, Pat and Jack "Java Man" Tackle began to venture onto dead vertical ice, as the ice tools became more sophisticated. I looked at vertical ice as something to be avoided if possible. I always claimed that superior route-finding skill would lead one around it. Alex Lowe arrived a few years later and began exploring the outer orbits of ice climbing possibilities.

Pat named the ice formation "Champagne Sherbet" for the streaks of green, blue and white ice. It was a curtain of ice pouring over a lip of rotten Hyalite Canyon volcanic tuft. The midsection of the flow on the right formed into jagged teeth, with a gap between the serrations and the less steep ice below. The left side was a steep column that connected to lower angled ice that reached the bottom.

The nearly vertical section at mid-height was steeper than anything Steve or I had climbed before. I had played around "bouldering" close to the ground on vertical ice—only to discover that swinging a 70 cm ice axe with four small teeth at the end of the pick and setting crampons on vertical ice was a very strenuous and serious business. Often, the spike at the bottom of the axe would catch the ice as soon as the climber initiated a forward swing, resulting in an underpowered, inaccurate placement attempt with no useful effect. I later filed the spike shorter on my axe.

There was no discussion of who would lead as we geared up. Gandalf took the sharp end. He reported that the lower part was "not too bad". I gave him a standing hip belay, anchored to a tree. Steve burrowed into his down parka and took a series of black-and-white photos of the professor.

The crux section came abruptly. Pat moved left where the rock met the ice column, forming something of a chimney between the two mediums. He leaned his back into the rock like a climber would in a rock chimney and maneuvered the Chouinard-Frost Piolet and Alpine Hammer in front of him. The stemming position reduced the strain of hanging on the tools; but it was tricky swinging the ice axe in the confined quarters to achieve adequate pick placements. He took short, precise swings and methodically climbed through the tough section, chopping starter holes and levering in several ice screws with his alpine hammer pick.

The chimney feature ended at the top of the vertical section. The agile man sidestepped to the right, just above the lip, and hacked out a stance in the ice the width of a 2 x 4. Then he levered in two more screws and put me on belay.

By the time I fought my way through the chimney, I was exhausted from too many flailing axe swings, my forearms were pumped and my hands were mush from over-gripping my tools. I front-pointed on my crampons over to Pat, in want of a good rest. I began to tie a figure-eight loop to clip into the anchors when Pat revealed the plan.

"Uh, we're not going to get three guys on this tiny ledge," he explained. The climbing mentor had clove-hitched in close to a biner of one of the ice screws. He had it adjusted so that he could lean back against it and not have to balance so much on his feet. It was tiring just trying to stand there. "Why don't you take the rack and lead the next pitch?" His question was more instructive than interrogative. "You should be able to reach the top of the ice. After you set up a belay, I'll belay Steve up to here, then you can bring me up."

"Uh, well, O.K., my arms are really tired, I could use a rest," I confessed, perhaps a little too meekly.

Either the wizard didn't hear my request or he ignored me. He handed me the one remaining unused ice screw and the one-inch webbing runner he had slung over his neck and shoulder. I had cleaned all the others except one that I left as a directional to keep the rope I trailed for Steve in a more optimal location. Pat reached behind me and unclipped the second rope from the loops of seat belt webbing that was part of my homemade harness and clipped it into the belay. I stayed tied into the rope on which Pat had led. "The next section looks fairly easy. There might be a section up there that's a bit steep."

I glanced upward. It didn't look too bad, except for one short, pretty-steep section at the very top. I'd worry about it when I got there. The next task was to extract the ice out of the tubular ice screws.

"Here, let me help you with those." Pat grabbed two ice-plugged screws off of the sling, and I took the remaining two. We went through the ritual of warming the threaded steel in our gloved hands and blowing into the end to melt the ice enough to blow the plug out of the tube. My lips froze to the steel at the end, where the carabiner attached. I waited for my breath and tissue temperature to free the delicate flesh of my lips, and continued the process. The frozen core eventually expunged out the end like excrement from a goose.

The process was repeated for each used anchor, taking several minutes for each one in the 10-degrees-below-zero temperature. If the cores were not removed, the ice screws could not be twisted into the ice for subsequent anchor placements. We rolled and squeezed the cold steel in our hands and blew hard, until our faces turned red and our eyes bulged. By the time the ice screws were cleared and ready, not only were my forearms still pumped but also my hands were frozen and I could barely grip my tools.

I wore a pair of brown-colored rubber gloves one could buy at a hardware store, with a pair of army surplus wool glove liners in them, which kept the hands drier than ski gloves; but did not provide a lot of insulation. The gloves looked like something a marine veterinarian might use for a prostate exam on a walrus.

"Don't wait too long to put one in," Callis advised. "You don't want to fall directly onto the belay."

"Right," I murmured. "I'll put one in just up there."

My hands remained numb as I climbed the first ten feet above the last guy to climb with Jerry Kanzler before the fateful journey to Mount Cleveland. I could barely grip my tools and fumbled around like I had all thumbs placing the first ice screw. I clipped in the water-soaked and frozen 11mm rope, now as stiff as steel cable. I went to work on my hands, swinging and shaking them vigorously.

As the blood returned to the capillaries, there came pain so intense I thought I would throw up or pass out. I just stood there on my front points, squeezing my eyes shut and gritting my teeth, arms folded as I leaned my helmet into the ice, waiting for the phenomenon climbers call the *screaming barfies* to finish its course. Once the vasomotor response was over, my hands were toasty warm and I was ready to move.

I thought I finally had my act together, running my lead out over a stretch of easy rolling ice. I could sense Pat's restlessness on his narrow ledge. He had to be very cold. Steve was out of sight, undoubtedly bored and freezing. I needed to get to the top and set up a belay so that Steve could come up to Pat, and Pat could get off of his perch. I climbed another 30 or 40 feet above my one ice screw and I arrived at a short but "very steep" headwall above me, just below the top. I didn't like the looks of it. Even though I had good feeling in my hands, my forearms still felt like mud.

I hacked my way up to the base; it was more like dead vertical. It was only 15 feet high at most, but was formed with icicles clumped together like partially cooked spaghetti. I knew this was going to be tough, and the possibility of falling off would be greater here than the chimney below. Did I want to place an ice screw at the bottom of the vertical section, where positioning was easy, or further up?

If I put a screw in the lower-angled ice and fell from the head wall, I would hit on the lower-angled ice and I could break an ankle or worse. If I were to place an ice screw in the middle of the head wall and I fell off, the fall would be short and I wouldn't hit anything. Besides, if I flamed out I could rest on my placement. I considered the possibility of two placements—one at the bottom, while I was on easy ground, which would give me protection while I placed another in the middle of the headwall.

I looked down at Pat. He had on a pair of wool Dachstein mitts. His right hand was tending the rope as it wound around his parka at waist level and into a biner at the belay. He was swinging the other hand vigorously, trying to keep it warm. His straight, black beard flowed out of his balaclava and his old, battered helmet. His dark eyes were trained on me. He was 50 feet below—far enough to not offer any advice.

I decided to go for one screw in the middle of the head wall. It was a bad choice.

I made sure my first stick with the axe was a good one. It took several blows to sink it in deep. I advanced my crampons, then bludgeoned in the alpine hammer as high as I could reach up. I kept telling myself to move quickly and precisely, to not waste energy holding a position too long; but all I effectively did was rush it. The pick contact struck different places instead of furthering a single placement hole. Trying to get the extra height put my body in an awkward position. I had to move my crampons again; but I was so stretched out that I could hardly see my feet.

"Look at your feet, Terry," I scolded myself; "You can't just kick them in any old place.

With effort, I turned my head downward to place my horizontal front points of my crampons. As I did, my next breath fogged my glasses. "Son of a bitch!" I had to wait for my lenses to clear a bit before sketching my front points up slightly. I was breathing hard.

The next time I looked down, I exhaled as if blowing out a candle to project my breath away from my glasses. The pick of my ice axe was at about head-level. It was buried deep into the last of the solid ice that didn't have the icicle texture. It was overdriven—in too deep. I weighted heavily on the alpine hammer through a wrist loop of ½-inch webbing attached to the hickory hammer handle. I kept my right hand located at the best gripping part at the bottom of the handle. A lanyard attached the handle to a shoulder-length sling.

"Shit."

Although the Chouinard-Frost ice axe only had five small teeth in the end of the pick, it could still be overdriven. I reached my walrus glove to mid-shaft for better control. I wiggled it up and down, back and forth. "Oh, this goddamn thing! Get the fuck out of there!" I grunted through clenched teeth. My Irish temper was starting to flare. My calves were burning, and that lead feeling in my right forearm was coming back. The ice axe pick would wobble, but not release. I twisted the shaft like the minute hand of a clock, and I could sense the torque on the pick.

"Goddamn, Kennedy, don't break the pick!" I implored myself. 'You break the pick and you will really be fucked."

I grasped the pick right behind its entry into the ice and pulled it up and out. The warning light for my right forearm came on; I needed to shake out my right hand, but I couldn't do so until I got the axe back into the ice. I gave a quick little upward throw with my left hand on the head of the axe and tried to catch the lower end of the shaft, but I didn't make it. The tool dropped to the end of the 70 cm wrist-loop sling and clattered against the ice. I was lucky the wrist loop stayed on my glove.

"That was stupid, you dumb shit!"

I lifted the axe high enough to trap it with my shoulder and grabbed it mid-shaft. I stuck the pick into the previous hole and gripped the metal ferrule at the bottom of the axe I had wrapped with athletic tape for a surer grip. By then, the warning bell for my right forearm was ringing furiously. I had sagged onto the wrist loop of the hammer so as to not have to grip the axe as hard; but now I needed full gripping power to stay on the ice while I placed the axe again. I would do my best to set the axe quickly; my arm was just going to have to take it. My calves were nagging me. I needed to change foot position.

"Tough shit, you are just going to have to wait," I cussed at my lower legs.

The first blow with the ice axe hit the rounded edge of an icicle and shattered it. No stick. The next one landed between icicles and sank deep, but with the fact that no teeth reached past that first inch and a half; it slid right back out of the hole as easily as a key from a lock. I made several swings, with similar results. Now my left forearm was pumped. Swinging the 70 cm axe felt like swinging a telephone pole.

With as much concentration as I could muster, focusing out of a thin, clear strip on my left lens at the very top of my otherwise fogged and ice-chip-droplet-obscured glasses, I finally managed to hit the same hole twice. The pick didn't sink in much further; but the way it set it seemed good enough. It just had to be! I didn't have the strength left to loosen it by testing it and then start over.

"Gotta get that right forearm shaken out," I grunted to myself. I quickly reset both crampons. That relieved the ache for a while. I had to trust they were in soundly, since I couldn't see down through my lenses (again). I might have tried climbing without glasses; but with my severe nearsighted vision, my feet looked so blurry it was a toss-up between the myopia and fogged lenses.

After more cussing, I got my right wrist out of the loop of the hammer and shook it wildly. It ached the way it does before it goes completely numb. When I could make a reasonably tight fist, I took hold of the hammer handle again. Then the right crampon popped out; but I held my position with the tools and the left crampon. By that time, I had lost all sense of how well either crampon was placed; but it was too late to worry about that. I shook the right foot out, felt around through my boot and found the same placement holes—I think. Then I shook some life back into the left foot, remembering where its front point holes were, and eased them in by braille method. Then the left forearm warning light switched on. The right one was aching again, and both calves upped the ante from nagging to screaming.

"Oh God, there is no way I'm going chop a starter hole, crank a dozen half-turns into hollow ice, reset the hammer and clip in the rope before I completely melt off this thing. This is totally fucked! Maybe I should try to climb down."

I pulled one crampon out of its placement and tried to see through the slightly clearing fog; but as soon as I pulled it out of place, the other one popped and I was suddenly hanging from both tools again. I kicked my crampons furiously back into place and managed to get my right thumb under my glasses and force them up onto my forehead, under my helmet.

I knew I was 40 feet out from my last ice screw anchor. Of course, at that point I wished I had taken the time to place one at the base of the head wall, on the easier terrain; but squinting hard, I still managed to trace the rope back down to that last anchor. That was a mental mistake! It looked about as far below me as the Titanic at the bottom of the Atlantic. Another ten feet directly below that was Professor Callis, leaning against his clove hitch, staring straight ahead, as though he were reading a book or maybe frozen in place, his mittened hands tucked under his armpits, right hand still holding the rope. Perhaps his neck had become stiff from looking up for so long.

If I fell from that point, I would go twice the distance to the next anchor—which meant I would land directly on top of him before the rope would tighten. The dynamic property of the rope would absorb much of the shock to my body— especially going that far; but if I landed on Pat, I might break his neck—not to mention what 24 inch-and-a-half-long chrome molly daggers would do to him. If I fell off, I might cartwheel when I hit the lower angle terrain. We might both wind up dead, me hanging below Pat at Steve Jackson's feet.

Bringing all that to my forethought was an inadvertent mistake. Suddenly I was very nervous. I started to get sewing machine leg; my hands were shaking not only from fatigue, but now also with raging mortal fear. I was between ice and a slippery spot. I was fighting for my life...and Pat's. My only chance was to finish the glowering headwall.

It's funny. I looked at the prints made by Steve Jackson of Pat leading the first pitch a few decades later. There were two short, steep steps on my pitch. Apparently I circumvented the first one, since I really didn't have to climb it. It made sense to avoid it with time, cold temperature and energy at a premium. That had been a good choice.

And the second vertical bulge? It could have been circumvented to the left just as easily. What in the hell was I thinking? For some reason, I had it in my head that I had to climb it; I didn't look around and consider other options. So much for superior route-finding skills...

I looked up and my glasses slipped back off of my forehead and onto my nose, setting a little too low but allowing me to see over them without fogged vision. The next ice axe placement would just about reach the lip. With a surge of adrenaline, I attacked. I looked down over the fogged glasses and saw roughly where I wanted my crampons. I kicked and clawed them in place like a cat at a scratching post. It didn't take much to get the pick of the axe out this time. On my next swing, the spike at the bottom of the shaft caught the ice as I swung and the pick glanced off of the ice weakly.

Strike one.

I allowed for this on the next swing. The blow was on the money; but the cold, brittle ice shattered, leaving a divot in the ice.

Foul ball; strike two!

At least now I had a target at which to aim. I used what was left of my mental capacity and made an accurate, if not a strong swing with the pick, landing in the middle of the divot and plunging in about an inch.

It would have to do.

The adrenaline rush was rapidly waning. Fatigue lights and system warning bells were going off everywhere inside of me. The cold, heavy, water-soaked, frozen rope between my legs kept me in a constant downward pull. I went to work with the alpine hammer pick.

Three more whacks and I had a marginal placement with the hammer pick. "Oh Jesus, don't let them come out now," I begged. I looked down at my feet. The lenses had cleared a little. I kicked hard with my crampons. My calves felt like they had knives imbedded in them. I looked up and was almost shocked to find that my face was suddenly looking over the top; but now I had another problem.

Rather than a transition onto low-angle terrain, the climb ended on a horizontal flat step. The ice changed from vertical to horizontal. With my shoulders still below the lip, I couldn't reach over the lip to set either pick into what lay over the top. I had to place my crampons higher so my shoulders had an angle from which I could swing the tools through eight inches of snow covering the flat spot. I worked my front points up, unable to see them at all, with or without glasses, since I had to lean forward, shoulders emerging over the lip, with my hands still gripping the tools below the lip on the vertical ice. I just bent my knees with my butt out in space, keeping my heels locked as low as they could go, calf muscles feeling shredded like so much beef jerky. From this stance, I had to grip even harder on the tools.

The sun was setting on the horizon of my strength. I needed to get higher to reach over the top. I reached up to the head of the ice axe with my left hand and mantled onto it, pushing straight down with my palm, locking my elbow. I could see at least one tooth sticking out of the placement. It wasn't in there very far!

"Dear Jesus, make the son of a bitch stay in there—please!"

I yanked the pick of the hammer out in one desperate motion, causing me to barn-door slightly to the right. My crampons might have popped off, but they didn't—no sir, not then, anyway. As I reached forward to brush the snow from the horizontal surface, begging the Almighty for there to be solid ice underneath, I could feel my legs begin to lever my front points off of their purchase. I willed them to stay in place.

The first desperate swing of the hammer found only slush under the snow—a sign there might be sticky ice underneath and not just rock, which would be of no use. I drew the hammer back and heaved it into the slush, hoping it would find home. There was a sloppy splat and some of the super-cooled slush plastered my glasses, freezing instantly. My lenses had already re-fogged, so it didn't make that much difference. The next blow was off-angle, and there was no pick placement; but I was pretty sure I had hit ice underneath. My left arm was shaking so much I thought it would rattle the ice axe pick right out of the ice; but it stayed. I made my last desperate, absolutely pathetic, life-endearing attempt to stick the hammer pick into whatever might lie beneath the slush. My life—and Pat Callis's – was contingent upon ice being present at the bottom of the slush, and my sticking the hammer pick into it within the next three seconds.

"Heavenly Father," I began to pray... my grip was gone. Not even the Great Camp Cook in the Sky could restore it. The sun had set. I tried to close my fist around the hickory handle, which by then was caked with frozen slush, making it twice its usual circumference. My fingers had seized half-open in the frozen walrus gloves, like the fingers of a mannequin.

"Jesus, help me make this fuckin' thing stick," I whimpered. "I'll never do this shit again, if you can just me off this goddamn—I mean doggone— fuckin' thing!"

The next sequence of events was like a slide show with the now-obsolete carousel slide projector. Between each slide cycle, there was a half-second during which there was no image...just black. The slide screen went to black as my hammer came down. When the image appeared again, the pick was buried to the head, but off angle. I pulled on the hammer from the wrist loop. At first, I thought I had stuck it in good ice; but the pick came out slowly, making a sucking sound. I was slowly sinking back down over the lip. My calves seized, and my grip strength—a puddle of goo.

I made one final last-ditch effort to swing the hammer, my walrus glove barely in contact with the ice-encrusted handle. The hammer landed parallel to the surface, a pathetic 90-degree rotation to the right. I tried to turn it to at least drag it like a ship anchor, hoping it would catch on something.

My mind faded to black, as the next slide cycled and I popped off of the lip of the ice column and launched into space.

I was a dead man. I could only think of how badly I did not want to die. I didn't want to kill Pat, either. The next slide dropped between the lamp and the lens. The panorama of upper Flanders Creek spun into view as I rotated 180 degrees, facing out and let out a blood-curdling scream.

There are no vowels in the English language that represent the sound that emanated from the depths of my bronchioles and bowels. Perhaps the high-pitch screech of the red-tailed hawk combined with the belch of an overfed turkey vulture coming in to roost would be close.

Perhaps the accelerating wind blowing by my face cleared the fog from my glasses, for I looked down and saw Pat well enough to note his Dachstein mittens tightly covering his helmet as he crouched on the ledge, right hand still on the rope. We were both belting out primordial death screams at the tops of our lungs, using that one "last" lungful we all reserve for expression of just how much we really do value life and how desperately we wish to keep a hold of it, at a moment when gravity suddenly is ripping life from our grasp...

And the next slide cycled.

I wasn't moving—at least, not downward. I was just hanging in space, looking directly at a steep, formidable free-standing pillar of ice at the same elevation on the other side of the drainage—an ice formation named Killer Pillar some years later. I wouldn't climb it for another 30 years, and only with the modern ice-climbing tools of the day.

My left arm was stretched straight above my head. I hung from the wrist loop of the 70 cm piolet like a horse thief from a noose. The adze of the ice axe was tilted back, and the spike was leaning into the ice like the bottom edge of a picture frame leans into a wall. The pick was still holding, but it could not have been by much. I had taken a 70 cm fall from ice axe head to axe spike. My shoulder did not dislocate, which was a very lucky thing.

I was about to suck in another lungful of death scream when I realized I was still in the living game. The motor was still running. I had a chance, hanging by a tooth. I had to squirm around and point my crampon front points at the ice again. I experienced a second adrenaline rush—bigger than the first. It was a reality all its own.

The slides cycled lickety-split through the projector, and it is impossible to remember the exact sequence that got me up over that lip.

It may have been one continuous motion, like a frog jumping out of a boiling pot.

There is one image of my right knee up arching over the lip like the old straddle roll high jumpers used before the Fosbury Flop. Then I was on both knees, with the pick of the alpine hammer buried into sticky ice under the slush, my boots and crampons hanging over the lip. I felt like a naked toddler climbing onto a greased countertop in a pair of roller skates.

I staggered to my feet, still well aware that I could stumble and fall over the lip again. Both tools dangled from their wrist loops, bonking and clattering against each other. The front of my parka and wool knickers were soaked and quickly freezing stiff. I tried to collect myself. I could barely lift my axe and hammer high enough to stick them into a bump of ice next to the stance. It felt like two weeks to lever in two screws.

"Off-f bee-lay." My throat was dry, and I barely had enough energy to shout.

I was grateful I had time to rest while Pat belayed Steve up the first pitch. When Pat arrived at my belay stance, he was stone silent. I've never seen anyone flip two loops into a clove hitch and clip in so fast.

"I can belay Steve," I said.

"I'll get him," Callis grumbled. Nothing more was said until Steve arrived at the belay.

"Wow, nice lead, T," Steve congratulated me with a big grin. "It was pretty easy until that last part. That was steeper than shit. Very bold. I probably would have put a screw in at the bottom of the steep step, myself."

Jackson hadn't seen any of it, being out of sight at the bottom. I felt my face flush. I glanced over at Pat. He didn't give me any eye contact.

"We can go left and rappel from a tree," was all he said.

After Pat dropped Steve and me off at our dorm room, I told Steve what had happened.

"Didn't you hear Pat and I scream?"

"I just thought you were yelling belay signals," he shrugged.

Steve and I spent many days in the spring and the autumn Indian summer rock climbing in the Gallatin Canyon, the Humbugs and Revenue spires and along the Madison River. Never were the days so new and infused with desire. Never was the rock so appealing and taunting. Never were our experiences so inspired or innocent. We did our best to be careful; but climbing is a game that is full of surprises.

The next weekend, Steve and I planned another ice climb up Hyalite Canyon. We had already knocked off Twin Falls, which forms early in the season. With Palisade Falls, the new route with Pat Callis and the scrape with fate behind us, we were ready to get back out there and continue ice climbing, honing our skills.

We picked up Dave Catlin and ate breakfast at the Western Cafe on East Main Street in Bozeman at 6 a.m. Dave was starting his second quarter of pre-med at MSU. Dave would follow his father's footsteps and become a veterinarian. It was a few clicks below zero, and the wind was drifting the snow in town; but that didn't stop us.

Halfway up the 14-mile-long Hyalite Canyon road south of town, we were pushing snow with the bumper of Steve's brand-new 1974 Saab, which he'd bought with the money he earned at his grandparent's ranch. We plowed along to Hyalite Lake reservoir and earthen dam. The wind continued, even in the confines of the timbered mountain drainage. Snow was blowing down the reservoir, forming a drift at the far end of the dam. Steve gunned the Saab and it blew through the drift like a Panzer through a rail fence. A few miles further, the snow got deeper and denser from the wind action; we knew the Saab was about to bog down. Our intention was to try an ice formation called Mummy Couloir, the first ice formation to receive serious ice climbing attention in Hyalite Canyon in 1971 by Pat Callis, Jim Kanzler, Peter Lev, Brian Leo, Dougal McCarty and others. We were still half a mile from the end of the road and trailhead. Just ahead was another formation as green as a lime Margarita. Brian and Dougal had just made the first ascent weeks before, and called it Green Sleeves. We stopped there and, with a little shoveling and pushing, managed to turn the Saab around and pointed back the way we came.

We strapped skins to our downhill skis, fitted with Silveretta cable bindings, and fastened the assembly to our leather single boots. It was so cold with the wind blowing and the snow drifting that I just wanted to get back into the car and turn the heater back on.

"We gotta watch out for avalanche conditions," I warned Steve and Dave, seeing how the snow was layered into slabs by the wind.

Steve and I were currently taking a snow safety course taught by a variety of ski patrolmen from Bridger Bowl and a geology professor, John Montagne— a former soldier in the Army Tenth Mountain Division of World War II. It was essentially the same course Jerry Kanzler, Jim Anderson and Mark Levitan were taking in 1969. Lectures were held in the evenings, with a few weekend field sessions. Steve and I intellectually understood that the wind was creating dangerous conditions by forming fragile snow bonds and slabs that could fracture, causing a whole slope to slide. Either one of us would have answered the test question correctly. I knew it was this condition that ultimately overwhelmed the Mount Cleveland Five and buried them all without a trace. One would think, even knowing what the wind had been doing to the snow pack we were in over the last 24 hours, that we might have elected to go ski groomers at Bridger Bowl that day and save ice climbing for less dangerous conditions, right? No sir, not a couple of young, hot upstarts. No way.

"There are so many trees that I think if we stay in them, we should be O.K.," Steve surmised, sizing up the terrain below Green Sleeves. "We probably ought to stay out of the creek bed leading up to the ice. I suppose something like that could go."

The three of us cut a trail through a clear cut, into some second growth and then old-growth timber. Each step broke through wind slabs that sometimes fractured a body length from our skis. Beneath these slabs, the snow was poorly packed and our skis sunk down until they contacted downed trees and buried branches. The sugary snow underneath the wind slabs was known as *depth hoar*.

Montagne had taught us about this. Wind slabs on top of depth hoar is to avalanches what flour and sugar are to cookies. This made skiing difficult, unappealing and certainly hard on both the skis and skins. At the streambed that descended from the Green Sleeves formation, we decided to cache our skis and proceed on foot.

"You're right, I think we should stay out of the creek bed," I concurred, looking up at the eroded gully meandering upward. It was ten or 15 feet deep, with loose dirt and crumbling bedrock sloughing into the wash from the sides—about 15 to 20 feet apart. The snow drifted deeper in the creek bed, with a trickle of water running underneath it.

"If we cross here, where it is low-angle, we can be in some trees along the edge of the gully, which ought to be safe," Steve suggested. We crossed the creek bed where it was easiest, and Steve and I took turns post holing a trail in knee-deep snow. By this time, Dave Catlin was some distance behind us. He had to make frequent adjustments with his ski bindings. We knew Dave would catch up with us as we started breaking trail on foot.

The streambed flared into a more open slope as we neared the ice formation. Here, Green Sleeves split into two separate formations at a Y in the terrain. We were interested in the higher and wider formation on the left. To get there, we were forced to re-cross the streambed. The best place was below the Y, where the trees on the other side were 20 feet away and represented safety. I was in front, so I prepared to go first into the streambed.

"This is spooky, Steve." The wind was strong and the trees were swaying. There wasn't any snow left in the branches. The rush of the wind through them added to the ambiance.

"I know what you mean, T. Be careful. I could belay you."

"No, I'll just go out a few steps and see what it feels like." I took one pah-loof, two pah-loof, three pah-loof steps out into the gully, each one breaking a soft crust about 18 inches deep, then sinking into sugary snow, until I was almost up to my crotch.

"What do you think, T.?"

"I don't like it. It gives me the creeps." I retraced my steps.

"Here, I'll give it a try," Steve offered, "my legs are longer and it won't be much work for me to break a trail." Hell, it was only 20 feet to the other side.

We traded places. "You want a belay? If this thing goes, at least I could keep you from going very far."

"Nah. I'll just be careful." Those famous last words. "Just watch me."

Steve Jackson easily stepped through my postholes, then continued making his own... four pah-loof. The soft crust of snow cracked out around his leading foot— about the diameter of a garbage can lid. Not a good sign. Five pah-loof. The next step did the same thing. Jackson was now halfway across.

"Be careful..." I reminded him.

He didn't let me break his concentration. Steve looked more like he was hunting, with the quarry just ahead of him and out of sight. The wind blew the drawstring of the hood of my parka and it flapped across my cheek, but I hardly noticed. Jackson lifted his trailing right boot out of the hole and swung it over the snow pack to punch another hole in the snow.

He gave his boot a good punch downward. As soon as it hit the snow surface, there was a sudden, unmistakable *whoomph*. Instead of a crack forming like a garbage can lid around his boot, a gaping crack formed in the snow 30 feet above him—three feet deep—and broke away from the slope above, buckling the snow surface into fractured plates ten feet below him. Immediately he was in motion, ushered down the creek bed. Jackson was still standing, but now buried up to his waist.

"Shi-i-it!"

Steve was sandwiched between blocks of snow and moving down

the gully faster than an Olympic sprinter. The only word he uttered was a gasping, "Terry!"

There was nothing I could do to help him—no rope to brace around my waist to stop his descent. I thought fast, hastening back to our training.

"Swim on your back! Swim on your back! Swim on your back!" I bellowed as Jackson disappeared around a corner. I frantically plowed through the snow along the edge of the gully, trying to keep Steve in view. I thought about Dave below. Would he be in the creek bottom at this point?

"Avalanche!" I yelled. "Get out of the gully! Get out of the gully, Dave! Get out of the gully!"

I looked for signs of Steve. Then, right below me, there he was—hanging onto a root protruding from the bank, where most of the slide had stopped.

"Shit man, are you O.K.?"

"Yeah, I guess so." Steve had gone perhaps 100 feet. I helped him out of the gully and we retraced my steps to our packs and waited for Dave.

A couple of minutes later, he arrived.

"Hey, were you guys calling me?"

You would think by this time we could take the hint. Conditions were hairball. But no-o. Not three 18 and 19-year-olds. There was still a luring ice formation above. We "carefully" picked our way to the bottom and roped up. Steve led a rope length to the top and we rappelled off of a tree and headed down.

No one will ever know exactly how the avalanche on Mount Cleveland started. Did the Mount Cleveland Five know they were in bad conditions? They might have. Steve and I knew we were. Clare Pogreba or Jerry Kanzler may have thought, or even said, "We'll just be careful."

When one is standing in wind slab on top of depth hoar (or temperature gradient deformed snow crystals or facets), on even easy terrain, there is no such thing as careful. There is only fate. Every man-triggered avalanche begins with a step too far. We know the avalanche on the west face of Mount Cleveland was massive. The crown fracture may have been as much as a half-mile wide, and may well have released and propagated far above the Mount Cleveland Five. It ran over 3,000 feet. Recovery crews reported that the bodies had multiple traumas. There was no way to fight out of the snow.

Steve, Dave and I made it back to the Saab wet and cold. We re-broke trail and fishtailed our way back into Bozeman with the heater running full blast, then clopped into the Haufbrau to dry off and rehydrate while we planned the next climb.

Pat Callis leading on the first ascent of Champagne Sherbet with first generation Chouinard ice tools in subzero temperature, January 1974. Photo by Steve Jackson.

CHAPTER 9

One Hell of a Nice Jump

The day had begun at 3 a.m., and my rear end was dragging. Steve and I had descended to the saddle between Mount Athabasca and Mount Andromeda, known as the AA Col, in the Columbia Icefield area of the Canadian Rockies. We had just climbed the Photo Finish route on Mount Andromeda.

We just needed a couple of hours to get off of the mountain and return to the campground for a night's sleep before driving back to Columbia Falls the next day. We were on the backside of a weekend raid to count coup and add to our list of accomplishments a mountain with an alpine ice route not available in Montana. It was August 24, 1974.

"If Steve and I can pull off this climb," I felt, "I will be worthy of climbing with Jim Kanzler, and Jim will want me as a partner to climb the north face of Mount Cleveland." I was 20—but I still thought like a teenager. I had a plan. My life was to follow an algorithm to Mount Cleveland. There was no room for deviation.

Steve and I had drooled all winter over a photograph of the ice face on the northwest bowl of Mount Andromeda. Climbing mountains was where it was at—not just one- or two-pitch frozen waterfalls.

We could be in the big mountains of the Canadian Rockies, with one tank of gas from Columbia Falls, driving the Tank to the Columbia Icefields in nine hours. With Steve driving his Saab, we got there in seven. I had a three-day turnaround from a shift change at the aluminum plant and Steve took an extra day off of work at his grandparent's ranch on the Dearborn River, north of Helena.

We swung leads up the ice face all day and got caught in a thunderstorm as we topped out onto the northwest ridge. The lightning strikes missed us; but lingering clouds socked in the mountain and created whiteout conditions. We inadvertently began descending the wrong ridge of the mountain. When the clouds started to lift, we could see we had made an error. We trudged back up 500 feet to summit and headed down the east ridge into the Athabasca, Andromeda Col. From there, we planned to descend directly to the Andromeda Glacier, which would bring us back to the road. We descended on intermittent hard blue ice that grew steeper the further we went. We repeated the routine of chopping starter holes for ice screws before levering them in with hammer picks, and belaying each other. It was a slow process. The sun dropped behind Andromeda and we were in the shadows, burning daylight.

We moved simultaneously, without belays, in the sections where snow had adhered to the ice from a storm a week earlier, which made climbing in crampons less strenuous. In late afternoon, the snow had become sticky, packing and balling up under our crampons to where it would not allow the crampon points to bite and caused dangerous slips when we weren't ready for them.

Jackson and I were experienced enough to know it was important to be careful on the way down when you were physically and mentally tired. Indeed, more mountaineering mishaps occur on the descent under these circumstances. In retrospect, we should have kept the rope through at least one ice screw between us as we moved together.

The slope rolled way from view as it steepened, not allowing me to detect the bergschrund we needed to cross until I was about 50 feet above it. Even then, I could not see the lower edge.

A bergschrund is typically a glacier's longest, deepest, and often widest crevasse. It is formed by the glacier proper pulling away from the often steeper but less massive permanent snow on the mountain above it. The downhill edge of this one was much lower than the uphill edge and impossible to determine how much gap existed between the two edges. As I moved closer, the angle of the slope above the 'schrund became steeper yet. I turned around, facing in, and began to front point backwards down toward the top edge. With each step, I became more aware of an abyss below me.

"Jackson!" I yelled up to Steve, who was a 150-foot rope length above me.

"Yeah!"

"I'm right above the bergschrund. Put me on belay."

"O.K. Gotta get screws in first."

"O.K."

The sun had just set as I looked around. Any crossing of the 'schrund was going to be complicated and dangerous. Directly below me was not promising, so I traversed gingerly 15 or 20 feet to the east to look for other options as Steve worked on a belay set up. Looking back, things may have turned out differently had I not deviated from the fall line of our descent.

I heard Jackson gasp. I looked up and saw he had lost his footing and was accelerating rapidly, the snow sloughing with him.

"Jesus Christ, stop!" I ordered. "God Damn it, Jackson, stop...sto-o-p!"

"I can't!" was his throaty reply as he desperately tried to self-arrest with his ice axe. The wet snow on top and hard ice underneath prevented him from applying the pick effectively. He traveled the length of rope in a matter of seconds. The rope gathered into haphazard figure eights, moving more slowly than the bobsled that was Steve Jackson. I looked in disbelief, realizing Steve was not going to stop. He was going to slide over the edge.

The sequence happened quickly; but time moved slowly. It was obvious to me (and probably to Steve) what was going to happen. Jackson would jettison over the lip into the blackness of the bergschrund, which might be 200 feet deep. He would fall until he pulled all the accumulating slack back out of the rope. Then he would pull me off of my feet like spitting out a cherry pit, and I would follow him into the bergschrund.

Mountaineers worry about what they would do in situations where they are roped together, but not belayed, and one climber falls. On snow, the protocol is to go into immediate self-arrest using your ice axe. If on broken terrain, one might hastily flip the rope around an outcrop of rock—if there is one. Or jump off of the opposite side if on a ridge.

If climbers do not belay one another on terrain too steep to self-arrest on, it is often better to untie from the rope so that if one guy falls, both climbers don't go. In our situation, we knew we had rope work ahead for the bergschrund crossing and glacier travel below, so we both had remained tied into the ends as we moved simultaneously.

Now there was nothing but a gathering rope between us as Jackson lunged past me. There was nothing to flip the rope over or a rock to jump behind to hold the fall.

Adrenaline rifled through my body. Surprise, bewilderment, fear, anger, regret, grief, and even acceptance streamed through me as Jackson plunged over the lip and disappeared. I stood in my tracks and screamed the death prayer:

OH SHIT!
OH FUCK!
OH GOD!
OH JESUS!
NO! NO! NO! NO!

I heard Steve Jackson's glottis snap shut as he took a final breath and disappeared. Somehow he turned and faced outward. The gathering rope suddenly began to hiss like a wire in the wind as it whipped wildly toward the place where Jackson went over the edge.

I knew what was coming. If we both went in, there would be no trace of us to be observed for the eventual search party. There would be no bodies to discover, no gear found strewn on a slope—maybe just a faint *sitzmark* leading to the upper edge of the gap—and that would melt away quickly. I wondered later if this was how the Mount Cleveland Five experienced their last moments.

I had three or four seconds to do something, and no plan. Instinctively, I took a couple of quick steps upward, away from the bergschrund and the sizzling rope. Then I realized how pathetically useless this was. I had consumed half of what precious little time I had before the rope would come violently for me. I tried to think rationally.

I had to place my axe pick in the ice and the rope over it and hope it held the fall; but I realized it would take too long to get a good stick through the mushy snow into the hard ice for any useful purchase— if I could get any at all. All I could think of to do was plunge the laminated bamboo shaft down as far as I could into the snow and maybe get the rope around it. I made a desperate jab. It went in about eight inches and stopped as the spike hit the ice.

My gloved hand was through the wrist leash. I would never get my hand out in time to get the rope around the axe. There wasn't much slack left in the rope by then. I knew the big yank was almost upon me. There was no time to do anything. I was down to the last, desperate option of self-preservation. I applied the primordial two-handed death grip—right hand gripping the head of the ice axe, left hand gripping the shaft next to the snow—and I gripped with every milligram of force I had in me.

Then I had a vision of my mother and father sitting next to each other on the couch in the living room of the house I grew up in, mourning my death. My mother had her arm around my dad and leaned into him, while he stared at his feet, elbows resting on his knees. "I am so very sorry for this," I tried to tell them. It was a simple peace. I accepted that in the next moment, I would be launched backwards out of my tracks, ice axe and all.

In that time-warped, slow motion scene of imminent catastrophe, I wondered, "Will I land directly on top of Steve in the bottom of the bergschrund, and if so, will he already be dead? At that point, it was no big deal. My question was simply pragmatic.

Steve and I were best friends. I thought we'd climb together until we were old men—no longer able to do the technical climb, but still enjoying a stroll up a hill together. Now, it looked like we were both going to get the big chop and join all the other mountain climbers who died before their time.

I was O.K. with it. I would at least get to meet the Mount Cleveland Five and compare experiences. I was ready for the moment of truth. I waited... and waited...and....

I became aware that the welded grip on my ice axe was beginning to fatigue. My jaw was tired of holding a grimace. The last precious moment of life sure seemed to be lasting a long time. I opened my eyes. I had squeezed them so tight, it took a while for my eyeballs to regain their shape and focus on the slope in front of my face. I no longer heard the sizzle of the rope. I turned my head toward the place where Jackson had disappeared. There was a lazy 'S' in the rope leading to the edge.

"What the...?" Nothing was moving. Everything was silent—dare I say, dead silent. Was the bergschrund less than 150 feet deep? Was Steve at the bottom, or on a block of rock or ice? Dead, or mortally injured? Did I have to, somehow, venture down into the bowels of the glacier to help him? Or was he only hurt a little—a broken leg or something?

I looked at the remaining rope, wondering if it would suddenly take off again.

"Steve! Jackson! Can-you-hear-me?" There was no reply. My heart sank.

"All right, Kennedy," I said out loud to myself, "you have to be ready for this. Be strong. Do what needs to be done. Steve might be dead. He might be hurt very badly and die soon. You've got to handle it. You can grieve later. Damn it, Kennedy, damn it, you have to handle this."

I pulled up on my ice axe and cautiously backed down a few steps toward the lip. I kept waiting for something more to happen: the upper edge collapsing, or my suddenly cutting out like Steve had and plunging into the gulf. I kept calling Steve's name and slowly inching toward the edge. Then I could see the far edge of the bergschrund and part of the hidden black chasm. Then...

"Kennedy, I'm down here." I looked around below me. "No, over here." He was on the far edge of the bergschrund, standing next to the gaping crack. "I made it. I'm O.K."

"Jackson, are you sure?" I couldn't believe he was standing there, looking up at me.

"No really, I'm O.K." He was far enough away that we still had to shout to be heard.

Next question: "How am I going to get down to you?"

(No reply.)

"Are there bridges I can get across within a rope length on either side of you?"

There was a brief silence and then, "No. Nothing."

Shit. "What if we traverse together, me up here and you down there, until we find something?"

"T!" That was what Steve Jackson sometimes called me. He used the nickname in casual situations. Our family lived next door to a retiring first grade teacher in Columbia Falls, who used to call me "T". I disliked it because I thought it was too feminine, but years later, when Steve started using it, I didn't mind. Hearing him call me "T" from the other side of the bergschrund had a calming effect.

"Yeah!"

"The 'schrund is very wide, as far as I can see, in both directions. There are no bridges. I can't see what's below me, but it's very steep. I can't move anywhere."

There was a longer silence. I tried to come up with creative options. I could unrope and keep traversing east toward Mount Athabasca, and either I would find a good bridge or I'd eventually come out on the lateral moraine. It was getting dark. I took a few steps back up the slope to get away from the menacing edge and carefully secured my ice axe and unshouldered my pack. It was only a minor disappointment to discover that my headlamp was no longer functioning. An external wire had broken off in my pack. Whatever we were going to do about this situation, it would be best to do it soon.

We had been on the move for 18 hours by then, and now a wall of space separated us. I was not keen on untying the rope and traversing to the lateral moraine, but I could do it. That would not solve the problem for Steve. I could tell the slope below him was steep because I couldn't see it, either. There were numerous open crevasses further below, which meant there would be hidden ones; this was no place to wander around in the dark, unroped. I began to get that— "oh-shit!" feeling all over again.

Jackson shouted again from below. He had been thinking, too. His voice was serious.

"Kennedy..."

"Y-yeah...?"

"...You're gonna havta jump!"

Three seconds later: "I know."

Nothing more was said for minutes; the idea had to sink in. The air was calm, and daylight was seeping away. Steve seemed to understand that I needed to gather myself. This was the only apparent option.

I can tell you right now that I do not like jumping off of things. I never did. I didn't like jumping off of merry-go-rounds or out of swings as a kid, or taking air off of moguls or cornices while skiing. When others jumped off of bridges into the river, I found excuses to do something else. I thought of myself as...well...a grounded individual. As a climber, I dealt with the air beneath my heels; but I could (usually) see no reason to jump.

Jackson was standing on a berm about as wide as the hood of his car that ran along the lower lip of the bergschrund in a zone where the snow spin-drifted off of the steep ice above and deposited during the previously mentioned snowstorm—the same snow that caused Jackson to lose his footing in the first place. Had there just been hard snow or ice, he would probably have received serious trauma from the initial impact and just kept going to the lower angle of the glacier below. A search party would have had something to find and package then; but we were both breathing and unhurt. The task at hand was to keep it that way.

It looked to be a jump from the apex of a two-story house. I had to reach down deep inside to resign myself to jump.

"Jackson!"

"Yeah."

"I'm going to ease up to the edge and lower my feet over and drop..."

"NO, NO— YOU CAN'T DO THAT!" Jackson became animated as he saw me appear at the upper lip. "You are going to have to clear about 15 feet! You need to get a running start!"

"Fifteen-fucking-feet! God o' fucking shit!" I began to recite the ol' death prayer; but I was so rattled, it came out backwards. I could not long-jump 15 feet—not even with track spikes and a tail wind. I was a short, slow white guy. I couldn't jump 15 feet with a grizzly bear chasing me— and certainly not in a pair of heavy boots, crampons and a pack. My heart thrashed beneath my wool jacket.

"T," Jackson continued, restored to his usual pastoral self. His voice became measured and encouraging. "You can make it. You will be O.K. It won't be that bad. Really."

"Oh man, I've got to do this. I can do this." My self-talk no longer contained profanities, which was probably a good sign. There was nothing else I could think of to do. I simply had to jump. "Don't dink around," I coached myself, "just cue up and DO IT."

"Kennedy," Steve's voice came up from below again, taking charge, trying to sound assuring and confident. "Just go to where I went over the edge and slide on your butt. That's the best place. Just make sure you are going fast over the edge. The snow is pretty soft. You'll be O.K."

"I don't know..." I started to waffle again. I traversed over to his slide mark. We could no longer see each other.

"You can do it, Big T." Jackson kept encouraging. He knew he had to keep me going. "Face out—be sure you face out. I'll give you a boot-axe belay."

"Tuh, BFD," I muttered. "If I don't clear the fucker, we're both dead men."

I took a deep breath and positioned ten feet from the edge. "It had better be enough." That last few feet to the lip pitched sharply downward. It was difficult to maintain my position, especially as I turned around to face out. I stomped my crampon heels into the snow. I could feel the ice a short distance underneath. My butt was touching the slope. The temperature had dropped to below freezing, and the snow was forming into corn crystals. I kept prodding myself: "Don't hesitate, just do it, you'll be O.K."

Steve could sense I was getting ready. He shouted up one final set of instructions:

"Make damn sure you face out! Get good speed. You are going to land right next to me."

Heels were dug in, butt against the slope, right hand on the head of the ice axe with fingers curled over the pick, thumb curled under the adze, left hand near the spike with the shaft diagonal across my body, levering firmly in a brake position.

I made a quick check. "Alpine hammer: in holster. Rucksack—God, maybe I ought to throw it over—no, stupid idea. Lower it? No, too much fuss, it would take too long. Besides, it will offer some padding. It might keep me from breaking my back."

"God damn it, Kennedy, DO NOT land on your back!" a voice inside my head yelled. "Land on your feet, land on your feet! Hold the axe away. Don't get impaled!" Rope: still tied in. Crampons: Shit! Crampons!

"You can't do this in crampons!"

"Oh, yeah? You ain't even going to stand here, stupid, without crampons," the voice chided with minor disgust.

"Yeah, but I might break a leg. Well, hell, I'll probably break 'em both, anyway."

"No, you won't," the voice said, more assuring this time. "You'll be okay."

In the next second, disaster nearly had us again. I pulled up on the ice axe ever so slightly—just to test things. The instant I relaxed the ice axe pressure, I lurched forward. Instinctively and reflexively, my body began to initiate a self-arrest, which meant twisting around to face in.

I twitched left as muscles preset to turn and plant the ice axe, waiting for the specific order; but something else at the last possible instant overrode the instinct. If I went into self-arrest position, I would not have stopped before I got to the lip and I would drop down into the bergschrund and then I would pull Steve in with me. My body twitched back to the right.

The ice axe shaft was partway out of its placement and I started sliding forward. I knew I could not get it set again to prevent dribbling over the edge. So this was it. It was time to go, and I was gone.

"Oh Jesus, here I come."

I pulled the ice axe all the way out and lifted the points of my crampons. I blew down Jackson's track and over the edge like a bat out of hell, like a fart out of a skillet, like a prune pit patuyeed across the Potomac, like uh—like a rolling stone. It was a profound moment of truth!

I spread my arms wide, ice axe in right, pumping, pumping, pumping, as the panorama of the Andromeda Glacier below me unfolded like a map. The arc of the bergschrund revealed itself, extending a quarter of a mile in either direction with the toothless grin of a snapping turtle. I could see the crevasses further below with rocks dotting the surface.

Steve looked up, tracking me. We almost made eye contact. In the separate reality of time moving slowly, I could see him grimace, close his eyes, tuck his head and turn away. I could see him shrug his shoulders and clutch his gloved fists around his helmet, the rope gripped in his right hand—not exactly in the textbook boot-axe belay position.

I have never appreciated 15 horizontal feet so intimately as I did flying through the air on that mountain. I could see my spot, about a double hand width off of Steve's hip. I was going to make it if I just kept pumping my arms.

The mantra in my head kept saying, "land on your feet, land on your feet, land on your feet;" but the only thing that came out of my mouth was, "shi-i-i-i-t!" I shut my eyes just before I torpedoed into the berm.

I struck with abruptness, punching into the surface up to my waist. My feet came to a firmer layer, stopped, and my upper body jackknifed forward with uncontrolled force. My face planted into the surface of the snow as if taking a quick bow, the temples of my metal-framed glasses flattening to almost 180 degrees. I was choking and gasping at the same time, trying to re-establish myself with the wind knocked out of me and my mouth full of snow. For a minute, I was completely consumed.

Gradually, I became aware of Steve's voice. He kept asking me if I was all right. I couldn't answer right away, but nodded upon regaining my composure.

"I'm O.K."

"God damn it, Kennedy, that was one hell of a nice jump!"

Well, it may have been; but it wasn't over. It was one or two clicks shy of dark. Steve and I were standing with a bottomless pit two feet behind us and a steep drop-off three feet in front of us. We still had 150 feet of slack in the rope, most of it dangling in the bergschrund, and no anchor. We needed to take stock. Were we on the top of a detached block of ice? The slope between us and the crevasses below seemed to be as steep as anything we had climbed all day.

"It doesn't look that far to where the glacier levels out," Steve estimated.

"Man, I don't know. That's got to be a rope length, at least. I am lighter; why don't you belay me down?" I suggested.

Jackson reset his axe and gave me a tight rope as I backed over the edge.

"It's steeper than hell, keep me on tension."

I backed down, most of my weight on the rope, hoping I could get to where the glacier leveled out before the rope ran out. My glasses frames were still twisted and didn't sit right on my face. The lenses were greased from face contact and spattered with water droplets. I couldn't see where the hell I was going. Just down.

Jackson was letting me out faster than I could set my front points. My feet struck something and I tipped over backwards and landed on my back.

"Tension! Goddammit!" I ordered. I struggled to get to my front points, but only got to my knees. What the f...? I was on flat snow! I felt kind of stupid.

Steve descended without incident, and the monster was snarling harmlessly behind us. We sat down and took a calorie and water break. There went the adrenaline. Within minutes, Jackson and I were transformed into a couple of stumbling drunks as we plodded down the glacier. I hooked a gaitor with a crampon and fell flat on my face. We remained roped up, of course, because we were on a crevassed glacier. A bit later, Steve stumbled to his knees and, when the rope went tight, I fell backwards onto my butt. All we needed was for one of us to fall into a crevasse.

The lateral moraine was a shifting pile of crushed boulders. We had boulders for sleeping pads, boulders for pillows, boulders for blankets and boulders for breakfast the next morning. Steve's helmet got away during the night and rolled back onto the glacier. We found it as we trudged out. We were a mere half hour from the car. Forty years later, that night remains the closest bivouac to a paved road I have ever made without a sleeping bag.

Jackson drove all the way to Columbia Falls, while I slumbered uncomfortably against the door. If they hassled us at the border, I don't remember.

I started the graveyard shift that night at the aluminum plant. I walked around in a stupor, holding onto a broom, trying not to get run over by fast-moving fork trucks with huge crucibles of molten aluminum. Steve finished another five and a half hours of driving to his grandparents ranch. He had more stamina behind the wheel than anyone I ever knew.

That is—except for that one time.

In December 1974, Steve, Dr. Z, Jack Tackle and I were returning to Bozeman after considering the first ascent of Tower Falls in Yellowstone National Park. Steve was driving his Saab. The trip included about a two-and-a half hour drive; and a few miles of cross country skiing on a road each way. We took a look at the falls and the upper portion was open water so we didn't try it. (Dr. Z and Emerson returned a couple months later and made the first ascent in somewhat better conditions).

It had been a long day, even without climbing, with a predawn start. Everyone was taking a nap by the time we emerged out of Yankee Jim Canyon, north of the North Entrance to the Park, and into the Paradise Valley south of Livingston. As it turned out—so was Steve.

Dr. Z was in the front passenger seat; Tackle was behind Dr. Z and I behind Steve in the back seat. As I slept, I became aware of the road getting rough and I thought to myself that Steve was hitting the construction zone a little fast—then I remembered there wasn't any construction zone. I woke myself up. Out the window, fence posts were flying by a foot from my face at 70 m.p.h. About that time, everyone else woke up too, including Steve, and there came a collective ga-a-sp. The pavement out Jack's window was at the level of the roof of the car. I made out a couple of reflectors zipping by as we bobbed and rattled along.

That was about the year seat belts were becoming standard issue—but only in the front. There weren't any in the back seats. (I guess automakers were only half convinced that seat belts were a good idea.) I knew instantly what this meant, if the car were to suddenly roll or hit a road approach and go end-oh.

It was every man for himself. I dove forward and hooked an elbow under part of Steve's seatbelt as it emerged beneath his seat and attached to the floor and waited for the car to start doing flips. Finally, I could feel us slowing down. I could almost count the fence posts. Steve did not panic.

He didn't jam on the brakes—but rather made an elegant ascent back onto the pavement, re-crossed the oncoming lane and made his way to the right side of the road and then to the shoulder, where we stopped. It was dead silent, except for the purring of the well- tuned Swedish engine. I returned upright. We just sat there bug-eyed and utterly speechless. Steve was the first to say anything and when he did it was simple and profound.

"Someone else want to drive? I'm getting a little sleepy."

Three weeks after the Mount Andromeda climb and the bergschrund incident, Steve and I quit our jobs before classes resumed at MSU. We packed into Mount St. Nicholas, the mountain the Blackfeet Indians called Three Feathers, and made the first ascent of the west face on a glorious September day. We bivouacked in the Great Notch, on the regular route on the descent.

The next morning, an aberration of the north face of Mount Cleveland silently rose with the sun over the horizon. Never did I feel so confident. I sat up and pulled my feet out of the same red rucksack I carried when Roger Newman and I climbed Mount Gould—the day Bob Frauson and the other rangers recovered Jerry, Clare and Mark. My pack now had holes and patches. I retired it after St. Nick.

"Jackson, you ready?"

"Yeah. Let's head down.

Steve Jackson on the west face of Mount St. Nicholas,
September 1974. Photo by the author.

Mount St. Nicholas, Glacier National Park. The Kennedy-Jackson
Route bisects the sunlit west face. Photo by the author.

CHAPTER 10

Bombs Away, Sir

During the last week of April 1975, Jim Kanzler and I drove the Tank to California and spent six weeks climbing in Yosemite Valley. I was in seventh heaven. My technical climbing capability surged to a new level in Yosemite that spring. It was like getting drafted into the Giant's farm system; I got a chance to play, but I hadn't quite made the "bigs" yet.

Jim insisted we climb every day, even in the rain. After a few weeks, I had to beg Kanzler for a rest day and, when he gave me one, he went climbing with a couple of guys he knew who we ran into in the Valley. I wandered around on the paths that led out from Camp IV, the walk-in campground where most of the climbers pitched camp. I had never seen oak trees before that trip.

That evening, at a picnic table in Camp IV, I asked Jim, "What about the north face of Mount Cleveland?"

"It's already been done."

"What?" My heart sank.

"Four guys from Minnesota did it."

"They did?"

"Well, up to the ledge 800 feet below the summit. They traversed off the face there. But they went to the top."

"Well, if they did not do the last 800 feet, then they did not do the face." My bravado returned.

"I suppose."

"Come on, we should go do it. It's still unclimbed."

"Nah. I have no interest in going back."

I felt like I had just been traded to the Washington Senators, the perennial doormats of the American League in the 1960s. This was at least the third time I had brought up the north face of Mount Cleveland question since Kanzler and I had climbed together. Over those few weeks, ours had become more of an older brother-kid brother relationship.

A couple days later Jim wandered back into camp.

"I have to get back to Big Sky."

"Huh, why?" I was too young and naive to understand the marital stress of being away from a wife and a child for weeks.

"Lindalee isn't too happy with me. I gotta go." He caught a ride back to Montana the next day and I climbed for a couple of weeks longer with Jim's friends.

When I returned to Bozeman in June, I was fresh off of my first grade V wall and had a handful of successful 5.10 (trad) leads under my belt. I was ready to rock and roll. Jim's expressed disinterest in the north face of Mount Cleveland was a letdown; but I decided I would stay on course and be ready the following year. Maybe he would change his mind. He had to.

I enrolled in the summer session at MSU to help make up for the absence that spring and stay on pace for earning a degree. I linked up with Brian Leo, and we hit the crags around Bozeman and made a couple of trips to the Humbugs. I flew up the Crack of Great Knack (5.10) this time after it had turned me back several times the year before.

Brian already had first ascents in the Beartooth Mountains and other Montana ranges. He was a favorite partner of Jim Kanzler's in the early 1970s and pioneered routes in Gallatin Canyon with Kanzler, McCarty and Jack Tackle. He was frequently recruited by Fred Becky to do some remote peak in Canada or the Wind River Range in Wyoming, sometimes with Dougal or Jim.

Brian was a ski patrolman, starting as a volunteer at Bridger Bowl in 1968 while in high school. Jim hired him onto the professional patrol at Big Sky in 1973, after Jim became the director of the Big Sky ski patrol the year before. Jim gave him the nickname "Breo." The Bridger Bowl and Big Sky ski patrols had the responsibility of avalanche control, which involved the daily use of explosive charges under tight federal regulations.

The Leo/Kanzler connection began when Jim and Jerry Kanzler moved to Bozeman with Jean just a few weeks after Hal Kanzler's death in 1967. Brian began climbing with Jerry Kanzler in the Humbugs and around Bozeman in 1969, as a high school senior, but did not become part of the Mount Cleveland expedition.

Breo's reputation as a *hardman* among the inner circle of climbers in Bozeman after the Mount Cleveland tragedy was well deserved. He became a go-to guy when things started to bog down on a climb. I felt privileged to be climbing with the guy who had taken the sharp end of the rope in the epic first winter ascent of the north face of Granite Peak. Brian had gotten McCarty off of the mountain with severely frostbitten feet after their legendary forced bivouac on the summit on New Year's Eve.

Leo and McCarty were part of a larger party, the other members of which attempted the standard route, but did not make the summit. It was shades of Mount Cleveland exactly three years later. The epic could well have ended in a tragedy like Mount Cleveland. Their survival hung in the balance throughout one of the longest nights of the year as they crammed themselves into a nylon bivouac sack, shared one waist-high half-bag, one short pad, a bag of lemon drops and a pocket watch that Dougal checked every five minutes for 14 hours as an Arctic blizzard raged and his feet froze solid.

"They were like a couple of roasts you might take out of a freezer," McCarty told me.

Breo was also on the ground floor of applying modern ice climbing techniques on the untapped inventory of ice in the Pine Creek drainage, south of Livingston and Hyalite Canyon, south of Bozeman, as the modern ice climbing revolution began in the fall of 1970. He was a key player among Pat Callis, Peter Lev, Jim Kanzler, Chad Chadwick, Dougal McCarty, Gray Thompson and a few others in the wake of Yvon Chouinard's redesigning the ice axe with a curved pick which transformed ice climbing.

Brian was finishing his bachelor degree in Still Photography that summer of 1975. His father had been an electronics expert in the Navy during World War II and a ham radio operator as a civilian. Brian spent time in his darkroom or tinkered with electronics when he wasn't climbing.

As summer approached, Breo and I turned our attention toward the Beartooth Mountains northeast of Yellowstone Park in Montana. We were both keen on Silver Pillar on the Silver Run Plateau. I thought of myself as capable, having climbed Quarter Dome, a grade V wall in Yosemite. I was gung ho about pursuing the prizes near home, continuing the steppingstones to the north face of Mount Cleveland.

Breo and I were thinking *big wall*. In mid-July, we went hell-bent for the granite goddess of the Beartooths. Silver Pillar is a three-quarter round cylinder that boldly faces the rising sun, like an ancient Egyptian monument. It has elegant folds of gray and blond granite and stands 1,000 feet high. Silver Pillar looks like a feature from Yosemite lost in Montana's highest mountain range. Jim Kanzler and Chad Chadwick climbed the first route on it in 1973, following a line just right of center. Their route was mostly free climbing, but included nailing over a roof and a bivouac in hammocks.

We had our eyes on a line dead center, which included a series of overhangs. We were prepared to climb with full aid-climbing regalia. We drove the Tank from Bozeman one evening and crashed at the trailhead up the West Fork of Rock Creek outside Red Lodge. The next morning, we humped heavy loads five miles to the base of the pillar and continued a short way up the snow couloir to the left of the pillar, then traversed right onto a ten-foot-wide sloping shelf to start the route. We dropped our freight at what looked like the most promising line up to the lower roofs.

I racked the hardware for the first pitch while Breo searched for a belay anchor. I was so laden with the vast assortment of Chouinard Hexes, Stoppers, pitons and bongs and weird aid gadgets that Breo called "tricky stuff" that I could hardly stand up.

"Wel-l-l, I'm having a little problem here finding an an-ker," he declared in his slow, craggy monotone drawl. I helped him search for a suitable crack from which to create a belay anchor. There was 100 feet of steep rock between us and the snowfield at the base of the pillar. The rock just above our shelf was blank, except for an incipient vertical crack about a quarter of an inch wide and ended five feet above the shelf.

"Maybe we ought to put in a couple of bolts for an anchor," I suggested. We needed a bombproof belay anchor in the event I should fall onto the shelf before I had a solid piece of protection along my line of ascent. Without an anchor, we could both be pulled off and fall to the bottom of the pillar and onto the snowfield.

"Wel-l-l, I sorta hate to use them now-w," Brian reasoned. "We're probably going to need 'em worse up above."

That made sense. We only had six quarter-inch bolts and four hangers—that's all we could scrounge up before we left Bozeman. I managed to noodle in a flimsy, wired nut into the crack three feet off of the ledge, which we used to aim the belay or keep the rope in front of Breo. The placement was shaky, and there was no point in him clipping into it. It would not have held his body weight, let alone catch a fall. We didn't even bother to hang any of the other gear from it.

"Just get something in as soon as you can and we will be O.K.," he figured.

"Alright, I will."

At last, I was ready to taxi off of the shelf and up into uncharted territory. I took off like an overloaded B-17. I could barely get off of the ground. Breo seated himself, leaning back against the wall like a tail gunner with the rope around the rim of his pelvis—the sitting hip belay.

I made a few moves, found another shallow crack, and beat a thin piton halfway in before it bottomed out. I tied a thin runner around the shank and used it for a point of aid; but I decided not to clip the rope through the carabiner because I did not think it would hold a fall and I didn't want the *rope drag* hampering me as I traversed up and left.

"I'll get something better in a little higher," I muttered to myself. In retrospect, I wished I would have gone ahead and clipped the darned thing anyway.

I thrashed and flagged my feet up a few moves here, a few moves there, procrastinating between every sequence, and feeling like I was about to be peeled from the rock with the equipment overload.

Savvy big wall climbers were using "zip lines" to ferry certain pieces of gear up to the leader, as needed, to keep the weight of the hardware rack manageable. We were not hip to the zip that day. Besides, there was something romantic, if not macho, about packing so much ordnance.

After a half hour, I had only gone 25 feet. I looked down at Breo, who was lounging with his English cap pulled down over his eyes. The early departure from Bozeman and my slow progress were making him sleepy. The only anchor clipped between my belayer and me was that tiny stopper—which I could have removed with a flick of a finger. It seemed like a long way down to the snowfield. I became more tentative with each unprotected move.

At last, I came to a deep parallel-sided crack that led upward. I whaled in an angle piton to the eye and clipped the rope and aid slings. Whew.

"Looks good for a ways," I announced. I wiggled to the top rungs of my aid slings, drew another piton and began to hammer it in.

On the third blow, something bad happened. The pin I hung from suddenly shifted, with the tip almost out of the crack.

"Oh shit! Leo, watch me! Watch me. I'm in trouble! I might fall!"

The cap was still over Breo's eyes. He didn't even look up as he took in a few inches of slack, and his brake hand moved a little closer to braking position. "Be care-ful," he grunted.

I had hammered the second piton into an expanding crack, meaning the sides of the crack were moving further apart as the top piton was being driven and the first piton was losing contact with the crack as I hung from it. It was ready to pop! There was nothing between us—except for that tiny nut, about as sturdy as a press pin in a corkboard.

Now events happen in time-warped, slow motion once again.

The bomb doors of the Flying Fortress swing open, and I think I hear the rushing sound of turbulence below the belly of the aircraft—but it's just the building tinnitus in my ears. The talus blocks on the shelf look like the tops of buildings. I am facing a long fall with no belay anchor, a grinning snowfield and a loose sphincter muscle. Red lights and warning bells are going off in the cockpit. I am talking to myself.

"We have trouble, sir! The piton is about to pop!"

[I see it.]

"OK, what are we going to do, sir?"

[Easy, airman, easy. Move slowly. Do not let your feet shift in the stirrups.]

"I've gotta do something...very soon here."

[Can you reach a different crack?]

"10-4, sir. I'll try."

(If only I had had a first generation #1 Friend active camming device! I could have plugged it into the crack, clipped it and the crisis would have been over. However, active camming devices were several years away.)

"Sir, what if this thing pops?"

[Go to crash landing protocol—land on your feet.]

"It is a hell of a long way to the shelf, sir."

[It's not that bad. Twenty-five feet. You can survive that.]

"I don't know, sir."

[Land on your feet, let your legs buckle; do not lock them. You could land this thing and not get hurt.]

"Hurt? Sir, I'll break every bone in my body..."

[Not if you are careful.]

"Careful! Careful? Let's carefully get something else in—preferably goddamn now!"

[Easy, Kennedy, easy. If the pin does pop, face out and push away. Are you listening?]

"Yes, sir."

[OK, then. You must not hit anything on the way down, because then you won't land on your feet. Do you copy?]

"10-4, sir. Land on feet. Don't hit on way down."

[Face out—push off—knees unlocked.]

"Oh fuck, sir. There is no belay anchor. We'll pull Breo off."

[You just worry about the landing. Face out, push off, land on feet, let knees buckle.]

"10-4, sir. I'm just going to look over here for another crack."

"Leo! Watch me!"

"Be care-ful up ther-r-re."

"Leo. I'm hanging by a thread. If this pin pops, I'll hit the ledge and keep going."

"Wel-l-l...Just tryn' land on your feet."

[Slow, easy, easy...]

PING!

"Bombs away, sir."

[Push off. Now! Feet, feet, feet, land on your feet!]

The sun shines on my face as I extend my left arm and turn outward. I drop through the bomb bay like a 138-pounder bound for Dusseldorf. There is a tinkling sound like an empty beer glass a split second after it smashes onto a floor—the sound of pitons, nuts and carabiners jangling as they become momentarily weightless on my shoulders.

The landing zone—the ledge—comes rushing up, and both feet find it. I fold into a squat, hands slapping the talus, gouging a small avulsion out of my left palm. There is a "cymbal crash" as the hardware and I make a sudden stop, before cartwheeling off of the ledge, and continue to fall toward the snowfield. It sounds like the whole percussion section has fallen from the back of the band platform.

Breo is wide-awake now, by golly, his cap cockeyed on his head. His arms are busy yarding in the rope. He orbits around my peripheral vision like a teddy bear in a dryer.

The rope must still be through the carabiner on the nut; but I have forgotten about it. I have a weird sense of joy, knowing I have not broken a single bone hitting the ledge.

"So far, so good, sir." I fly on for the snowfield below.

"We're falling a long way, sir. Why are we falling so far? Sir, we don't seem to be stopping. Why are we not stopping? Uh-oh—I know. No belay anchor, right, sir?""

I am cruising in the frog position—like skydiving. Belly first, knees bent, arms out.

"Sir, I guess we will be pulling Breo off about now, right?"

I look up, if only in my mind's eye, expecting to see him come winging over the edge, too. "That nut ain't gonna hold nuthin. I guess we should have put in a bolt. Well, it won't be long, and we will be making cherry snow cones. B-r-r-r, that's going to be cold..."

BO-ING...!

"What the hell, sir? The rope must have caught on something..."

[Leo caught you.]

"He caught the fall? He didn't get pulled off?"

[That's right.]

"Way to go, Breo!" I shout, elated over the new outcome. The piton that pulled out, the aid slings I had been standing in above and a couple of carabiners, are dangling from the rope just below my face. "Way'da go!"

I look up. The rope is as straight as a chalk line. Weird—I don't see Breo. The rope just seems to end in the middle of the cliff. He does not respond.

My euphoria lasts about one second. There is trouble!

"Bogies at 12 o'clock high, sir—30 feet and closing fast!"

[I see them.]

The rope has swept along the shelf as it went tight between Breo and me, raking loose rock over the edge. A squadron of granite Messerschmitts is diving straight at me, following the course of the rope. I freeze in disbelief.

[Evasive action, Kennedy—Now!]

"Oh God! They have me." I feel crosshairs dancing on my forehead.

[If one hits you, Kennedy, you are dead—MOVE!]

The first chunk—the size of a dictionary—just misses. I see the black flecks of feldspar arranged like letters on a tablet. The language I cannot read; but the meaning I understand...

"Oh Jesus, sir! I am not wearing a helmet..."

[Move, Kennedy, NOW, NOW, NOW!]

I lurch hard left. Then there is a moment of undeniable truth.

Thwack! The second rock strikes the back of my skull. My head snaps forward, and my forehead hits the cliff in front of my face—bonk.

"Uh-oh... it got me... I guess I'm dead..." I look around to see if things look different, being dead. The snow looks close, but not any different. I don't know what to expect. I cannot remember ever being dead before. Am I supposed to be doing something?

"Sir. Any suggestions?"

[Feel your head, Kennedy. I don't think you're dead.]

"I don't think I can do that, sir..."

[Why not?]

"I don't want to feel the fragments of my skull. I don't want to feel my brains!"

[I do not think you are hit that bad.]

I reach my hand to the top of my head. A strange, detached feeling comes over me—as if I am about to pick up a sleeping child. The child is me. I feel my head and bring my hand back. There is nothing.

"There must be something, sir—after all, the rock did hit us."

I reach my hand to the back of my head; it is warm and slick. I bring it back. It is bloody, from fingertips to elbow. There is a four-inch lock of hair in the palm of my hand.

"We're all fucked up, sir."

I reach up again and feel around. "I feel the wound, sir. An inch long, edges are gapped." And between the edges there was something hard.

"Holy shit, sir, I feel my skull. Sir...?"

I had touched my bare skull! It did not feel broken...there were no brains coming out! I could feel the whisker-like texture of the severed ends of hair that had been chopped off. A chunk of Beartooth granite had been the cleaver, and my noggin had been the chopping block. The difference between life and whatever happens after that was about an inch.

There was still a possibility that I had a serious injury. I needed to get up to the shelf. It was the only time I ever *Bat-manned*, hand over hand, up a rope for 30 feet.

"Leo! I've been hit in the head! I'm bleeding—bad! I'm coming up the rope!

Get the first aid kit out! I might have a closed head injury..." I managed all that in one breath. I was barking instructions like the captain of a disabled bomber, dropping out of formation.

I hauled up over the lip, surprised to find Breo in my way, lying flat on his back. He was not where I remembered him, next to the haul bag. We both had our hands on the rope, not more than a foot apart, like we were having a tug-of-war. I crawled over the top of him. He was ten feet from the haul bag. The rope was not around his hips but gripped with both hands at his knees. There was a furrow through the scree made by his Robbins Shoes. His left foot was at the lip. I had bulldogged him to the edge when I hit the end of the rope. It was a wonder I did not pull us both over the edge right then and there—a testimony to Brian Leo's natural strength. The tiny, wired nut was at his ankles, still clipped to the rope.

I twisted around with my back against the cliff, catching my breath. Breo crawled over to me, dragging the rope. We sat there, silent for a few moments. Then I asked, "Did I just take a really long fall?" We burst out laughing together. There was snot flung from my nose and blood running down my face.

"It was a pretty good one," Breo reckoned.

"Check my pupils and my ears. We might need to get out of here while I still can," the adrenaline rush continued. "Let's leave the rest of this stuff in the haul bag and get it later, the Chevy key is in my back pocket. Maybe I'm not hurt that bad—I don't feel that bad—I suppose I'll just need a few stitches... " I was just babbling, while Breo took charge of the damage assessment.

He examined me like a 110-year-old ophthalmologist. His nose was wrinkled and he was squinting. Either he couldn't find the place where the blood was coming from, or he needed glasses.

At last, he had a diagnosis.

"Wel-l-l, I sup-pose we should use the big com-press...."

He emptied the haul bag to access the first aid kit at the bottom. The day had arrived to open the sealed pouch of the olive-drab army surplus battle compress Breo had packed up and down the mountains for years.

The following October, at the annual Dirty Sox Club meeting, we showed the slides of the Leo/Kennedy route on Silver Pillar. Of course, I could not wait to show the one of me sitting on the shelf with blood running down both sides of my head, covering one lens of my glasses. The big compress was lashed to the top of my head like an Easter bonnet. That drew a few chuckles. There had been such a mess of hair and blood that it was hard to find the actual wound. The gash, as it turned out, was further back and not under the compress. The bleeding had stopped on its own.

We left the haul bag on the shelf attached to the tied-off pin with a series of runners, descended the couloir to the snowfield and hiked out.

Three hours later, in Red Lodge, we figured I would live, so we rumbled on. The university health-service doctor could stitch the wound. I washed most of the blood off of my face and some of it out of my hair while Breo drove the Tank.

We were back in Bozeman in another three hours. By then, we were hungrier than I was hurt; we stopped off at the Haufbrau to wolf down Lanny Burgers and celebrate a successful crash landing and the Hollywood belay.

"When I heard the jangle of hardware," Breo explained, filling my glass, "I knew you were going to take a long one." He brushed peanut shells off of the table onto the floor. "I started pulling the rope in hand over hand to shorten the fall. I knew I'd better start getting the rope back around my hips, but I couldn't figure out which loop was which. I just went, 'oh shit! I better do some thing pret-ty quick he-r-e'. I just grabbed the rope with both hands and thought, 'this is going to be interesting.' It was sort of a Spencer Tracy belay like in that old movie, *The Mountain*."

We swilled another pitcher and called it a day. When I finally called the health center at MSU, a doctor informed me that so many hours had passed since the wound had occurred that he could not suture it without the risk of a deep infection. I carefully washed the laceration with soap and water in the shower—just like any other bodily orifice—and it healed without much fuss.

The bump on my head had a tendency to swell during approaching storms, and became something of a barometer over the next ten years or so. The bump is still up there somewhere, among the other knots and barnacles.

Breo and I returned to Silver Pillar the following weekend and retrieved the haul bag with our gear. We started our route from a different ledge and established the second line on Silver Pillar, left of center, with a bivouac three quarters of the way up.

I was no longer a three-year man. I was battle tested and ready for the north face of Mount Cleveland.

The author after Breo's miraculous belay. The difference between life and death was about an inch. Photo by Brian Leo.

Silver Pillar, Beartooth Mountains. The Chadwick-Kanzler Route
is just right of center, and the Leo-Kennedy Route follows the left-
hand edge, as viewed in this photo. Photo by the author.

CHAPTER 11

The Face Looks Good

On a Saturday, April 24, 1976, Steve Jackson and I climbed the Wedge in the Humbug Spires, Bozeman to Bozeman in a day—years before the Bureau of Land Management trail was established through the Humbug Spires, terminating near the base of the Wedge.

This was the last Humbug trip of the spring, with final exams looming and summer jobs starting thereafter. We hiked an extra mile each way because of the demolition of the log bridge, and made the approach to the flagship of the Humbug Spires from the cabin by dead reckoning.

I was gunning for the first free ascent of the West Face, the most coveted route on the Wedge in the 1970s. Steve Jackson and I had already climbed the hairy 5.10 test piece called "Gandalf"(Callis, Jerry Kanzler, Pogreba) on the south face of the Wedge, without falls or hangs. The West Face was the fourth route on the Wedge: a creation of Jim, Jerry, Clare and Ray, with the Kanzler brothers completing the climb some time after the foursome figured out the tricky traverse on the first pitch.

The climb began on friction slabs without protection, until a "chicken head" was slung with a runner for protection along a run-out traverse. A blind knife blade piton placement protected a delicate move into a shallow corner, facing away from the traverse. From there, 15 feet of aid was used on the first four ascents. There was talk among the Dirty Sox Club that this section could "go free" at the level we were climbing.

I tapped the inch-and-a-half-long thin piton in and worked my feet left, committing to a narrow crack. I smeared my EBs on shallow depressions with my left foot, scouring loose grit, and torqued the outer rand of the smooth-soled canvas boot into the corner with my right. I stemmed and lay-backed, inching upward until I could jam my fingers into the crack and twist them for purchase into the abrasive stone. I snatched a straight-sided Chouinard Stopper from the gear sling suspended below my shoulder, wiggled it into a small pocket within the crack, and clipped in the rope.

I was on top of my game, moving well. The sequence was repeated until the crack opened for perfect hand jams, and the difficulty eased. It was the first time the section had been climbed without standing in aid slings connected to pitons. The lead was difficult for the day in Montana at early 5.10. Jackson gave a congratulatory shout from below. We traded leads to the top.

Ten years later, another climber hung and placed a bolt (retro-bolted) on this section of the climb, making it easier and more convenient for those who came later. A connection to the first pioneers of the Humbugs was lost.

We raced back to Bozeman and the Haufbrau to celebrate. I could hardly wait to tell Jim Kanzler and Pat Callis.

Halfway through the second pitcher of beer, I dropped the big question on Steve: "Are you ready to go do Mount Cleveland?" Before he realized what I had just asked, I kept hammering my line, "Come on man, let's go get it! I think we can do it. Whadda yuh think?"

Jackson grinned, drew a deep breath between his teeth and slid back in the booth, clunking a size 12 1/2 boot onto the bench across from him. He folded his hands around his beer on the wooden table, into which many a patron had carved his name, and exhaled slowly, pooching his cheeks.

"O.K., let's go for it, T. It's something we have to do."

With each second of silence that followed, the concrete set harder in our commitment. We would attempt the north face of Mount Cleveland that summer. I had a good idea what was in store up there. The north face of Mount Cleveland was twice as high as the west face of Mount St. Nicholas. Nothing on St. Nick had been as foreboding as the final headwall of Cleveland looked.

"Maybe we should get a third guy," Jackson suggested, gazing at the last two inches of beer in his glass before leaning his head back and swilling it.

I was sobered with introspection. "Jim says he's not interested."

"He would be the best guy to do it with, that's for sure."

I still wanted, in the worst way, to climb the face with Jim Kanzler; but if Jim was truly not interested, then I was prepared to tempt fate without him.

"What does Pat say about it?"

"I've discussed the North face with Pat many times."

"And...?"

"Well, I'm not sure exactly how he feels. He certainly has a connection to the face. He went into the base of north face by himself a month after the bodies were recovered. He looked at the face."

"What did he think?" Jackson knew of my frequent consults in Callis's office to present future projects of unclimbed faces in Glacier. I always steered the discussions back to the Mount Cleveland tragedy.

"Well, he got up on the northwest shoulder, where he could look out onto the north face. He said he was intensely drawn to it. He also said he didn't want to create a vendetta, but thought it could turn into one."

Pat Callis, Peter Lev and Jim Kanzler did have a plan to climb the face over Thanksgiving break in 1970, and had informed the Glacier Park rangers of their intentions. This prompted a letter from Glacier National Park Superintendent William Briggle. Briggle strongly urged Montana's strongest alpine climbing team—who had discovered the first evidence of the Mount Cleveland Five's fate— not to pursue the climb. Mel Ruder got wind of the exchange, and a two-column article appeared in the *Hungry Horse News* shortly thereafter.

Other circumstances caused a cancellation of the plan, and the whole north face idea hung in limbo for the next six years.

"So is there any chance we could get Pat to do it with us?" Steve asked hopefully.

"Probably not this year. I already asked him. He can't do it because of building his new house."

"Oh, that's right." Jackson tapped his fingers on the gouged tabletop, as if playing a piano riff. "It would be great to have somebody like him with us."

"I know."

"What about Breo or McCarty? After the north face of Granite Peak, you'd think those guys would want to start getting after all the big prizes."

"I've brought Mount Cleveland up to those guys before. I tried to get Breo interested right after we did Silver Pillar last year. Neither McCarty nor Leo is too keen on Glacier Park and the sedimentary rock thing. Brian has done easier things up there. He's done the regular route on St. Nick."

"I didn't think the rock was too bad on St. Nick," Jackson recalled. "Would the north face of Mount Cleveland be any different?"

"Nah, not really."

I straightened up in the booth seat.

"I mean, it's all loose, with lots of debris on the ledges; but, hey, that's the way it is everywhere. The Tetons—even Yosemite has loose rock." I didn't want to risk losing Jackson. Mount St. Nicholas had the best rock in Glacier, as far as I was concerned. It was not typical of all Glacier Park Mountains.

"Here, I'll get another pitcher." I emptied the remainder of the one on the table into Steve's glass and stood up, fumbling around in my baggy dungarees for another buck and a quarter among the Humbug rock granules and lichen that sifted into my pockets during the climb that day.

I returned from the bar with another half gallon of liquid courage, and we discussed strategy.

"The best time would be in August," I submitted. "The weather should be the most stable, the rock fall minimal, and hopefully enough snow to get water."

"Boy, that's when my grandparents' ranch will be in full swing, getting the second cutting of hay," Steve replied, slurping foam as it ran over the top of his glass.

"That's kinda what I thought. You don't think you could get a weekend plus three or four days in there somewhere?" The long weekend Steve and I had taken for our climb on Andromeda two years before had been too much of a squeeze. I wanted a cushion to spend time at the bottom of the face, to reconnoiter the route and have at least two days for weather contingency.

"Well, I don't know, T. I could probably take an extra day and a weekend, but I don't think I should take more time than that. My grandparents are getting older and they really need the help."

I was silent, hoping Steve might feel he could bend and commit to at least four days. Four days would be tight: Travel, boat ride, approach. Two days for the ascent and descent with a bivouac. Hike out, boat ride, seven or eight hours of driving again, border crossing hassles both ways. Four days was crazy. I wanted enough time to be organized and rested and give the face our best shot.

"It would be a lot better for me in September," Jackson went on. "We had great weather on St. Nick in September."

"Yeah, that's true." I was hoping to use September to fall back on if an August attempt failed. Now it looked like it just had. I hated the idea of squandering the prime weeks of the summer. "I guess we should plan on giving it a shot before school starts." I tried to hide my disappointment.

"Then, I could quit a week or so before school, because things at the ranch will be winding down."

Midnight came and went. To anyone else, we might have appeared drunk. No doubt the beer had taken a toll; but considering the wee-hour get-up that day, the glorious day climbing in the Humbugs, and hours of driving, we were probably in decent shape compared to the other patrons of the Hauf. Our state of sobriety notwithstanding, we left the watering hole with a date for the highest precipitous rock face in the Continental U.S.

Steve left Bozeman for the Dearborn River country, north of Helena; and I for Columbia Falls and a summer job at the aluminum plant, which would start during the second week of June. On the way home, I felt bored and restless. How was I going to pass the summer until September and see the alpine season waste away, with Mount Cleveland only 40-some miles away and no partner?

Within a week, I wrote Steve a letter:

> Hey Stever,
>
> How are things at the ranch? I've been thinking...I should go into the north face and have a look at it. Maybe I could get a partner and go partway up, just to get a feel for it. Maybe it won't be that bad. Maybe I could climb to the 800-foot ledge and traverse off and we could do the whole thing in September...

He wrote me back, saying it was okay with him if I wanted to take a shot at the face with a different partner. He understood not getting on the face during the best time of the year. We would still go in September if I wasn't successful before then.

By July, I had recruited Barry Frost to attempt Mount Cleveland. Barry was an early technical rock climber in southern Montana, his exploits coinciding independently from the Butte contingency. He became friends and climbing partners with Jim and Jerry Kanzler soon after Jean and her two sons moved into a mobile home in Bozeman during the winter of 1967, just weeks after Hal's death. Barry was a fan of Jerry Kanzler's enthusiasm and extraordinary ability.

When Barry got word his friends were overdue on Mount Cleveland, he rallied with Pat Callis, Peter Lev and Jim Kanzler and rushed to Glacier on January 2, 1970, as part of the search team. He was given the role as an observer on the lower Goat Haunt Mountain, just north of Mount Cleveland, where he and several others constantly scanned the north face of Cleveland for any signs of the Cleveland Five.

Steve introduced me to Barry during the winter of 1973-74. Steve and I got together with Barry to climb Palisade Falls in Hyalite Canyon one subzero day just after New Year's Day. Steve climbed with Barry during Steve's early rock climbing adventures in high school. Barry was seven years older, and had a hand in teaching Steve the rudiments of the craft.

Barry and I developed a friendship, climbing together off and on after that. Conveniently, Barry and his wife lived in a basement apartment a block away from where I lived. We spent more time reminiscing about Jerry Kanzler and playing records of Crosby, Stills, and Nash's "Wooden Ships" and the Doobie Brothers' "Dark Eyed Cajun Woman" than we did climbing.

Barry Frost and I were not a strong enough team for Mount Cleveland, should he and I attempt it before Jackson was available. We both knew it. I was the young upstart with an undisguised drive for the north face. I was stronger leading technical rock and had been making local first ascents for a couple of years. Frost, on the other hand, had little opportunity to climb while in the Army and was just rekindling his interest. Barry had been married for about a year, and his wife was expecting a child. Barry was concerned with getting a higher-paying job than what he was making at a local grain elevator. His domestic situation demanded much of his climbing energies.

I needed to be paired with someone with greater strength and experience than myself. I needed a Pat Callis, a Peter Lev, or, of course, Jim Kanzler as a partner. The chemistry professor who had climbed high onto the Emperor Face on Mount Robson with Jim Kanzler had excluded himself from any serious alpine undertakings that season, because he was building a house. An opportunity to climb with Peter Lev never presented itself. I had met Peter only one time, and was not brash enough to ask him to pair up with me.

Naturally, Jim Kanzler's declining my invitations to climb Mount Cleveland was a letdown. Would Jim just put the Mount Cleveland tragedy behind him and carry on with a "normal life?" How could he? Jim Kanzler had too many of Hal's traits.

If Hal was driven by the loss of young men during World War II combat, then Jim must have been driven by the losses of Hal and Jerry; and the losses of Clare Pogreba and Ray Martin and Jerry's new friends: Jim Anderson and Mark Levitan. I had a feeling Jim would be dogged for the rest of his life if he did not return to Mount Cleveland. Was this not his destiny?

My parents' generation thought it was foolish for Jim to continue to climb at all after the Mount Cleveland search and recovery that dragged on for seven months.

As my father frequently liked to say, "You can't be too careful."

Certainly, climbing bigger and steeper faces did not fit that philosophy. To me, life was about quality, not quantity; and to Jim, pushing the envelope was "where it's at."

Jim once commented, "Creating an intangible line up a face–by climbing it—is probably as valuable a thing as you can do..."

In 1976, I was the same age as Clare and Ray when the Mount Cleveland Five disappeared. The prime alpine climbing season arrived, and the days slid off of the calendar. If older climbers made the first ascent of the north face, or if I made it when I was older, the legitimacy of the Mount Cleveland Five attempting the face so young would be forever challenged. The scathing "There is no such thing as an experienced 18 year old" and "Too bad Jerry and the other boys didn't take the ranger's advice and blah, blah, blah..." kept ringing in my ears. 1976 had to be the year— when I was 22.

The year before, I had talked Dad into hiring a private pilot to fly around some of the big faces in Glacier. Dad, Dan and I made several passes by the north face of Mount Cleveland with a Vietnam veteran Navy pilot, who must have been pushing the single-engine wing-under aircraft to its limit. We traversed the north face of Mount Cleveland at three-quarter height, and he dipped the wings as I opened the window, stuck my camera out into the wind, and snapped 35 mm Ektachrome film with an old Argus camera that left scratches on the slides.

On another pass, the pilot flew directly at the face until there was nothing but jagged limestone in front of the plane, then veered left just over the saddle between the main summit of the Cleveland and its eastern peak. On the last pass, he approached from the south— so close to the summit ridge he could have knocked a goat off of the mountain— before diving over the north face. The wall, the sky and Waterton Lake were all stirred into one. So much for being too careful; yet my father never complained. I got the feeling later that he privately liked going to the edge—and then over it!

I could visualize Barry and me making it to the 800-foot ledge below the headwall. Above that, it looked as though we could be in over our heads.

Rumors circulated to me from Dougal McCarty about a "truly crazy" climber named Don Claunch, who in the mid 1960s had allegedly made a solo ascent on the north face to the 800-foot ledge a number of years ahead of the Minnesota climbers. Dougal was trying to keep me from getting my hopes up too high about making the first ascent of the north face. My objective, however, was plain and simple: climb the entire face. McCarty had never seen the face; he did not have a good enough mental image to understand that if you didn't climb the headwall above the 800-foot ledge, you had bailed; you did not climb the face.

At the end of the day, I just had to get up there and see what might become of it.

Barry Frost arrived in Columbia Falls the third week of July of 1976. We organized our gear on a tarp on the front lawn of my parents' house in Columbia Falls. My mother and father (Betty and R. Glenn) had not met Barry previously, but they were always interested in my friends. Mom loved the opportunity to meet someone new and engage him or her in conversation.

"Oh, I just love it when you bring your friends home!" she said more than once. "They are always such nice young men."

Betty continuously engaging Barry served to distract us from the task at hand. Barry was a quiet guy, and I could sense he was becoming a little overwhelmed with Betty prying him for his life story while I grew impatient due to the delays she was causing. We needed to get our food, climbing equipment and bivouac gear organized and into our packs. We had the Glacier Park concessionaire's tour boat, *The International*, to ride from the Waterton townsite in Alberta to the Goat Haunt Ranger Station in Montana that afternoon. It would take at least three hours to drive through Glacier, over Logan Pass and make a border crossing. If we missed the boat that day, there was no way we could make an attempt on the north face within the four days we had.

Every minute counted.

R. Glenn, the former Master Sergeant, stood surveying the operation. The finer details of climbing and the equipment eluded him, as well; but he got the gist of it. He had concerns, but was keeping them to himself for the moment.

The neighbors across the street could see all this to-do going on over at the Kennedys' and wandered over to investigate. Mom and Dad hovered while Mr. and Mrs. Nelson stood watching a couple of paces off. Frost and I knelt on the tarp, manipulating hardware, making trips to and from our vehicles, trying frantically to get everything together and on the road. Having all these other people in close proximity was making Barry and me giddy.

Mom was a nervous person by nature, as I have already explained. Her variable emotional demeanor had been held in check by her otherwise gregarious nature— until she took stock of what was on the tarp.

"Oh...are you boys going to be taking ropes and those things you pound into the rock—those whatchamacallits?" she asked.

"Uh...yes," I replied. "We are." (Uh-oh, I thought to myself, Houston, we may have a problem...)

"I didn't think you were going to be doing that kind of climbing, " her voice revved up as she spoke. "I thought you said Mount Cleveland was a walk-up..."

"Well, it sort of is—from the backside," I explained, realizing I was not going to maintain a coy sense of deception by omission any longer without telling an outright lie, which I was not brought up to do.

"We aren't doing the backside, Mom."

There was a pause. Even the robin in the birch tree stopped chirping. That could only mean one thing. (Houston, can you read me? Houston, we've got a problem. Over.)

"Well then, you aren't going to..." Mom started; but I gently cut her off.

"The north face, Mom. We are going to the north face."

The silence grew louder.

"You boys aren't planning to do the north face, are you?" she asked, as if she hadn't heard me. "Oh, but oh, I don't think you guys should be going up there."

"Uh, well, we're going to be very careful, Mom."

"I don't want you going up there. Not where Jerry Kanzler and the other boys were killed. I thought you weren't going to climb the north face for a few years yet. I thought you were going to go with more experienced climbers, like Doctor—oh, what's his name—the college professor." Her voice was turning sorrowful. "Oh, oh-oh-oh I don't want you to go."

Well, hell, the cat was out of the bag now! Mom's little chipmunk self was headed for the big Douglas fir across the fence in the Kimzey's yard. I hoped the lid on the Tabasco sauce bottle was screwed on tight. Mom was starting to lose it. The ring of north face of Mount Cleveland struck like a bolt of lightning on a nearby ridge. There was silence while everyone waited for the thunder. R. Glenn began pacing, massaging his scalp. Mr. and Mrs. Nelson looked at each other, their feet shuffling, not sure if they should head back across the street and let the Kennedys sort out a family crisis or if they should stay and see how the drama was going to unfold.

Barry and I tried to go about our business, but it was impossible. I was afraid I was going to overlook something important.

Dad asked me questions as he padded back and forth along an eight-foot stretch of sidewalk.

"Are you sure you should be doing this? Are you sure you are ready?

Maybe you should give it a few more years. What about this college professor, maybe you should wait and go with him. What about the older Kanzler brother—Jim?"

"Dad, I've been training for this for six years. I'm ready," I more or less lied. I really didn't know if I was ready. With every passing second, I felt less so.

I glanced over at Barry. It wasn't just the idea of preparing for such a big climb, but also interacting with my parents, whom he had never met before, that made him uncomfortable. He stood up and discretely backed away from the circle. He reached into his shirt pocket and pulled out a pack of cigarettes.

Oh, man! I thought. There was something I had failed to tell Mom and Dad about my friend: Barry smoked. I had meant to explain that he had been in the Army and smoked once in a while. I had explained, before he arrived in Columbia Falls, that Barry was a good guy and a careful climber. I was not sure if I ought to bring up the smoking thing. Barry would only spend enough time at my parents' house to organize our gear; then we would be on our way. I figured Barry would not need to light up in that short period of time, so I did not say anything. Even in those days, parents had a disdain for young people who smoked. Truth be known, Barry had a pack-and-a-half-a-day habit.

I was the first to notice the cigarette in Barry's mouth. The flame from his lighter caught everyone else's attention. Barry did not notice everyone looking at him at first, because his eyes were narrowed to thin slits as he got his cigarette lit and took a deep drag. His eyes remained shut until he took the cigarette from his lips. When he at last opened them, everyone was staring at him.

What could I say?

Barry buckled under the mounting stress from my parents' concern and the neighbors' curiosity. The moment had become ripe for a cigarette. Hell, I could have used one.

Frost held his cigarette near his thigh, as if to dampen the impact of getting busted. No one moved, not even Barry, with a chest full of smoke. The moment created new curiosities: When was Barry going to exhale? How long could he hold it? Would he start coughing?

Barry deferred as long as he could, then creased the corner of his mouth and let a steady stream of smoke escape into the air, away from the group. He looked like a Yellowstone Park geyser going off sideways. The smoke then drifted back, right over the tarp—and straight at the Nelsons.

"Uh...I smoke," he said apologetically, "occasionally. I hope no one minds." The rest of us took a step back to avoid the effluvium that was now streaming directly into the group.

Barry's smoking habit and the novelty of someone doing it openly in the Kennedys' front yard began to pale as the gravity of the larger crisis— the quiet, obedient neighborhood kid heading to the north face of Mount Cleveland returned to the public's consciousness. Mount Cleveland had far greater health risks.

Attention swung back to me, and pressure continued to mount. I considered gathering up the gear on the tarp and stuffing the whole thing into the Tank, and getting the hell out of there.

Barry took another drag, then dropped the lit cigarette at his feet out of habit and crushed it on the grass. The group-stare returned to him. He glanced up and was met by everyone's eyes again, then bent over, picked up the smoldering butt and tucked it into a back pocket of his knickers.

I was about to insist that Barry and I split when R. Glenn spoke:

"Well, son," he began, cool, calm and collected: his difficult-situation trademark. "One thing I've always admired about you is you always know when to turn back."

It was simple and profound. Not just admonishing, but also encouraging. It was a turning point. Everyone turned to R. Glenn as he spoke, pondering my father's statement. He was still the chief.

Attention arched back to me like a beacon in the fog. Barry appeared relieved to be out of the spotlight. I stood there for a moment, staring at a dandelion in the lawn, a faint ringing in my ears.

Yeah, he's right. We don't have to go up, I thought to myself, as if I had never considered it before. We can always turn back...

Dad, Mom, Barry and the Nelsons stood like wax sculptures as I gathered myself to respond.

"You're right, Dad," I said softly, and the tension sloughed away. "We can always turn back."

As I repeated my father's words, everyone began to melt into softer forms. The boiling pot of noodles had been removed from the burner. Peace of mind was restored. Of all the stress I must have induced upon my parents with my climbing aspirations, neither my mother nor my father ever forbade me to pursue anything. I was always left to my own judgment.

Mom spoke next.

"Well, then, I'll go fix you guys a couple of 'san-riches.' You'll need a lunch for the way over to Waterton," she chirped. Ah, yes, the chipmunk was back. "What would you like, Barry?"

"Uh, anything is fine, ma'am." Betty darted into the house, the screen door slapping the frame behind her. I could hear her flit up the stairs of my parents' split-level house.

The next morning, Barry and I climbed in crampons up the snow apron at the bottom of the north face of Mount Cleveland. We were terrified out of our gourds, but nonetheless determined to at least set foot on the face. The overcast sky had been growing thicker by the hour.

The moat between the snow and the rock was 10-15 feet wide in most places, and looked bottomless. Water ran down the prominent couloir stretching up into the towering cliffs just right of center on the face. It cascaded behind the top of the snow apron into the moat, disappearing like the paintings of water pouring off of the edge of a flat Earth. We positioned ourselves on the snow to the right of the gully, at the narrowest crossing we could find.

Barry belayed as I carefully straddled the lip of snow and eased myself over and down, using crampons and an ice axe, to where I could bridge one foot onto rock. I pivoted around, both crampons on shattered limestone, and continued toward the couloir. It was creepy. I belayed Barry up. A more sound mountaineering strategy at that point would have been to unrope and climb quickly out of the gully to minimize exposure time in the funnel. We instead belayed a couple more rope lengths along the edge of it, indicative of our insecurity.

If there was ever a time I was on a mountain and happy to see rain, it was then, starting as a light sprinkle from a gray overcast. The shades rolled down on Mount Cleveland, socking-in the mountain, and intensifying the rain. Thank God, I thought to myself. There was no reasonable choice but get off of the mountain and retreat back to Waterton Lake. I felt a hundred pounds lighter after re-crossing the moat and descending the snow. In spite of good rain gear, we were completely soaked and our packs felt like a ton of cooked spinach by the time we reached Goat Haunt Ranger Station and the boat landing. I was so glad I was not high on the face as the rain hammered down, I did not mind being drenched.

I would always regard Barry Frost's and my attempt on the north face as an important experience— not only from a mountaineering standpoint, but also from a friendship perspective. I imagine Barry felt a sense of closure by setting foot on the face, having been on the search team for his younger climbing friend, Jerry Kanzler, and the Mount Cleveland Five. Barry's climbing activity faded over the next few years, and eventually he dropped out all together. Barry Frost was one person who understood how I felt about the whole Mount Cleveland saga.

I cached my crampons, ten pitons and a few carabiners in a cairn I hastily constructed in the terminal moraine below the face. I was committed.

The next two months were an exercise in restlessness. Keeping in shape was difficult—and boring. I no longer had partners to climb with, there were no rock gyms in those days, and there was very little decent rock in the Flathead Valley to climb. I *bouldered* on the rotten cliffs in Bad Rock Canyon, an activity more like picking fruit from a rickety ladder. I did hundreds of chin-ups on a 2x2 and dozens of fingertip chin-ups on the moldings above the doorjambs throughout the house. I scrambled a few mountains in Glacier and Dan belayed me on a top-rope while I climbed laps up a crack in the center concrete pylon of the Old Red Bridge over the Flathead River, south of Columbia Falls. I scrambled Teakettle and power-hiked up Columbia Mountain.

I ran a two-mile route up the North Fork Road north of Columbia Falls twice that summer, once with my old friend and track star, Eddie Woster. I ran until my chest felt like it would explode and I was about to puke at the end, certain those supreme efforts would get me in top warrior shape. I whiled away the remainder of the summer, waiting for September to arrive.

On September 10th, I rode my bicycle to Kalispell and back for a workout. I stopped at a bridge over the Whitefish River and walked along the top of a steel bridge structure to get used to exposure. Steve Jackson would arrive on September 13th.

No one was home when I returned; but there was a note from Dan next to the telephone:

> Jim Kanzler called
> in Waterton
> the face looks good
> will meet you and Steve
> at St. Mary in three days
> says to load your quiver!"

I had not heard from Jim all summer. I exploded into a war dance and placed a call to Steve.

Barry Frost on Practice Rock near Bozeman,
December 1974. Photo by the author.

The author, circa 1976. Photo by Brian Leo.

CHAPTER 12

The Tall Horizon

O n September 13, 1976, Jim Kanzler, Steve Jackson and I drove to Waterton, Alberta, boarded *The International* tour boat and arrived at the head of the lake in Montana. We acquired a backcountry permit at the Goat Haunt Ranger Station, the same outpost that served as the field base for the Mount Cleveland search, six-and-a-half years before.

The next day dawned gray, but we headed to the north face anyway. By the time we broke out of the timber, the clouds had socked-in the face halfway down. It wasn't raining but it looked like it was about to.

"I think we could go ahead and start up the face," Kanzler said. He was still stoked and ready to do battle. "The weather forecast for today was supposed to be just ten percent chance of precipitation, but better tomorrow."

The sight of clouds on the face made me giddy. I was nervous about starting up the big face anyway and any excuse to postpone the climb was comforting. Kanzler understood not starting in less than perfect conditions. His six weeks in the Canadian Rockies had been spoiled by one storm after another and he returned to Montana without climbing anything substantial. He was thirsty for success. We hemmed and hawed for a few minutes. It was a tough decision to make. I had a moment of brilliance.

"What would Pat Callis do?" I asked Jim.

I saw the expression on his face change and his shoulders drop. He knew instantly. "Callis would not go up with clouds on the face." We knew the decision rested with those words. We stood humbly gawking at the face for another minute. "Well fuck it. Let's go back." Kanzler muttered and shouldered his pack. Steve and I fell-in behind Jim.

"I know! Let's go to the desert and climb some sunny sandstone." I suggested as we scraped through the brush.

"That's a great idea, Kennedy!" Kanzler said, "I am sick and tired of hanging out in the mountains, waiting for the weather to clear."

"I've never climbed in the desert," Jackson declared. He was excited by the idea.

"Oh, you would love it," Jim responded. "Let's crash at the shelter and head out tomorrow. We won't make the last boat anyway."

Sure enough, the next morning dawned clear.

"It's probably a sucker hole," I warned. We brewed instant coffee and packets of instant oatmeal.

"I'm gonna head over to the ranger station and get an update on the weather forecast," Jim announced. Ten minutes later, Steve and I heard a clomping noise approach the shelter. It was Kanzler running back in his mountain boots. "Alright you guys. It's going to be sunny and warm for three days."

"Three days? Are you sure?"

"Yup. Let's repack and go climb that Goddamned thing."

We arrived at treeline less than an hour before sundown. The two-mile bushwhack through the firs and spruce was like walking through a closet. We emerged into an empty courtyard and stood beneath a wall a mile wide and almost a mile high. The north face seemed even taller than it had the day before.

The evening sun cast alpine glow on the mountain, giving Mount Cleveland the appearance that she was carved from amber. The textures of the cliffs were distinct. Towers stood out from the wall, casting shadows behind them. The mountain gave me a spooky feeling as though it was a sentient being, staring down on us with a knowing beyond the scope of ordinary men. If we could make our way up the steep cliffs, perhaps we could acquire some of that knowing. I understood what Jerry Kanzler meant when he said, "The north face of Mount Cleveland silently beckons to me." The new camaraderie was absorbed in that silence. There was a mutual recognition between mountain and warrior, as if the mountain had been expecting us. The torch, at last, had arrived.

My heart was pounding more from the intimidation of the face than the exertion of the approach. My mind raced with questions. If I climbed the north face of Mount Cleveland with Jim and Steve, then what? Was following the tracks of the Mount Cleveland Five to the north face and making the ascent the end to the quest? What was carrying the torch supposed to accomplish, anyway? Release the souls of the Mount Cleveland Five? I had packed these questions up and down the mountains for the past six-and-a-half years. Not a single day went by that I did not think about Jerry Kanzler and the Mount Cleveland Five. I had sat down and pondered these questions next to streams, listening to the water; on rocky outcrops, listening to the wind; and in front of sunsets, listening to nothing.

I caught a glimpse of the answer. I would keep following the tracks of the Mount Cleveland Five until I came to the place where they disappeared. Then I would decide what to do.

"Come on, you guys; we'd better find a place to bivouac," Kanzler said, breaking the silence.

Below the north face of Mount Cleveland, the terrain was not steep; but there was only one area flat enough to invite a camp. The Mount Cleveland Five must have put their base camp here, near the well-defined tree line, where dead wood could be gathered for a campfire to help pass the long, cold hours of December darkness.

We spent the night without sleeping bags or pads, because everything we carried to the base was going up the face; sleeping bags were too bulky and would hinder the climbing.

Each of us picked a spot in which to lie down for the night. Jim and Steve organized gear while I scrambled up the moraine to the cache of crampons, pitons and carabiners I had left behind in July with Barry Frost. Jim Kanzler was reciting Shakespeare as I returned, the timber of his deep, gravelly voice amplified by the surrounding rock walls.

Just as Kanzler's performance concluded, I heard an eerie sound coming from far away.

"Listen. You guys hear that?"

A chorus. Geese.

A V-formation of a hundred Canada geese flew over us, so high that it was difficult to see them—even against a clear sky. Could they already be migrating? It was only mid-September. Why would geese be flying straight toward Mount Cleveland? We wondered if they were high enough to make it over the mountain, or if they would have to bank and turn to avoid crashing into the face. As the V of geese neared the skyline of Mount Cleveland, multitudes of two-pitch calls began to reverberate off of the wall, resulting in a distorted collage of calling. The flock never missed a wing beat, and flew over the summit of Mount Cleveland. The haunting serenade ended abruptly, five seconds after they disappeared, leaving behind an even more eerie silence.

Were the geese harbingers of success or failure? Were they trying to warn us? A short time later, it was dark. A breeze came up at sundown and blew erratically throughout the night, adding an extra chill to the autumn air. It was impossible to stay comfortable without a sleeping bag. It was like lying on a gravel road for ten hours with only a bathroom rug for padding. I shifted my body on an uncoiled rope all night long, the drawstrings of my parka pulled tight.

A minute of sleep was a luxury. The belt of Orion emerged over the eastern summit of Mount Cleveland at about 3 a.m. At 4 a.m., Sirius peered through the endless multitude of stars and the blackness that bore them. Mount Cleveland's silhouette was a tall horizon, obscuring a third of the sky with even greater blackness.

An hour to go. I was wide-awake. A little ripple of anxiety fluttered through my gut. What would the day bring?

"OK, you guys—time to get going." Jim Kanzler grunted. It was 5:30 a.m. On went the headlamps. We were already in our mountaineering duds. We unrolled ourselves from fetal positions like dry leather. I was shivering. My feet were cold. Kanzler lit the stove, and we shared tea from a single plastic cup.

By 6:30 a.m., we had trudged up the moraine and donned crampons at the snow apron then headed toward the familiar deep recess in the face, our steel crampon points making "skritching" sounds on rock fragments embedded in the snowfield.

I had warned Jim and Steve of the spooky moat crossing Barry Frost and I had encountered seven weeks before. I anticipated that further melt would have made it wider. As we arrived, I was astonished to find the entire gap filled with rock debris. The broad gully stretching into the face above had divulged enough talus and scree to fill the deep moat for as far as we could see in either direction, and spilled down the snowfield, leaving a streak of debris on the surface more than a rope length wide. There were heaps of new deposition on the terminal moraine 500 feet below the moat. An event of colossal magnitude had occurred since I had been there.

"This mountain is alive!" Kanzler proclaimed. "Let's get over on the rib. I don't want to be here when it wakes up." We simply walked across the moat.

We moved left, out of the recess, greatly reducing the probability of being taken out by rock fall. The climbing was easy at first, and we climbed side by side. Jim and Steve were on a rib closer to the couloir. I was further left.

The climbing became more difficult and exposed. The weight of my pack with a rope, not yet uncoiled, and a sling of hardware around my shoulder, was making me feel off-balance and insecure. I could hear Jim and Steve out of sight to my right. They were getting ahead of me, which made me nervous. I was encountering steep steps between ledges; any one of those could have spit me off, resulting in a sure tumble to the bottom, now hundreds of feet below.

"You better get some help now, Kennedy, before those guys get so high above you they can't hear you," I told myself.

"Kanzler!" He did not hear me.

I whistled as loudly as I could. "Kanzler! Jackson!"

Kanzler responded, "Kennedy! You okay?"

"No! I'm stuck!"

"Hang on! I'll throw you a rope!"

The other rope came sailing down, and the end landed at my feet. I was embarrassed when I joined Jim and Steve above.

"Don't worry about it," Kanzler said. "Let's get going. It looks easier over here."

We stayed closer as we worked toward a chimney behind a tower. I was eager to redeem myself and recover my psych; so I volunteered to lead the first section of roped climbing. I placed two pitons at a ledge after leading a full rope length and had just called 'on-belay' to Steve when I heard a commotion around a corner behind me.

It was Kanzler. He had untied from the second rope and third-classed outside the chimney, while Steve and I were going through the tedium of climbing with the rope. This saved precious time. Kanzler was on a roll, which gave Steve and me more confidence. Kanzler tied back in and swung onto a more difficult pitch.

High above was the menacing crown of the last 800 feet, leering down at us. It didn't seem to be getting much closer. I wondered how we were going to get through it. We climbed through the morning and into the afternoon.

A left-leaning cleft was full of snow and ice. A 20-foot-high chockstone with icicles dripping around it blocked the bottom portion. We strapped on our crampons again and readied our ice tools as we filled our water bottles from drips. Steve worked up a short ribbon of snow to the base of the chock stone and stemmed his long frame around it, crampons screeching on the walls.

"How's it look above?" Kanzler shouted. We were all eager to know what lay ahead.

"It's ice, but not real steep."

"Does it lead to the 800-foot ledge?"

"I can't tell from here." Jackson drew his ice axe and alpine hammer and moved out of sight, stabbing the ice.

We arrived at the 800-foot ledge just above Steve's pitch, which served as a viewing deck for the 3,000 feet we had just ascended. The crown of the face was now just above us. It looked tough.

"All right, let's get on with it," Kanzler ordered. He adjusted the coil of rope around his shoulders and checked the wraps of one-inch webbing of the swami belt around his waist. "I'll lead the next pitch."

He began to head straight up from the 800-foot ledge, and I could see he had in mind to attack the crown of the face straight on.

"Wait a minute, Jim. We don't have to do this lower part, remember?" We had discussed this next section using photos, as well as on the approach. We could traverse along the 800-foot ledge and then cut left on a ramp, which would shorten the crown by a pitch—maybe two. It was as if Kanzler had forgotten.

"I think we ought to just go straight up from here," he insisted. "This is a better line, and it doesn't look that hard."

"Yes, but..."

"I just want to put up the best line." His voice took on a stern quality.

I heard shades of Hal Kanzler in that voice: the Marine Corps captain, the man on a mission. There were stories about Hal circulating through the previous generation of the Montana mountaineering guild that he was not only driven but also could become stubborn on his forays into the mountains. Apparently, Hal and a couple of his partners from Columbia Falls had doubled the Little Matterhorn and Edwards Mountain near Sperry Glacier and were headed back when Hal spontaneously thought the trio should climb Gunsight Mountain. His buddies were content but Hal was insistent. What resulted was Hal ascending Gunsight Mountain himself, while his partners headed back to Sperry Chalet to wait for him.

It was mid-afternoon on the north face of Mount Cleveland, and I didn't feel like arguing my plan for the route. It wasn't my place. After all, this was Jim Kanzler's saga.

Before Hal died, he had forbidden Jim (then 18) and Jerry (then 15) to try the north face of Mount Cleveland, in which his sons were already expressing interest. Jim took a summer job in Glacier in the summer of 1966, just after he graduated from high school. He wrote to his father back in Butte requesting more climbing gear from the Kanzler arsenal. Hal mailed Jim a box of pitons with a note: "These are not to be used on the north face of Mount Cleveland or the east face of Mount Gould."

Hal was gone, and Jim was no longer a teenager. The lure of the north face only became stronger for the Kanzler brothers, and Jerry had died in its pursuit. Jim was now my mentor, and there was no way I would insist anything of him. On the other hand, I was the one who had taken over the study of Cleveland's north face. I had been prepared to attempt the face even if Jim never came back to it. So I appealed to Jim Kanzler's practical side.

"Okay man, starting from here is a better line. But we could save an hour or more if we did the traverse and bypassed this section. It would be nice to make the 200-foot ledge by nightfall."

I was prepared to fully give in and let Jim do what he thought was best. This was his day. The north face of Mount Cleveland was now his baby. Kanzler was the one on a roll. Jackson and I needed to support his effort. His response took me by surprise.

"Yeah, you're right. We should do the traverse."

We shouldered our packs without further discussion and zigged west on the 800-foot ledge, then zagged eastward up the ramp. Two inches of icy snow crust made the footing tricky. We crept single-file beneath the overhanging wall above as the ramp leveled out into a ledge. No one was sure what would happen at the end of the ledge. It was hard to tell from the photos, other than that the climbing would be technical.

Jim stopped as we turned a corner, and I about crapped my knickers. The ledge didn't just end—it inverted. We were going to have to deal with the overhanging wall!

"Jesus!"

"This is fuckin' steep."

"No shit." I took off my pack and sat on it. I felt I could better control my bowels if I sat down.

"Well, I guess this is it," Kanzler said matter-of-factly. "You want the lead, Kennedy?"

"Fawwk." I turned around and looked at Jackson.

"No way, man. Remember—you lead the rock, " he said with a nervous chuckle. "I'll lead the ice." He leaned against the wall.

"Kanzler, it's up to you, man." He knew it.

The band of rock immediately above the ledge was shattered and crumbling. Something bad must have happened in the mud of the old ocean bed here, millions of years ago, which eventually became the mountains of Glacier Park. The rock was loose, but I hammered in a thin blade piton anyway.

"Don't use too many pins," Kanzler ordered, "I'm probably going to need them all on this lead."

Jackson stacked the ropes. Kanzler organized the rack of hardware to his satisfaction, then drew a deep breath and exhaled through pursed lips.

"Okay man, here I go. Don't give me too much slack."

He knew his station. He was the best. He had climbed the Northwest Face of Half Dome and the Nose of El Capitan. He and Pat Callis had the high mark on the Emperor Face on Mount Robson. No badge-flashing, Smokey-the-Bear-hat-wearing ranger dude or armchair mountaineer could ever call him inexperienced now. Kanzler was the director of the Big Sky Ski Patrol, and knew more about avalanches than any of the park rangers on the Mount Cleveland search team.

He tiptoed off of the ledge and began a 30-foot traverse on loose, bulging rock. He had 3,500 feet beneath the heels of his mountain boots. Jackson and I hardly breathed.

"If it had just been you and me, I don't think we could have done this," I whispered to Steve.

"No shit," he whispered back. "We would be in trouble here." I'd never felt so sober.

The rope went out in light tugs. Kanzler found a place for the number nine Hexentric nut—the biggest piece we carried.

"Watch me!" Kanzler insisted. He was breathing hard. "It's very loose here. My foothold could pop."

"Please, Kanzler, don't fall!" I prayed.

He moved steadily away, horizontally, at the same level as Steve and me. He brushed loose rock off of the holds that rattled down the face.

"It's steeper than an elevator shaft," Jackson muttered.

"Okay, I'm going to have to push a big block off. Be ready." Kanzler gave a shove with his left hand, and a block the size of a file cabinet tipped away from the wall, separating into two blocks as it turned a half-somersault and disappeared from view. It was silent for what seemed like minutes. I braced for the impact. I wanted to cover my ears. Suddenly, the blocks exploded below. The impact started a chain reaction; rock exploded everywhere below. Kanzler resumed climbing before the face was restored to silence.

"This is as steep as El Cap, but a lot scarier," Kanzler informed us.

I drew a breath and let it out with a sigh, cheeks puffing out. "Kanzler, you don't have to do this," I assured him. "You can come back and we can drop down to the 800-foot ledge and traverse off this damn thing."

It would not have been difficult to regroup on the ramp, return to the big ledge below and traverse off. We still might have made the summit; but we would not have climbed the face.

The upper crown was the epitome of the mountain. From both the north and the south, Mount Cleveland's higher western summit bears a resemblance to the Great Pyramid of Egypt. From the northwest, it takes on the posture of the Sphinx and glowers. The last 800 feet make up the headdress and cobra.

Either Kanzler chose to ignore me, or his concentration was so focused that he did not hear me.

"I think there is a ledge above me," Kanzler yelled back. "I'm going to head for it." He sounded more self-assured now. "This is it, goddamnit! We are not going back now!" He cut straight up.

Kanzler hammered pitons into thin, horizontal cracks and wedged nuts into vertical fissures in the steep limestone as he made his way to a perch (on which one guy could barely sit). There was no discussion of who would lead now. Jim and I had to switch ends of the rope in tight quarters to set him up to go again. The cliff above us disappeared into sky and we could not tell where it led. However, Kanzler climbed like he had done the pitch before and knew the way.

A hundred twenty feet above, Kanzler reached a narrow ledge. "I'll bring you guys up to here," he shouted down.

Steve and I reunited with Jim, and the three of us stood elbow-to-elbow. Jackson and I switched ends so we could leave the ledge in the same order we were standing. We were very exposed. Below, the cliff overhung. When I looked down, I could only see the next 15 feet; then nothing until the moraine and the forest thousands of feet below, which looked like different colors of carpet. I promised myself not to look down anymore.

Kanzler re-racked as I brought the rope around my pelvis and clipped it to my waist loops.

"Am I on?"

"You're on."

He unclipped from the anchor and took off. The climbing was hard right off of the ledge. His boots were right above my face.

"Get something in right away, if you can," I said in a coarse whisper.

"I think I can get in a pin a ways above." Kanzler was in sharp focus, moving deliberately and sounding like a steam locomotive as he exhaled. He cut left at half-rope and disappeared from view. He popped his head back down to get my attention.

"I'm traversing left. There's going to be a lotta' rope drag. Keep the rope slack."

The rope went out steadily for a minute, then in short jerks. It would stop, then go an arm's length out and would slide back into my lap, then back out. It went on like this for an hour.

"How's it look from there?" Jackson yelled. There was no reply.

"He's having trouble," I sighed.

"I think you're right...maybe he's setting up a belay," Jackson tried to sound hopeful. It was late in the day, and we had been in the shade of the north face shadow since dawn. I could feel the sweat on my back and neck turning cold. Steve and I were starting to shiver. We needed to put on another layer of clothing, but getting our packs off and opened without dropping something was too problematic. We decided to just go ahead and shiver.

The rope moved out a little more.

"He's still going up."

Then, as if from a mile away, " 'awl-ling!" and the rope went suddenly slack.

"Oh Jesus, I think he fell!" I pulled in two, four, six feet of slack. "Kanzler! You okay?" I yelled at the top of my lungs. No reply.

"Oh fuck. Now what?"

"I don't know. Just wait, I guess."

I tried again to make contact, but the wind had picked up, and it was no use. The sun was almost to the horizon. Jackson blew warm air into his hands. Were we going to get benighted right here?

Then there came a faint tik-tik-tik-tik-tik.

"He's putting in another pin." Jackson stated.

"Thank God!"

The rope started to go out again in little jerks.

"Twenty feet, Kanzler! Two-ze-ro!" The rope eked out.

"Ten feet! One-ze-ro!"

The rope kept going. I had to get the rope back around my hips before the last foot ran out to my knot.

"That's-all-the-rope!" I screamed. I had no choice but to unclip from the anchor and start climbing as Kanzler continued to demand rope slowly. I was about 15 feet above Jackson when there was another faint shout from somewhere.

"T. You're on belay," Jackson reported.

"Are you sure?"

"Yeah."

I continued to climb and the rope steadily went up in little jerks. Halfway to the belay, I was out of contact with both Jackson and Kanzler. I was alone, with one rope disappearing above and one disappearing below.

The sun set as I climbed on. I looked up—there was Kanzler.

"Just pull through on that pin," he instructed. "I couldn't make the move because of the rope drag, so I had to use the pin and keep going. I almost fell off."

I grabbed Jim's shoulder to mantle up to his position. He was sitting on a small pile of scree.

"Kanzler, are you tied into anything?"

"Right here, under my ass." He leaned to one side. There was a short angle piton driven into what looked like dirt. "It's good," Kanzler assured me. "Still, it is a good thing that you didn't fall," he said, smirking with one corner of his mouth.

"She-it."

"I was so exhausted, I couldn't muscle my way any further with the rope drag. I couldn't get back to the wall. I was totally wasted, man. Here, give me Jackson's rope; I'll belay. Go get us set up on the ledge."

"Right."

By the time Steve reached Jim at the belay, the stars were out. Jackson had climbed the scary pitch in the dark, without a headlamp. There was no place to slide his pack off and fish his light out of his pack. The piton we all used for aid had been a little too big for the crack. Kanzler had to "weld it" to the rock, forcing it with many hammer blows. He instructed Jackson to just leave it and not waste time trying to get it out.

The piton is still up there. I wondered if anyone would ever find it. It was the only piece of gear we left behind.

The 200-foot ledge was a catwalk that spanned the upper headwall, about 200 feet below the summit. I was able to get in a string of good anchors. Each guy excavated a platform to lie down on head-to-toe, and stayed clipped into the anchor system to keep from rolling off during the night. We spent an hour manufacturing semi-comfortable resting spots. The longer we fiddled around, the shorter the night would be. Then we rallied on Kanzler's perch. We were hungry lads, not having eaten much during the fourteen hours of climbing. We dined together in the ambiance of headlamps. Jim and Steve had Norwegian Herring fillets in tangy tomato sauce, and I a Norwegian Herring fillet marinated in succulent vegetable oil.

I could feel a little draft of warmer air licking my neck and face. "You know, I think we might be only 50 feet below the summit ridge," I submitted, wiping my fingers on my wool knickers.

"No way, Kennedy!" Kanzler exclaimed. We started looking around.

"I got the impression we were getting close when I was doing that last lead," Jim reconsidered. "You know how the foreshortening effect can jade your perspective."

"Right; but in the photos, the 200-foot ledge runs across the summit pyramid all the way to the eastern summit ridge, and there is only another 150 feet or so of this ledge to the horizon."

"Man, you might be right." It was hard to believe, but we had nearly climbed the entire face in a day!

"Maybe tomorrow, we should just head straight up and have breakfast on top," Jackson suggested. We really could not determine how far the summit ridge was above us. The rock was steeper than vertical, and would be very difficult.

"Well, I think we should traverse west and get back closer to the middle of the face and go up that cleft just east of the summit," I explained, "I think our route should do it all. I don't want to leave it for someone else to say we didn't climb the whole thing."

"I like that idea, Kennedy," Kanzler said. "What do you think, Steve?"

"It's fine with me. I just like the fact that we are here, and the weather is perfect; and tomorrow, we have all day to finish it."

"Okay then— it's up to you two to do the leading tomorrow."

"Sounds good."

"We've almost got this thing in the bag."

"Yeah, we just can't let ourselves do anything stupid."

"Right."

One of us bumped an empty sardine tin off of the ledge, and it rolled on edge and into the dark. Tink-tink...tinkle-dink, dinka-dinka...tittle-dinka-dink.

We could hear the tinkling chimes grow further and further away. A minute later, "I still hear it."

"Me too."

"It must be going all the way to the bottom."

I thought I could still hear it halfway through the night.

Before we crawled to our respective resting spots, we sang a few Bob Dylan songs. Kanzler had all the early Bob Dylan albums. One of the many tragedies Jim Kanzler would experience in his life was Lindalee divorcing him earlier that year. Their energetic, blond-haired, blue-eyed son named Jamie, was seven years old the night we spent on Mount Cleveland.

Little did I know then that Jamie would play an important role in the search of the Mount Cleveland Five. Little did Jim Kanzler know that, 30 years later, he would have a grandson named James Dylan, named after his grandfather...and his grandfather's favorite singer-songwriter.

About the time Orion was rising above the Great Plains, somewhere in the direction of Great Falls, while Kanzler snored and Jackson dozed and I fidgeted, there was a commotion of sliding rock— then a crash of a large rock— just below us. Everyone bolted upright. Did someone fall off?

"Jackson-Kanzler...Jackson!"

"Sorry, guys. My platform just gave way," Steve said.

"You okay?"

"I'm fine."

The block falling off of the 200-foot ledge started another cascade of rock falling down the face. The night was so still that we could hear every matchbook-sized flake find its way to the moraine. We just sat there in the dark and listened to it. When at last the last bits of scree had found their stopping places and total silence was restored, Jackson said. "Well, maybe my rock landed on the sardine can and smashed it." We broke into knee-slapping, rib-hugging laughter.

When Kanzler recovered enough breath, he added. "Yeah, now Bob Frauson won't be able to find it and come up here and bust us for littering." We broke into belly laughs again. I wonder if someone standing on the shore of Waterton Lake at midnight would have heard faraway laughter coming from high on Mount Cleveland— from a place no one had ever been before.

The next morning, we traversed two rope lengths west on the 200-foot ledge, closer to the center of the face. It was easy, but exposed. Above, I could see the cleft of the chimney that would be the final passage. It did not extend all the way down to the ledge. The rock below it was wet, indicating hidden snow and ice in the cleft. I led a pitch with sparse protection but moderate climbing to an alcove. There was 15 feet of steep, wet rock barring the way. Jackson carefully led on. Above, the chimney was wide and full of hard, icy snow. Jackson cruised through it. The terrain opened to the broad summit area of Mount Cleveland.

The north face was below us.

I don't suppose there were three more jubilant guys on the face of the planet. With great pride, we signed the summit register. On the small tablet rolled up in a canister with the other entries by those who had climbed other routes, there was an entry from three guys from Minnesota. Kanzler knew the names from his days as an Outward Bound rock-climbing instructor in Ely the two summers following the tragedy. It went something like this: "Tried the north face. Couldn't do the last 800 feet. Good luck, Kanzler or whoever."

We walked to the apex of the north face, not far from the summit cairn, for a look down. It is funny how giddy we were, cautioning one another to not get too close to the edge, when we had just spent a day and a half on the face. Kanzler rolled up the tablet and returned it to the canister.

"Okay Kennedy, what's next?" he demanded, a huge grin on his face.

"Well, there is the north face of Mount Siyeh or the south face of Merritt. I've looked at them both closely. I don't think there is anything more intimidating than the final head wall of Merritt. I think Siyeh should be next."

"Oh, boy—here we go!" He was still on a roll. It would last for another three years.

"Then we go for Siyeh next year."

"Next year, for sure."

"I have a feeling we have our work cut out for us."

"No doubt."

From the day I had made my precocious vow to climb the north face of Mount Cleveland, I also promised to perform some kind of ceremony when I did so. The summit would have been the obvious place.

A few people who know me have asked how I felt on the top of Mount Cleveland after finally achieving the north face of Mount Cleveland. Did I feel any connection to the 1969 tragedy? I wondered too if I would feel I had exonerated the Mount Cleveland Five—or even myself—after we reached the summit.

As it turned out, the hour we spent on the summit was in celebration of having finished a great climbing experience more than it was a tribute to Jerry and the Mount Cleveland Five. The eulogy would come a bit later in the day and the remembrances of the Mount Cleveland Five would continue for a lifetime.

We left the broad summit area and selected the best place to drop into the west face bowl. This was the shortest route back to the head of Waterton Lake. Jim Anderson had climbed the west face of Mount Cleveland twice before he was 18; and Mount St. Nicholas with Chuck Kroger (raised in Kalispell, and a future Yosemite and Colorado climbing legend). Neither Jim, Steve nor I had been to the summit before. I had purposely saved Cleveland's summit for success on the north face. We picked our way through the upper ledges and short cliff bands.

The angle of the west face diminished after several hundred feet, helping create a bowl shape to the face. It was in this vicinity the avalanche released, the crown fracture being visible to Bud Anderson from his airplane and the Lev-Callis-Kanzler team, and swept the Cleveland Five out of this world and into the next.

I could sense the lateness in the day of December 29, 1969— the gloom of winter overcast and the wind licking the mountain, depositing drifted snow on the place where we now descended, creating a fragile wind slab across the bowl. I could feel the five cold faces and sweaty backs, the wet gloves, and cold toes in single boots. I could hear the deep breathing and sense the rapid pace necessary to reach the summit of Mount Cleveland in the winter from a base camp on another side of the mountain. No doubt they were burning daylight. I could feel their strength and ambition. I could hear that fateful "whoomph!" as the bonds along lines of tension in the snowfield disconnected, causing an instantaneous fracture across the bowl as the whole surface settled upon a weak lower layer, forcing what air was in the snowpack outward in a single breath. The whole slope would have moved initially as one uniform slab, then broken up into pieces and powder and accelerated downward, becoming a rushing stream of frozen water racing over the ground, billowing through the air with the confusion, fear and panic of five Montana sons and brothers tumbling like rag dolls.

I could see the west face bowl empty downward, thundering over the lower cliff band, rumbling and hissing. I watched the river of snow slithering and sprawling onto the apron at the bottom of the mountain, filling the stream bed below as it reached the edge of the trees and the white dust cloud settling back to the ground. The whole thing may have taken only a minute. Maybe less.

Then there was nothing, just the wind blowing along the rocky outcrops, whispering the call of the Awe. The countless snowflakes that had gushed down the mountain, busting apart and melting on their fringes from the friction of 3,000 feet of tumbling snow, refroze together as a cohesive mass, never to slide again.

When the Park Service team recovered Jim Anderson's body, on June 29th, 1970, his watch calendar had stopped on December 29th— which just so happened to be Hal Kanzler's birthday. Hal would have been 49. As the recovery crew lifted Anderson's body out of the snow, his watch started ticking again.

We found an easy way through the diorite sill and continued toward the lower face. Jim was moving faster than Steve and me, and was now a 100 feet ahead of us. He continued to descend, as if he were deliberately avoiding the significance of our location. I expected him to stop and say something. It would be irreverent not to acknowledge the place where the Cleveland Five had perished.

Jim, Pat Callis and Peter Lev had climbed through this location late in the day on January 5, 1970. Darkness overtook them as they searched for Jim's younger brother and friends. The search trio had dug a snow cave and waited a long, troubled night for morning.

The next day they descended. It was a short distance below where Jim, Steve and I were now that Pat Callis had looked off to his left and saw the tip of a pack protruding through old avalanche debris that changed the course of the search in an instant.

Kanzler continued toward a ramp that angled to the northwest, allowing passage through the lower cliffs of the west face, as if he was on familiar terrain. Steve and I were near the terminus of the upper snowfield. The moment was slipping away. If there was to be a ceremony for the Mount Cleveland Five where their bodies were recovered from the mountain, then it was going to have to happen soon.

I took three more steps and stopped. Steve nearly ran over me.

"Hey, Kanzler! Wait up a minute. Let's take a break! I could use some water."

Jim turned around and scrambled back up to where Steve and I were. Jackson and I dropped our packs.

"This is it," Kanzler said as he reached us, catching his breath. "This is the place where my brother and my friends were buried."

"I know," I said softly.

"Callis, Lev and I walked right over the top of them and never knew they were here."

There was little emotion in Jim's voice. If he felt sad, he sure wasn't going to show it. It disturbed me that he might have just walked on had I not requested a water break. Maybe Kanzler was a master at forgiving and forgetting, at living only in the moment. Maybe none of this mattered. Sometimes living and climbing, dying and remembering all seemed so confusing. Perhaps Jim Kanzler had simply transcended the whole thing. Maybe I was the one stuck in the Mount Cleveland tragedy and the aftermath.

There was a flat spot a few yards away, just above the next cliff band. The water draining the west face ran under the remnant of the snowfield, which was now at its lowest volume at the end of the summer. It splashed over the cliff below. This was the place.

The June 29, [1970] entry in Park Service Report of The Mount Cleveland Tragedy...December 26, 1969-July 3, 1970 read:

> It was planned on this date to make a summit climb of the probable route taken by the climbers. [five rangers]... started...at 5:00 a.m. At 9:00 [a.m.] the party reached the base of the snow in the middle bowl [of the west face] just above the falls at the head of the slide run-out area. The odor accompanying the water from beneath

the [cavernous] snow was immediately noticeable and a gaze upward from the stream bed revealed the first body about 30 [feet] from the lowest edge of the snow...held in position by a red Perlon rope. (Two bodies were located on that day.) Most of the day's operation was conducted in alternating rain and snow flurries.

The stream was now small enough to step over and the edge of the snowfield well above us.

"Let's fill our water bottles here," I proposed, trying to keep the mood upbeat. "Let's fill our bottles and make a toast to the Mount Cleveland Five."

"Good idea," Jackson chimed in, rummaging into his pack and pulling out a near-empty water bottle.

"Yeah...it would be a good thing to do," Kanzler agreed. We topped off our bottles, mixing the water from the north face with that of the west face.

"Here's to five great guys. May they find happiness and adventure wherever they are now," I toasted. We raised our water bottles, touched them together, and took a drink.

"Here is to Jerry Kanzler..." We touched again. "...To Clare Pogreba, to Ray Martin, to Jim Anderson, to Mark Levitan." We touched bottles for each one.

"Here's to us," Jackson added.

"Here's to the north face of Mount Cleveland. We finally did it, Jer." Kanzler was smiling. We touched our now–half-empty water bottles one last time. We stood there rehydrating and looking around with the joy and sense of accomplishment that come from being in the mountains on a warm, sunny day.

I gazed up at the snowfield above us one more time.

"Let's get out of here," Kanzler said, picking up his pack and heading for the break in the cliff band below. "We need to figure out how we are going to get back to the Waterton townsite without the boat. (The last day of operation of the tour boat had been the day we approached the mountain for the second time.)

There was no reason to hurry—other than to get back to civilization and announce our success, that is. None of us cared at that point about how we got back to the cars. If we had to walk the ten miles around the lake, so be it. Our descent brought us back to the stream course, Camp Creek on the maps. The weather was perfect, and by the time we got to the lower elevation and into the vegetation, we were getting hot in the afternoon sun. Steve thought it would be a good idea to splash some water on our faces.

At a waterfall from the same west face watercourse, we stopped to cool off. A certain bravado took over and, one by one, we stripped naked and stood under the force of the freezing cold water. Literally and figuratively, we were cleansed of the great face and the mountain by the waters of the burial ground of the Mount Cleveland Five.

"Do you think we should call Mel Ruder?" I asked Jim as we strode the last few hundred yards of trail to the ranger station to announce our return. "I'm sure he would be interested in what we have accomplished."

"Shrrr," Kanzler replied in a way that belied his confidence and contentment. "I'm shrrr Mr. Ruder would like to hear that at last we have climbed the Great Face. He has written enough about dead Kanzlers. He'd probably like to write about a Kanzler triumph for a change."

We clomped through the open door of the ranger station, into the subdued light of the well-preserved log structure, requisitioned from its winter hibernation for the base of ground operations the first week of the 1970s. The seasonal ranger, who emerged from the radio room in the back, met us.

"We'd like to check back from our climb," Steve Jackson said, unable to control a smile that lit up his face.

We provided the ranger with details of our climb. He knew climbing the north face was special, and he probably knew of the tragedy that had occurred on the mountain behind the ranger station some years before his days in Glacier National Park. He just didn't know the details. He didn't make the connection with Jim Kanzler, but could feel our excitement.

Steve and I were about the same age as Bob Frauson when he was a private, hauling dead and wounded soldiers off of Riva Ridge in Italy in 1944. I doubt the young seasonal ranger knew any of this. He excused himself for a moment and stepped into the radio room to make a transmission to Bob Frauson at the Hudson Bay Ranger Station in St. Mary, 26 air miles to the southeast. Without a doubt, the six-foot-four, barrel-chested World War II veteran was anxiously awaiting word of our return—successful or otherwise.

"221—Goat Haunt.... 221—Goat Haunt."

"This is 221. Go ahead, Goat Haunt."

"Bob, I've got Kanzler here. They made it."

Of course, the transmission signal was broadcast park-wide and beyond. Every ranger and location with a radio monitoring the National Park frequency heard the news simultaneously. The north face of Mount Cleveland had been climbed. Jim Kanzler had done it! Another little slice of Montana history could now be inked.

We did not hear Bob Frauson's reply. We were too caught up in the moment of glory, laughing and cajoling. Indeed, we were having fun. There was little doubt at that hour, if not that whole day, that we were the greatest climbers in the world.

Alex Lowe, who represented the next generation of Montana climbers and took alpine climbing to a whole new level, and was once considered to be the greatest climber in the world, was quoted as saying, "The greatest climber in the world is the one having the most fun." Alex would be starting his first day as a high school senior in Missoula about then. None of us knew there was such a guy; but Alex's day was dawning.

The ranger returned to the front desk.

"Bob Frauson offers his congratulations." I made a sideways glance at Montana's newest hero. He was smiling triumphantly. It wasn't the chipped incisor that stood out so much as it was the longer, undamaged tooth. I just remember that grin pasted on so firmly that nothing in the world could have wiped it off. That tooth gleamed like Sirius, the Dog Star, which follows the hunter Orion.

There was another crackle of the radio in the next room. Call numbers were coming over the air. The ranger excused himself again. Apparently it had been his call number. We ignored the interruption and followed Kanzler to the topographic map of Glacier mounted on the wall near the door. He had located Mount Siyeh.

"Oh my God, Kennedy, look how close the lines are on the north face of Siyeh. They run together. It's simply dead vertical."

"I know—D.A.V," I said, "dead-ass vertical." We laughed.

The ranger returned with another message.

"Headquarters was relaying a message from Mel Ruder. He wants you to call him as soon as you get back to Columbia Falls. He said not to call the *Daily Interlake* until he's had a chance to speak with you in person. I think you guys are going to be famous."

Twenty-two years later, I was interviewing over the phone with author McKay Jenkins. He was writing his book *White Death: Tragedy and Heroism in an Avalanche Zone*, an account of the Mount Cleveland tragedy.

"So when you, Kanzler and Jackson got to the top of the north face of Mount Cleveland, how did you feel?" McKay asked me.

I thought for a moment and then replied, "like winning a gold medal in the Olympics." I just left it at that.

Was climbing the north face of Mount Cleveland the end to the saga? I hardly think so; not when the proverbial tracks lead over the horizon of Mount Cleveland and down the other side. The way I felt about the Mount Cleveland Five did not change over the years, and I wanted more than ever to reach beyond Mount Cleveland with Jim Kanzler.

There is little doubt in my mind that Jim and Jerry Kanzler along with Clare Pogreba or Ray Martin would have climbed the north face had tragedy not intervened; nor the mountaineering ambitions of any of the Mount Cleveland Five have ended on that mountain.

A better question to ponder was: had the Mount Cleveland tragedy not happened, would I still have become a mountain climber myself? I wish I had a dollar for every time I asked myself that question. The conclusion I made was: life just keeps happening no matter where you are.

Mel Ruder likely would have painted the front page of the September 23, 1976 issue of the *Hungry Horse News* with the success of Jim Kanzler on the north face of Mount Cleveland had not another incident occurred in Glacier the night before "The Horse", as my father used to call the paper, went to press. A young woman was dragged from her tent at the Many Glacier campground in the middle of the night, fatally mauled and partially consumed.

That must have been a tempestuous 24 hours for the two, one-man writer-photographer-editors of the Flathead Valley. The North face of Cleveland story was bumped to a full-page spread on page three in the *Hungry Horse News*, "Trio Presents Details of North face Climb" with a large photo of the face and the route traced on it. G. George Ostrom's *Kalispell Weekly News*, reached the newsstands a day before the *Hungry Horse News* and ran a front-page headline on September 22, 1976 that read "Cleveland Conquered". The headline overshadowed the story of a raging fire in a building in downtown Kalispell the night before the *Kalispell Weekly News* went to press. Ostrom was a mountaineering partner of Jim Kanzler's father who anguished over Hal's suicide and Jerry's disappearance. Ostrom's Mount Cleveland coverage included three large photos of the mountain and a story that took half of the front page and most of the third.

Most daily newspapers in Montana carried a story about the Mount Cleveland climb with a recap of the tragedy six and a half years before. Jim, Steve and I became local celebrities for a while.

I wowed Diane Dugan, an attractive woman in one of my college classes, with the Mount Cleveland tale and we got married a few years later. The sheen eventually wore off.

Looking down the north face of Mount Cleveland.
Photo by Jim Kanzler.

Jim Kanzler leading after the ledge inverted to overhanging. Photo by Steve Jackson.

Jim Kanzler and the author the morning after the bivouac high on the north face of Mount Cleveland, September 1976. Photo by Steve Jackson.

Steve Jackson and the author on the summit of Mount Cleveland, September 1976. "Hey Kennedy, you're standing on the rope!" Photo by Jim Kanzler.

CHAPTER 13

On the Path of Mad Wolf, Part 1

iyeh is a Blackfeet Indian name. Since the language of the Blackfeet was an oral language only, the English spellings of names are phonetic. Si-yeh means Mad Wolf. There once lived a Blackfeet Indian who earned the name Siyeh, for whom the mountain was subsequently named.

James Willard Schultz, an explorer, trapper, trader and historian who periodically lived with the Blackfeet—wrote a book, *Signposts of Adventure*, copyright 1926. He wrote of this proud old warrior, a member of the Piegan tribe of the Blackfeet: "[Siyeh] was so recklessly brave that after some years, none would go with him on raids against the enemy... [and] had more hatred for white men than any other Indian I ever knew."

Hal Kanzler owned a copy of *Signpost of Adventure*, and Jim read it when he was a Boy Scout in Columbia Falls. Hal had a special affinity for the indigenous people of this country, especially the Blackfeet; perhaps because he lived near and often visited the Blackfeet's sacred mountains, which the white people took over by invasion and occupation and later named Glacier National Park. Jim adopted his father's respect and appeal for the Blackfeet Indian culture.

Schultz went on to write that Siyeh—Mad Wolf— had once prayed after finding out that the whites had named a mountain after him: "...I have given him [the white man] a name of our people. And O Sun pity me. I pray you give this white man continuous unhappiness under that name. Utterly destroy him and soon."

Jim Kanzler and I knew climbing the north face of Mount Siyeh was going to be risky—even sacrilegious.

August 1977

Pat Callis, Jim Kanzler and I stood at the terminal moraine of the Siyeh Glacier, shading our eyes. We represented three generations of climbers.

The mid-August sun peered over the summit rim of Mount Siyeh as we looked up into the shadows of the north face.

I was making the case to the professor to climb the whole face, bottom-to-top. I had studied Siyeh's north face even more thoroughly than Mount Cleveland's, simply because it was more accessible. The lower third would be relatively easy compared to the upper two thirds, and most of the lower part would go third class without belaying. A broad ledge ran the width of the face, separating the two sections. The way I saw it, the first ascent needed to bisect both sections. Once on the broad ledge, we could relocate to attack a line on the upper two thirds of the face— which represented the true difficulties.

"Why do that?" Pat countered. "We should follow the ramp at the bottom of the face leading up and left to get on the big ledge. Then we can start on the part of the face we are really interested in. We don't need to do the lower part—it's not necessary. We should save our effort for the serious part of the route."

Ever the pragmatist. This was the way Callis approached problems. It gave Jim Kanzler and me pause. I was surprised and disappointed in the conservative approach of the Dirty Sox Club's mentor. The route had been my project, my Master's thesis. The lower, easy section was necessary to do a nice line. I wanted to climb the entire face. I would have thought that, after Pat and Jim's gallant attempt on the Emperor Face on Mount Robson, Gandalf would have wanted to leave nothing on the table.

"The first ascent should go up the easiest way," Callis explained. "That way, you maximize your chances of succeeding. Let the second ascent party do the lower part if they want to add something to the route."

Jim Kanzler was with me. He and I had discussed the route variations before. Of course, we knew the ramp was there, but we both wanted to do the entire face. When Kanzler and Callis were waiting for the right conditions at the base of the Emperor Face, piecing together a route, it was Jim who had wanted to go right up the middle. "I didn't want to leave a better line on the face for someone else to come along and do, and claim we didn't do it all, " Jim explained to me a few years later. "I wanted to do a bold line right up the gut."

Pat was still the senior climber, and always would be. Following social tradition, he had the final word. Jim and I were resigned to adopt his reasoning—for the time being.

My disappointment was short-lived. I was just happy to be going to Glacier's big, unclimbed face of Mount Siyeh with the likes of Kanzler and Callis. Scrambling up the ramp was still the dream come true. In seven years, I had gone from being a kid rappelling from a clothesline rope to teaming up with Jerry Kanzler's big brother, continuing the quest to champion the Mount Cleveland Five. Now I was pursuing the next challenge with the heroic mountain climbers who had gone searching high on Mount Cleveland in the winter, seven and a half years before.

Pat, Jim and I traversed onto the broad ledge, where the three of us leveled a place to bivouac under a low shelf. There was no point rushing onto the face late that day. We had as comfortable a site to bivouac as one could hope to find on such a big face. We pondered the foreshortened features of the cliffs above as the setting sun changed the drab sedimentary rock to a temple of gold in perfect August weather. I had a sense of security being with the best alpinists of the day in Montana. If the going got too dicey on the expanse above, as it surely would, there were Callis and Kanzler to lead the attack. I rested well that night.

The next morning, we missed the predawn start. I had expected the two seasoned gunfighters to strap on their six-shooters and stride to the OK Corral like Doc Holliday and Wyatt Earp, taking me with them. Instead, we just sat there procrastinating. Neither Pat nor Jim took the initiative. I did not feel it was my role as the junior member to rally those who's wake I drafted.

An hour passed. Then two. If we were going to have a go at the big face, then we should have already been in motion. We just sat there rehashing what might lie above us, letting time and clear skies slip away.

At last, Pat spoke. "Well..." he began in a quiet voice, his coal-black beard angled down from the sharp, thin features of his face and jutting forward as he looked up. "There was a reason why I came here to do this climb," he said with a puzzled look, "but right now, I don't remember what it was."

Huh? What did he just say? Was Gandalf submitting a resignation to do the climb? No way! Not on the most heralded precipitous face among mountaineers and scramblers of Glacier National Park! Ed Cooper had published two views of the north face of Mount Siyeh in the December 1969 issue of *Summit* magazine, on the inside cover feature "Know Your Mountains". Jim and I took the dazzling photos as a harbinger. These were bound to attract serious alpine climbers from around the country to vie for the first ascent. Jeff Lowe and Mike Weiss, honed alpinists from out of state, had already slipped in and copped the east face of Mount Gould three years before.

I could see Mount Siyeh from the tops of Teakettle and Columbia Mountains, once I became familiar with the peaks of Glacier. These mountains were in Jim Kanzler's and my back yard. The north face of Mountain Siyeh became high on the "torch list" and I knew that Kanzler and I had better get with it.

Pat couldn't bow out now; but he did.

There I was, sitting part way up the north face of Siyeh with the two climbers I idolized the most, with perfect weather in position to get, perhaps, the biggest prize of all. I could feel the wind leave my sails.

I began to wonder if it was me. Perhaps Pat was not confident in me. I wasn't in Pat or Jim's league yet, but I was working on it. I thought back to the day on Champagne Sherbet, when I came so close to taking a huge fall that could quite conceivably have killed us both. Maybe that was it.

"You two can go ahead and go if you want," Callis said. "It'll be even more efficient with two guys, anyway. Don't let me stop you guys from going," he encouraged. "You ought to get up there and do it. You should go right now, though; we've already wasted too much time."

I wasn't sure what I wanted to do. I could not have felt more dejected if I had gotten a scratch in the vinyl of my new Who's Next album, my favorite climbing "psych-up" music.

Gandalf shouldered his rucksack, bid us well and scrambled east on the ledge, disappearing around a corner like a puff of smoke.

Kanzler and I watched Pat reappear far below us, moving quickly as he descended several hundred yards of the ramp. We waited for him to finish the exposed step near the bottom; then, he appeared as a tiny speck moving along the low-angle flank of snow of the glacier. He turned around and looked up as if to locate us. We waved, but the professor could not find us on the labyrinth above him. He disappeared into the moraine.

"What do you think, Kanzler?"

"We're here," Jim grunted lethargically. He sat slouched on a block of talus without moving, his elbows resting on his knees. We were in a minor crisis—and I was at a major crossroad.

"The Boy Scout and the Cub Scout," I thought. Would Jim think I was worthy as a partner? Did he think I would be able to climb as a near equal and not just rely on his strength and determination, like I had on Cleveland the year before? I felt I had steeled since then. Kanzler and I had become steady climbing partners. He knew what I could do. Maybe Siyeh was the level of endeavor that called for a partner Kanzler could rely on to share the dirty work. I could understand that. Maybe we could bail off of Siyeh and choose an easier objective. My mind wandered to a route I also wanted to do up the east face of Little Chief Mountain, a few miles to the south. We could hike out and relocate.

I wasn't listening when Jim spoke.

"I think we should go get up on the son-of-a-bitch." Huh?

"Well, I'm uh, up for giving it a try. We can always turn back. It's easy to get off from here."

Gandalf was right. If we were going to go, we had better not wait too long.

"'We'd better git to gittin,' as my dad would say." I do not think R. Glenn had any idea of what his son was about to embark upon—nor did he want to.

"Right," Kanzler agreed. He drew a deep breath, pursed his lips and exhaled, getting his climbing mojo going.

We reorganized the rack of hardware. Jim found a way to third-class through the first barrier above the broad ledge. It was scary with a pack and gear, but it led to a couple of hundred feet of easier terrain. We belayed the first technical pitches below the diorite sill. Jim led the first one to set up on a more serious pitch I led, using a spot of aid. At the base of the diorite, we traversed right for two rope lengths to avoid the overhanging wall above, and climbed a difficult pitch that got us through the diorite and in position to follow a line of weakness leading to the dizzy heights above. The next pitch turned out to be moderate but the next one looked tough.

It was here we began to stall out. I was intimidated. The whole face from there looked like the three-pitch crux Kanzler had led on Cleveland. I just couldn't rally my courage; I certainly wasn't filling Jim with any confidence, either. I suspect he was thinking that he didn't want to lead everything if I crapped out.

"Fuck, man. I dunno," I stammered as I caved. "It just looks incredibly steep."

Well, shit. I just blew any momentum we might have had. My guts just spilled down my wool knickers, onto my boots. I drained the enthusiasm out of Jim like puncturing an air mattress.

"Yeah, I don't think we have a big enough rack to deal with it," Kanzler surmised, his eyes going over the menagerie of forbidding limestone cliffs above. I wasn't sure if he really meant it. "We might get up there and get all fucked up and not have enough gear to get down."

There is nothing more anguishing than watching your partner dragged out of his tree because you lost your moxie. Kanzler's apparent indifference made it easier on me, though, and I felt somewhat better.

"Let's get out of here. Let's get off this thing before it gets dark."

We bailed. As we coiled the ropes on the broad ledge we referred to from then on as the Escape Ledge, a sense of security returned.

"Hey, I've got an idea," Kanzler piped up. "Let's follow the ramp to the ridge and scramble to the summit."

"Hmm. Well, O.K. When was the last time you stood on the summit of Siyeh?'

"Oh, man. Probably with my father and brother, 15 or 16 years ago."

We stashed our gear at the end of the ledge and scrambled with renewed joy to the summit.

Out from the main wall a short distance and to one side, it was easier to see what the face held more three-dimensionally. The north face of Mount Siyeh was a thing of terrifying beauty.

We returned a few hours later and descended to Cracker Lake. I turned around for one last look.

"Well, Kanzler...I guess we'll have to climb this one in our dreams," I blurted. Indeed, I was relieved to be walking away. It felt strange to hear myself say such a thing. On the other hand, I just wanted to hear what it sounded like to admit failure out loud. I was curious how Kanzler would react to my defeatism.

"No doubt."

His ready remark sent me reeling emotionally. I really did not expect him—did not want him—to agree with me. I thought he would be upbeat. I expected the guy who insisted the first ascent of the Emperor Face go right up the middle would rant and rave about turning back and insist upon another charge. Kanzler sounded just as morose as I did. It helped me realize how unsettled, restless and uptight I was.

We turned and began shuffling along the cerulean lake, while fat, wingless crickets the size of the last phalanx of your thumb crawled and hopped off of the trail as we passed. I stopped and picked one up. It was a nice distraction. One day, someone was going to climb the north face of Mount Siyeh. I had just talked us out of it—with perfect weather, no less. I did not like being such a wimp. For a while, I didn't like myself.

We hiked out in silent rumination. Kanzler pushed the pace just shy of a canter. With every mile he went faster, trying to drop me. I could tell he was pissed. We clopped along with our mountain boots unlaced to reduce the pressure on our heels (already taped to minimize blisters).

Jim would pull away, 5-10-25 yards at a time. I was determined to keep pace. I had to throw in surges to catch up, stumbling on roots and rocks sticking up in the trail, nearly taking a header on one occasion. I might as well have been wearing steel-shanked snowshoes.

Kanzler never looked back.

The sun set behind Mount Allen and nightfall was not for another hour or so. We reached the Tank at the trailhead before dark. It was funny how our mental states changed so quickly.

Before I got the 54 Chevy unlocked, we were making plans for another attempt.

"It'll have to be after I finish guiding," Kanzler stated. "I can't afford to miss out on any more work. I've got to make those child support payments. Exum is done for the season on September 11th. It's a long dry spell, without a paycheck, until ski-patrolling starts."

"That's fine. I'll quit work at the plant about then, and there will be plenty of time before I have to be back for classes in Bozeman."

The north face of Mount Siyeh from the air. Photo by the author.

CHAPTER 14

The Directissima

On the Path of Mad Wolf, Part II

September 1977

We were on the north wall. Again! There was no denying the taunt of ambition from climbers in their 20s. During the month following the first attempt, Kanzler returned to the Tetons to guide for Exum Mountain Guides and I to the aluminum plant to help load pigs and ingots onto flatcars. We both had to finish our summer jobs. We were no trust-fund tigers. We were blue-collar climbers from Columbia Falls.

If distance makes the heart grow fonder, then time makes the heart grow bolder. We were eager for a rematch. We had to climb the big face, and we were convinced we could after we had chickened out the first time. I suppose if I had shown more confidence at the belay on the last pitch, Kanzler would have opted to go for it; but I had been freaked out. We both knew that when it came time to climb Siyeh, I was going to have to climb at Jim's level and share leading the hard pitches. In August of 1977, I just didn't feel I was there. By September, I had myself psyched. I imagined myself capable of leading any pitch on the big face.

This time, Jim Kanzler decided we would hike the approach and climb as high as we could on the same day, since we figured we were certain to spend at least one night on the upper face any way we cut it. On Gandalf's advice, during the first attempt, we had avoided the lower section. After minimal discussion, the lower 1,000 feet of cliffs, previously avoided, was added to the agenda. We would do it all, right up the middle...the directissima.

We third-classed through most of the lower face, roping up for just two pitches owing to our packs full of bivouac gear and two days of water. The vagrant wind brought clouds upon us and I grew giddy. Kanzler maintained his machismo and kept driving. I led the hard pitch below the diorite sill. We scrambled a ways; then, Jim took the traverse to the right, setting up the key pitch that led through the diorite band. The idea was to get above the high point of August and bivouac at dark.

Late in the afternoon, as we finished the traverse, black clouds began pouring over Mount Gould and the Garden Wall of the Continental Divide. We had trouble on our hands. We were soon to be ravaged. Instead of retreating, we opted to throw down our lot on a narrow ledge at the top of the diorite sill—even though a more comfortable one was a pitch higher. It was best to get set up and get inside the bivouac sack before the storm hit.

"Siyeh is a mountain," I had proposed as we planned a strategy for the first attempt with Professor Callis. "We should approach this as a mountain climb. We should wear mountain boots." Seemed simple. Jim didn't make any counterpoints. When the professor agreed to join us, he was content to climb in boots, too; but once Jim and I got into the thick of it, after Gandalf parted company, we were taken aback at how difficult the upper face appeared when actually confronting it. We calculated there would be over 20 pitches above us. There was one strategy Kanzler and I revisited before the second attempt: mountain boots versus EB rock shoes. We wanted to give ourselves every advantage we could to succeed. Jim started thinking smooth soles.

"We could climb a lot faster," he ascertained. Jim was the master of efficiency within the Dirty Sox Club. Far and away, he was the most progressive climber of the day. "If we climb in boots, we'll probably wind up aid-climbing in a bunch of places, and that takes up too much time. We'd probably have to bivouac—maybe more than once."

"Yeah, but what if we got caught in a storm—What if it snowed on us? We'd freeze our feet. It would be like wearing roller skates on the ledges," I countered. I was the conservative one— always wanting a place to retreat to, not wanting to commit until it was absolutely necessary. "Rock shoes on a face like Siyeh would make the climbing easier, alright; but if we were in a bad storm, we would be in serious trouble."

"We'd take approach shoes. We'd need them to get to the base and scramble off the top, anyway. We could retreat in those if we had to."

"In snow, they wouldn't be a whole lot better. Boots would keep our feet dry."

"True."

"Carrying approach shoes would take up too much room and add weight to the packs."

"Good point."

"We'd still have wet, freezing feet. If we are up there in September we could easily get a winter storm. If we were in EBs we'd be in trouble. We'll have enough trouble on our hands up there as it is."

"True. But if we climbed in rock shoes, we'd be faster and less likely to be caught in a storm."

"Okay, I agree. Speed is safety." I throttled back a little. "But if it storms up there in mid-September, it will likely be snow. Siyeh is a mountain; we should climb it like one."

I ran the play again. It was good for a few yards. I think Kanzler was ready for that line.

"Besides, stiff-soled boots edge well. Glacier limestone is just about all edging."

"That's true."

"George Lowe and Chris Jones climbed the north face of North Twin in boots."

"Yeah, but, there was a lot of hard ice climbing; they didn't have a choice."

"No; but they still had to climb very hard rock in boots. The cruxes were the rock pitches."

"That's a good point."

"Jeff Lowe and Mike Weiss did the east face of Mount Gould in boots. I'm pretty sure."

"Really?"

"Yeah, I think so."

I had to pat myself on the back for presenting my case so well to the logical and pragmatic Jim Kanzler. Jim was six years my senior, and my mentor, if not a big brother figure; prevailing in discussions was infrequent. Our discussion plugged in the variables, and it was about time to crunch the numbers. Each guy mulled over the other's points. If Kanzler had made one more point in favor of rock shoes, I was ready to accept the rock shoe argument. I trusted Kanzler's judgment.

Then I conjured up one more piece missing from the equation. It was another fear factor, different from the fear of dying violently. It was the fear of failure. Tie the fear of failure to a line and throw it out there and Kanzler would surely come and get it like a cutthroat trout to a salmon fly; like a grizzly bear to a winter kill. It was the seldom-discussed (but privately perceived) fear of failure in the climbing world that is an undeniable component of bold within the psyche of the alpine warrior. Kanzler's higher than average FF factor might well have been an acquisition of his Marine Corps father. I was getting to know my partner well.

"If we get up on the face and the weather turns marginal, wearing boots might be the difference between going up and retreating."

I presented the line with as little detectable pretense or telltale emotion as I could.

Kanzler paused for a moment, considering my last point. Ripples dissipated and the salmon fly sat on the water, silent, with no place to go while its wings dried before it could fly.

"That's a good point," Kanzler nodded. His eyes narrowed as he gazed out of the open door of the mobile home he rented in Big Sky, toward the rough-graded road cut through immature lodgepole pines.

"Yup...maybe we should wear boots."

We had enough room to sit on the ledge, leaning back with feet hanging over the edge, once we hastily excavated the debris on the ledge and anchored ourselves to three pitons.

We donned every stitch of clothing we carried, including down parkas and outer shells— cocoons for the night to come. We just made it.

Darkness was enhanced as Mount Siyeh became enveloped by a heavy shroud. Side-by-side we waited, feet inside rucksacks. The tied-off climbing rope tugged at my groin as I slowly oozed toward the edge. All that could be seen was the ledge suspended in a muffled, spaceless sea. Visibility was ten feet. The thin covering of the bivouac sack was pulled over our heads so we might hide from the gloom. There was no conversation as sleet cut through the void and spattered on the coated nylon envelope. Thoughts were confined to the realm within our hoods. It seemed as though our ambitions were sealed in an urn on a big ship, going down.

About 10 p.m. came the realization that it was no longer snowing. Jim checked outside and announced it was clearing. He could see stars— "Hurray!" but there were four inches of sloppy, wet snow plastered to the ledge, the ropes and hardware hanging from the pins. Everything was a sopping mess; but at least we could see the lights of Cardston, Alberta across the Canadian border to the north. I shook our gear off and Jim brewed a cup of tea with his Salewa bivvy stove from a pot full of slush. The temperature was rising, for we could hear the snow melting from the face as a faint chorus of millions of drips. Jim reckoned the damage had been done, however; in the morning, we would have to retreat.

I pretended to be optimistic, dancing by shifting my weight from one foot to the other on the narrow gangway in the middle of the night—an insignificant speck on a morbid, crumbling wall, wet with snow. "Tomorrow we can give the face a couple hours to dry and then start up," I rationalized. "It won't be so bad."

I knew it was over. There was no way we were going to continue in such conditions. I think I just wanted to say something out loud that sounded bold, something with courage and commitment even though I knew Kanzler would not let us do something so foolish.

"Kennedy, you are weird," the alpine ship captain said, calling my bluff. We drank the tea and then settled back into the bivvy sack.

I must have been asleep, because something awoke me. I was shivering. The wind had picked up, and I sensed that Jim was wide-awake, too.

Suddenly, a brilliant flash of light stabbed through the night. It illuminated the inside of the bivvy sack well enough that I could see the scar on the bridge of Jim's nose. I gulped in a deep breath, from which would come a string of startled expletives; but before I could release it, there followed an ear-splitting concussion from the thunder that jostled my innards. I thought we might bounce right off of the ledge.

"Holy fucking @#$%!" Kanzler beat me to it.

Over the next few minutes, the mountain was struck by lightning at least a dozen times. At first Jim figured we would be okay, 1,800 feet below the summit. A few moments later another simultaneous strike and explosion were followed by a barrage of rocks from above.

Kanzler lurched. He was hit.

"Oh shit, oh fuck, oh God! Kanzler are you okay?" I turned and grabbed him, fearing the worst. A fractured skull, a compound fractured femur; bone and blood, a dying friend and a desperate attempt to get him off of the face.

Kanzler writhed in pain and, through clenched teeth, grunted, "I'm alright; nothing is broken."

I helped him struggle out of the bivvy sack and onto his knees. The onslaught continued; we crouched as close to the wall behind us as we could, Kanzler rubbing his thigh. We were holding on to each other like a couple of Rhesus monkeys to the cloth mother in a Harry Harlow experiment. I expected that in the next moment, we might get torched and welded to the wall, or one of us would be dismembered or decapitated.

Gradually, the violence drifted off of the mountain and onto the Great Plains, eventually dissipating in the distance.

It got colder.

We returned to the bivouac sack. The rock that had struck Kanzler's leg had also made a small hole in the sack. Jim's injury was not serious; but our predicament was. The snow started again, and did not relent for the rest of the night.

When daylight finally came, we were horrified. The face looked like January. At one end of the ledge, the snow had drifted waist-deep. We carried no ice axes, no crampons and no gaitors—since the north face of Mount Siyeh was all rock.

We contemplated reversing what would then have been a descending traverse through the diorite with the exposed moves. Vertical cliffs were plastered with snow. It made my gut churn.

"Maybe we can rappel from here," Kanzler suggested. "It would even be a shortcut. It would cut out those two-and-a-half pitches of traversing."

"And get through the diorite and the steep cliff below it? I don't know...." I had always adhered to the principal that the known is always easier to deal with than the unknown. "I'm not sure the ropes will reach that far."

Kanzler rose to the occasion. "They might. Let's at least find out."

We packed our wet gear and I put Jim on belay. He moved to the end of our ledge and down ten exposed feet to a stance.

"I can get in a couple pins in here."

He belayed me down to his position. We tied the ropes together and threw the ends off with knots in the tails to prevent sliding off of the ends into oblivion. Kanzler attached his figure-eight descender and leaned out and jostled the ropes as he looked down. "Looks like they just make it." He disappeared over the edge. It was a very good call.

This brought us to the top of the lower-angled section we had third-classed the day before, which had been hairy enough. In such dicey conditions, we needed careful belays; but, to our dismay, there were no places to anchor. No cracks for nuts or pitons, no blocks to loop a runner around. —Not even a seam to force in a knife blade after pawing through the snow. Ahead were 500 feet of snow-covered ledges and 1,500 feet of exposure to the shrinking Siyeh Glacier below. So we picked our way down slowly, sometimes 300 feet apart, with the two nine- millimeter ropes tied end-to-end between us.

"Goddamnit, Kennedy, some of these wind-slabbed pockets could slide," Kanzler moaned. "If any of this pulls out, we are fucked."

"Oh, well, at least we wouldn't have to sit here and freeze to death," I muttered.

I went first, with a sliver of security, knowing Kanzler's weight might keep a slip from becoming a fall. If Kanzler should lose it, we both would be toast. Thank God we were wearing boots and not smooth soles! Gripped as we were with fear, it was essential to maintain a certain composure and alertness in detecting potential micro errors in judgment with every loose, snow-covered hold.

—∞○⚬◦⟨◉⟩◦⚬○∞—

It was after that epic night and retreat that I adopted a new nickname for Jim Kanzler: Mad Wolf. The name caught on for a few years. The Big Sky Ski Patrol and some of the Dirty Sox Club called Kanzler both Rat Hole and Mad Wolf for a period of time. A funny thing happened a short time later, when Big Sky Ski Resort expanded its terrain; a ski run was named Mad Wolf.

We rappelled to the Escape Ledge. Relieved, yet dejected, we decompressed at the moraine below the face. We took off our harnesses, loosened our wet boots and repacked our rucksacks for the trudge out.

I turned around and looked upward to where we had been. The wind had picked up and was licking across the face, causing streams of spindrift to pour downward, only to be swept away and vanish into thin air high above us in the wind. "I guess it's next year, then."

I wasn't sure if I really wanted another go at the big face. Jim's response would hold sway.

"Yeah, it's going to be a long winter."

He slung his rucksack onto his shoulders and cranked the waist belt tight.

"Come on, Kennedy, let's get outta here."

We sat through the night and the storm with our feet hanging over the edge, September 1977. Photo by Jim Kanzler.

Jim Kanzler rappels off of Mount Siyeh in the storm,
September 1977. Photo by the author.

CHAPTER 15

The Trestle

On the Path of Mad Wolf, Part III

Kanzler finished guiding for Exum Guide Service on September 10, 1978, and met me at the Monastery the next day. Late the following afternoon we headed for Glacier. The weather in Montana that autumn was unsettled. Cold fronts moved through western Montana every few days. In the valleys, there were showers and cool weather. It was often windy with periods of rain, and the mountains socked-in, and mixed with snow, making conditions incompatible with serious climbing on high rock faces. The weather would improve for a couple of days before the next front moved through. The season was changing rapidly. There was snow visible high on Mount Blackmore south of Bozeman as we drove through the Gallatin Valley. We complained constantly to each other about our circumstances, whining like a couple of tied-up dogs.

"There is no point in trying the face again until this weather pattern changes," Kanzler said. "It's the jet stream. We won't get reliable weather until it moves north again."

"Yeah. And when is that going to happen?"

"I don't know, man. Life is just strange."

I gnawed my fingernails as I tried to think of revisions in the itinerary. "Maybe we should just knock off a few rock climbs in Gallatin Canyon and wait for stable weather."

"That's an idea."

"I'll bet you could free the section of aid on the second pitch of Orange Crack on Gallatin Tower."

"Yeah? I climbed it with Leo a while back and thought it would go free. I have also had my eye on a crack across the river."

"Maybe we are heading in the wrong direction." That brought a period of silence while we each gave the idea some thought. I ripped a hangnail down the side of my left index finger. It would be sore for a week.

"Hell, we paid our dime," Kanzler decided. "We might as well head for

Mad Wolf. What else are we going to do with our lives?" We crossed the Madison and the Jefferson Rivers at Three Forks and turned north toward Helena and Glacier on U.S. Route 287. We rolled our pads and sleeping bags out in the grass at a rest area near Wolf Creek north of Helena. At 2 a.m. we were suddenly getting drenched.

"Oh shit, it's raining!" I barked.

"No it's not, the fucking sprinklers just came on! Grab your stuff and run!"

The sky was overcast with streaks of darker gray, like long strokes from a watercolor brush. There was a lenticular canopy capping the summit of Mount Merritt to the north. We knew what this meant. High winds aloft. For the third time, we began climbing the north face of Mount Siyeh at first light anyway and on into the day.

I took the rack of gear from Jim and led up onto the difficult pitch below the diorite sill once again, hoping in vain that the weather that day would improve. I was 40 feet out from the belay on double 9mm ropes. I felt twitchy. I drew a long, thin piton and held it in my mouth and stepped up onto small holds. The chromoly steel produced a weird electrical sensation in my fillings, but I just put up with it. I reached up and stabbed the pin into a horizontal crack as far as it would go. I reached for my hammer, struggling to get it out of a homemade leather holster that insisted on twisting and not letting go of the tool. "Someday I am going to buy a real one," I growled to myself. My left boot was on a hold at knee-level and started to bounce up and down involuntarily with a motion climbers call "sewing machine leg." If my foot shook off of its perch, I would take a very serious fall.

Above us, gusts of wind thundering against the rock face sounded like doors in a castle dungeon being slammed by a giant. I was nervous. My vibrating foot was pissing me off. I was climbing like shit.

I wiggled the pin back out and returned it to my mouth. I dropped the hammer, letting it hang from the lanyard and shoulder loop to free up my hands, and backed down to the bigger holds for a rest.

The summit rim was like a mysterious trestle thousands of feet above our heads. We clung to its structure as swift, laboring locomotives belted across. Seconds after each violent gust, the face around us chattered with rock fall as the wind blew scree off of the ledges. There was a surrealistic impression that the wall—the trestle—would collapse, but it was we who shuddered.

"I dunno, Kanzler, " I hollered, fiddling the hammer back into the holster. "I don't like it."

"I don't know what to tell you, Kennedy," Kanzler shouted back. "Fred (Beckey) would go down. George (Lowe) would go up. Whatever you think."

The situation had the look of an identity crisis. Who were we in the big game of north faces? The chessboard was a yawning plane of complexities, and even the pawns were so tall! What seemed most puzzling was that all the pieces were black. We really didn't know where we stood. Among men. Among knights.

I shifted my feet gingerly on fractured footholds to continue to rest, leaning the lead pack against the steep sedimentary rock. I was shackled by hesitation. I wondered what Jerry Kanzler or Clare Pogreba or Ray Martin would have done. Would they have kept going? Was I as compelled as they were?

I had been carrying the torch for eight years by then. Turning the calendar back eight years from when the Mount Cleveland Five had disappeared, Jerry Kanzler and Jim Anderson would have been ten years old again. Jerry had already scrambled up dozens of peaks by then, with his dad and big brother. In a way, Jim had become my big brother. A lot of life happens between fourth grade and college; and from there, it just keeps happening. It goes by quickly...like a falling stone.

I thought I saw a raven stalled in the wind high above us, a short distance from the wall, silhouetted against the darkening sky. He rapidly grew larger and for a moment, I thought it might be a golden eagle diving toward us. Then I suddenly realized it was no bird at all, but a rock the size of a coffee table, wheeling and turning—heading right towards us.

"ROCK, ROCK, ROCK, get down Kanzler, get DOWN, get DOWN!" Whee-oo- whee-oo-WHEE-oo. It made a sick twisting, swishing sound as it approached and flew past us at terminal velocity. It had never touched the wall above us, and exploded on a ledge just below and a little to the right of Jim—perhaps 30 feet away.

"Bigger than a bullet, faster than a train," Kanzler declared as I downclimbed back to him. For the third time, being far short of our destination, we cashed in our tickets for a one-way token home.

I looked up and saw the rock coming toward us near this
point. September 1978. Photo by Jim Kanzler.

CHAPTER 16

No Piss Stops

We rappelled and downclimbed off of the face, and hiked back to the trailhead at the Many Glacier Hotel in downcast mode but happy to be alive. Jim opened the bonnet of the VW bug and we changed out of wool knickers into jeans and running shoes in the parking lot when people weren't looking our direction. I peeled off my good-luck gold acrylic turtleneck, which had not been washed in a month. I changed into a souvenir t-shirt from the Beartooth Run, an eight-mile uphill road race I ran in the previous July outside of Red Lodge after I had adopted the run-more-miles-but slower approach to fitness. It smelled only half as acrid as the turtleneck. I put a wool ski sweater over the top of it, which helped cover the smell. We walked into the hotel bar.

The mid-September tourist population had thinned out; most of the people who remained were older, distinguished-looking types. The wind and spatters of rain had brought the majority indoors to roam the spacious Swiss Chalet, built of huge cedar logs and lacquered several layers deep.

"I'll meet you in the bar," Kanzler announced, pulling a razor out of his pocket, "I'm gonna shave." He turned toward the restroom.

"You might as well take a bath in the sink, too," I quipped. "I can smell you from here."

"Yeah, well... I don't mind smelling bad, I just wanna look good," Kanzler said, grinning out of one corner of his mouth, revealing his chipped tooth. It had been a week since either of us had bathed; yet Kanzler's thick hair looked full-bodied— except for the telltale crease from his helmet. My oily, straight hair made me look like a wet dog with a scruffy beard. There was no point in trying to comb it. It would just look greasier.

When Kanzler found me in the lounge, I was slouched on a couch with a couple of drafts from the bar. A pair of Lucky Lagers was tucked into a coat pocket to stretch the overpriced beer of the Many Glacier Hotel lounge. In another week, the lodge would be closed for the season.

Kanzler and I stuck out like sore thumbs. We drew curious looks from well-heeled travelers patronizing the lounge, but welcomed the disapproving glances and whispered comments to each other like "they're just a bunch of re res". We were, after all, crazy, and proud of it. No one else had any idea what we had just been through on the north face of Mount Siyeh earlier that day, nor did they sense the battle that raged within us.

"Let's head for the Tetons," Kanzler suggested. "We can do something there. The weather is probably okay. I don't think the jet stream dips that far south right now. Peter Lev should still be there, and we can stay on Guide's Hill. It's going to be a while before Mad Wolf is ready again—if we get another chance. We might as well stay on a roll."

We drank up and bolted south. Two days later, we approached the west face of the Grand Teton. Kanzler wanted to do the whole enchilada from Cascade Canyon. We bivouacked at the base of the Black Ice Couloir and front-pointed over to the West Face route early the next morning. The climb went smoothly and we arrived at Jenny Lake at the base of the mountain before dark.

The next morning, we slept in— sort of. I awoke to the expected stiff muscles and the lethargy. Kanzler already had the stove going on the picnic table. After a second cup of Cafe Vienna, Rat Hole announced he was going to the Jenny Lake Ranger Station to get the latest on the weather. When he returned, I was back on the ground, snoozing partway inside my bag.

"Goddamnit, Kennedy. We might as well go now," he said, gathering items on the picnic table. His size 8E feet poured over the edges of his sandals. He had nasty callouses on his big toes, which angled inward— probably from tight EBs and approach sneakers. His feet were so calloused they looked like he could make it to the Lower Saddle of the Grand barefoot, like Bilbo or Frodo. "Any window we get is going to be a short one," he informed me. "If we wait here for the next one to develop, it will be over with by the time we get on Siyeh. We might as well be moving while the weather is bad and be there at the beginning of the next window."

"You mean, leave right now?"

"Yup."

"Geez Louise." I rolled over in my bag on top of a bivvy sack. I just wanted to sleep a little bit longer. Jim could sense my lack of enthusiasm, sensitive guy that he was.

"OK, let's have one more cup of coffee." He began pumping the filthy Optimus stove with great purpose. I could sense his thought process. The sooner he could get the pressure up in the tank, the sooner he could get the brew going and the sooner we could be on our way. We drank up and bolted north.

As the Rat Hole mobile sputtered down the long grade just above Mammoth Hot Springs in Yellowstone Park, Kanzler pulled into a short, unmarked loop. Above the pavement were 30-foot-high limestone boulders leaning over the narrow pull out.

"I've always wanted to climb on these," Kanzler said, "what do you think?"

"Well, what about getting up to Glacier? We won't make it by dark if we don't press on." I was still feeling a little miffed.

"Come on, Kennedy, we're here. We could use a little pump to stay in shape. I've had my eye on these boulders for years, and this is a good time to jump on them. Come on, let's do it."

"Oh-h, okay-ay..."

"It won't matter if we make Glacier today or not. We wouldn't hike into the base of the face tonight, anyway." Kanzler scrambled out of the bug and reached back behind the seat for a rope. I followed reluctantly. Kanzler had just started using a commercial harness. I still used three wraps of seatbelt webbing, tied around my waist, and a pair of leg lops sewn with heavy thread by a cobbler in Bozeman to fit my legs which stayed in place with parachute cord laced through the wide belt loop of my wool knickers or whatever I happened to be climbing in. We squeezed into EBs. Jim placed a sling around a tree above, and we "shredded" our hands in an abrasive, overhanging crack.

"I hope the rangers don't see us," I said nervously, "this is probably illegal."

"I don't know. It's not illegal to climb in the Tetons or Glacier."

Our discussion was interrupted when another car pulled up and two attractive females about Kanzler's age got out. Jim wasted no time striking up a conversation. They were both nurses from Rhode Island, on a late season tour of Yellowstone. Kanzler turned on the charm while I settled for practical matters, asking their advice about painful in-grown toenails, and I learned the trick of filing a V-notch into the end of the nail.

The two ladies began the short walk around the roadside exhibit. Kanzler quickly formulated a plan. I pledged loyalty to my future wife in Billings and reminded the distracted son of a Marine Corps Captain of our mission. It was not without some difficulty that I managed to drag Kanzler back into the kraut-can and down the road.

"I still think we could have scored with them," he said as we rolled through Gardiner. He was a little peeved. I just kept my gaze out of the window, grateful that we were back on the road.

We reentered Montana and continued along the Yellowstone River and the Absaroka Mountains. As we reached Livingston on the big bend in the Yellowstone River and Interstate 90, the wind caused the bug to rock and lurch. The sky was even darker than it had been since we left Montana a few days before, and a few raindrops spattered the windshield.

"This ain't good. Let's just head to Billings," Kanzler suggested. "I can visit Chadwick and you can spend a night with Diane. We will still be closer to Glacier than we were in the Tetons. Chadwick has a T.V. and we can keep a close eye on the weather forecast and take off again when we see good weather coming."

"Might as well." Spending the night with my sweetheart sure beat sleeping in a rest area or under a bridge.

The next morning, at 7:30 a.m., Kanzler called me at Diane's apartment. It was not a particularly good time to be bothered.

"The weather is supposed to improve. Let's go."

The bug screamed down the winding, two-lane Highway 89. The speedometer needle indicated we had just reached 57 m.p.h. The vessel could not have gone one knot faster if the floorboard had been six inches lower. She was crammed with nearly everything either one of us owned: climbing gear and another case of Lucky Lagers in bottles.

We shared the same ambition. We wanted to climb the biggest unclimbed faces in Glacier National Park, by their easiest and safest lines, under good conditions. The idea was to control what variables we could while accepting those we could not.

The same formula was applied to driving. We chose to drink beer as we traveled. It was part of our game and who we were at the time. It helped keep reality a little fuzzy. Fuzzy helped oil our feathers and let the pall of the Mount Cleveland tragedy roll off of our backs.

"You know what? I'm just about sick of people back in Columbia Falls ragging on you, and I guess me, sometimes, about Mount Cleveland and climbing," I complained to Kanzler as the beer grew warmer and we belched like a couple of toads during the rut.

"Yeah, well, what do they say?"

"I heard two women, my mother's age, talking in line at the Columbia Falls grocery store just after we climbed Cleveland and one said something like, 'For God's sake, wasn't it enough for the older Kanzler boy to have climbed the north face of Mount Cleveland once and for all?'"

"Yeah, well, what did the other lady say?"

"Oh, I don't know. I just walked away before they recognized me. But I did hear one of my mother's friends say at a card party my mom was hosting something like; 'He did it for his brother and his father.' Then someone went, 'Oh, Betty, to think Terry was with him?'"

"So what did your mom say?"

"Oh, I don't know, something like, 'Oh-h, I kno-ow.'"

"'Those boys were too inexperienced.'"

"'They should have listened to the rangers. (Blah, blah, blah).'"

"Yeah, well, whatever," Kanzler replied. *Whatever* was becoming a popular catch phrase about then. When Jim used it, it meant the same thing as nothing matters. For Jim, I began to realize, nothing matters was a safe-zone to which he could retreat, when he needed to; whatever sounded less philosophical to others and blew people off with less impact.

People of my parents' generation were not cheering us on. No one was saying, "Hey, go get the north face of Cleveland, you guys!" After the ascent of the north face of Cleveland, no one was saying, "Hey, you guys are hot! You should go get that big face on Mount Siyeh!"

Other Dirty Sox Club regulars did not have much interest in Glacier Park. Leo, McCarty and Dr. Z had never set eyes on the north faces of Siyeh or Cleveland. Jim Emerson and I had talked about doing the east face of Gould, even after Jeff Lowe and Mike Weiss snagged it in 1974. Then Emerson had a second heart attack and was forced to quit climbing for six years until he received the first of a series of pacemakers.

The only real hometown fan Jim and I had, who really knew what we were up to, and understood the gravity of our endeavors, was Dan. "Go kick ass!" he told me when we crossed paths at home that summer. "Leave nothing on the table." He was the only one encouraging Kanzler and me. Indeed, Jim Kanzler and I were on a two-man frenzy, paddling a leaky canoe up the backwater of American alpinism.

On this mad dash back to Glacier to catch an elusive window in the weather, we made one additional rule: We would only stop for gas. Kanzler had calculated that if we drove straight through [from Billings] and averaged 55 m.p.h. we could arrive at Many Glacier, organize, approach the six miles to the base of the north face of Mt. Siyeh and bivvy before night fall. This could happen only if we made one stop in Helena for gas. Thus, we were to take no rest stops, no stops to change drivers and no stops to piss.

We stayed loose by doing Kanzler-style yoga in our seats and rolling down the windows periodically, hanging our heads out like blue heelers from a farm truck to let the rush of air sharpen our alertness, which tended to lose its edge mile after mile, beer after beer.

I took over for one stretch. The switch was made on a long, straight stretch between Wilsall and Ringling on a "short cut" to Helena. Jim let up on the gas and I bridged to the ceiling with my feet on the dash, my head in the space behind the seats that had been converted to cargo bay. Jim slid under me, maintaining one eye on the road, one hand on the wheel and the other on his beer.

Initially, we started relieving ourselves into paper cups and it was my job to pour the warm liquid out the window, but the aerodynamics were so poor above 50 m.p.h. that I left telltale streaks along the right side of the land-craft module.

"If we get stopped by cops, Kennedy, we're going to have a hard time convincing them that we haven't been drinking with piss stains all over the car. We've got to start pissing back into the bottles."

"Well, it's only on the passenger's side," I rationalized, "if we get stopped, they won't see it."

"Oh, they would find it. We can't take any chances." Of course, we had the case of beer under a parka in the back where it was both hidden and accessible. "Start refilling the bottles," he ordered.

"You gotta be kidding. This is going to make a huge mess."

"You won't have any problem."

"Right, and you can just snake it out the window."

"No more pissing out the window." We laughed.

The new challenge was entertaining, and we mastered several techniques before we reached Glacier. Kanzler had remarkable accuracy in the cockpit (no pun intended). I've never seen anyone who could maintain as steady a foot on the gas pedal, arch his back, and refill a beer bottle doing 50 like Kanzler could. As co-pilot, I took over steering during the procedure.

We rambled along the upper Smith River, then cut west and dropped into Deep Creek, on to Townsend and into Helena. Jim gassed up while I discarded the recapped bottles, which saved weight and theoretically improved fuel efficiency for the remaining six-hour drive to the trailhead at Many Glacier.

We roared through Wolf Creek Canyon, perked by the high cliffs along the highway, but they appeared too rotten to waste time on. We sped along the Missouri, hell-bent on the first ascent of the north face of Mount Siyeh.

As we approached Great Falls, Kanzler had an idea.

"Hey, you know what we ought to do, Kennedy? We oughta stop by the Great Falls International Airport and speak to the meteorologist to get a detailed weather forecast."

"Great idea, Kanzler."

"Yeah, we gotta find out if this weather is going to last. We sure as hell don't want to get suckered again and get hammered like we did last year. That really sucked."

"Yeah. And they could give us information like freezing levels and how strong the winds might be above 9,000 feet, that sort of thing."

"Okay, we'll do it," he said, bottoming the accelerator, "I'll try to push a little harder to make up for the time we will lose there."

We exited I-15 and the Rat Hole mobile swung around the curves of the airport thoroughfare. So much for one stop. Weather information trumped everything. "Why don't you talk to the meteorologist and I'll start racking some hardware?" Jim schemed. He was a master of efficiency when he wanted to be. He might not answer a letter for months or return a phone call for weeks, or he could show up two hours late for a day's climbing in Gallatin Canyon; but by God, when the man was on a roll and on task, he never wasted a second.

"I'll drop you off here," Kanzler said as we pulled up to the departures entrance. "I'll be back in 20 minutes. I'm gonna check the oil, too. I'll be over there," he indicated an open field not far from the airport. We weren't the type of guys who would pay for parking. "Be sure to find out if we can count on three days."

"Right."

I returned about a half-hour later. The Rat Hole mobile was parked along the curb, but Rat Hole was nowhere to be seen. I finally located him at a nearby phone booth. He was already in his wool knickers.

"Who you talking to?"

He covered the receiver, "This chick I know in Great Falls," he whispered.

"Come on, Kanzler, we gotta get going. Let's get on the road!"

"Okay, okay, I'll meet you at the wagon in a minute."

Half an hour later, we were rolling again. "Well, how does it look?" Kanzler queried.

"Not great," I replied. "The guy said it would be good for another 36 hours, but that another front should come through."

"Rain?"

"Most likely in the mountains."

"How about for now?"

"He thought no chance of rain today, 20 percent tomorrow, 40 percent by Thursday."

"Pfff."

"I know. 20 percent means rain in the mountains. I don't want to be up on that wall again when it rains...or snows! On the other hand, if we don't get a chance soon, the season will be over. What do you think?"

"I think we pay our dime, we take our chances," Kanzler blurted. "What the fuck. We're in motion. Let's go do it!"

"Well, I suppose. I mean we might as well go up there and have a look. Things could change. We might have to sit it out a while. Better to be near Glacier and nail this thing when the window opens than to be too far away and spend the good weather driving," I said, quoting Kanzler nearly verbatim from the day before.

"Yup" he croaked. It was little things like that that brought us back into harmony after a few bars of dissonance in our fugue in D minor. We sputtered on. A minute of silence passed; then Kanzler spoke. "Sitting around on your thumbs gets old too. You know what I think? I think if we get to Glacier and the weather doesn't look good, and the forecast being shitty—I think we ought to come back to Great Falls. You know that lady I was talking to on the phone? I spent a couple of sweet nights with her in Big Sky last winter. And you know what, Kennedy? She's got a foxy roommate. I'll bet I could set you up. It would great. You could learn some tricks. It would be a great time. What do you think?"

"Sure, Kanzler," I quipped. It irritated me when he went on like this. Jim had a reputation as a driven climber throughout the 70s, and he had charisma. I think a lot of single women in their 20s and 30s fell for him. Jim's climbing had none of the conquistador attitude he seemed to have in romantic relationships. In spite of this distinction, Jim had prowess with both climbing and women. Rumor had it that Hal had been a womanizer on business trips.

We arrived at the trailhead in Many Glacier at about five in the afternoon. There were two hours of daylight at our disposal. The east slope of the Rockies was cold and windy, typical of Many Glacier. Cirrus clouds streamed in the sky overhead. The east face of Mount Gould was in shadows. The steep, iconic triangular east face and the long arête that borders the face on the left and drops even further into the valley were indistinguishable. This would be the fourth time Jim and I would be on the north face of Mount Siyeh.

"I don't like these clouds, " I said.

"I don't, either. Mare's tails." Kanzler grunted.

We knew exactly what we wanted to take on the 3,500-foot-high face. Every piton, every sling, every ounce of food, which pairs of socks, how many squares of toilet paper. We had rehearsed it many times. It didn't take long to pack our rucksacks. We stuffed our feet into loosely fastened steel-shanked mountain boots.

"Got everything? Harness, helmet, hammer, holster, hardware? Boots, bivvy sack, water bottles?" Kanzler took a couple of big chugs of water from an orange juice container and tossed it back into the VW, shouldering his battered rucksack. His mustache cascaded over his upper lip and swept over the corners of his mouth. A bead of water clung to it for a moment, then rolled onto his turtleneck.

"I guess so. You got both fuel canisters?"

"Yup."

I let out a deep sigh. It was very tough pushing off from the security of the pale blue kraut can. We didn't need to be doing this—we simply felt as though we had to do it. No one, not even other climbers, would have thought any less of us if we didn't go back to the north face of Mount Siyeh. Three tough battles would have been enough. Neither one of us was pointed enough to discuss why we felt we had to keep battling Mount Siyeh. It may have been that our reasons were quite different. Deep down, the answers had to exist; but getting to them would be a task for someone else, like a psychiatrist or Jesus or somebody. I shouldered my pack and clicked the waist and sternum buckles. Kanzler took a quick look around for anything that may have been left behind, and locked the bug. "The key is under the back bumper, on the driver's side."

"That's the first place I'd look," I scoffed.

"That's why I put it there. Come on, let's go, Kennedy. Tell the world as we know it goodbye."

We tromped off to test destiny. Again.

The aspens and cottonwoods along Josephine Lake and the windswept, glacier-carved valley that led east to the Blackfeet Indian Reservation had turned yellow, but the winds had not yet plucked leaves from branches. There was a heaviness in the air. Summer was over. I could feel the lower angle of the sun. Shadows were longer and seemed darker. Evening would be brief. The mountains were lurking. We were walking into grizzly bear country and soon it would be dark. The longing for summer to stay a little longer made me melancholy. It added to the fatalistic outlook and the macabre aura that already hovered over us.

I followed Kanzler to the end of the parking lot. I felt tethered to the humpy car by a bungee cord. It became harder to move forward. We entered the trail to Cracker Lake, which lies at the foot of Mount Siyeh's north face. We walked half a mile or so when I stopped. I could not take another step.

"I don't like it, Kanzler, " I announced, unsnapping the buckles of my pack and dropping it to the ground.

"Yeah, I know," he replied, pretending not to notice my impulsiveness.

"Let's take a look at this. 20 percent chance of rain tomorrow, right?"

"Yeah."

"That's not a great day in the mountains. Then what? 40 percent chance. That definitely is bad news. Look at the sky. Harbingers. Strong wind. It must be 25 miles an hour. Any Boy Scout can tell you this means a change in weather. It's one thing to go up on that son of a bitch and end up getting hammered. That's bad luck. We've done that. It's another thing to go in there knowing you are going to get hammered. That's just stupid."

"Yeah, you're right," Kanzler agreed, without any emotion or need for discussion.

"We've got to follow our own instincts here. I say we get outta here."

"I agree." It never ceased to amaze me how easily Jim could change his mind. One moment he was an erupting volcano or a charging rhinoceros, headed for a climb, and the next moment he was willing to go back at the drop of a handkerchief, like it was nothing.

Most people have mood swings. Kanzler had a built-in channel changer.

"Well, what do ya wanna do? We could go back to Great Falls."

"Great Falls? Great Falls! There ain't nothing to climb in Great Falls," I exclaimed. God, Kanzler had a one-track mind. He was about the most unpredictable man I'd ever known. He could derail a logical plan and come up with something that was even more logical or he could insist upon an idea that exceeded the boundaries of rational thought altogether.

"Oh, there might be something to climb into there," he chided me as that shit-eating grin spread across his face, causing about five days of unshaven stubble to protrude from his chin like porcupine quills. I knew exactly what he had in mind. There was no question that Kanzler had promiscuous tendencies, of which I was, of course, exceedingly jealous.

"I already have a girlfriend and one is all I can handle," I lied. I just didn't think it was a good time to go chasing sirens on a distant island.

"Yeah, okay. Let's just get outta here." We re-shouldered our rucksacks and started to hike back to the trailhead.

"You know what I'd like to do? I'd like to lay around in sunshine and climb on some warm granite. I know! Let's go to the Humbugs! Let's go climb the Wedge."

"Hmm. We could climb something on the west face. There are three discontinuous parallel cracks that could be linked with the West Face route that haven't been done. We could go do that."

"Or a thin crack to the right of the West Face route that leans left and makes a right-angle dogleg to the right and merges into the Southwest Face route."

"Oh-h, I know the one. That would be really hard."

"Yeah. I bet you could do it, Kanzler."

The weight of Mount Siyeh slid off of my back. I felt unencumbered, warm and comfortable, like putting on clothes right out of the drier. "We could go fire up the stove, crash under the Windy Creek Bridge, and head out early in the morning."

"Why don't we leave right now?"

"Right now?"

"Sure, why not? It's what, two, two-and-a-half hours over Logan Pass to Columbia Falls, and what, another four or five to Butte."

"Shit, Kanzler, it would be after midnight before we got there."

"So?"

"So, we could gas up in Columbia Falls. Mom and Dad would be happy to feed us."

It was about 12:15 a.m. when we rolled up to the gate at the barbed wire fence that used to have a horse skull on it. I had taken over the driving somewhere between Missoula and Drummond on Interstate 90. We had emerged from under the weather system dominating the northwest corner of the state. Kanzler was asleep in the passenger's seat, a stuff-sack with a wool sweater in it tucked under his head, against the window.

"Hey, Kanzler! Wake up. We're here."

"Hmm? What's that? Where are we?"

"It's the new stretch of the interstate highway I-15. They finished it. They filled in the whole ravine. We drove over the ravine and took the interstate exit at Divide, then backtracked on the old road. But this is it, this is the gate."

"I don't get it." Kanzler had crashed hard. He was still a little disoriented.

"Remember last spring they were filling in the ravine below the road leading into the cabin?"

"Yeah."

"And those huge culverts lined up out in the sagebrush?

"Yeah."

"Well, it's done. This is the road. Up there, the thing that looks like a dam is the interstate. See the guardrails? And that dark spot that looks like a hole in the side must be the culvert. The road must lead through it."

"Holy God. That is disgusting."

"Humbug trips will never be the same, Kanzler. Maybe you should drive?"

"No. Go ahead, I'll get the gate." He piled out and held the posts and barbed wire to the side. The Beetle leaned and lurched up the rain-washed ruts through the sagebrush. The full moon was at the zenith, and the landscape was bathed in its light. We were far enough south to be out of the unsettled weather.

We approached the huge landfill breaching the ravine, barring the way. The black hole on the right side, part way up, looked like the protruding mouth of a giant goldfish with 50 feet of displaced earth above that seemed like 500 feet in the moonlight. The guardrail of the southbound lanes rimmed the top.

"Turn off the headlights, Kennedy," Kanzler ordered as we pulled up the ramp to the level of the entrance. He was wide-awake now. "We don't want to disturb anything or anyone that might be inside. It might be bad Karma."

The lights were extinguished and I turned off the engine as the VW rolled up to the oppressive breach.

We sat there silently for a few moments.

"You can barely see the far end of the tunnel," Kanzler said in a coarse whisper, staring into the blackness.

"I don't think it would be wise to go in there without first doing a ceremony or a sacrifice or something."

"Right. We'd better get out the stove and brew up. Let's be careful not to make a lot of noise."

We exited from the lunar module. Jim lifted the bonnet and rummaged for the stove. Soon we were sipping Red Zinger and Roastaroma in the moonlight.

"I think we ought to walk through it first, before we drive through, " I suggested. "It may be an opportunity to experience total darkness."

"Great idea. It would be neat to walk in there and not be able to see your hand in front of your face." Kanzler walked over to a clump of sagebrush and snapped off a small branch with its pungent leaves. "I don't think we ought to go in there without smoking some weed first."

He reached the sage into the blue flame of Coleman fuel and it caught fire reluctantly, popping and emitting small bursts of light. We each took a whiff of the smoke and "smudged" the opening of the cave, like the ritual of some Native American tribes, to cleanse a space of unwanted spirits. We walked into the corrugated tomb with only the sound of shifting gravel under our feet.

"I guess we are at the center," I whispered.

"Let's just stand here for five minutes and not say anything."

"Okay."

We entertained ourselves all night with such mischief as climbing the bolt heads on the inside of the culvert with the aid of the VW's headlights; then turning the bug around and amplifying the music of the Butte's all-night rock station by orienting the door speakers of the car into the culvert. We blew up a fuel canister of the bivouac stove in a small campfire we built in the middle of the culvert, the blast of which was disappointing. We pretended to be Bigfoot with Kanzler giving me a camel ride on his back and me wearing a small pack and draping a poncho over us and jogging across the four lanes of the interstate ahead of oncoming vehicles. We knelt behind the guardrails, positioning our chins on the posts, making ghoulish faces at the infrequent motorists passing by in the wee hours.

"Hey Terry, it's starting to get light, " Kanzler said, looking to the eastern horizon. "I think we ought to go climbing."

We managed to get the car to the cabin area and slept for a few hours in the grass close to where the cabin once stood. We climbed a new variation of the West Face route on the Wedge by combining the three parallel cracks as the first pitch. The next day we climbed an elegant crack of moderate difficulty on an obscure rock I have been unable to find again since. The following spring, Jim led a dogleg crack on the southwest face, which was the hardest pitch on the Wedge up to that time.

Jim Kanzler, the author and Jim's VW Bug,
circa 1978. Kennedy collection.

Jim Kanzler on the West Face route of the Grand Teton,
September 1978. Photo by the author.

CHAPTER 17

The Consolation

October 1978

Jim and I returned to Columbia Falls after the Humbugs and helped Dad shingle the roof of the Kennedy home as October rolled around. We still held out hope for stable weather and another shot at the north face of Siyeh that year.

R. Glenn wasn't too keen on the idea. He was a little suspicious that Jim Kanzler had an element of reckless abandon, just like Hal, but Dad always gave me the freedom to choose my own destiny, without insistence or overbearing criticism.

We finished the roof and the skies remained gloomy. Jim and I loaded our gear and headed back into Glacier for one last assessment.

The Rat Hole mobile chirped around the curves of Going-to-the-Sun Highway along McDonald Creek, on the west side of Glacier. The Beetle roared like a lion as Kanzler downshifted on the steepening grade up to the hairpin turn at "The Loop" and continued toward Logan Pass. My fingers drummed on the dash and my knees swayed back and forth. Kanzler and I could see the evidence, and we knew the verdict. The snow level maintained a presence at 8,000 feet, no doubt to stay. We could not justify going back up on the big face. A part of me was actually glad. I felt the tension slough off my back with the decision to postpone another attempt until the next year.

We pulled into the empty parking lot at Logan Pass. We looked around, a bit taken aback by the silence and emptiness. It was like being a janitor after a packed auditorium had vacated. The painted parking stalls on the pavement resembled auditorium seats; we could still hear the ovation, like wind in aspens, and feel the final chord resonating. At the same time, we were overwhelmed by the shattering silence that had been left in its place.

The wind blew hard at the pass. The air mass moving from west to east accelerated as it squeezed through the low points of the Continental

Divide. Was it a cold front moving through, or a big low pressure in the Great Plains somewhere?

I looked over at Jim. He was checking out the nearby buttress of Pollock Mountain, habitually looking for routes. The wind blew his shoulder-length hair like flags. The guy needed a shave.

The two of us were performers, not janitors. Here was our chance to take to the stage. For all we knew, there was not another single, solitary person in the mountains at that time.

Kanzler finally spoke, "I still think we ought to do a climb."

"I know." I reached for the binoculars behind my seat and scanned Mount Reynold's north face. I traced the route up the center of the crown Kanzler had soloed two years before to warm up for Mount Cleveland. "We need to do a consolation or something."

"I can't stand it," he went on. " I'm going crazy." There was my cue. I waited for him to deliver his next lines.

"Kennedy, we just can't leave Glacier, we must do something!"

"It doesn't look all that bad," I said, in reference to the weather. "Maybe we could do a climb nearby. A short approach— not too committing, but technically interesting."

The former Boy Scout and Teton mountain guide seemed not to hear my suggestion. "I've been doing this for so long. My whole life has been spent in anticipation of climbing mountains," he went on, lamenting with an increasing impetus to his words. He was staring at the left front tire, which was missing a hubcap. "As a young boy, I came here with my father and brother and climbed these very mountains."

I brought the binoculars down and flipped the strap around my neck. Shakespeare surely would have coveted an actor like Jim Kanzler. He was a natural: Sturdy frame, chiseled looks, deep voice, melancholy and theatrical. He was magnificent.

His lyric continued, climaxing with a crescendo and the gestures of a buffoon. "I'm going crazy, I'm losing it, Kennedy. I must climb. Gotta go climbing." Then he began doing Gene Wilder in Young Frankenstein. "Upward, Kennedy, climb, climb, climb!" He clutched his breast skillfully and sagged to his knees. "Help, I'm having it, I'm having it."

I moved in with the supporting role. I did my best Marty Feldman. "Your medication, Master, where is it?" I rummaged around in the glove box. "Here, here, Master. Hold on."

He groped about, clutching his breast with one hand, reaching out with the other, gasping, "Medication, medication time!" He took the elixir and a deep breath. At last he was able to relax and a more normal insanity was restored.

We narrowed our choices down to three: The direct north face of Mount Reynolds (adding the lower face to the Harrison-Sanders Route, which ascends the headwall after traversing onto the face on an easy ramp); the imposing northwest face of Citadel (Dusty Star) Mountain; or a direct line up the east face of Little Chief Mountain. Kanzler wasn't interested in repeating Reynolds. He wanted to do something new. Citadel looked like a hideous bushwhack to the base. Little Chief became the logical choice, especially because I had been on it a couple of years prior and had retreated in wet conditions.

We packed quickly, for it was late in the afternoon. I organized a rack of hardware and Jim the food. I noticed it didn't take him long to figure out the menu.

"Not much in that stuff sack," I observed.

"We're going light, Kennedy. I'm convinced the lighter you go, the lighter you are, the lighter you are, the faster you climb. Faster is better. It's safer."

Seemed logical to me. I looked in the stuff sack. Eight granola bars and two cubes of margarine.

"Shi-i-sh!"

"Callis and I took margarine with us on the Emperor Face because it was more calories by weight than anything else."

I didn't immediately respond, trying to let the idea of all that greasy, oily fat soak in. Kanzler could see my upper lip begin to curl and my nostrils flare involuntarily. He swiftly beat me to the punch: "The granola bars will make the margarine more palatable."

"Gee, are you sure we aren't a little heavy on the granola?" I was stupefied. My face continued to curl up like a piece of dried birch bark. I could feel a cube of margarine bubbling in my stomach like a Yellowstone Park mud pot.

"I think we ought to bring the bivvy stove, " he continued, trying to distract me and ignoring my question. "It might be nice to have a cup of tea or hot chocolate tonight, and in the morning."

I certainly agreed with that. "How about a cup-of-soup or a freeze-dried dinner tonight?" I could visualize hot soup keeping the margarine melted and the gut able to keep working on the greasy muck.

"Only if you carry it," Kanzler responded. I snatched up a couple of envelopes of chicken noodle and, when Kanzler wasn't looking, threw some dried apricots, nuts and a chocolate bar into the stuff sack, which was going in his pack.

We gave our boots a quick shot of snow seal, then sought our vestments to suit the next set of our act: soiled wool knickers, pitted-out polyester turtlenecks and scaly wool socks. A true north face alpinist never washes his climbing trousseau before the end of the season. We threw our loaded packs behind the seats, piled into the bug, and sped off to St. Mary to book the show with the mountaineering nemesis, District Ranger Bob Frauson. We were relieved to discover the barrel-chested magistrate had just stepped out of the ranger station so we scratched out our plan on a piece of paper and left it wedged in the door.

The only flat spot near the face was down low, in a thicket of alders. Jim unstuffed our sleeping bags while I searched for water. The alders were dense—thicker than hair on a dog's back. I'd gone 100 yards or so and found the first streambed dry. I became aware how dark and spooky it was becoming.

A reoccurring nightmare flashed across my mind. I was in Glacier National Park on a windy, moonless night, bushwhacking through the alders, alone, miles from anywhere. At any moment a grizzly bear would rear up like the Devil and there would be the ripping of claws, the slashing of teeth, and the crunching of...

I thrashed my way back to Kanzler as fast as I could.

We set out again, together, this time with our weight-saving one headlamp. At the dry streambed, I said, "Must be another hundred yards to the next one; I thought I could hear water earlier." The wind was picking up and rustling the remaining dry, dead leaves clinging to the branches.

"I know how you feel," Kanzler said sympathetically, "it sure is tense."

"I don't like it, man. There could be a g-bear anywhere in here and we wouldn't have a chance."

"It's too weird," Kanzler concurred, "let's get outta here. We can find water in the morning." So we spent the night chewing granola bars very slowly, to mix them with saliva. The margarine turned out to be helpful in lubricating the granola bars. There would be no tea.

Up at first light, we were off quickly, not having much to prepare for breakfast. There would be no hot chocolate. Certainly, there would be water at the snow apron at the base of the face.

The apron was a gray mass of hard, compact residual ice, containing rock fragments that had accumulated in the snow since Little Chief had become a mountain. What had been trickles of water were now icicles. We had left the stove back with the bivouac gear, 800 feet below, and we wouldn't burn daylight going back for it.

If water couldn't be found at the base, it certainly was not to be found higher on the face. The first ascent of the direct east face was dry. Very, very dry.

Chouinard north wall hammer picks shattered the brittle ice, and crampon points scratched the surface of the apron. The sky was as gray as the ice and windy, not especially inviting to start a serious climb, but we had to get up something. We roped up 300 feet higher in a shallow gully. Jim did the first lead and then we swung pitches up the face, tending right as difficulties increased. I led what turned out to be the crux pitch. I was on steep terrain in fingerless gloves, sifting through snow to feel for holds. I placed pitons as often as I could find placements and then came nose-to-nose with a headwall I knew I could not free climb in boots and cold conditions.

After some hesitation, I traversed right on my belly on a narrow ledge under a bulge—until the ledge became so narrow that I had to lower myself off of the lip and hand-traverse along the edge for eight or ten feet. I ran the rope out and belayed Jim from a questionable knife blade piton. The higher we climbed, the greater the snow factor became. We gained the lower 1,000 feet of cliffs with careful climbing and route finding.

The weather began to squall, but we were determined to reach the top. Rappelling down was out of the question. The hour grew late and it was cold enough to wear all our clothes, even while moving. We certainly didn't want to spend the night out so we coiled the rope and continued through the easier terrain of the upper face third-class to reach the summit.

We headed down the southeast ridge of Little Chief Mountain that connects with Mahtotopa Mountain. My lips and fingertips were cracked and sore. Our only concern became water. It had been 24 hours since we had a drink and we were tiring rapidly with dehydration.

We found our oasis in the middle of the western slope of Mahtotopa, where a six-foot band of rock protruded through the scree. In spite of ice around the edges, there was enough water in which to shower. We drank frigid water until we both had splitting frontal headaches, then made our way down the rest of the slope and ledges with a single fading headlamp, moving as fast as we could to keep warm after filling ourselves with the icy water. We flopped down on our ground cloth, fixed a brew of hot tea and settled into the comfort of sleeping bags.

Sometime later, while Kanzler was in a deep sleep and I drifted in and out of consciousness, the disturbance of scree from the slope above us penetrated my senses. A charge of electricity rifled through my spine—red alert! I lay paralyzed, eyes wide open, straining to hear, heart beating in triplets.

The wind was erratic and I strained hard to listen. I wasn't sure what, if anything, I'd heard. Moments passed. Then, yes. There it was again. More scree rattled down the slope. I turned to alert Kanzler.

"Did you hear that?"

"Huh, what's going on?"

"I heard something out there, could be a bear."

"What? A bear? Are you sure?"

"Listen in the talus above us." (Moments pass.)

"I don't hear anything."

"Shhhh..." (Pause.)

"I don't..."

"Shhhh...there! Hear that?"

"Yeah."

"Oh, shit!"

"Be quiet. I want to hear it again," Kanzler insisted. He sat up, letting the sleeping bag drop off of his shoulders and pulled his balaclava back to listen better. "Could be the wind. Or just rocks rolling downhill. You know, these mountains are always changing. How do you think the scree got here in the first place?"

"Jim, that slope has a lot of vegetation on it. It's stable."

"True. It could be mountain goats."

"If it were goats, we'd hear something more, like animals walking around, or perhaps more than one. It sounds like a bear above us, digging roots."

"You might be right. It does sound like that."

"Listen. There it is again."

"Okay, let's start getting rid of the food and start making some noise."

"Good idea." I reached into my pack and pulled out a remaining half of a granola bar and what was left of my margarine, which was smashed flat and oozing out of its foil wrapper. Fortunately, it was contained in a Ziplock bag. I heaved it as far into the alders as I could. Kanzler searched the perimeter with the dim headlamp. We sat quietly to listen.

"What's that fish smell?" Jim asked after a minute or so.

"Oh, no! The Desitin!" I exclaimed in utter dismay. "Oh shit!" I had been using Desitin earlier that night, once Jim had fallen asleep, to treat my split fingertips and cracked lips.

"God, that stuff is 80 percent cod liver oil, Kennedy. Get rid of it!" he ordered.

"Oh man, it's all over my hands."

"Wipe 'em off. Hurry!"

I took off my gloves and wiped my hands with them as thoroughly as I could. Then I rolled them up into a ball and launched them into the alders, but the odor still lingered, just as strong as before. I was living bear bait, in the middle of an alder thicket, in the middle of a windy, moonless night, deep in grizzly country in Glacier National Park, miles from anywhere. Our paranoia grew as we listened into the night. We didn't hear it again for a while. Then on the other side of us—a rustle.

"Over there!"

"Shhhh, listen."

"Sounds like a squirrel or a rat or something."

"I'm not so sure, start making noise, Kanzler!"

"Okay! Bob! Help! Over here!"

"Kanzler, what the...?"

"There is only one guy who can save us now...it's Bob Frauson," Kanzler declared, standing on his Ensolite pad in his wool knickers and knicker socks. "Help! Help, over here!" he shouted with cupped hands in the direction of St. Mary. "Baaawb!"

"Very funny," I said, thinking at first that Kanzler was just mocking me. It was like him. I could see he was serious or somewhere between serious and the lunatic fringe. Then I understood. It didn't matter. Kanzler was right. We needed to make noise, any noise. I fell in with Jim.

"Bawb! Ba-awb! Help! Up here! A bear! A big one!" Shouting at the top of our lungs, mixed with the hysterical laughter of another Dirty Sox Club outing gone daffy, we bore forth into the night, calling for help from Glacier's top bear gunner and body recovery ranger.

Our wee-hour-of-the-night antics were not without some historical origin. In September of 1976, just days after Jim, Steve Jackson and I succeeded on the north face of Mount Cleveland, a 22-year-old woman car camping with four other University of Montana female students was fatally mauled by two grizzly bears and dragged into the woods. Two men guarded the body as armed rangers investigated nearby. The bears returned to their kill and chased the men up trees. Frauson heard the commotion and raced to the scene. As he arrived, one bear was reaching up the tree, about to pull one of the men down. The former Tenth Mountain Division soldier quickly shouldered his shotgun and killed the bear with one slug. Frauson's partner killed the second bear minutes later.

"These bears are park bears," Jim gasped between breaths of shouting and laughter. "They also know if they take just one bite out of us, that Frauson and the other rangers will come after them with guns. So keep hollering."

The frivolity wore off and the previous day's effort reminded us of sleep. "It's no use," I conceded, "Bob is ten miles from here, no doubt asleep in a nice warm bed, in Park Service housing with reinforced windows and doors to protect himself and his family from grizzly bears. There is no way he can hear us up here."

"You're right, Kennedy. If I'm going to get eaten by a grizzly bear, I am at least going to get some sleep first." With that, he was snoring in a matter of a few minutes. The torture of the darkness reminded me that it was no laughing matter. I pulled my sleeping bag over my head. What else could I do? A bear was going to do damn well as it pleased. Eventually, I drifted into sound repose.

The next thing I knew, I was being shaken roughly! My heart stopped completely. For all I knew, my entrails were about to be torn from me like a string of link sausage. My eyes popped open as I bent my legs up to fend off the attack. I was staring into a grizzly face!

It was Kanzler. He sure needed a shave!

"Hey Kennedy, it's getting light. Let's get the hell out of here." We stuffed everything into our packs as fast as we could and bolted.

An hour-and-a-half later, the Beetle was rolling through St. Mary as we left Glacier Park, chirping like a songbird. Gaining elevation, the panorama seemed to rise with us. Little Chief and Going-to-the-Sun Mountains stood vigil over deep, cold St. Mary Lake, which was speckled in white caps, the climax of the mountain-plain threshold. There also stood Mount Siyeh, north of Going-to-the-Sun and further within the range. A small break in the racing cloud cover caused a patch of sun to briefly illuminate the gentle south flank of the mountain— ending like a knife cut, defining the side that casts the shadow. A parting wink, no doubt. The desire to boldly venture into that shadow and pass through the contrasts would persist.

The clouds were starting to lower again. The summits would soon disappear into the veil of deep, dark moods. Snow was surely coming. It is funny how snow and whiteness come from such gloom and darkness. I'd always thought that to live was to risk death; perhaps also, to die was to risk rebirth.

We just knew the alpine season was over. It would be another cycle of seasons before the chance to go for the north face of Siyeh would come again. The mountains that held our imaginations sank beneath the timbered ridge and we headed for the monotony of life with the masses. A familiar cadence returned. My fingers were drumming again. There was little fulfillment in being patient.

"Next year, man."

"Next year, for sure." I pressed my lips together and shook my head, staring out of the window, at nothing.

Halfway to Browning, before the aspen and alpine fir yielded to the prairie, Kanzler suddenly pulled into a wide place in the road.

"What's up?"

"Fifty push-ups."

"Fifty push-ups?"

"And 50 sit-ups. We can use my pad."

"...forty-eight, forty-nine, fifty. Okay," I said, breathing hard. "Twenty-five pull-ups on that tree over there."

"We won't get twenty-five on that branch. It's not level."

"Okay, in two sets, then."

"Alright."

"I'll go first.

Little Chief Mountain, Glacier National Park. The Kanzler-Kennedy East Face Route ascends the central buttress and stays in the center of the face to the summit. GNP stock photo 34528.

Chapter 18

Life in the Monastery

Dejection did not last long.

Retreating from the north face of Mount Siyeh in the 1977 storm made life simpler. We now had our destiny defined and became steeled for the Path of Mad Wolf.

Bob Frauson, as quoted in the *Great Falls Tribune* a few years later, stated, "Kanzler and Kennedy had created a monster for themselves when they didn't make the north face [of Siyeh] the first time; they were on their own up there, and they knew it." We had our canines sunk into the beast.

I finished a degree in elementary education at the end of winter quarter in March of 1978. Student teaching had been a rude awakening. I loved one-on-one instruction; but the realization that I did not possess the organizational aptitude to juggle five or six subjects multiplied by 35 kids hit me across the face like the tail of a 14-pound Flathead River bull trout. I was unable to spread myself that thin. I could also see that my greatest stress factor with teaching was going to be social interaction with the rest of the school staff. I reached the conclusion that teaching school was just like going to school all over again. It didn't matter if I was a pupil or a teacher; I took my place on the fringe.

I returned from the classroom to my cluttered apartment on the north side of Bozeman every night exhausted and discouraged. I had waded through four and a half years of college only to realize I would not survive. There was only one thing I could do: climb.

About the time I finished my degree Jim Kanzler called.

"Why don't you move to Red Lodge with me after I wrap up the ski season at Big Sky?" he suggested. "We can climb all spring and get into awesome shape."

"Great idea! We could go back to Yosemite and do a route on El Cap. That would get us into shape."

"I think we should hang out in Red Lodge and go shred the East Rosebud." Kanzler had already hatched a plan. "There are tons of things to do in the lower East Rosebud. It's in the rain shadow of the higher

[Beartooth] mountains, and the best rock formations face south. We could start climbing right away. We could go try the Bear's Face or the First Wall in May."

Whoa. Kanzler was talking big, unclimbed stuff. Untouched walls. I tried to shift my mindset away from Yosemite.

Jim continued: "We can go finish Siyeh and then," he dropped the big one on me in the same sentence, "...climb the Emperor Face."

"Emperor Face! The Emperor Face?"

"Sure, we could do it."

"What?"

"Come on, Kennedy, we could do it."

All of a sudden, spring, Yosemite and the eastern canyons of the Beartooth Mountains were shoved to the back of the table.

"I don't know, man. I'm not sure I'm up for that. What about Callis? I mean the Emperor Face is yours and Gandalf's gig."

"I'm not so sure Pat wants to go back."

"What? Why not?" I had not imagined myself as part of the monumental undertaking of making the first ascent of the Emperor (north) Face on Mount Robson, the highest peak in the Canadian Rockies. It was the biggest trophy to be taken in North America at the time. I saw Jim Kanzler and Pat Callis as figures out there on the frontier, leading the way. I somehow needed them as role models to emulate.

"I don't know," Kanzler continued, "I think Callis has had enough of it. C'mon, you could do it, Kennedy. It won't be any harder than Siyeh. It's longer, but most of it is ice. Pitch for pitch, ice is easier."

"Yeah. Well, what about the rock bands? That's the real problem. Look what happened to you and Pat."

"We just didn't take enough rock gear. If you and I took the same rock rack we did on Siyeh—plus ice screws—we could get up the bastard. You and I could do it."

The best alpine climbers in the U.S. and Canada were vying to be the first to climb the Emperor Face. I thought of myself as still fledging and not quite yet in the Big League. I needed to rise to Jim Kanzler's level by swinging leads on our hardest climbs. I was the kind of guy who could only focus on one project at a time; I wanted to finish Mad Wolf and see what doors opened after that.

"What about all the avalanches and rock fall?" I felt myself leaning as I spoke.

"We wouldn't go unless conditions were bomber."

Conditions were key. Life and death on the Emperor Face was a judgment call and a crapshoot. The danger was more obvious than getting hoodwinked by a shallow snowpack on Mount Cleveland's west face in early winter.

"Just think about it," Kanzler went on. "We'll go back to Siyeh this September. If we do that, we won't be able to do the Emperor Face this year, anyway. September will be too late. We need to try Robson in the summer—maybe even early summer, to have more snow covering the unstable rock. We'd probably be looking at next year...if someone else doesn't knock it off first. I can't go to Robson this summer. I've got to guide. I need the money. By June, I will be behind on child support payments. Let's just do big stuff close to home this spring."

I packed my belongings into the old Tank and left Bozeman for Red Lodge and the eastern edge of the Beartooth Mountains in a mixture of rain and sleet. It was snowing before I pulled into the sleepy town, which was inhabited mostly by the aging offspring of underground coal miners.

Red Lodge is considered one of the ten snowiest towns in the United States: two miles long, four blocks wide, with a population of roughly 1,700 in 1978. It was built along a creek bottom like many late-19th-century Montana mining towns and was known more for its coal than its gold. Rock Creek rushes over granite boulders through the east side of town. An old mountain man known as Liver Eatin' Johnson was the first marshal.

Jim and Lindalee Kanzler bought a house in Red Lodge for $12,000 in 1972. Jamie was three, then. Jim had linked up with the entrepreneurial Chad Chadwick from Billings, the most prolific technical climber of the Beartooths in the 1960s and 1970s. Chad was a self-taught climber who experimented with short lengths of hemp rope at age 12. Chad and Jim began a small climbing instruction and guide service business in Red Lodge in 1972 called Mountain Craft (named after a book of mountaineering techniques written by renowned British mountaineer of the day, Geoffrey Winthrop Young, copyright 1920). Hal Kanzler had a copy of *Mountain Craft* and taught himself and his partners basic rope work from it, just before more modern techniques emerged through the influences of the Pacific Northwest and Yosemite in the 1960s. Alas, Mountain Craft, Inc. was active for only three years.

By 1976, Lindalee and Jim were divorced. Many years later, long after she had remarried, Lindalee told me, " I left Jim because I knew if we stayed together I would never have anything. I knew living with Jim would be living from paycheck to paycheck for the rest of my life. I wanted to have more than that for Jamie."

When the 1977-78 Big Sky ski season ended in April, Jim moved back to an empty house in Red Lodge. I followed a week later.

"Welcome to the monastery," Kanzler greeted me as he opened the door to the small, two-story house. "Welcome to the house of lonely, wayward climbers. Please leave your mountain boots on the porch." Kanzler pressed his hands together and bowed, Buddhist style.

The little house became known as the Monastery by mountain culture people of Montana and the Tetons. Monks (climbers) with few possessions would come and go for the next few years. Two small-town mountain climbers as hard-driven, self-pressured and psychologically labile as we were would have been hard to find.

It rained or snowed almost every day that April. That much was not unexpected in the Beartooths in spring. Kanzler maintained a scaled-back manic presence and a positive outlook most of the time. My mood swings tended to reflect his, sometimes in synch, sometimes not. Surely, the weather would break at some point; we needed to be ready to launch ourselves at the First Wall, which was located several miles up the trail, beyond the road in the East Rosebud.

A man, who was at least in his 80s, lived across the street from the Monastery. He appeared outside every day in a pair of old leather shoes and work clothes, rain or sleet. He made laps traversing back and forth on the narrow sidewalk from his front door to the gate that cordoned off his tiny backyard, a distance that could not have been more than 30 feet each way. He had a strange form of locomotion.

"What is he doing?" I asked Jim the first time I saw the exhibition.

"Running."

"Running?" He looked more like an ancient primate chasing a wounded armadillo through a tar pit.

"Yeah, he runs every day. He was doing it when Lindalee and Jamie were here. I call him 'the jogger.'"

"Jeez, it looks painful. It looks like his hips and knees are killing him. He can't even stand up straight."

"I know, man; he just does it anyway."

The Jogger seemed determined to maintain a semblance of physical conditioning, in spite of his advanced age and joints that barely moved. He was at it within 30 seconds of the same time each day. How far he ran, we did not know. No doubt, he had a prescribed number of laps he covered, but we never counted them. It was simply too painful to watch. Besides, the battle he waged was a personal affair.

"I wonder if we will be like that when we are old men?" I asked. If Jim responded, I don't recall his answer.

Our morning routine consisted of taking turns walking to the local bakery at 7 a.m. and purchasing a loaf of French bread, just out of the oven. The nutritionally devoid white flour mixture was a staple; neither one of us could afford better.

One morning, we sat on the porch drinking instant coffee and eating handfuls of bread smeared with margarine. The temperature was in the 30s and raining, but we sat outside anyway, just to keep ourselves conditioned to the elements and maintain an edge of toughness.

"Do you smell something dead?" Kanzler asked.

"Maybe. Yeah, I think so..."

"I wonder if a cat or something died under the porch."

"I think it would smell much worse if there was a dead cat under there. Maybe it's a mouse or something." There was not much space under the old wooden deck. We checked around the porch and the yard. No dead creatures. The breakfast routine on the porch persisted for several days, the same question always dominating the conversation.

It was my turn again to head for bread. When I returned, Kanzler was kneeling on the porch. The chairs had been moved to one side, and several boards had been pried off of the deck. One hand was covering his nose and the other balancing a half-liquefied cat on the end of a shovel. It looked more like a rainbow trout than a cat.

"Oh my God, that's disgusting, Kanzler!" I stepped back from the stench and turned my head away. "What are you going to do with it?"

That familiar, sardonic, asymmetrical smirk emerged onto his face. He turned around and advanced the shovel toward me. "I think we should slice the bread and make sandwiches out of the leftovers."

Oh-h, shit! I took a couple of scissor-steps to the left and suffered a sudden bout of (w)hirling disease.

I managed a trip to Yosemite with two other guys I had never climbed with before. The weather was not much better in Yosemite than in Montana. I returned to the Monastery a couple of weeks later without having climbed much of anything.

On a dry but windy day, about a week after I'd returned, Jim and I climbed the Tower of Innocence in the lower East Rosebud. Jim and Chad Chadwick had established the first route (eight pitches) on the prominent feature in November of 1973—the day Richard Nixon declared himself innocent of the Watergate scandal. The next break in the weather was five days later, and we pioneered a four or five-pitch route up the middle of the southeast face of a wide formation in the middle of the group I referred to as "The Boiler."

April showers brought May showers, and worse. The poles of psychological temperament reversed. We began spending most of our time moping around the Monastery, complaining. Periods of frenzy became fewer. Some days we continued with our fingertip pull-ups above the doorjambs. We managed to put together a big wall rack and enough food for six days. Kanzler read several novels, cover-to-cover. I daydreamed while listening to Pink Floyd, trying to draw inspiration.

"Maybe we should do some running to stay in shape," I suggested. "With all this shitty weather, we're going to lose our fitness, not getting much climbing done."

We laced up our sneakers and charged out of the door, pushing a chest-splitting pace for 12 blocks south on Haggin Avenue, along the rows of small houses, stride for stride, side by side. My legs felt like leftover oatmeal. Jim had the "inside lane," as the street turned right to avoid Rock Creek. He gained a step on me. I drew to his left shoulder again.

Kanzler may have thought we were just on a training run; but our little serendipitous workout was an all-out race, as far as I was concerned. My goal was to outrun my ropemate. Pride and manliness were at stake. If Jim Kanzler took the hardest leads when the climbing got tough, then I needed to show my mentor that I had prowess in other areas of endeavor that suggested a certain level of capability, especially if I was to one day find myself on the Emperor Face.

We headed into a second right turn, completing a hairpin onto Platt Avenue, and headed north, back in the direction of the Monastery. I could see an opportunity unfolding, and I made my move.

I stayed off of Kanzler's left shoulder, a stride back. When he cut into the second right turn, he predictably swung wide. I was already wide, and cut behind Kanzler into the turn, throwing in a quick surge as we rounded. When we came out of the turn, we had traded positions, with me on the inside and Kanzler two strides behind. Encouraged, I tried to break contact with another surge. Jim's footfall receded. He had to know we were racing by then.

My legs adapted to the torrid pace. They felt strong, perhaps from the climbing and the approaches with full rucksacks, but my sternum felt like a busted zipper. I was slowing down. Kanzler reeled me in over the next two blocks and tucked in behind me.

"Okay man, you want to draft me? Go ahead. But you ain't gonna go by me," I announced telepathically.

As we came to the next intersection, a car approached from the right. We were going to have to slow down or even stop to let it pass in front of us. I didn't want Kanzler to pull even, so I quickly turned right to avoid the car all together. This brought us back to Haggin, and we continued up the long straightaway back to the finish line. We had a mile and a half behind us, another half-mile to go. We were both sucking for air. I could hear Kanzler behind me, wheezing.

"Faw-Kennedy," he gasped when I glanced back.

I've got him, I thought. Steady now. Keep it goin'. Try to relax without slowing down.

In an effort to win a letter sweater in high school, I went out for track as a freshman. I had hopes of being a miler; the two-mile race seemed too darned long. I had watched Jim Ryan and the short, feisty Steve Prefontaine with long, blonde hair and a mustache on The Wide World of Sports on television. Ryan blowing the mile field away down the stretch and Prefontaine running away from the pack in the three-mile were inspiring moments to witness. I wanted to be like them, but my arches were intolerably painful when I ran.

A podiatrist made me wear a rigid pair of orthotics (custom shoe inserts). The forward edge dug into the balls of my feet. I couldn't run with or without them. I gave up on the idea of being a track runner and went fishing instead.

As I led Kanzler back down Haggin Avenue, I imagined I was Steve Prefontaine in the 5,000, heading into the bell lap, the race down to two guys on the Hayward Field track in Eugene, Oregon. The dueling runners passed in front of the covered bleachers full of revved-up fans, clapping and stomping in unison. Clang-clang-clang-clang. The crowd rose to its feet and the rhythm was lost to screaming and wild cheering as Pre surged, George Young on his heels.

Two blocks to go. The crowd was still on its feet, and the cheering grew louder! With no additional effort, I found that I could run harder.

Pre surged, and a gap widened between the two men gunning for the top spot on the Olympic team. Pre stole a quick glance back as he pulled away and pandemonium erupted from the stands.

I looked back. Kanzler had dropped off. The suffering felt good. The last block was tougher than the 25th chin up of the fourth set.

The broken gate in front of the Monastery marked the end of 12 minutes of self-inflicted torture. I lunged forward, arms raised as if breaking an imaginary tape; then bent forward, elbows on knees, sides heaving. Kanzler stumbled in behind me and dropped to the sparse, soggy grass on his hands and knees. He crawled a couple of steps and began barking at spiders.

"Great workout, huh?" I puffed when I started to get my wind back.

"Wonderful," Kanzler replied, wiping his mouth with the back of his hand, "run 'til ya puke. It doesn't get much better than this."

On May 30, 1975, just a few days after witnessing the historic first one-day ascent of the Nose of El Cap with a trove of other climbers in El Cap meadow, Jim Kanzler and I ate ice cream cones near Yosemite Lodge. We had finished a day of crack climbing. Jim pointed out Billy Westbay, one of the famous trio, as he sauntered by. We were talking with some other climbers when one of them said, "Did you hear the news? Steve Prefontaine was killed in a car accident." My heart dropped like a rock into a paper bag, and I slinked off into the oaks to grieve the death of another hero.

We climbed Shepherd Mountain, above East Rosebud Lake, in snow flurries. May 31, 1978, was a blustery day, too cold to rock climb. We headed up Rock Creek below the Beartooth Plateau. Jim soloed the established June Couloir, while I climbed the next couloir to the (climber's) right, where I had to suck it up by climbing the final 20 feet of vertical cornice above the couloir by jamming in the shafts of my ice tools, because the snow was too soft for the picks. We appropriately called the route "May 31st Couloir".

"Here we go..." Kanzler announced, reading the newspaper one morning in the first week of June, after two months at the Monastery. "We've got two pretty good days before the next front. Let's haul gear up to the base of the First Wall and cache it. We'll let the front pass through and, if the weather behind it is stable, we'll have a go at it."

So we humped ropes and virtually all of our rock gear, hammocks, food and water jugs up an unstable gully to the cavernous undercut of the First Wall. The roof out of the gully was so long that when Brian Leo had led the first pitch during an attempt in 1972, the haul rope was 40 feet from the wall and the belay was only 40 feet off of the ground. That was as far as anyone had gotten. The remaining 1,500 feet would only be a little overhanging. Kanzler and I left our gear in a safe place and returned to the Monastery.

Two days later, we woke up to a foot of snow in Red Lodge. It dumped four feet in the mountains.

"This is fucked," Kanzler declared. It took two weeks for the lower East Rosebud to dry. Only our rock shoes and harnesses remained in our possession. The rest of our gear was marooned up high— in severe avalanche terrain. We drove to Billings and climbed the sandstone rims above the city with Chadwick and Jim Williams.

A few days later, Kanzler got a call from Chad. "He wants me to go run a foot race with him this weekend," Jim reported. "It's going to rain anyway, and we won't be able to climb."

"Foot race? What kind of foot race? On a track?"

"I don't think so. It's on roadways, I believe."

"How long?"

"Ten kilometers."

"How far is that?"

"I don't know, about six miles or so."

"Six miles! Are you crazy? Don't you have to qualify or something?"

"I guess not. Chadwick says anybody can run in it." That was the darnedest thing I'd ever heard.

"The run we did last week was bad enough," I cautioned Jim. "That was a little over two miles. Six miles will fuckin'-near kill ya, Kanzler."

Jim headed to Billings and ran the race. When he came back to the Monastery, I asked, "Well, how was it?"

"It fuckin'-near killed me. Chadwick told me we're doin' it all wrong. You're supposed to run more miles, but not so fast." That seemed nuts to me. Wasn't the idea to run fast?

The snow eventually melted in Red Lodge. The May accumulation would stay into the summer on the 12,000-footers in Beartooths. The top of the First Wall was only 9,000 feet in elevation, and the steep wall would be free of snow much sooner.

"The approach gully should be pretty stable by now," Kanzler declared. "I think we ought to wait until Thursday and then go get on it. We're supposed to get another front tomorrow. Then it looks like the weather will get better. Hopefully this one won't be as bad."

The next night, it snowed another foot in Red Lodge. It snowed another four feet in the mountains.

"This is really fucked!" Rat Hole conceded, as we stood on the porch, assessing the damage. We pooled our money together, lamenting not having gone to Yosemite together in May.

Depression set in like the cloud mass enshrouding the mountains. It was the end of what might have been a romantic time in my life, when carefree abandon trumped the mundane responsibilities life had in store for me, in the years to come. All I wanted was to play in the outfield with Jim Kanzler and bat ahead of him in the lineup.

Huge, wet avalanches bulldozed berms of snow higher than the leafing aspens in every gully of the Lower East Rosebud. We couldn't go anywhere. Kanzler would leave for the Tetons in another week.

We could hear the rush of Rock Creek at high water a block away from the Monastery, even with the windows closed. At night, as I laid upstairs under my sleeping bag on an old mattress in a tiny bedroom and Kanzler crashed in a rickety old bed frame downstairs, we could hear the boulders rolling and clunking along the bottom of the torrent. A deep heaviness set in; we would never have that much time together again.

I slogged to the bakery. It was still snowing heavily.

To hell with bread, I thought the next morning. I returned to the Monastery with a fifth of cheap whiskey, instead. Mad Wolf and I got shit-faced. Just plain ol' doo-doo brained. I passed out on my sleeping bag later that morning. Kanzler shoveled the sidewalk along the street in front of the Monastery to work it off. He was a good neighbor.

Two significant events happened that summer, while Kanzler guided with Exum and I continued to live at the Monastery.

Toward the end of July, Kanzler called me. "The Emperor Face has been done."

"Huh?"

"Two guys from Colorado did it."

"The Emperor Face?"

"Yeah. Mugs Stump and Jim Logan—they climbed it." There was a moment of dead-air silence as the news sunk in. Kanzler tried to be matter-of-fact without emotion, but I heard the disappointment in his voice.

I tried to sound disappointed, too, mostly because I knew this had been Jim's dream and he had put so much time and sacrifice into it with

Pat Callis. In a way, it had cost Jim his marriage to Lindalee, and signaled the end of another era, not just for Kanzler and Callis but for other teams of climbers as well. There was no sense in rushing up to the Canadian Rockies to make the second ascent. A door had closed.

Truth be known, I was more relieved than disappointed when Stump and Logan took the prize. Now Kanzler and I would only have one focus. After Siyeh, we could find another goal.

By the middle of the summer, I got engaged to my first lover; unwillingly at first, but I eventually gave in. "Caved in," as Kanzler described it.

The following March (1979), after living for nearly a year in the Monastery, I married Diane Dugan, a women I met in the Elementary Education program in 1976, just after Kanzler, Jackson and I got off of the north face of Mount Cleveland. My stories of the climb wowed her, and I seized the opportunity to make myself available for a romance from my otherwise deficient repertoire of dating skills. She took the bait; but I was the one that got hooked.

Diane finished her teaching degree before me and took a job in a rural grade school, about 80 miles northeast from Red Lodge. During the summer of 1978, while Kanzler guided in the Tetons, Diane spent most of the summer at the Monastery. We hiked in the backcountry in the Beartooth Mountains and scrambled a few easy peaks. I filled out teaching applications, but only landed an assistant teaching job in Billings the following November, just after Kanzler and I had made a trip to Devil's Tower in the northeast corner of Wyoming and climbed several routes.

The wedding was held just outside of Red Lodge along the Beartooth Highway on March 7, 1979. Many of the Dirty Sox Club climbers came and lit up the Monastery with a bachelor party while I attended the wedding rehearsal the night before.

When that was over, the bride went to her quarters and I to the Monastery. Dougal McCarty called for the groom to do a little *space truckin'* on back roads in his bile-green Volkswagen bug the night before the big day. Jim Emerson and Mark "Kal" Kalitowski hunkered in the back seat as co-pilot and navigator, should it become necessary for the front seat crew to be replaced.

If Dougal McCarty wasn't best known for his climbing or ski patrolling at Bridger Bowl and Red Lodge Mountain (a.k.a. Rock Dodge), he was heralded in wide circles as the guy who could take charge of the fun and merriment. Key words: take charge. McCarty was the Bacchus of the Dirty Sox Club.

We reentered Red Lodge and the almost-empty main street from the south, just before midnight. Up to that point, we had been keeping a lid on it; (when not swigging out of it) keeping the hatch battened down, you might say, and behaving in a responsible manner, as far as we were concerned. The only other car coming in our direction had to be at least nine blocks away.

In the middle of town, another ski patroller Dougal knew came out of a tavern and crossed the street in front of us. The unsuspecting downhiller looked up and recognized McCarty's dented Kraut can at the same moment Dougal recognized him. Feigning terror at the sight of McCarty's approach, he sprinted for the sidewalk. McCarty took the cue and feigned chasing him onto the sidewalk. The pedestrian darted for the recessed doorway of the bakery and Dougal kept the charade going by driving the entire machine onto the sidewalk, making tracks in a skiff of snow.

I started freaking out.

"For God's sake, McCarty, I'm getting married tomorrow! Don't get me throw-ed in jail!"

"It's O.K., man, I know that guy, He's a Rock Dodge 'troller.'" Dougal rolled his window down and exchanged a greeting with his colleague, cranking the Cessna and huffing the goose call. "Let's get out of here, McCarty!" I barked. In one momentary lapse of reason, felony, DUI and worse loomed large. We were exposed and vulnerable, not more than the length of a loaf of French bread from the bakery window. If the police were to round a corner, we would be... (Never mind, you get the idea.) Emerson and Kalitowski fidgeted, wishing they could dematerialize. I was ready to run for it. McCarty could fend for himself.

"McCarty! Get this piece of hot, steaming dog doo-doo off this fornicating sidewalk—right fornicating now!"

"Okay, okay." McCarty eased the green hump back on to the street and we continued in stunned silence. The other car had closed to within four blocks. Iceberg, mate, straight ahead. Two blocks. "Turn, damn it, turn, turn, turn!" One block.

"Holy shit! Is that a light bar on top of that car, or is it just a ski rack?"

"Relax, Kennedy. It's just a ski ra—oh, shit! It's a cop!"

"Duh! Ya think?" The pair of headlights a mile down the main street had belonged to the one cop on duty in good ol' Red Lodge.

"Turn right, Dougal!" I ordered, "maybe he didn't see us on the sidewalk." I tried to take control of the situation, but I was totally freaked.

Dougal turned onto East 12th Street, his eyes riveted to the rearview mirror. The rest of us craned our necks to the stern. Ten seconds of intense anticipation passed as fate awaited us. My mother and father, brother and sister, aunt and uncle, and all of the bride's party slept in motels not far away. They had no idea of the monkey business the groom had indulged in and what bag of monkey wrenches were hurling toward the wedding party as it slept.

The black and white sedan with the light bar appeared at the intersection and turned our way.

"Oh shit! I am done for!" I could feel my face grow hot.

McCarty pulled over and came to a stop.

I was not so worried about what the cops would do with us and the trouble I might be in; I just could not fathom explaining it to all those relatives who had come to Red Lodge. Diane Dugan, my wife-to-be, was a rural first grade teacher and would not have been nearly as shocked. Disgusted, yes; but shocked? No. It was her parents and my family about whom I was most worried.

For two full seconds it was deadly quiet, except for the chirp and sputter of the diminutive rear-mounted engine. We could all hear it missing on one cylinder, but no one thought to mention it.

The cop car made a couple of "yelps." Patches of red light raced through the interior of the tiny capsule like vicious demons, as the policeman angled in behind us.

McCarty drew a deep breath and exhaled forcefully. "Okay boys. I'll take care of this." He had a determined look as he opened the door and tried to get out, but Das Grun Auto lurched forward like a billy goat ramming a fence. Dougie had forgotten to take the engine out of gear. The four mountain climbers were sent piling forward. That must have looked impressive to the cop. We don't have a prayer, I thought. I'm a dead man.

McCarty replanted his mountain boots outside and strode back to the cop car before the police officer could get the cruiser in park. Dougal approached the driver's side like a five-foot-eleven-inch, 211-pound root beer stand waitress dressed in a trench coat. That poor cop must have been making a bowel check about then, or trying to unsnap his .38.

"Fuckin'-a man, this doesn't look good," Emerson remarked.

"No, it doesn't," Kalitowski concurred.

McCarty was back there for what seemed an extraordinarily long time. I stole a quick glance. McCarty was bent over, talking to the officer through the window, which had been rolled down a few inches. The cop never got out of the car. Dougal looked as though he might be taking an order. "Two scoops in that root beer float, sir?"

The light bar strobed on in raging silence. Exhaust fumes were seeping through the floorboard of the bug. Kal rolled his window down a few inches.

Certainly, the cop would notice Dougal's breath and know that he had all seven sheets set firmly to the wind. It was just a matter of time before we would be hauled to the other end of town. To whom would I place my phone call? I didn't know the phone number of the motel in which my parents were staying.

Minutes passed; then, finally, Dougal returned.

"Whew. Man, that was close...heh, heh, heh. (Cessna)"

"Wha-what's happening? Are we busted?"

"Okay man, here's the deal. I explained that you were getting married tomorrow and that we were just out having a little fun tonight. I apologized for driving up on the sidewalk and told the cop I knew the guy. I promised to never do that again."

"Yeah, okay. So?"

"Well, he is going to follow us back to the Monastery and we have to promise not to drive anymore tonight."

"Really—that's it?"

"No shit. You're still getting married tomorrow, mate."

"Wow! Good job, Dougal!" I fell back into the seat. McCarty had pulled off yet another miracle.

We rolled up to the Monastery with the cop right behind us. The DSC flight crew climbed out of the lunar module. "Houston, the Beetle has landed." I started talking to the cop. He looked as though he was just out of high school and sang in the church choir. Of course, that may have been a distorted perception since I was "drunker than a boiled owl."* The Dirty Socks Club contingency emerged from the Monastery, one by one. Ambassadors of the DSC and the RLPD stood in the street and socialized for a while. Brian Leo offered the cop a beer. Jack Tackle nudged Leo in the ribs. Later, Tackle told Leo he didn't think that was a good idea since he didn't think the cop was old enough to drink.

By the time the encounter was over, everyone had shaken hands with the cop and I had invited him to the wedding reception. It turned out to be a pretty good bachelor party, after all.

The next day, I left the monkhood. Jim Emerson performed the duties of best man, dressed in a borrowed suit and a brand new pair of blue Royal Robbins (climbing) shoes he had bought for the occasion. Only Steve Jackson and Jim Kanzler were missing. Steve was in Florida, attending graduate school. Kanzler was ski patrolling at Big Sky. He didn't think the marriage would last, so he didn't attend.

*From *A Tough Trip through Paradise* by Andrew Garcia, 1878-1879.

Jim Kanzler on Westminster Spire with the
Beartooth Highway below, April 1978.
Photo by the author.

The author hauling loads below The First Wall, May 1978. Photo by Jim Kanzler.

The bachelor party at the Monastery. Left to right: Jack "Java Man" Tackle, with his wife Pam, "Chief" Dan Hogan, Rick "Hooblie" Hooven, and a friend, "Dr. Z" Craig Zaspel, Jim "Emer-something-son" Emerson, Gary Skaar, Bill Havalin, Jim Williams, Doug "Dougal" McCarty. Standing in front: Mark "Kal" Kalitowski. Seated: Brian "Breo" Leo. Photo by Mark Kalitowski.

CHAPTER 19

A Ticket to Ride

On the Path of Mad Wolf, Part IV

September 1979

After our third failure at Siyeh, in the autumn of 1978, and our climb on the east face of Little Chief, Jim Kanzler and I took a trip to Devil's Tower and the Needles of South Dakota to climb on sound rock without the dangers of alpine climbing. That winter we did a climb on the snow-covered rock of what is called the West Wall of Lone Peak in the Big Sky Ski Resort. The following spring, Jim climbed, unroped, nine pitches of rock in Gallatin Canyon, starting with the Joker (by an easier third pitch, bypassing the more difficult original). He continued up the tiers of cliffs above the Gallatin River, ending with the classic Spare Rib at 5.8, a route in which he had made the first ascent with Pat Callis ten years earlier. A few days later, he free-soloed the Standard Route on Gallatin Tower, including the bulging, in-your-face 5.9 hand crack of the Direct Finish that Jerry had led on sight with Barry Frost in 1968.

I had led the Direct Finish a few times by then, but with the pitch sewn-up tighter than a catcher's mitt with gear.

I followed Jim's bravado by third-classing some of my favorite climbs on Practice Rock in Hyalite Canyon and worked my way into unroped ascents in Gallatin Canyon and the Humbugs. Spare Rib became my favorite free solo.

Jim made his seasonal journey to Jackson Hole to guide for Exum in June 1979, while Brian Leo and I hit the Canyon and the Humbugs. Brian and I climbed a nondescript route near the south buttress of Mount Moran in the Tetons. Dougal McCarty and I climbed a 16-pitch new route, Pyro de la Calico, in the Beartooths in mid-August.

Dan had lived in Alaska for several years after finishing a business degree and took a job as a CPA in Anchorage. When he came home to visit

Mom and Dad in Columbia Falls that summer, I drove up from Bozeman and we trekked into Mount St. Nicholas, where we climbed the standard route.

To train further for Siyeh that summer, I ran road races, bagged peaks and did hundreds of pull-ups. One day I cranked 365 in sets of 20, one rep for each day of the year. Someone pointed out that day that the following February was a leap year, so I did one more. My arms were sore for a week. My moods spooled up and down like a yo-yo as I waited for Kanzler's last day of guiding.

Early in the summer, three months after Diane and I were married, we rented an apartment in Bozeman. She had a new job teaching first grade that began the first week in September, and I got work with lay-out at the *Kletterwerks*: Dana Gleason and "Starvin'" Darvin Vandegrift's early pack design and manufacturing company.

We had another member in the party by the time Kanzler finished guiding— his new girlfriend, Margo Erjavek. Margo worked in the office at Exum, scheduling the guides and helping in the mountains frequently. She was as good looking as she was fit and she could outrun either one of us at any distance over ten miles. Margo and Kanzler began climbing together frequently. Margo planned to help carry our gear into Mount Siyeh and hike out when Jim and I started up the face.

Unsettled weather moved through Montana as I drove the Tank to Columbia Falls a day ahead of Jim and Margo, who drove the Rat Hole mobile. I could see fresh snow on the summits of the Mission Mountains and I got that we-should-have-been-on-the-mountain-last-week feeling. Jim and Margo arrived at R. Glenn's and Betty's house on September 11 and the three of us left for Mount Siyeh the next afternoon with both vehicles, since Jim and Margo planned to head for the Canadian Rockies after Siyeh; and I would head back to Bozeman.

We rolled through St. Mary; Bob Frauson and the Hudson Bay District Ranger Station at the east entrance, and continued to the Many Glacier entrance, arriving about an hour before sundown. Near the Many Glacier entrance is the only location in Glacier Park where the north face of Mount Siyeh can be viewed from a road. When the dark wall stepped into view to the south, we parked the vehicles and got out.

"Faw-wk!" Jim and I growled in unison. The ledges held new snow almost to the bottom and we could see wet rock. Wet rock meant more rock fall and trickier climbing. I continued the routine of pissing and moaning, which Kanzler and I did a great deal of during the Siyeh Years.

"Well, (flock) a (gall-darned) duck, now what should we do?" I quacked. "How long do ya think it will take for the face to dry off? A couple days?"

Kanzler ignored me for a moment as he studied the face with binoculars. One corner of his mouth grimaced as he squinted through the cheap glasses. "You know, Kennedy, I think we have a ticket to ride."

"Waddya mean?"

"I don't think there is that much snow up there. Sure, there will be some wet rock, but do you know what else this means? We won't have to carry much water. There will be water up there. We can catch drips or melt snow with the bivvy stove. Not carrying several days of water will lighten us up considerably. We could get by with one wide-mouth water bottle apiece."

Kanzler had a good point.

"You're right! It's doable." The prospect of technical rock in less than perfect conditions bore less anxiety upon me than waiting for the face to dry off. It was already mid-September, and we had been blown out by weather at this time during the past two years.

"What about the rockfall?"

"We got high pressure now, Kennedy. Let's go slay the dragon."

September 13, 1979

Jim, Margo and I awoke to clear weather after rolling our sleeping bags out under the Windy Creek Bridge in a dry creek bed and made breakfast further down the road on a picnic table. (We were not the type of people who were going to pay to camp in a campground.) We split the climbing gear load three ways and hiked to the base of the north face. Margo wished us good luck and watched us disappear above Cracker Lake before hiking out.

Jim and I reclimbed the lower face and stopped on the Escape Ledge instead of bivouacking at the base. If the weather looked problematic the following morning, we could traverse off. The weather remained clear all night.

September 14, 1979

Kanzler had decided we should climb in blocks. Each guy would lead all the pitches one day, and the other climber would lead all the pitches the next. This had the advantage of not exchanging packs and the main sling of hardware at every belay stance, which is precarious in vertical terrain, and increases the risk of dropping something vital. More often than not, we could exchange ends of the ropes. Retying knots took less time and energy than re-stacking double ropes after every lead.

The weather remained clear. I took the first block above the bivouac on the Escape Ledge, which included the hard pitch below the diorite sill for the fourth time, if you counted the third attempt the year before, when we bailed mid-pitch after near-obliteration by falling rock in high winds. We figured it was better for me to re-lead this pitch, for the sake of familiarity and efficiency. The less time we spent on the face, the less food and water we would have to carry and the less time we would spend bobbing around on ledges like rubber duckies, with Mad Wolf trying to smash our heads off with rocks. This also meant less time for our old nemesis, Zeus, to throw another tantrum.

To one who believes in such things, it might appear that neither Jim nor I had particularly good karma. Along with turning back from the north face in perfect weather on the first attempt, the heinous bivouac in the storm on the second, and the rockfall on the third, there was the spring of 1978, when Kanzler and I lived in the Monastery. That spring, we tried to get super climbing fit together—only to be rewarded with two four-foot dumps of snow in the Beartooths. Jim Kanzler and I would never have that much time to climb together again.

I knew it wasn't just me chasing the echo of the Mount Cleveland Five tragedy as we scurried around the countryside, ranting and raving, sidestepping catastrophes of our own. It seemed unlikely that the deviant, small-town mountain climbers from Columbia Falls were ever going to encounter optimal conditions again on the face, feared and revered by the generation who preceded them. Not when an indigenous warrior, the namesake of the mountain, had levied a curse on the white man. Siyeh saw his people devastated by a race motivated by greed and fear, while the Blackfeet people, motivated by the spirit of the Earth and their connection to it, competed for space and buffalo with others like themselves.

No, sir. Jim Kanzler and Terry Kennedy were bad medicine. A price would have to be paid.

If our sacrilege on Mount Siyeh did not cause us continued unhappiness, our single-minded ambition to climb Mount Siyeh caused us frustration and restlessness for three years. We had often felt the slight of the coupe stick, even while we were not climbing. We were nearly destroyed on several occasions. Spared, thankfully, but nonetheless humiliated.

Come what may, Jim Kanzler and I needed to climb this thing, atone ourselves for the sins of our forefathers, or whatever it was that seemed to be lodged sideways in our craws. I was becoming exhausted. We needed to move on. The fortune of excellent conditions would be left for future climbers, perhaps more pure of soul, decades later.

Verglas poured silently, like candle wax from ledges, covering some of the holds. Sometimes I could climb around it and sometimes I chipped the ice off with my alpine hammer pick. I brushed the snow off of holds with fingerless gloves, and my hands instantly became wet and cold.

I came to the place where I was perched when the slab of limestone came hurling at us the year before, and kept going. I fudged a move here and there with a boot in an etrier clipped to an anchor. I worked up to the ledge at the bottom of the diorite sill and set up the familiar belay anchors. I felt strong and confident.

The double strands of 9mm rope came steadily in as I belayed Jim up the icy pitch. I could feel him on the other end, moving fast. I looked westward toward Mount Gould and the Garden Wall. There was not one damn cloud in the sky. A perception came over me. I felt light. I stood there in the shadow and stillness of Siyeh's north face, stacking the rope at my feet. I could hear Kanzler's breathing as he neared my position, and I made room for him at the stance. He pulled onto the ledge carrying the pack with the bivvy gear and provisions. He drew up a clove hitch and hesitated for a moment before he clipped into the belay.

Kanzler's head was cocked back, and locks of his thick, dark brown hair flowed from under his helmet, licking the collar of his yellow wind shell. His Adam's apple stuck out as he began to gawk upward at the steep, greenish-black rock above us. The diorite sill was once a molten intrusion. The intensity of the heat had turned the adjacent limestone white. The intimidating cliffs above us stretched upward, beyond our view.

"Why don't we just go up here?" Kanzler suggested. Was he serious?

"We don't want to go up there. That's way harder than the route we've planned. We'd be in etriers most of the way. It would take us another day, at least."

"Come on, I'll lead it." Shit—he was dead serious.

"It doesn't make any sense to go up there. It would be like Heckmair and Harrer, going for the Rote Fluh on the first ascent of the Eigerwand." Kanzler knew what I meant, but he wasn't listening.

"Kennedy, we are modern climbers; we have the experience and the gear. This would be the perfect line. Nobody could climb a better line than this in years to come."

The icon of my youth was making me nervous. If we went banging our heads on this stupendously steep wall, I knew we would lose our momentum. We might eventually bog down, and it would ultimately cost us another year. Kanzler was obviously on a roll. It is not that I doubted we could climb the wall above us, given enough food, water and even more gear. We had food for two days and one water bottle apiece, relying on the snow on the ledges to keep us hydrated. We didn't know if we could count on more than two days of good weather. We didn't need to throw ourselves at the nastiest part of the wall.

Kanzler was feeling strong and confident—which was good—but his spontaneity was threatening to derail the train.

"Here, give me the rack." He reached an arm toward me, still holding his gaze above. This definitely was not good. Now we were locking into a disagreement.

"Kanzler, let's just get through the traverse and we know what we've got ahead of us." He was silent and started to slide the heavier pack off so he could take the lighter lead pack. I needed to say something to keep Kanzler surging forward, but disrupt his tunnel vision.

"Well, there is one thing about these faces...," I began, as if I had been holding out on important information, which, in a way, I had. I said faces, because the vision I held for the two of us was to finish Siyeh and go in pursuit of other steep, unclimbed faces in Glacier. Who knew what might lay beyond that? The Canadian Rockies, Alaska, Patagonia...the Himalayas? First, we had to do this face.

For a second, I lost the flow of words. The pause snagged Kanzler's attention, and he took his eyes off of the wall above and looked over at me.

"What's that?"

"These faces," I continued, "will only be climbed for the first time—once."

There was silence. Here came that fear-of failure thing again, which we both understood so well.

"Okay. Okay, you're right," Jim responded without reproach, "we should do the route you figured out."

Just like that, we were on our way.

I restacked the ropes quickly to place me on top to lead again as Jim transferred the gear he cleaned from the pitch below and clipped it onto the lead rack, which was still slung around my shoulder.

"We're in motion," Kanzler proclaimed. He loved to use the Shakespeare quote, "In motion there is life, in stasis—death." To us, "in-motion" was momentum enhanced by throwing caution to the wind—or stifled by hesitation. We were a conservative pair of climbers, rarely throwing caution to the wind and often subdued by hesitation, but we could be bold when things felt right.

Right then, at that moment, when the kids in school were going out for morning recess in Columbia Falls, I knew we had it. We were going to climb the big face on that attempt. All we had to do was not make any stupid mistakes. I led on into the best day of alpine climbing I have ever had, rotten sedimentary rock notwithstanding. The truth is, it wasn't that bad. Loose granite is worse.

By 6 p.m., I had grown weary. I had led 11 of 13 belayed pitches, plus some heady third classing climbing to start the morning. After the traverse right in the diorite sill, I kept taking options left to line us up with a deep, hidden chimney that was difficult to see while on the route. Occasionally the rope drag became overbearing. I had to muscle up slack and then climb the slack out. It was exhausting. We had not come across enough running water to fill our water bottles, and I only had about an inch of water left in mine. We did manage to find seeps to stick our lips on and suck in small amounts of water along with lichen and grit.

From a tied-off piton, I belayed Jim up 40 feet to an anchor. He put me back on belay and I kept going. I whaled in a couple of pitons and sagged onto them. It was time for Kanzler to take over before I got too flamed out.

"Good work, Terry. I can take it from here."

"Okay, man. It's all yours."

Jim held onto the three wraps of seat belt webbing tied with a ring bend that made up the waist portion of my harness while I grabbed the pitons with my right hand and held the rope through the stitch plate with my left. He maneuvered around me to the other side of the narrow stance, with drastic exposure below us, and clipped in. I took him off belay.

There was a methodical exchange of gear. Kanzler slipped the left shoulder strap of the heavier pack off of his shoulder and I gripped it with full concentration as he slipped out of the other shoulder strap.

"You got it?"

"Got it."

Jim unbuckled the waist belt and I had the precious cargo. We kept a shoulder-length runner girth hitched through both the loop at the top of the pack and left shoulder strap. The redundancy backed up the sewn loop should it be ripped out and the pack drop. I clipped it in, then slipped out of the lighter lead pack and carefully handed it to Jim.

The sun would set in less an hour.

"Man, where does this thing go from here?" Kanzler inquired as he studied the cliffs above.

"We want to get into the slot straight above us. I think you can get it on this pitch."

"I see it. It's going to be dicey getting there."

Above us the rock bulged to overhanging, with a crack cleaving the steepest part. It looked like something one might find in Yosemite. It would have been an inviting route to try in sunshine, in a t-shirt with E.B.s laced up tight. The toes of Kanzler's wooden-shanked Peter Habeler Super Light mountain boots were much too thick to enter the crack. The face surrounding the crack was devoid of holds along which to edge.

"I'll try out left," Kanzler decided. The rock just past the budge didn't overhang as much, but was like potato chips, making commitment to hand and foot holds risky. Kanzler probed the section, hoping to find adequate protection. The cracks were too loose for pitons or nuts between the wobbling blocks.

"This is fucked." He climbed back down to the level of my stance. "I'll have to try the crack."

On the fourth attempt on Mount Siyeh's north face, we had one distinctive mechanical advantage over our previous attempts: Friends. The first commercially available active spring-loaded mechanical camming devices developed by Ray Jardine, an aeronautical and space engineer who was also a front-running Yosemite rock climber. The progressive Jim Kanzler quickly invested in a set. We carried the original rigid-stemmed whole, sizes 1-4. Kanzler and I climbed with them the spring of 1979. When it was time to head to Siyeh in September, he bought an additional set of sizes 1-3, dipping into his savings to do so. I had just been married and couldn't justify buying my own when I earned far less income than my wife. Half sizes were not available for another year. I splurged the following season and bought the half-sizes, with the idea that Kanzler and I would continue as a climbing force. We employed the new gadgets throughout the fourth attempt, no longer needing to carry several sizes of Hexentrics or bongs for wider crack sizes.

Kanzler racked the Friends and his etriers at the front to his gear sling and engaged the overhanging crack. He plugged a #3 Friend into the crack and clipped it. He backed off to easier holds and gingerly made a progression of bounces to place more weight on the piece while holding onto the rock. Satisfied that it would hold, he clipped in an etrier and carefully ascended the four rungs, clipping in the double ropes. The crack was uniform in width, and the only other piece of gear that would fit was the other #3. Jim placed that as high as he could reach, advanced his webbing ladders and stepped into them. Kanzler had only one option: reach down, unclip and remove the first #3 Friend, clip it to his gear sling and climb to the top rungs of his etriers; place the first piece higher, then repeat the retrieval of the lower one and leapfrog it higher.

Kanzler was 30 feet above the belay, hanging on the single piece of gear. If the placement popped or the rock surrounding the crack was loose and gave way, Kanzler would fall, unloading onto my belay after a fall of 60-75 feet. The numbing realization of our commitment precipitated an eerie silence as the sun caught highlights of the cliff towering above us, turning the rock golden and casting long shadows. Kanzler's grunts, and the sound of the hardware jangling on the rack, grew further away as the toes of his boots thumped against the wall. My pulse beat beneath my sternum like an idling locomotive.

The crack widened at the top of the bulge and Kanzler stuffed in the one #4 we carried; he stepped out of his etriers and continued free climbing.

The sun set as I pulled onto the snow-covered ledge at the end of Jim's critical pitch, humping the pack with the bivouac gear. I felt wasted.

We excavated the ledge to make it suitable to recline and Jim melted water from the snow. One large block rolled off of the ledge as if from a ship into an ocean that had no surface. I had taken several breaths before we heard the splash of pulverizing rock far below us.

"Oh God, I'm sure glad we're not down there!" I muttered.

"I'm glad we are right here, high on this wall." There was confidence and satisfaction in Kanzler's voice.

"Yeah, me too. We're gonna do this thing, Kanzler." Hot tea and envelopes of instant soup were shared from a single cup, which was scraped clean with a piton. The ropes were laid out to insulate us from the semi-frozen dirt and scree on the ledge, and we hunkered down for the night.

In the middle of the night, with Kanzler snoring inside his hood, I had a sudden revelation.

"Jesus, I didn't have to jump!" I blurted into the darkness. Kanzler's snoring ceased abruptly, and he bolted upright.

"Kennedy, what's going on?"

As if in a trance, not noticing Kanzler had suddenly sprung to life, I repeated, "I didn't have to jump."

"Kennedy! Wake up! You are having a nightmare."

"No, no, it's, I'm awake. I just realized I didn't have to jump."

"You're scaring me, man—are you still tied in?"

"It's O.K., I'm tied in." Kanzler relaxed a little. "Do you remember when

I told you about Steve Jackson and me on Andromeda in '74, when I had to jump off the lip of the bergschrund?"

"Of course. You've told that story many times. Scary. You both are lucky to be alive."

"I know. But I didn't have to jump."

"I thought you said you did."

"I did. But I didn't."

"Whaduya mean?"

"Well, remember Steve slid the length of the rope and plunged out of sight over the upper edge of the bergschrund, and I was certain he would go in and pull us both in, but his trajectory took him to the other side..."

"Yeah."

"... and I was left to voluntarily jump off the lip and over the crevasse?

"Yeah?"

"Well, I just realized I didn't have to jump."

"Yer shittin' me. Didn't you have to jump?"

"No."

"Well, what else could you have done?"

"This is really stupid. Get this. All I would have needed to do was put in a couple of ice screws and rap off; one ice screw would have probably have been fine. The ice was as hard as concrete. Jackson could have pulled me across the gap."

"You mean you didn't think of that?"

"No. I guess not." I could just see Jim out of the corner of my eye. We were both staring into the darkness over Cracker Lake and the eastern flanks of Glacier's mountains, with the broad shoulders of Mount Cleveland silhouetted beyond Mount Wilbur and Mount Merritt. There was enough breeze playing along the face, changing direction frequently for us to want to keep our hoods on, but we loosened them to hear each other better. My hands were tucked inside of my down parka.

"Maybe Jackson had all the screws with him." Kanzler replied, searching for a justification for me.

"He might have. But I doubt I would have descended a full rope length below him without carrying some of them. I was looking for a place to cross the 'schrund and set up a belay. No, I'm sure I had to be carrying several of the ice screws."

Kanzler listened like a psychiatrist to the details of my confession.

"I don't know. I suppose I had this ingrained idea that we must never lose an ice screw. We only climbed with six or seven of them, I think. It just didn't occur to me to actually leave one."

"They're expensive."

"You know, if I would have thought to leave one I certainly would have. But it just didn't occur to me."

"Apparently Jackson didn't think of it, either."

"I guess not. It was a stupid mistake. I don't jump far enough and we both get gobbled by the bergschrund. Too far and we cartwheel for hundreds of feet. I couldn't even see where I was jumping until I launched over the edge."

"Well, you are still alive."

"Older and wiser, I would think. I would hope." Jim Kanzler and I sat there for perhaps ten minutes without saying anything. I was still ruminating the naivete of the jump. Of all the times Steve and I had told the story, no one else had ever suggested I should have simply rappelled off of an ice screw.

The sky was black with twinkling stars poking pinholes in the universe. The wall behind us was even blacker. The outline of Siyeh's east and west ridges arched overhead, from eight o'clock to four o'clock, forming edges as sharp as broken glass. We were in the geometrical center of the face, midway between the diorite sill and the summit cairn.

The conversation ended. After that, I had no idea what Kanzler was thinking as we sat staring into the night, leaning against the face with our old buddy, Orion, tiptoeing along the summit rim, his bow drawn for who knew what.

There were times when I felt Jim Kanzler's and my mental sine wave crests were in resonance, that he and I and were of one soul. There were also times when our sine waves were in complete chaotic dissonance and we disconnected, like pulling the toaster cord out of the wall socket. Sometimes the wave crest matches came quickly and sometimes they were weeks or months apart. I lived for those times—when we were connected and my world felt at peace.

Not a day went by on which I didn't think of the Mount Cleveland Five and just how slippery the line between life and tragedy could be. It just took one step to trigger a slab avalanche that released half a million square feet of five-foot wind slab plunging down into their laps.

Two weeks after Jim, Steve Jackson and I were enjoying a certain amount of notoriety in Montana newspapers, following our ascent of the north face of Mount Cleveland, I visited Jean Kanzler at her home in Three Forks, Montana. She told me she was always disturbed at the thought of how Jerry and his friends had suffered, suffocating before they expired. She related an experience she had about a year after the avalanche.

"Jer came to me in a dream. He was walking across an alpine meadow with beautiful wildflowers. There was this other tall fellow with him. It had to be Ray Martin, but I really couldn't see his face. Jer came up to me and said, 'It is okay, Mom, it was just like being tackled.' He turned and walked away, across the meadow, with his companion."

Jim Kanzler and I were climbing the big face of Siyeh. Jerry, Clare, Ray and the other guys were not. I had to wonder: If there hadn't been the tragedy on Mount Cleveland, would I be up here, on this wall? My own life might have taken a completely different turn.

"Let's get some shut-eye," Kanzler murmured, reclining on the rope and cinching up his parka. He was snoring in minutes.

"Kennedy. Hey, it's going to get light pretty soon. Let's get going." Kanzler reached over and lit the tiny blowtorch. My teeth were chattering. The pot was loaded with corn snow—12 ounces of frozen diamonds. We passed a hot cup of instant coffee back and forth, sipping the brew as quickly as we could before it cooled off. Kanzler got into his boots like a fireman responding to a call. He had the lead pack on, the gear slung over one shoulder and the runners over the other before I could get my own boots on.

"Got me?"

"Almost."

Kanzler reeled off the next six pitches like he was riding a bicycle.

"Thirty feet—threee zee-row! Twenty feet—twooo zee-row! Ten feet!" The rope stopped. Kanzler could hear the audibles. I unclipped the rope and started banging out the anchors. We fudged the fundamental belay procedures a little to save time. I could hear the ringing of driven pitons above me when they were employed. I couldn't wait to get going. Moving meant warmth. The rope came tight. I yanked three times. The rope yanked back. I climbed, and the rope went up with me.

We arrived at a narrow ledge we called the Cat Walk, spanning the width of the face, 400 or 500 feet below the summit rim. One of our two 9mm x 165-foot ropes was cut halfway through by routine leader rock fall. We had to use it.

It was about noon and a good place to eat something and rehydrate. We discussed our position. I crept along the ledge with a belay in boot-deep snow, looking at possibilities above, and returned.

"This is it. I'm pretty sure we're where we want to be, according to the photo."

"All right, Kennedy," Kanzler blurted as he shouldered the light pack and checked his knot. "Let's go count coup."

"Go get 'em, Mad Wolf!" We spontaneously let out top-of-the-lung war whoops. We were burning daylight, racing the sun to the horizon.

"You're on belay."

"Climbing."

"Keep a tight ass up there."

Sixty feet up, Jim was confronted by another crux section. He secured the lead pack and gingerly stepped off of a teetering block, edging right to an off-width crack. It was the only option. Kanzler wiggled and arm-barred upward for 50 feet. The right side of his body jammed inside and his left foot and fingers searched outside the crack for small holds that helped him push upward. Big boots were an advantage. None of our anchors came close to fitting the crack. A horizontal crack just over halfway would have taken a thin blade, but Kanzler couldn't get to his hammer off of his right hip.

It really didn't matter. He could not have released his right arm torqued inside the crack to swing the hammer, anyway. He just had to keep shoveling without protection and maintain his composure with 3,000 feet of vertical exposure sweeping away below him.

Here we hauled the packs. The pitch wasn't so strenuous for the second because the top rope belay relieved me of having to jam myself so deep into the crack for security. When I reached Jim he was still breathing heavy.

"Wow, way to go, Kanzler! That was very bold."

"Thanks, man. I still need some recovery time. Can you lead the next pitch?"

"Sure."

I ran the full length of rope up vertical rock with ample holds and decent pro.

"Good job, Terry," Kanzler said when he reached me. "That was a good lead, too. Okay, I'm ready to go again." We carefully traded packs and gear slings, and he was on his way.

The climbing got more involved. Kanzler disappeared into a deep corner, and for the next two hours, chunks of ice and rock poured out of the depression. I turned my collar up and shrugged my shoulders as I leaned into the cliff to miss the bigger pieces and prevent the sifting snow from running down my back. Jim seemed to be keeping me informed of conditions and progress, but I couldn't understand a word once he disappeared from view. All I could do was tend the rope and hope things were going well above.

Then, from far above came an urgent yell and the rope went slack, with six feet dropping into my lap. Jim told me later he was aiding on a nut when it popped and he rattled down the recess, grabbing a runner on the way down, stopping his own fall before the next piece caught him. I could never figure out how he did that. I Jumared on the damaged rope while Kanzler belayed me on the good one, wearing the heavy pack. Jim was forced to leave the lead pack clipped to an anchor part way up the pitch, so I suspended it from my harness below me and towed it along. My left side was soaked from trickling meltwater.

At last the summit rim looked within reach: one, maybe two pitches away. The sky remained clear, with a couple of hours of daylight remaining. Kanzler was fidgeting like a hyperkinetic child, waiting to get on with it as we re-racked the lead gear sling. His idea was to go straight up. We both agreed the line would require aid climbing and consume precious time. I persuaded Jim to traverse around the corner to the right, where I was sure easier terrain existed. He was happy just to go up.

Kanzler was off belay. Part of me wanted to climb quickly to reach the next stance and get Kanzler set up again to finish before dark. Another part of me wanted to slow down and just enjoy the climbing. I knew Siyeh would one day become a dusty milestone in both of our lives.

Halfway up the pitch, communication was less strained. I shouted up to Jim, "How does it look above?"

"Looks good."

Thirty feet from Jim, I looked up. A draft of warmer air streamed against my face. I could see parts of the rock highlighted by the evening sun. Jim Kanzler leaned forward and peered down at me, and his chipped-tooth grin slipped his face.

"Smile, Kennedy." He was already there.

Jim Kanzler with snow and verglas on the
ledges—the ticket to ride.
Photo by the author.

The author in the diorite sill. Photo by Jim Kanzler.

The author high on the north face of Mount Siyeh,
September 1979. Photo by Jim Kanzler.

Jim Kanzler leads into the unknown on the north face of
Mount Siyeh, September 1979. Photo by the author.

CHAPTER 20

Alone Together

I placed one hand on top of a block leaning over the face, swung a boot onto a hold and pulled over the lip—almost into Jim's lap. We shook hands and embraced.

"We did it, man!"

"We did it!"

I crawled away from the edge as I shed the gear sling and pack. Kanzler unclipped from the last belay anchor. We rolled around in the scree like a couple of bear cubs, laughing as if we had just pulled off a huge practical joke on the rest of the world.

"No one else has any idea of where we are now or what we have just done," Kanzler declared, staring down into the drop-off from which we had just emerged.

"I know."

"No one else gives a rat's ass," he went on, raising his voice, as if escalating an argument with someone unseen.

The feelings of elation and success were short-lived; the celebration quickly morphed into brooding. As I stood on the summit, I began to feel lost. Jim and I had spent years of our lives in pursuit of Mad Wolf. I didn't have a plan for what should happen next. I stood at the threshold of unlimited freedom, and I didn't know what to do.

In a way, I think we had not anticipated ever finishing the climb. The Path of Mad Wolf had been a process; now it was over. The algorithm had reached its logical conclusion. There seemed to be no place to go from here.

I took a victory photo of Jim at the edge of the face, which became the original logo of the Glacier Mountaineering Society, to which neither one of us belonged, but who would bestow upon us their "Outstanding Individual Achievement Award" anyway.

Psychologists say a person can feel a loss, like the death of a loved one, in many ways. Certainly, Jim Kanzler had experienced many "deaths" during his first 32 years. More would come.

I felt I had to come up with a future before we left the summit, like we had on the summit of Mount Cleveland. The sun was melting through layers of gold, mango and crimson.

"Man, this is really cool," I said softly.

"Yeah. Why don't you stand over there and I'll get you in a nice sunset shot?"

The air was still, a contrast to the wind that had ripped us on the face in 1978 and threatened to blow my brother and me off of the top when we were kids. Without a whisper, it was gone. The rest of the time on the summit felt like grieving.

"I suppose we should get down before it gets too dark."

"I suppose."

"I don't know," I muttered, "I don't really feel like going down yet."

"Yeah, it's gonna be pitch black before we get to that exposed section above the moraine. I guess we could just use the headlamp."

"I guess. I'm not too crazy about walking out the Cracker Lake trail in the dark."

"Me neither, especially now that we smell like bear bait."

"How much water ya got?"

"A quarter, maybe a third. You?"

"About the same. Maybe we could just bivvy up here."

"On the summit?"

"Yeah, what's one more bivouac?"

Other climbers might have been in a hurry to return to the bottom to punch the clock and record a faster time on the route. Going super light, with less, but more sophisticated gear, and climbing simultaneously meant fewer or no bivouacs on a big route. It became the trend in years to come. Bivouacs were who we were. Racing over the holds or standing on the summit holding a stopwatch wasn't the essence of mountain climbing for us. Placing our backs against the mountain was.

"Let's go down the ridge a ways out of the prevailing wind, in case it comes up," Kanzler advised. "We've still got a tin of sardines. It would be better to eat them up here rather than down there in the dark, with grizzly bears lurking behind every bush."

"We'll be facing the rising sun when it comes up in the morning."

"It will be nice to wake up with the sun on us, for a change."

Just like that, the Siyeh years were over. The crests of our sine waves had eclipsed, and began to move rapidly out of phase. By the time we leveled a place in the scree toward the prominent eastern shoulder of Mount Siyeh and laid the ropes out like damp bathroom rugs, our wave crests were like teeter-totters moving in opposite directions. Fewer than ten minutes after leaving the summit, the dissonance became palpable. For the rest of my life, I would not understand why.

Kanzler wanted to be left alone with his thoughts; bad timing to be laying side-by-side. We would have been better off scratching out separate holes a hundred feet apart. We should have been celebrating our hard-won success. Instead, a black cloud precipitated out of *now-here* and continued all night. The mood turned rancid. We curled up on the ropes like a couple of Neanderthals fearing a saber-toothed tiger.

We were alone, together.

It was just a few days before the autumn equinox. Except for the hump of Siyeh's summit a short distance behind us, there were dazzling stars in the half sphere that stretched overhead. They crackled in ghostly silence.

One would think after the stresses of a big climb like we had just finished, a few hours of good sleep would have been easy. Not for me. I flipped from one hip to the other every 15 minutes, hovering on the verge of sleep, the universe's fundamental questions of existence seeping in and out of my consciousness.

Kanzler was as silent as a tombstone. I knew he was awake; he wasn't snoring. He flipped from one side to the other like turning pages in a book.

About the time Orion's bow began to emerge over the vast horizon to the east, I was ready to break the silence.

"Kanzler, have you ever thought that between any two points there is another point?"

"Of course," he answered instantaneously. "You mean you just thought of that?"

"Well, no—I mean, yeah, I was just thinking of that. I've been thinking about it for a while. I remembered it from a geometry textbook. It was in the first paragraph of the first chapter."

"So?"

Whoa. What one syllable could present more disdain and defiance, or be more demanding?

"Well, I was just thinking about how neatly that axiom defines infinity."

"Everybody has thought about that at some time," he lashed out.

Now he had me on the defensive. Kanzler was a smart guy. He was well-read, much more so than me. He was a hard nut to crack when it came to having an intellectual, never mind a philosophical discussion. He often played devil's advocate or just became contrary. Every time I tried to begin a philosophical conversation with him, which had become sparingly as the years progressed, I received a response that suggested I lacked keenness of mind. It pissed me off.

"Well, yeah, of course," I responded, "but..." I got the familiar feeling I was just going to bang my head on an invisible barrier. No matter how I would try to phrase my thought, the shield was always going to be there, pushing me back.

More than pissing me off, it made me sad. After all, we had persevered through, and finally succeeded together. I had looked up to Jim all these years, and now he had to act like a jerk on the most perfect night anyone could describe in the mountains. Kanzler was the proton; I was the electron. At the innermost level, we would never get together.

Staring up into the night, on a mountain with a face that had captivated both of us from our youth, I found myself fumbling to establish myself as worthy of a philosophical discussion. What I really wanted to do was revel in the universe with my surrogate big brother.

What I was trying to express was how the simplest geometry was so profound. Maybe the axiom of existence, suggests that sentience, too, just goes on. Once a conscious being, you cannot cease being conscious, whether you liked it or not. Just by the act of moving from one place to another, from one point to another, you cross an infinity. When at last you think you have reached a destination, you are left bewildered by the unfathomed possibilities in all directions, even a line that leads to within. Maybe there was an axiom like, "Within any given point, there exists another point." Or...

"It implies life after death," I blurted.

Great. Now I was mired in the tar pit. "I mean..."

"When you die, you just go to the worms," Kanzler informed me with certainty. "It all fades to black, and it is like that forever. Get used to it, Kennedy."

The last bivouac became another tragedy, if not for Jim, then for me. Kanzler had been sucked into the black hole that seemed to dog him. We just laid there, alone together for hours, until it finally started to get light.

I watched the horizon intently for the first dot of the sun. At the first sighting, it was already a crescent, an arc—infinite number of points.

We let the sun warm us for a while in our fetal positions before stirring. Then we stuffed the packs and slung mountaineer's coils around our shoulders. The only snow remaining on the mountain to melt for tea was still in the shadows of the north face.

For all intents and purposes, Jim Kanzler and I went our separate ways that morning. It was the fourth day of a long run of warm, stable weather. It would have been a good day to start a serious climb, but we were done.

Jim Kanzler and I were interviewed by several Montana newspapers and enjoyed some local notoriety. We climbed a little here and there together, but the forthcoming years eluded us. Kanzler went on an expedition to China with some big names and soon became disillusioned. He came back no longer wanting to be part of the Big Time. I was a poor provider, and my marriage failed in just a few years. It did produce a daughter, Lindsay, who grew up to be a brilliant artist and the loner I always thought I was.

As I descended Mount Siyeh, I turned to look at my friend ambling over Glacier's blonde talus and scree, as he had done so many times with Hal and Jerry, but he was gone. Life would never be the same.

Alone together on the summit of Mount Siyeh
at sunset, September 15, 1979. Photo by the author.

CHAPTER 21

Carnage Patrols

In the summer of 1981, two years after success on Mount Siyeh and the year Lindsay was born, I was hired by Glacier National Park as a seasonal ranger. My mountaineering experience and intimate knowledge of the Glacier mountains and backcountry no doubt gave me a leg up on other applicants. Interestingly, I was assigned to the Hudson Bay Ranger District. This meant I would be working for Bob Frauson, the Hudson Bay District Ranger, who had coordinated the search for the Mount Cleveland Five.

I was in the east entrance station kiosk at St. Mary one evening. I had been monitoring the radio traffic of the east side of the park while greeting visitors. At about 5 p.m., there came a report of a missing hiker who had separated from his friends at the Hidden Lake overlook, near Logan Pass. The man was a doctor on leave from the Navy. The rest of the party returned to Logan Pass while the Navy physician planned to make a jaunt down from the Continental Divide to Hidden Lake itself, about a mile further and 800 feet lower in elevation. The man failed to meet his friends at Logan Pass at 4 p.m. Other hikers had not seen him. Uniformed Park naturalists were on the trail daily, interacting with visitors; they had not seen him, either.

Hikers returning later than they had planned is a common occurrence, and not in itself a reason to mobilize a search until a sufficient amount of time has lapsed. A missing healthy man in his prime, a member of the armed service, no less, was not cause for alarm.

At 7 p.m. I heard Bob Frauson contact his Subdistrict Ranger, Gerry Ryder, and the Assistant Subdistrict Ranger, Richard Altemus on the district-wide radio channel, requesting a "landline" call to the district office. Half an hour later, the phone rang in the entrance station kiosk. It was Gerry Ryder.

"Have you been monitoring the radio with the situation of the overdue hiker at Logan Pass?"

"Yes, I have," I replied.

"Okay then, we are going to send you, Altemus and Bishop to Hidden Lake and look for this guy. Go ahead and close the kiosk and meet me in the subdistrict office as soon as you can get here. The road patrol is going to close the Hidden Lake trail. We're concerned the sow grizzly and her two cubs may have returned to the Hidden Lake area, and we have to consider the possibility of a bear incident. I'm going to send you three in there. Altemus and Bishop will be armed."

"Okay Gerry, I'll be there in 15 minutes."

The popular Hidden Lake trail from the overlook down to Hidden Lake had been closed earlier, for two weeks, while a mother grizzly bear and two cubs foraged in the area. When the ranger patrols stopped sighting her, the trail was reopened and had remained so for a little over a week, until this hiker failed to return from a two-and-a-half-mile hike.

Richard Altemus was the leader of this search patrol. "Okay, we'll go to Hidden Lake Overlook and shout down into the lake basin if the wind isn't blowing too hard," the ranking seasonal ranger decided. "He might hear us, and we might hear him if he is hurt, but can still shout."

"Or he might be up a tree, with a grizzly licking its chops at the base," Kevin Bishop, a seasonal backcountry ranger, offered. Kevin was a graduate student back East somewhere and had been a seasonal backcountry ranger for several years while he completed his degree. Kevin was enthusiastic about his duties and tended to be a bit impulsive. He also had potential as a comedian.

I was not allowed to carry a firearm in an official capacity. The only weapon I had was a pocketknife in my pack, with a one-and-a-half inch blade, used primarily to slice salami or to cut rope or cord; but, as they say in grizzly country, you just have to outrun one other member in your party to assure your survival during a violent encounter with a grizzly bear. Both Altemus and Bishop were pretty fast, and we were all in decent shape. With a three-step head start, I figured I could stay ahead of those guys long enough for a charging bear to reach one of them first. Since I didn't have a firearm, the other guys consented to let me take up the rear as we hiked. There was no wind when we reached the overlook, 500 feet above Hidden Lake. Bishop was the least bashful about unleashing his voice into the stillness of a beautiful night. Kevin and Rich took turns calling the man's name and requesting a reply. We were surprised to hear very clear echoes off of the flanks of Bearhat Mountain, Mount Reynolds, and a ridge called the Dragon's Tail that formed a wall around most of Hidden Lake.

"I'm sure he could hear us if he were able," Altemus said after ten minutes of calling the man's name. "It's a question of whether or not he is able. If he were up a tree and uninjured, I'm sure he would have returned a shout."

Kevin and I agreed.

"If he had broken an ankle, you'd think he would have contacted someone. He had four hours of daylight, at least," I submitted.

"Yeah, I'll bet a hundred people reach Hidden Lake everyday—at least. If you hurt yourself before early evening, there would still be enough people down there to get help before it got dark. It doesn't make sense, " Altemus said.

"Unless a bear got him," Bishop added.

"Apparently, nobody sighted a bear down there today. That's what Gerry and Bob were told by the naturalists at Logan Pass."

"It doesn't mean the guy didn't go to the far end of the lake and get mauled way down there. Not many visitors go to that end of the lake," Bishop continued.

"Well, we can't rule that completely out. A bear could show up at any time and the guy could have been at the wrong place at the wrong time," Altemus agreed.

The maintained trail to Hidden Lake ended at the outlet, but one could continue along the west shore for a ways until brush turned most people back. The eastern shoreline was easy travel for a short distance before high cliffs dropped down to nearly lake level, making travel in that direction unappealing.

"I'll call Gerry Ryder and let him know what we've got so far," Altemus said, drawing the brick-shaped Motorola handset from his belt holster. He keyed the transceiver.

"221-223." (Click.) "221-223." (Click.)

"221, go ahead, Rich." (Click.)

"Yeah, Gerry. The three of us are at the overlook. We've been shouting for the subject without an answer, over." (Click.)

"What's your impression? Over." (Click.)

"The winds are calm and we got a good echo, so he's either unable to respond or he's not down there, over." (Click.)

"Any bear sign?" (Click.)

"Negative." (Click.)

"But you cannot rule that possibility out." (Click.)

"10-4, Gerry." (Click.)

"I don't want your team going down there in the dark if there is a possibility of an aggressive bear." (Click.) The St. Mary subdistrict ranger was explicit.

"I copy that, Gerry." (Click.)

"You want to come back and return in the morning? Over." (Click.)

"Stand by Gerry, we'll discuss it, over." (Click.)

"10-4." (Click.)

"What do you guys think?" Rick Altemus said, turning to us.

"Well, by the time we hike back and drive to St. Mary, then rally early enough to be here at daybreak, it's going to be a short night anyway. I'm up for staying here, if you guys do," I presented. I had this thing about bivouacs. I liked the mountains at night.

"Right. We could monitor the trail, in case he does show up," Altemus furthered, "good idea. Bishop?"

'We could listen for animal activity. It's quiet. I think it is worth staying up here."

"You guys got enough clothing to spend the night?"

"I'm good," I replied, "it's a pretty warm night."

"I brought a space blanket," Bishop stated. "We could huddle under it."

"We could just walk around to stay warm if it gets that bad." None of us had taken sleeping bags or pads, but extra clothing and wind and rain gear would suffice.

"221-223." (Click.)

"Go ahead, Rich." (Click.)

"We are good to stay up here. We can drop down to the lake at first light, over." (Click.)

"I copy you want to stay at the overlook until morning, then continue the search at the lake at first light, over." (Click.)

""10-4." (Click.)

"Rich. Let me confirm that with Frauson, over." (Click.)

"10-4. Standing by." (Click.)

"221-222." (Click.)

"221—go ahead, Gerry." (Click.)

"Bob, did you copy any of this?" (Click.)

"Ah, 10-4, Gerry," Bob Frauson confirmed. He was the man. "Just be sure they don't go down to the lake tonight. They will be in a radio dead zone down there. Be sure they stay together." (Click.)

"223, do you copy?" (Click.)

"10-4, Gerry, copy. We'll move closer to Mount Clements under some ledges for shelter. We'll stay up high tonight, over." (Click.)

"10-4, Rich. Be advised I will be to the overlook at 0630 to relay radio traffic," Ryder informed us. "Have a good night. 222 clear." (Click.)

"223, clear." (Click.)

There was no movement that we could detect coming from the lake basin that night. As soon as it started to get light, we descended to Hidden Lake.

"Keep a sharp eye out for any bear sign," Altemus reminded Kevin and me.

"I think we should be sure to scour the shoreline," I pointed out. "I have a feeling we might find a pair of sneakers and a pack next to the water... and nothing else. After all, this guy was in the Navy. Maybe he had a tick list of the places he swam."

"Right; we need to make sure we cover the shore. Kennedy, you do that. Bishop and I will check more in the brush, since we have weapons."

We spread out, about 30 yards apart, and moved southward. I took the shoreline, Rich was in the middle and Kevin Bishop was furthest into the brush. We found no bear scat and no sneakers on the shoreline. We covered 300-400 yards, staying abreast. The vegetation became more difficult to negotiate, which made it less likely that a hiker would have bothered coming this far unless he or she had an agenda of climbing Bearhat or fishing the upper end of the lake. The missing man did not have fishing gear.

We regrouped near the lake edge after combing the terrain for more than a half hour. No bear sign, no answers to calling; no trace of anything. Bishop was still pretty revved up and wanted to search the brush further. Altemus didn't have any problem with him exploring nearby. We all had radios that were good within our line of sight. We just couldn't hit a repeater and get out of the basin to inform headquarters of our search.

Altemus and I sat down. "What could this guy have done?" Rich asked out loud.

"Oh, good question." I took a deep exhale. "He didn't get mauled or chased up a tree, and he didn't drown."

"Well, we can't be 100 percent sure," Altemus corrected me, "because we didn't check the other side of the outlet. But there isn't much to cover there. There's only a small strip of beach and a small thicket, and that won't take long to check out."

"Right."

Then our radios crackled. "223-221."(Click.)

"There's Ryder," Altemus said. "223—go ahead, Gerry." (Click.) It was 0625 hrs.

"How you guys doing down there?" (Click.)

"We're fine. No sign of anything." (Click.)

"10-4. Whereabouts are you?" (Click.)

"Kennedy and I are 300 yards south of the outlet. Bishop is about 100 yards to the west."

"10-4, I see you now. Be advised, I've got 20 fire crew personnel en route from the West Lakes district to join in the search. Curt Buchholtz is going to assume incident command. They left Logan Pass about 0615 and should be here shortly. Jim Kruger is airborne; his ETA is ten minutes. He's approaching Sperry Glacier now, you copy?" (Click.)

Rich Altemus took a breath before he answered Gerry Ryder's last transmission.

"Damn it, Kennedy," Altemus said, "we need to figure this out before all these other guys get here. If we don't find something or figure this out, Ryder is going to start a grid search and we'll be here forever." Then he keyed his transceiver to answer Ryder, who was now silhouetted against the sky at the overlook, 800 feet above and a quarter mile away from our line of sight.

"10-4, Gerry. I copy Kruger inbound." (Click.)

"Rich, you, Kennedy and Bishop start heading to the outlet, unless there is any other place you want to check down there?" (Click.)

"10-4, Gerry. We'll search just east of the inlet." (Click.)

"10-4, Rich." (Click.)

"Maybe the guy tried to take a short cut out of here," I offered to Altemus.

"Well, there's the saddle between Mount Clements and Cannon Mountain," Altemus mused, "but that doesn't make any sense. That's no shortcut; you couldn't miss the trail going that way. Maybe he followed the outlet down."

My eyes stayed on the cliff band across the lake. I wasn't paying much attention to Altemus. Rich responded to his own supposition. "... No, it wouldn't take you long to figure out that wasn't right. There is thick vegetation and cliffs just below there."

Suddenly the hair on the back of my neck stood up and my pulse started to race. Adrenaline unloaded into my blood stream. "He's over there!"

"What? You see him?"

"No, but he's over there."

"What makes you say that?"

"Because that is where I would go. If you were here and you wanted to take a shortcut out of here and not take the long traverse the trail makes below Clements, where would you go?" I quizzed the assistant subdistrict ranger. Altemus turned and looked across the lake. I continued, "I'd go along the cliff band and cut up that lower-angled corner in the cliffs." I pointed it out to Rich.

"The one to the left of that rib?"

"No, to the right of the rib. The one to the left gets steeper near the top; I'd take the right-hand corner. That's where he is, Rich. He tried to climb the cliff right there and he fell. We'll find his body at the base of the cliff." My heart was pounding. I could feel my neck pulsing. I looked at Altemus. His eyes had grown wide, and I could see his chest heave with deep, rapid breaths. His adrenaline rush was beginning.

"Jesus, Kennedy. You might be right." Then we could hear a soft thump, thump, thump as Jim Kruger's Bell G3B helicopter, similar to the helicopters in M.A.S.H., approached the area. Ryder called Altemus.

"223-221" (Click.)

"Go ahead, Gerry." (Click.)

"Kruger is approaching, is there anything...?"

The helicopter entered the gap between the Dragon's Tail and Bearhat Mountain and instantly the hammering of the rotor filled the deep basin of the mountain lake with loud echoes of thumping and it was hard to hear oneself think, let alone the radio transmissions. Rich and I both put our radios up to our ears.

"Have Kruger fly the cliff band," I shouted to Altemus. He nodded. He held his radio to his ear and mouth with his right hand and plugged his left ear with his left index finger.

"221. Have Kruger check the base of the cliffs east of the lake." (Click.)

"10-4. Tango Delta Alpha, you copy 223?"

"Roger that. You want me to fly the cliffs east of the lake shoreline?" (Click.)

"10-4. Tango Delta Alpha." The helicopter with the bubble-shaped cockpit was over the middle of the lake, and the pitch of the rotor began to change as the aircraft slowed. Jim Kruger eased his machine closer to the cliff band, then slowly edged along the 300-foot wall of rock at the level of its top edge, the way it looked to Rich and me at lake-level.

Kruger was Glacier's number one helicopter pilot. He had contracted with Glacier since 1970. He had flown the bodies of Jerry Kanzler and the Mount Cleveland Five from a precarious landing zone not far from the recovery site. I'd never met Jim Kruger, but I would about an hour later. Kevin Bishop rejoined us; he had found nothing. We could see a line of people in yellow fire shirts descending the last switchback above the lake.

When they arrived, command of the search would be handed over. The helicopter moved steadily along the cliff and floated past the two corners Altemus and I had discussed. It reached the end of the cliffs. "223—Tango Delta Alpha. I'm not seeing anything..."

"He's there, I know it," I said to Altemus.

"Well, maybe not."

"Rich, Kruger wouldn't see the base of the cliff from his position. He was too high. He had the sun in front of him, and he was trying to look down into the shade. We still need to get over there and look for ourselves."

"Okay, we will."

The helicopter settled down about 100 yards from the outlet of the lake, in an open meadow. Bishop, Altemus and I quickly returned to the outlet and Rich called Ryder, informing him we were planning to make one more foot patrol along the east side of the outlet and the cliffs.

"223. Go ahead and check the shoreline and cliff band. Meet us at the L. Z. (landing zone) when you are finished." (Click.)

Rich Altemus and I didn't discuss our hypothesis with Kevin Bishop while he was searching the brush. As far as Kevin knew, we were just going to cover the east side of the outlet. "Okay, Bishop," Altemus ordered, "you stay on the shoreline. Kennedy and I will traverse along the base of the cliffs. Stay even with us. Take the round out of the chamber of your weapon. Let's go." Altemus and I looked at each other. The adrenaline rush renewed itself. I followed Altemus to the base of the cliff band. It was prudent to stay behind the guy with the weapon.

"Where are we, Kennedy?"

"We still have a ways to go. The first corner is still up ahead."

We raced over the terrain. Even with the easier footing next to the lake, Bishop was having a hard time keeping up with us. I could clearly see that there were no shoes, packs or other signs of human activity along the shore from where I was. Rich and I arrived at the rib.

"This is it, Rich. The second corner is just around this rib."

"Okay, you ready?"

"Yeah."

We were breathing heavily, not only from the exertion of scrambling fast over loose talus and scree but also because we were so revved up in wild anticipation.

"Okay, let's go." Altemus's voice sounded an octave higher than usual.

A wide ledge ran along horizontally about ten feet above the base of the cliff. I scrambled up onto it to give myself a different vantage point than Rich's. He quickly gained about 50 feet on me; he was almost to the corner.

Then something caught my attention; I could see it out of the corner of my eye. Something didn't look right. I looked over the talus below me, but could not immediately tell what had, a second earlier, seemed so out of the ordinary. I hoped whatever had provoked my peripheral vision would do so again.

Altemus was now at the corner. He stopped abruptly, as if he had been poked in the ribs with a stick. My peripheral vision picked up on something again, and I turned to look for the strange object. It took a moment for it to register.

"Oh, Jesus, oh, Jesus!" Altemus exclaimed. "There's a shoe here..."

I stared at the object I had finally pinpointed. At first, I thought it was a six-foot-long chunk of cottonwood log that had been bleached gray in the sun. Maybe that was what had seemed out of place. There were no cottonwood trees at 6,400 feet in Glacier. Those weren't twisted limbs of a cottonwood tree I was seeing; those were the broken limbs of a human body.

"Here's a camera lens. Oh, God; there's blood everywhere."

"I see him! I see him!" I exclaimed, staring at the gray object.

"Where!"

"Oh, God, he's dead! Oh, Jesus—he's very dead." I believe it was the first time I'd ever seen a dead person, other than at funerals, that is. He was certainly the first dead person I'd ever seen in the field. It wasn't anything like in the movies.

"Where?"

"Right below you, Rich. Fifty feet below you."

"Hey! You guys see him?" Bishop shouted up from below.

"Yeah, he's just above you."

"Where, I don't see him."

"Halfway between you and me."

"Is he hurt?"

"Oh, Bishop!" Altemus muttered.

The 24-year-old graduate student and seasonal backcountry ranger set his shotgun down and began to dart up the slope like a 160-pound squirrel.

"He's dead, Bishop. He's very, very dead," I repeated.

Bishop didn't seem to hear me. His arms and legs were scrambling, and the talus was rolling.

"Bishop! Slow down!" Altemus bellowed. Kevin didn't seem to hear that, either. He approached the gray corpse and immediately placed his index and middle finger over the body's neck, as if to find a pulse in the carotid artery. He lowered his ear near the corpse's chest.

That's disgusting, I thought.

"Damnit, Bishop, leave him alone!" Altemus roared.

My knees were shaking. The wide ledge I was on angled down to the base of the corner, where Altemus was standing. He fumbled for his radio in its belt holster and had a hard time getting it out, he was shaking so hard. I reached an arm out to the cliff above my head to steady myself.

I looked up at the rock in the corner, above me. "Oh my God, did he fall down that?" It was then that I noticed the blood spatters, not just at the base of the cliff but on the rock above.

Movement caught my eye, 20 feet above me: a group of flies. They landed on an outcrop of rock that jutted out. On it was a chunk of flesh.

"221-223." (Click.)

"Go ahead, Rich." (Click.)

Altemus gripped his radio. It was trembling. The ranger cleared his throat and tried to moisten his lips with his tongue.

"223. Go ahead," (Click) Ryder answered again.

"Uh, Gerry, we've made a find. It's a 10-54 [ranger code for a fatality]." (Click.)

While Rich and Gerry made arrangements for the West Lake teams to join us, I made my way down to Kevin Bishop and the dead man, who had been clad in running shorts, t-shirt and running shoes. A blood trail could be seen between the base of the rock and where he took his last breath. It was as if he had gotten out of the shower and laid on the floor, creating a puddle—only it wasn't water.

There was hair on a flat section of exposed limestone that had served as a pillow before the man continued to crawl on his back toward the edge of the lake, apparently facing out. His left lower leg was compound fractured at mid-shank, twisted backwards and held together by tendons. The foot was in a shredded sock. His right femur was gouged deep, with the muscle showing. Both arms were broken, and the fingers of one hand looked dislocated. He had a large flap ripped back on his scalp. It made my skin feel twitchy. Heavy, excited breathing became shallow and inhibited. I could hardly stand up.

Bishop sat two feet from the body, facing away. He looked pale and stunned.

Altemus walked up behind me. "God, it looks like he was alive for a little while."

"He must have rested over there." I pointed to the puddle. "He tried to get out in the open, in hopes someone would see him and help him."

"Yeah, it looks like it." The adrenaline had run its course. What had been a walking, talking, warm human being only yesterday was now strangely silent and broken, staring at the sky with eyes that didn't move or blink. Bishop retrieved his space blanket, and we covered our fellow traveler. We withdrew from one another to comfort ourselves as the West Lake fire crew began its adrenaline rush, knowing it would soon handle the remains of a man who had died violently.

What kept rolling through my mind was, "This is what happens to you when you fall off."

My second season as a ranger in Glacier was in 1982, Bob Frauson's last summer before retirement. The highly regarded ranger retired in the Flathead Valley, seven miles south of Columbia Falls.

That August, there came a report of a missing climber on the remote Mount Stimson, in the southern part of the park. Mount Stimson is the second highest mountain in Glacier, located in the West Lakes District, so the search was commenced by personnel on the opposite the side of the park from St. Mary.

The missing young man had separated from his two other companions on their attempt of the standard west face route. Apparently, the missing man had gotten so far ahead of his companions that they could no longer see him. With the hour late and thunderstorms threatening, the other two climbers elected to descend to tree line and wait for their macho friend. Hours later, he had not returned, and the two finished the descent and hiked the 12 miles of trail to report their buddy missing in the middle of the night.

The search went on for two days, with more personnel being added to the search. Permanent Park Ranger Steve Frye was the incident commander, along with Bill Conrod, who had served in the Grand Teton National Park as a climbing ranger with numerous searches, rescues and recoveries to his resume.

By the third day of the search, everyone was thinking the same thing: they were searching for a body. Most likely the gung-ho scrambler, who didn't see a problem with not keeping a party together, had met with his demise.

"229-221." (Click.) It was the only radio call I ever got from Bob Frauson in my career or his. Bob Macabre was summoning me to his office. I knew if I had done something wrong and was to be reprimanded, it would be by either Rich Altemus or Gerry Ryder, not the general.

I had an idea what the meeting was all about; I had more technical mountaineering experience in the mountains of Glacier National Park than the other rangers—which is not the same as having solid rescue tactics, but is nonetheless important. Frankly, I was a little miffed that I had not been added to the search and rescue operation sooner, but that is not the way the National Park Service operates. The west side does its thing, and the east side does its thing. Looking back, I suspect it may have taken Frauson two days to pull enough strings to get me involved in the search. At the time, I found it interesting that I hadn't been asked to get involved until everyone knew this was a body recovery mission.

I walked up the steps to the Hudson Bay District Ranger Station. It was a simple Army barrack-style building containing four rooms. The door of the ranger station opened into a small space with a countertop. Behind it, a ranger could stand and look authoritative, with a topographical map on the wall behind him or her. To the left was a larger open area and desk where a clerk sat answering calls and filing the copious paperwork, the hallmark of the bureaucracy that is the National Park Service, a branch of the Department of the Interior. The right end of the building was Gerry Ryder's office. I glanced inside; he wasn't there, but his coffee pot was on, with an inch at the bottom, distilling into a layer of acrid residue.

The door to Bob's office was offset slightly, in the center of the building. The door was open and Bob was at his desk, shuffling a few papers. His wide-brimmed premium beaver Smokey the Bear hat hung from a hook next to another copy of the topographical map behind his desk. He undoubtedly had heard me come in, expecting me, not ten minutes after he called me on the radio. Bob didn't look up until I had removed my own premium beaver Smokey the Bear ranger hat and knocked on his door.

"Come in, Terry," he said, his voice subdued. Bob Frauson always used a soft voice. He was a man of few words. If there was more than one conversation going on in a room and Bob Frauson said something, the din would drop to a hush. When he spoke, people listened. He was "the man." The General. I doubt Bob Frauson ever had to repeat a word. I am equally certain Bob was capable of matching his voice to his stature and bellowing like a range bull should he deem it necessary. He could probably pick up a full-grown man by the lapels and fling him across a room.

"Would you like a cup of coffee?" he asked. It was 10:35 in the morning.

Bob had his own coffee pot on a small table in a corner near the door.

There were about two inches left in the bottom. I figured it was exactly two-and-a-half hours old.

"No, thank you, Bob."

"We've decided to send you over to the Mount Stimson search," the Tenth-Mountain-Division World War II-private-turned-park-service-general said.

"Okay. I thought you might use me," I said, trying to act official, but what I was really thinking was, "You son of a bitch, why didn't you send me two days ago?"

"We've got the staging area at the highway gravel pit at Nyack Creek, on the Forest Service side of the river." For the first time, Bob lifted his hazel eyes from his desk and swung them over to me. They were steely, like a pair of .44s.

"I want you there at 1400 hrs. You will have to drive yourself to West Glacier. We'll reimburse you for the mileage. Someone from headquarters will transport you to Nyack Flats. I've arranged to have Kruger chopper you in." He swiveled his chair around to the map and pointed. "We've got an L.Z. at thirty-nine-twenty [feet elevation] up the Nyack drainage and a base camp, at forty-four-forty below the west face." He placed a finger the size of a 12 gauge shotgun shell on the map. "You will have to proceed on foot from the L.Z. Kruger has sling-loaded in supplies. Frye and Conrod have an advanced base in the cirque at sixty-two-sixty below the snowfield. You will help search the lower cliff band above the base. I've got a few things for you to take over. Wear your 'class Bs' [informal uniform] and take your personal mountain gear. Any questions?"

"No sir, I don't believe so. I'll get packed and leave right away," I said politely and officially.

"Damn you," I was thinking, "you just want me to get in on bagging the poor bastard. You want me to be down in the brush because after two days, that's where you are sure we'll find the guy because if he were high on the mountain, Kruger or one of the upper team members would have spotted him by now. You just want me to have the experience of picking up a corpse that has been there for three days, right?"

I sat in the rigid metal chair, staring at the once white coffee cup that sat on Bob's desk. It looked like a cup you might find in the 1950s at a bus stop diner, stained as if lava had once flowed from it. We shook hands, mine disappearing into his. It was like shaking hands with a grizzly bear. I walked out of his office and around the countertop, toward the outside door.

"Mister Kennedy." I turned around; he had a little smile on his face. His eyebrows arched upward, the lower creases making furrows in recovering sunburn and the upper crease rolling into the territory of a receded hairline, white from the protection of his sweat-stained Smokey the Bear hat. I detected a twinkle in his eye I had never been privileged to see before.

"Be careful up there," he said. He knew he had me right where he wanted me. He knew Jim Kanzler and I had poured it on in the years after the Cleveland disaster. The little hotshot, I could hear him thinking. This ought to cool his jets.

"I will, Bob." I turned and headed down the steps. I just might bring you a little piece of that poor bastard back in a plastic bag, I said to myself. You can add it to all the other bodies and pieces you've bagged.

I stomped to my quarters to put the finishing touches on the rescue pack I kept near the door. There was a mixture of excitement, adrenaline and disgust flowing through me. I kissed my wife, Diane, and our one year-old daughter, Lindsay, goodbye, loaded the gutless Chevrolet Vega and putted over Logan Pass. Chevrolet didn't make 'em like they did in 1954. I missed the Tank.

The Bell G3B came thumping over the gravel pit. I could see Jim Kruger, in his jeans and cowboy boots, manipulate the stick and pedals as the ground crew and I held on to our hats and loose gear. It was the first time I'd been in a helicopter. It was the same bird that flew the bodies of the Mount Cleveland Five off of the mountain. Their wet, saturated, frozen and thawed remains had been placed into body bags and strapped to the same struts I now placed my boots on to crawl inside of the bubble, next to the pilot.

Kruger had a warm smile. He looked like a guy who was just having some fun flying his helicopter around in the mountains on a nice, summer day.

"I'm Jim Kruger, this is my helicopter," he said with a grin, nodding to me. "Snap the buckle in here," he shouted above the engine and whopping rotor, "and we'll get in the air."

"Terry Kennedy, pleased to meet you," I shouted back and started to extend my right hand across the seat. Kruger ignored it. He had his right hand on the stick, and he still had to control the helicopter. How naive of me!

"Put these on." He handed me a headset across with his left hand.

"Dispatch. Tango Delta Alpha. Leaving Nyack Flats en route to Mount Stimson. Two on board." (C-click-ch.)

He opened the throttle and the sound of the engine rose to a searing pitch; then the rotors made a heavier, whopping sound. I could see the shadow of the blades change from almost countable flicks to a nearly continuous blur. The machine rocked slightly, then lifted upward. We were suddenly above the trees and flying over a semi truck on U.S. Highway 2, then the Middle Fork of the Flathead River.

The ride fascinated me. I realized I was now glad Bob Frauson had sent me to the scene. I was already looking forward to the flight back. I hoped I wasn't going to have to hike out!

Even an old Bell G3B covers 12 miles quickly. I was busy squirming around, trying to take advantage of looking outside, watching the trees go by like so many matchsticks. I was digging the machine. Fuckin'-A, man, as Emerson would say.

Jim Kruger took off his headset and yelled above the cacophony. "I guess they don't know what happened to this guy."

"I guess not."

"'Must have fallen off somewhere."

"Probably."

"It's too bad." He started to put his headset back on. I could see the base of Mount Stimson coming up, and I suddenly realized I had a fleeting opportunity to ask Jim Kruger a question.

I really didn't know what information I wanted from him, but I simply asked, "You flew the Mount Cleveland recovery mission in 1970, didn't you?" Of course I knew he had; but he didn't know I knew.

"Yeah," he nodded. "What a tragedy! That slide got all of them."

The noise wasn't so bad now that we were just cruising and not climbing or descending. He still kept his sentences short as he continued. "So young! You know 'em?"

"Kinda."

"Good climbers?" Kruger continued looking out of each side of the bubble and below him. The mountain slopes were beginning to close in around us. Nyack Creek was much closer than it had been.

"They were," I nodded. "The best."

He nodded back. "Didn't you climb that face?"

"I did." I was flattered Jim Kruger would bring that up.

"How was it?"

"Pretty gnarly in places," I responded.

"It sure looked like it. Never catch me up there," he smiled.

"Less dangerous than flying one of these," I grinned back. We stole a glance at each other.

"I don't know about that." He gripped the stick briefly in his left hand while he gave the glass on a gauge a double-flick with the nail of his right middle finger. It was probably the altimeter. He switched his right hand back to the stick and put his headset back on. I did the same.

"Dispatch. Tango Delta Alpha. Descending to Nyack Creek." (C-click-ch.) He pulled the voice activation mic away and said to me, "Lean back a little." He looked over my lap and then at a mirror mounted on the starboard strut. The rotors bit hard and made that heavy sound again as debris blew off of the gravel bar and the two guys on the ground took cover. Then we were on the floodplain of Nyack Creek. Kruger reached over and grabbed my knee. "I'll tell you when to get out," he spoke in a serious tone while the engine idled down and the whistling of the slowing blades dropped an octave or so. "Go in front of the helicopter. Keep looking at me. We are on a little slope. Duck down low."

I nodded my head sharply. "Okay!"

It didn't take me long to hike up the creek bed of the avalanche run-out zone of Stimson's west face. There were only a few patches of snow left down low and a diminishing mid-August water flow from a snowfield at mid-height on the mountain. I was a little surprised to find the two search team members at the tent, not doing much of anything. It was just four o'clock in the afternoon.

"I would have thought you guys would be out searching," I said.

"We were searching the base of the lower cliff band, then Steve Frye ordered us back to the base camp area. He and the other three guys are traversing about 1,800 feet above us, and he didn't want us working right under them."

"Oh, I see. That's a good idea."

"Yeah, they've already knocked down some rock. We'll probably get out again later, after they traverse back. The brush is very thick in there. I don't know why he'd be down this far. It's way off the route. We're all thinking he fell, so I guess he could be anywhere."

We hung out at the tent. I got my first opportunity to sample K-rations. We monitored the radio channel, keeping track of the progress of the search above us by listening to Steve Frye and Bill "Willie" Conrod. They each had another guy with them, but only Steve and Bill would use their radios, for simplicity.

At 1730 hours, Bill Conrod (423) called Steve Frye (522). Bill was about 200 feet above Steve and 500 feet to his left as one faces uphill—or the "climber's left."

"522-423" (Click.)

"Go ahead, Willie." (Click.)

"Steve, I'm looking with binoculars at something on a ledge that might be 100 feet below you and possibly 300 feet southwest of your location. It seems to have color. Could be clothing. Can you see it?" (Click.)

There was a pause of about one minute.

"Negative. Repeat location."

Bill Conrod explained again and, five minutes later, "423-522." (Click.)

"Go ahead, Steve." (Click.)

"I've got a visual with my binoculars, below me and maybe 250 yards away. It's blue. Could be a baseball cap." Steve Frye confirmed. "Meet me at my location in fifteen. We'll take a look." (Click.)

"10-4. Meet at your location in fifteen minutes." (Click.)

The three of us at the lower camp and those at the L.Z. below all knew what this meant. Finding any item should define a fall path of the missing man. If the item with color turned out to be something man-made, it undoubtedly would have belonged to the missing scrambler. Mount Stimson might only get a couple of ascents a year. Everyone figured Frye, Conrod and the two other guys were very close to making the find.

Glacier Park's sedimentary rock, once the bottoms of oceans, was laid down in horizontal layers, typically resulting in mountain terrain that has eroded into series of parallel ledges that often stay perfectly horizontal, allowing uninterrupted traversing for considerable distances. I waited with the two other rangers at the lower camp in anticipation as the four rangers above us traversed further to the southwest, on a broad ledge. We were glued to our handset radios.

We didn't have to wait long. About 30 minutes later, we heard a radio activate the repeater (with the c-click-ch sound) and a transmission go park-wide. "Dispatch-522. Dispatch-522." (C-click-ch.)

"Go ahead, 522." (C-click-ch.) I recognized the smooth, deep voice of the dispatcher. It was Jerry Nelson, the neighbor across the street where I grew up in Columbia Falls. Jerry and Mary Nelson had come across the street to watch Barry Frost and me prepare for our attempt at the north face of Mount Cleveland, six years before.

"Be advised, we have a 10-53 [person down]," (c-click-ch) Steve Frye reported solemnly. His park-wide transmission would be heard by many people, not just the rangers. Members of the missing man's family or his friends could likely be in a ranger station, hearing the broadcast transmissions from the repeater. It was necessary to use ten codes in order to keep the specifics under wraps until the park was ready to officially release information.

"And ...?" The three of us in the tent said out loud.

There was a short pause; then:

"Be advised we have a 10-54 [fatality]" (c-click-ch), Frye continued. Now everyone monitoring the park radio that knew ten codes knew the missing scrambler had been found and he was dead, as we all had expected. The searchers on Mount Stimson breathed a sigh of relief, but, of course, this meant the real dirty work was just about to begin. It was now after 6:30 in the evening.

"10-4, 522. I copy you have a 10-53 and a 10-54. How do you wish to proceed?" (C-click-ch), Jerry Nelson asked.

"Uh, stand by one, dispatch." (C-click-ch.)

Several minutes passed.

"Dispatch-522." (C-click-ch.)

"Go ahead, 522." (C-click-ch.)

"Be advised we'll make the package and delivery tomorrow. Have Kruger on the Nyack Creek L.Z. at 0800 with a lead line. We'll attempt a sling load." (C-click-ch.)

With the basic plan outlined, the incident commander switched back to Channel two, keeping transmissions local. The field command worked on recovery logistics. There were two men on the creek at the L.Z. camp, three of us at the middle camp, and four at the high camp.

The next morning at 0530 hours, the three of us at the middle camp shouldered our packs, including climbing harnesses, helmets, leather gloves and a body bag and scrambled 1,500 feet to the upper camp. In Glacier, the rangers referred to the body bag as a pouch over the radio, a code word invented by Bob Frauson, who no doubt was closely monitoring the operation from St. Mary. There had been extra concern about grizzly bears, especially at night, knowing there would be an odor wafting about the mountain, serving as a beacon to Ursus horribilis. At 0700 we joined Frye, Conrod and the two others who had spent the night in the upper camp, making seven men high on the mountain.

During the first two days of the operation, the weather had been unsettled. There had been occasional brief showers mixed with sunshine and windy conditions up high. The night after I arrived on the scene, a front moved in and the cloud cover lowered on Mount Stimson to 8,500 feet— about 100 feet above the diorite sill, and roughly 300 feet above the body.

Our unfortunate subject had fallen over the steep diorite cliff band, most likely on his way down after getting off route. He was a quarter of a mile from the route he and his companions were following. On the correct route, the diorite sill cliff band was broken and posed only a moderate obstacle that could be climbed unroped. Apparently, our subject couldn't find this key passage on the way down.

It threatened to rain or sleet at any moment as the recovery team carefully scrambled through low cliff bands above the higher camp. We carried several ropes and a cluster of Park Service rock anchors.

Before we traversed to the body, Conrod prepared the rest of us for what we would find. "He really augured in," Bill said. "This isn't going to be pleasant. There are pieces."

Bill Conrod had been a climbing ranger in the Tetons. He had more technical rescue experience than anyone in Glacier at the time. He and I talked a few times after our work was done on Mount Stimson, and over the next year. Bill had been a good technical climber and had done many routes in the Tetons. He had climbed with some of the big names, but after he became a climbing ranger, frequently going on rescue missions and participating in recoveries like this one, his interest in climbing as a personal pursuit diminished. He told me the mental anguish of finding other climbers badly injured or dead and in pieces messed him up psychologically, making climbing less fun and more frightening. He warned me that the same thing might happen to me, and I should decide whether I wanted to follow a career as a climbing ranger or not. I understood.

Along the avalanche pathway on Mt. Cleveland, Jerry DeSanto and Larry Feser found the lower half of a hickory-shafted ice axe at the 8,300-foot level, during a climbing reconnaissance to locate the bodies on May 25, 1970. In August the following year, Bill Conrod made an ascent of the west face of Mount Cleveland to privately commemorate the Mount Cleveland Five. There, he discovered the other half of the ice axe.

Eighteen years after Bob Frauson sent me to the Mount Stimson search and recovery, McKay Jenkins wrote *White Death: Tragedy and Heroism in an Avalanche Zone*. The book documented the search and recovery of the five Montana climbers. Jenkins implicitly depicted Bob Frauson as the main hero.

By the time I went to work for the National Park Service in Glacier, I had already experienced the satisfaction of reaching some of my greatest mountain climbing ambitions. It seemed to me at the time that Bob Frauson saw in the Mount Stimson mission an opportunity to teach me a lesson.

Or maybe he just wanted me to know what he had gone through internally since his war experience derailed his mountain climbing ambitions.

Bob Frauson was a strapping six-foot-four-inch, barrel-chested young man. I could not help but wonder if, had he not been privy to so much human devastation, he himself might have gravitated toward a passion for difficult mountaineering. Perhaps, the heavy exposure to death and suffering that came from first being in World War II combat turned his greatest mountain ambitions to fodder. The harsh reality of handling so many bodies of other young men his age would take its toll on anyone. I became more understanding of Bob Frauson's dire approach to men in their teens and twenties placing themselves in dangerous situations for valor, pushing themselves into the unknown.

Jenkins quotes Frauson:

> "I never tell climbers (no)...I just tell them war stories...and what the end might be. Some...come back and thank me, and some come back dead."

—*White Death*, page 64.

The Mount Stimson recovery team came to the place on a shelf where three days of searching had ended. The body had been covered with a thin tarp the evening before. It was our task to place it in a zippered vinyl body bag called "the pouch." By then, it was 0800 hrs. Jim Kruger had already been on the gravel bar of the Nyack Creek L.Z. for a good half hour and was making preparations with the helicopter for a short line pick-off if the weather held.

The most daunting prospect was lowering the body some 2,000 feet to lower-angled terrain and hand-carrying it to the bottom of the mountain. That would not only have been very time consuming and might well have taken two days with our limited equipment, but it would also have been extremely dangerous to the recovery team because of the unavoidable rockfall. It would have been an effort of heroic proportions and miraculous to pull off without injury to the team. That prospect was our last choice.

Less treacherous would have been to traverse, with the body, the way we had come. This would have involved lifting the load several times up short cliffs to reach the main traverse ledge then lower the cargo down a descending-traverse route to the vicinity of the high camp and the permanent snowfield. Moving a dead weight anywhere but down the fall line is problematic. Raising a 160-180 pound load would have required multiple rock anchors and the assistance of a ratchet system, such as Jumar ascenders reversed or Prusik knots. We could have managed that. Seven men could have muscled the load up ten or 15-foot cliffs two or three times. It would have been exhausting, but we could have managed if the vinyl body bag didn't shred.

Hoisting the body any higher would have required mechanical advantage and pulleys. We weren't equipped for that. Dragging the body bag along the ledge would have been doable, providing the "pouch" held up. Making 1,000-foot diagonal descent on more moderate terrain would have been more desirable than lowering the body down 2,000 feet of ledges and cliffs replete with loose rock, even though climbing through such terrain for sport would not have been difficult.

Clearly, what everyone on the Mount Stimson recovery team wanted was for Jim Kruger to maneuver the Bell G3B into position so that we could clip the load into a 40-foot line below the helicopter. Jim Kruger could lift the body off of the ledge and fly it out.

Try not to look at the body too much, I repeated to myself. Just don't look at his face. I tried to dampen the adrenaline rush rising within me as we approached the tarp by being philosophical and pastoral. "After all, the person who once inhabited that body wasn't there...right?" I knew there would be ghastly injuries and deformities. Seeing such defacement would not serve any useful purpose to a climber. There would always be that image etched on my mind and haunt me with, "That is what will happen to you if you, someday, take the big one." Thoughts and images like that might surface while in the midst of climbing a desperate section, where a fall would be fatal.

"Okay you guys. Everyone is going to want to wear their gloves," Steve Frye informed us. We laid out the pouch and unzipped it, full-length. Steve Frye positioned everyone where he wanted us. He would remove the tarp, then we would lift the young man in one piece as best we could and place him in the pouch. We would take the pieces and what personal items we could find within the immediate area with us.

The thick cloud cover maintained a definitive demarcation line just above the diorite sill. "If the ceiling gets any lower, we're screwed, " Frye muttered, looking upward.

"We'd better get Kruger going, then," Conrod advised. "He can always abort. I think we've got a small window to do this thing."

"Bill, I think you are right." He keyed his transceiver pinned to his jacket. "Tango Delta Alpha-522." (Click.) There was a pause.

"Go ahead, 522." (Click.)

"Are you good to go, Jim?" (Click.)

"Uh, 10-4. If that ceiling doesn't get any lower, I'm willing to try it."

"10-4, Jim. We're going to package the subject and we'll tell you when to go." (Click.)

"10-4, 522. Tell me when you're ready." (Click.)

The body was lying in a slight depression or shallow gully as it intersected the ledge, extending down from the diorite sill above. This was the reason he had been so difficult to spot. If I had learned one thing from my experiences recovering fall victims, it was that falling bodies are like falling water; they tend to flow into depressions and pool where it is flat. Look for their line of descent in gullies and expect to find them in a low-angle areas of the gully, below steep drops.

Our subject was on his back, descending feet-first, with his arms flailing overhead. He was wearing jeans and a flannel shirt, which told me he was probably inexperienced. A serious or experienced climber would not be found on a high, remote mountain in cotton—especially not in unstable weather.

Every limb was obviously fractured, twisted and deformed. His shirt was shredded and ripped off of one shoulder, trailing behind him like a banner, exposing his back as he took a huge run down the gully on ledges, talus and scree taking several hundred feet of air off of the sill. We scooted him around parallel to the ledge and brought the pouch up to him.

"Don't look at his face," I reminded myself, "Don't look, don't look, don't look." There was a certain carnal curiosity within me that disregarded any request for chastity. I stole a glance at the dead man's face and caught his stony gray gaze for perhaps only a second. Brief though it was, the image was burned indelibly into the emulsion of my memory. I can look at it whenever I want, which is seldom, and often when I wish not to do so. I can tell you there was almost no blood on his face. He did have an odd shape to his head. One eye socket was higher than the other. His eyes were wide open, a pale bluish-gray, with pupils large and black, staring straight out into the sky as if he had been stargazing for three nights.

His eyes were beginning to dehydrate and sink into their orbits.

I was positioned on the downhill side. I placed my gloved right hand under his pelvis and my left hand under his left knee. We were all in a bit of a hurry to get this done. Steve Frye called 1-2-3, and four of us lifted the corpse. His torso was as stiff as beef jerky, but his left leg flopped, limp, and

I realized it was about to fall off. So did Bill Conrod, and we hastily clasped hands underneath. Steve slid the pouch in place and we lowered him.

About 75 feet above us was his daypack. One of the guys scrambled up the gully to retrieve it; another guy picked up scattered items. A few feet above where our subject had come to rest was something on the scree. It looked like scrambled eggs, only gray. I was pretty sure I knew what it was.

"Steve. Are we going to put that in the pouch, too?" I pointed in that direction but refused to look again.

Frye turned to me slowly, refusing to look where I was pointing. He had seen it.

"I'm not going to pick it up," he said quietly.

"I'm not going to pick it up, either," I whispered back.

He gave me a short nod. "I'm sure our young friend won't mind if we leave a piece of him up here," he said softly.

Conrod produced about 20 feet of nine-millimeter rope and, with the skill of an experienced loadmaster, proceeded to lash the body bag with the rope to secure the cargo anatomically inside and prevent it from sliding. He ended with double figure-eight loops to be clipped into the hook of the static line below the helicopter, which Jim Kruger had assembled at the L.Z. on the creek below.

"Tango Alpha Delta, 552." (Click.)

"Go ahead." (Click.)

"We're ready, Jim." (Click.)

"10-4, 552. What's your wind?" (Click.)

"Ten knots from the west southwest. Slightly variable." (Click.)

"10-4. Copy 10 from west southwest." (Click.)

"10-4." (Click.)

"Keep a close eye on it. Let me know if that changes. I'll get underway." (Click.)

"10-4. Conrod will be with the cargo. The rest of us will be together 60 feet to your right." (Click.)

"10-4, Steve. I copy that."

"Okay, men. Let's pray to God this works." Steve Frye said with a heavy sigh. Six of us huddled together as far back on the ledge we could get, so we would be as far from the rotor as possible and Kruger could see everyone at once. Conrod was the only man on his feet.

"Dispatch-522." (C-click-ch.) (Short pause.)

"Go ahead, 552." (C-click-ch.) The voice of Jerry Nelson, again.

"Be advised we are getting underway to attempt a static-line pick-off."

"There he goes, he's starting up," someone said. The helicopter on the gravel bar was partially obscured by the alders along the creek and difficult to see until the rotors started turning. The tips were painted white for better visibility, and they were easy to see when moving even from 4,000 feet above. We could hear the increased pitch of the engine. The ship lifted off before the whop-whop-whop of the rotors bit deeper into the air to get it off the ground, due to the delay of sound traveling almost a mile.

Jim Kruger maneuvered his ship around and around in spirals to gain elevation in the deep mountain valley. We watched from the ledge, captivated. It must have taken Kruger a full five minutes. We were all edgy. We knew this was a very dangerous undertaking for Kruger. One strong gust of wind or a miscalculation, and the helicopter could nip the mountain with a rotor tip and crash violently. We looked down on the pilot as he maneuvered the helicopter up toward us. Kruger's eyes were busy looking upward through the Plexiglass bubble to be sure where he was in relationship to the cliffs. He never looked directly at the six of us huddled on the ledge, but I think he kept track of us out of his peripheral vision.

The cloud ceiling was maintaining. He was going to take a shot at it. It was strange watching the pilot working his way up to us from below. As he got closer, he made brief eye contact with Conrod. Bill held the knot above his head for Kruger to see his target.

"Looks good from here, Jim!" Steve Frye reported. (Click.)

"10-4. I'm not going to be able to maintain a hover. I'm going to come in low enough to get Conrod the line, but I've gotta keep going forward. He's going to have to do this fast." (Click.)

"Hear that, Bill?" Frye shouted.

Conrod nodded his head vigorously.

"We copy, Jim!" (Click.)

"10-4. I can see you Bill. Here I come." (Click.)

The reverberations of the rotors and the engine at full throttle became so loud it was no longer possible to hear communications with the handsets we carried. The G3B was briefly level with us as Kruger brought the ship toward us, slowly ascending, cowboy boots working the pedals. He wore no helmet— just amber sunglasses. The rotor wash began to reach us. Conrod had the double figure-eight knot in one gloved hand, while the other covered his helmet. He was watching the line approach below him.

Suddenly the hook hit the rock below and began to bounce. We all shouted at once, standing up from our protective crouches and pointing at the hook. Everyone knew if that hook had caught anything at all, a lip or protrusion, it would pull the helicopter into the mountain and it would crash right on top of us. It would happen in about a second-and-a-half. We were all yelling and screaming and pointing to the hook, which was bumping along below Conrod.

Bill reacted quickly. He thrust himself off of his perch on the small outcrop jutting out from the ledge, like a hawk diving onto its prey. He descended ten feet with amazing agility, considering the heavy mountain boots and gloves he was wearing. Had he tripped, or had loose rock given way, he would have tumbled to his own death. Conrod grabbed the cable about ten feet from the hook and flipped it away from the rock. He held the cable out in one hand and madly reversed direction, scrambling one-handed, as the helicopter bore up the slope right over his head. If something happened at that point, Kruger and the G3B would have crashed right on Bill.

The cable kept sliding through Conrod's hands. The hook was at Conrod's hand as he reached the body bag. By this time the helicopter was forward of Conrod, I doubted Kruger could see him. The pilot's attention could only be focused on the narrowing space between the mountain and his rotors.

In one continuous motion, Bill Conrod grabbed the double figure-eight knot and brought the knot and the hook together, like he was lifting two dumbbells overhead in a gym. In spite of the chaos from the down wash of the rotors, the small bits of scree blowing from the ledge, and the intense concern for both the pilot and Conrod, we could hear a faint "tink" as the clasp on the cable hook closed shut, trapping the knot.

The cable went tight a nanosecond later, and the ship hesitated ever so slightly as it took on the weight of its new passenger. It cleared the outcrop and the ledge about two feet per second at first. Conrod had to push it away from him to keep from getting knocked off of his position.

"You've got him, Jim! He's all yours!" (Click.) Steve Frye shouted into his radio. There was no reply.

The cargo was 5-10-15 feet off of the ledge and hung in position briefly as Kruger swung the tail around slowly and began to lean the ship away from the mountain. He banked hard to the left and cleared the slope of Mount Stimson.

Within a few seconds, he was out into the valley, 4,000 feet above Nyack Creek, the body bag swinging 40 feet below. The cargo reminded me of a picture I saw of Royal Robbins in his hammock on the North American Wall on El Cap during the first ascent.

"Dispatch. Tango Delta Alpha." (C-click-ch.)

"Go ahead, Tango Delta Alpha." (C-click-ch.)

"I'm en route to headquarters from Mount Stimson with a sling load. One on board. ETA 15 minutes." (C-click-ch.)

"10-4, Tango Delta Alpha, I copy you are inbound with cargo from Mount Stimson. One on board. ETA 15 minutes. The crew will be waiting for you at the L.Z." (C-click-ch.)

In an odd way, it had been a compassionate and consoling experience to take the quick glance into the face of "our friend". In having done so, I felt a connection with all of us who run around in bodies, knowing that somehow, in our own way, we will all be cargo one day.

CHAPTER 22

Tracks in the Snow

Thirteen years passed like cottonwood bark down the Flathead River since Jim Kanzler and I emerged onto the summit of Mount Siyeh and bivouacked one last time. I had been married for five-and-a-half years of that time, and was now a single dad myself, struggling to maintain a relationship with my eight-year-old daughter, Lindsay. I had climbed new routes in Glacier, but nothing of the magnitude of Cleveland or Siyeh. I had survived an epic on the Super Couloir on Deltaform Mountain in the Canadian Rockies in poor conditions. I had been a climbing ranger in Rocky Mountain National Park for a season and climbed the Diamond of Longs Peak wearing a badge, teamed with the supervising climbing ranger, Billy Westbay, of Yosemite fame. I had guided for Colorado Mountain School, including an expedition on Mount Logan in the Yukon of Canada.

Jim Kanzler had left Big Sky for the Jackson Hole Ski Patrol and continued to guide for Exum in the Tetons during the summers.

By June of 1991, I had put another five years of school behind me and took my first Physical Therapy position in Eugene, Oregon, because Lindsay had moved there with her mom. It was a novelty to have a real job. I could buy climbing gear and still have money for food and rent. I could pay child support. I could set money aside for the future. A year later, I had accrued vacation time and could buy an airline ticket and go somewhere. I had not been to Alaska in seven years, or the Canadian Rockies in ten. It was time to get back to where I once belonged.

A line caught my imagination in 1984, when my brother, Dan, Montana mountaineers Tom Cladouhos and Ed Sondeno, and I made an ascent of the South Buttress of Denali. On the approach, we skied underneath the southeast face of East Kahiltna Peak (13,340 feet), connected to the Cassin Ridge of North America's highest mountain. I saw a route between granite buttresses that avoided a dangerous icefall. A narrow hose of ice curved behind a cylindrical pillar that reminded me of the Silver Pillar in the Beartooth Mountains.

Early February 1992

Eight years after the Denali climb, I called Kanzler.

"C'mon, Kanzler, we need to get back on the old warpath," I said over the phone "Let's get out there and start counting coup again. There are still unclimbed faces out there, and we need to go do them. This route on East Kahiltna Peak will be a dandy."

I was hopeful he would get fired up to do something big. It had been six years since we had climbed a big desert tower in New Mexico and I suspected Jim, like me, had been out of form for a number of years. It might take a little encouraging, but it would be like the Blues Brothers getting the band back together.

"It won't be too outrageous," I prattled on, "but challenging enough. I'll send you copies of the photos I took in 1984."

"I know it's a neat face," Kanzler replied. "Jack Tackle and I skied under it in 1980, when we took a cache partway up the south buttress of Denali." Jim had joined Jack Tackle to make a second attempt of the route Jack would later climb and name Isis, on a feature leading from the West Fork of the Ruth Glacier to the ridge of the South Buttress of Denali. On the attempt with Kanzler, Tackle got sick and they never got on their route. Jack Tackle climbed the route a year later, with David Stutzman.

"It should be a good route," Jim said. His voice had a vacant quality, distancing him from my enthusiasm. There was a moment of dead air.

What Jim Kanzler said next wrenched my guts.

"I'm over it, Kennedy."

"What? What do you mean? Kanz-lerrr!"

He had to be pulling my leg. I wrung my hands, praying that he was.

"I don't want to go wandering around on glaciers and crevasses," Kanzler droned. "I don't want to subject myself to avalanches anymore."

It was like a confession. I quickly launched into damage control mode, trying to cushion the impact of Kanzler's words. I needed to buy a few seconds for him to reconsider what he was saying.

"It's not too crevassed up there. We'd be roped up, of course. The line is pretty safe. We can avoid the icefall."

"I'm done with alpine climbing" Kanzler cut me off.

"Kanz-lerr..." He was killing me.

"I don't like getting my feet cold, Mr. Johnson." He tried to laugh, but his voice was too dry.

My heart sank further. I had to work to pull my next breath in. Kanzler. No. I felt pained by his self-degradation. It was thick and heavy, and he was attached to it. I had seen it throughout the years. Climbing had always had a palliative effect; now it was different.

"But why, Kanzler, why?" I could only force a whisper. "Forty-four is nuthin'. I'm 38, and I feel the same as when I was 22. You can't be that far over the hill. Let's just start on something easier—less dangerous."

I was stunned. An era had come to an end. Perhaps it had died on the summit of Mount Siyeh, and I had just refused to acknowledge it then, but there was no mistaking it now.

I slumped against the bare wall in my cluttered apartment in Eugene. My grip loosened on the telephone receiver as I hung up. It began to sink in that Jim Kanzler and I would never team up to do anything big again.

I had seen Kanzler's drive sputtering through the years following Siyeh, but I had pretended not to worry. Both Kanzler and I had periods of time when we were not on our game. I had gone through periods where I was not in shape, when family obligations or school forced climbing to the side. Whatever the reason, the lure of the mountains always came roaring back.

Something in his voice and choice of words—"I'm over it" –had a crippling effect on me. I never felt so lost.

Jim was approaching the age when Hal had shot himself. Jim had his dad's chiseled features. One spring day in 1977, he and I were walking along the Gallatin River en route to a rock climb in the towers of Gallatin Canyon. "I always wanted to live long enough to walk my dad's butt off, but he never gave me the chance." Jim said, referring to Hal's endurance on the trails and his untimely suicide. Now there was another dying, this time for me. It was the loss of my best mountain climbing partner.

Throughout the 1980s, I had thought Jim Kanzler and I would get back on the path of Mad Wolf. One year, Jim Kanzler and I nailed our way up an aid route on El Capitan for a few days, rappelling off before a huge storm hit us. That wasn't exactly getting on a roll like we had been on in the 1970s; but it held some promise.

My life had taken some twists and turns. My first marriage failed, and it took a few years of wandering about to decide where to go from there. At least I had climbing. I began rock climbing consistently with new partners in Eugene. I linked up with Tom Bauman, a local legend—the first guy to solo the Nose of El Capitan in 1971, belaying himself with Jumars! I bagged the Oregon Cascade volcanoes solo, sometimes in the winter. I put up new routes on established local crags and discovered other rocks in the Oregon forests that had never had previous climbing activity on them. I ran in all-comers track meets on the Hayward Field and got into decent shape.

Kanzler had been guiding. He rock climbed sporadically with Jamie and other members of a younger generation. If you don't count guiding the north face of the Grand Teton, which he did more than once, Kanzler had not done anything big in years. I always assumed he and I would get back into knocking off other unclimbed routes and faces sooner or later— if not in Alaska and Canada, at least in Glacier Park.

I hung up the phone and went to work, convincing myself that it just was not a good time for Jim to head out on a two-week trip to Alaska. After all, it was pretty short notice. The following year would be better. If I was successful at putting the southeast face of East Kahiltna Peak together, then another project would likely spawn from that. Kanzler would have time to get back on track, and he and I would rock and roll, just like old times.

On a night in July 2002, 32 years after the Mount Cleveland tragedy, with our best climbs now behind us, Jim and I sat around a small campfire at the base of the Wall in the Humbugs, passing a flask of Yukon Jack back and forth. We had climbed a new route that day on the Nose, which we named "The Twelfth Planet." The second pitch had been, possibly, my strongest Humbug on-sight lead, requiring brushing coarse grit from the crack and the foot-smears with a wire brush while maintaining awkward stances.

"If Jerry had lived, do you think he would have gone on to be a great climber?" I asked.

"Yeah...probably." Kanzler seemed ready for the question.

"Like first ascents in the Canadian Rockies and Alaska...the north face of the Eiger, routes in the Himalayas?"

Kanzler took his time indexing my references; but that wasn't the question I really wanted to ask. "I mean...if Jerry had lived..." I hesitated. I had long since come to understand that Jim was—in a practical interpretation—the sole survivor of the Mount Cleveland tragedy. This was dicey.

"...Would...there have been... an Alex Lowe before there was Alex Lowe?"

"I don't know," Jim muttered. He stared deep into the coals and shifted his position on the ground, searching for a keener reply.

Jerry Kanzler and Alex Lowe were mountain warriors—mountain gods—who disappeared into the thundering whiteness 30 years apart. Alex was killed October 5, 1999, walking across an avalanche run-out zone below a 26,000-foot-high peak—Shishapangma, in the Himalayas of Nepal—with a mug of coffee in hand (so the story goes). Alex had been world-class for 20 years. He had been featured in a variety of periodicals, including *National Geographic*. Everyone knew who Alex Lowe was.

Jerry and Alex both had thick, dark hair; medium builds, and were exceptionally strong. I remembered them as outgoing and engaging, with an unusual presence in their eyes. To those who knew them better, they had been regarded as fearless, with extraordinary climbing abilities and ambition. Alex was known to have done chin-ups by the hundred. Jerry had been a gymnast in high school and had been seen doing one-armed chin-ups, gripping the bottom edge of a floor joist.

Jim had known Alex through the climbing circles and guiding at Exum. Alex entered the scene after the Mount Cleveland climb, some time during the Siyeh years. He would earn a reputation from cutting edge climbs around the world and rescuing other climbers. I climbed a route on Devil's Tower in Wyoming with Alex and Rick Hooven in the early 1980s. Alex made the cover of the February 1997 issue of *Climbing Magazine* in an insane photo of him climbing an overhanging iceberg—unroped—with nothing but a black, frigid ocean beneath him.

Alex gave an autographed copy to Kanzler: "Jim—You started this nonsense—chasing you."

I could see flickers of light reflect in Jim's glasses. I thought he was about to make a proclamation that would have substantiated 30 some years of wonder, and vindicated me—never mind the Mount Cleveland Five.

Instead, Jim slumped forward, shaking his head almost imperceptibly. "I don't know," his voice came like a breeze entering the old Douglas fir overhead. "I just don't know."

We were silent for a while. A few soft pops came from the waning fire. "Jerry was a much more talented climber than me. He was the best climber in our little group. He was full of enthusiasm and life, and he always wanted to lead. He always seemed happy."

Maybe that was what made Jerry Kanzler and Alex Lowe such heroes to me. The chin-ups and the amazing climbs I could fathom. Always being happy and high-energy, I could not.

A fellow expedition member was killed with Alex and one of his best climbing partners was injured—yet walked away from the debris. How ironic that Alex Lowe, with all of that extraordinary experience, would be killed walking across easy terrain. Jim and I would always mourn his loss.

We lapsed, once again, into separate contemplation, disconnected by questions that had no answers. I felt left behind in the world of mortality.

The embers shimmered and grew dim. I imagined the Mount Cleveland Five sitting around a campfire nearby, yet worlds apart; telling stories and making plans for adventures in a time yet to be. I never asked Jim such questions again.

Mid-February 1992

I called Kanzler again a week later. Things might be different now. Maybe Jim had just been in one of his dark moods. Maybe he had clawed his way out of the black hole. Maybe our sine wave crests would come into synch.

We exchanged chitchat about the weather and new rock climbs I was putting up near Eugene. I was careful not to broach the subject directly. I felt him out for ideas for other partners. If he was not serious about quitting alpine climbing, he had a chance to end the charade.

He didn't.

Then, Kanzler took me by surprise yet again.

"What about Jamie?" he asked.

"Jamie? Your son?"

"Yeah. He's climbing well. He's led a few 5.12s and has done quite a bit of ice climbing the last year or two. Jamie has a friend, JP, who is his best partner, and I'd bet the two of them would be up for something like this."

I rocked back on the legs of my chair. If Jim didn't want to subject himself to crevasses, cold, falling ice and avalanches, why would he so willingly offer up his son? This would not be piddling around on half-pitch bolt clippers. Alaskan climbing is worlds apart from that. There are numerous ways to get chopped on big, glaciated mountains.

"Jamie has a good head on his shoulders," Kanzler went on. "He's got a lot of experience with snow conditions, with all the backcountry skiing he's done and the work he is doing with ski areas. He's cautious, and I'd say he is the more conservative of the two when it comes down to not taking on too much danger."

The first time I saw Jamie Kanzler, he was two years old. Larry Wilson, the wrestling coach, had mentioned Jim, Lindalee and their son were going to visit him while they were in town, staying with Lindalee's parents for a few days. I contrived to look at Kanzler slides at Wil's house when I knew Jim, Lindalee and Jamie would be there. It was like walking into a house with the Beatles sitting around the living room.

The last time I had seen Jamie, he was a lean, shirtless 14 or 15-year-old at Whitefish Lake, in the northwest corner of the Flathead Valley. He was having a day at the lake with some of his downhill ski racing buddies in the summer of 1983. I was taking a weekend from Helena to visit my parents with my Lindsay, who was two, and her mom, when we were still married. We drove ten miles from Columbia Falls to Whitefish Lake to play. I recognized Jamie and introduced myself. Jamie remembered me from a few years before at Jenny Lake in the Tetons, when he spent time with his dad there. Jamie frequently had to look after himself while Jim was guiding. The shy teenager was a little taken back by an adult he did not know well addressing him in front of his friends. Jamie was polite, if not overly engaging.

Jamie was a chip off the ol' Kanzler block. He represented the last of the Kanzlers. If something happened to Jamie, then Hal, Jim and Jerry's bloodline would come to an end. That torch would be extinguished. It was also not lost on me that Jamie and JP were in their early 20s, just as the Mount Cleveland Five had been.

With all of this weighing on my mind, I called Jamie in March of 1992. His voice had the same heavy timbre as his father's. For a moment, I thought I had accidentally dialed Jim. Jamie accepted my invitation without hesitation; then he contacted JP, who also accepted. There came a ring of familiarity.

On May 2, 1992, Doug Geeting landed Jamie Kanzler, JP Gambetese and me on the Kahiltna Glacier, and we began pulling our plastic toboggans of gear and provisions up the West Buttress track of Denali. The next day, we left the trade route and ferried loads four more days up the East Fork tributary of the main Kahiltna Glacier, setting up a base camp below the southeast face of East Kahiltna Peak.

We moved well, roped up on the glacier. Jamie and JP were both as good as I was technically, and probably stronger. My only concern was that the three of us had not climbed together before. I knew this might be asking for trouble, but I accepted the risk, knowing that Jamie was so much like his father. I suggested we do a "warm-up climb" when we got to the mountain to get used to climbing together, thus making us more efficient on the face. If the weather held, we could get in two routes with the ten days we had between Glacier flights to and from Talkeetna.

The American Alpine Journal had documented a 1961 ascent of the south ridge of East Kahiltna Peak, and I was thinking this feature might be what we were looking for; if we were successful on the southeast face, we would descend the south ridge. If we climbed the descent route as a warm up, we would have a big advantage should we come stumbling off of the summit in bad weather or fatigued.

As we moved our sledloads up the glacier toward the base of the face, I kept an eye on the approaching south ridge. A hidden S-shaped couloir came into view, cutting the corner on the left side of the southeast face to a notch in the south ridge, 1,500 feet below the summit.

The three-man caravan stopped for a good look when we were adjacent to it. The S-couloir would have ice climbing similar to the main face, and would finish on the ridge to the summit. We would have an option to camp or bivouac in the notch, either on the way up or down. We formed a plan to climb to the summit via this new line.

We left our base camp below East Kahiltna Peak at 7 a.m. on May 10th, and headed for the S-couloir. It wasn't exactly an alpine start by Rocky Mountain standards; but it really didn't matter, since days were very long in May in the Land of the Midnight Sun. The sky does not fully darken until midnight in most of Alaska that time of year, and predawn light begins just four hours later.

We roped up in camp for the glacier travel to the bergschrund and the base of the S-couloir, aware that there was a series of crevasses over the quarter-mile stretch, and we would have to carefully negotiate it.

A thin mist of ice crystals hung on the surface of the glacier, making it difficult to see the details of the snow surface. One could not be sure exactly when your crampons were going to contact the snow. It was like walking on clouds, yet we could see the peaks and ridges bathed in sunlight above the ground fog.

We agreed that Jamie would go on the point, with me bringing up the rear. I figured I could see what was going on better and slow the younger guys down if necessary. JP tied into the middle of the rope. Jamie tied in 40 feet in front of him. This left over 50 feet trailing behind Jamie, with the loose end slithering along as we traveled. Similarly, I tied in 40 feet behind JP and trailed another 50 feet with a loose end behind me. The loose ends of rope served as a second rope, which would become invaluable if someone were to fall into a crevasse. Each member attached to the main rope with one mechanical ascender and one Prusik knot with foot loops that functioned as ratchets on the rope, should one find himself in a crevasse and need to climb out. We carried a second rope in a pack to use in the more difficult climbing on the face proper.

Jamie led us out of camp. We hadn't moved 100 yards before I found myself stepping on a faint depression in the snow that extended in either direction, indicating we had just crossed a hidden crevasse and each of us had stepped right in the middle of it. I didn't see the lurking hazard until I was right on it because of the light conditions. I shouted up to Jamie to be very careful with conditions so deceptive.

Moments later, I lunged forward involuntarily. I thought JP had hurried the pace, and was dragging me. I looked up. At first I couldn't see anyone. Then I could make out one guy through the mist, on his hands and knees—Jamie. JP was nowhere to be seen.

It took about a second and a half to process what was going on: JP had fallen into a crevasse. The rope had been tighter between Jamie and JP, so Jamie took JP's body weight until JP had dropped far enough below the surface, and then he engaged me. The jolt caused Jamie to take one awkward step backward, and he instinctively dropped to his knees, and then prone, with his ice axe in self-arrest position.

I shouted through the fog. "Jamie, are you OK?"

"Yeah! JP fell into a crevasse!"

"I know! Can you hold him?" I still had some of his weight on me, but most of it was on Jamie.

"I think so." The slope was not steep. Had it been, there would have been a greater propensity for JP's body weight to drag Jamie backward toward the hole JP had broken open and plunged through, and JP's weight would have gone to me. The rope sawed into the lip of his entry portal and helped slow him down. There was no visible indication of him. The rope just disappeared into white.

"OK. I'm going to give you all of him," I yelled to Jamie.

"Okay."

"I'll try to get over to you and we'll work on getting him out."

"OK, man... he's really heavy. Try and hurry."

"OK Jamie, I will. This is going to be tricky. If I go in, we are all going to be fucked."

"I know, man. Be careful!"

Not all crevasse falls and extrications would be this complicated. Others could be much worse. I was just thankful there were three of us, not two.

JP's plunge had made a hole the diameter of his shoulders and pack combined. It was literally a manhole. The ropes disappeared into the hole, with Jamie's end cutting four feet into the snow, toward him.

I took a deep breath. First, what we needed to do was establish whether or not JP was hurt. I was now fewer than 40 feet from him, but there was no way we would be able to hear each other until I was right up to the hole. I had no idea how wide the crevasse was. It was possible JP had plunged through a ceiling and dangled in the middle of a room with the floor 200 feet below him. I've looked down into crevasses like that. It was possible that I was already standing on the ceiling. The one thing I could not let happen was to fall into the crevasse myself. If I did, I would fall 40 feet below JP and shock-load Jamie or get wedged, either of which would yield dire consequences.

JP and I had to communicate. Only JP could inform me of the characteristics of the crevasse. I drew the rope through my ascender and Prusik knot to minimize the amount of rope between us. I took my pack off and attached it to the end of the free section I trailed behind me, to minimize my weight. Then I got down on my belly and started to crawl like a crocodile to disperse my weight like a snowshoe, pulling the rope through the ascender.

I could make out a faint sag in the snow ahead of me that stretched perpendicular to our line of travel. Fifteen feet from the hole, I shouted. No reply.

Twelve feet. No reply.

Ten feet. No reply.

I began to imagine JP upside-down with his pack on, not able to get upright in the middle of an elevator-like shaft. It does happen. JP was very strong, though, and hopefully could get himself upright. It would be just like a wrestling move.

Eight feet. I shouted again.

"JP! You OK?"

Nothing.

I inched closer, drawing in the slack. I was becoming more and more jittery, fearing the snow would suddenly collapse and I would plunge in, colliding with JP on the way past him. I bit my lip. I didn't want to get any closer. I raised myself on my hands to get a more direct shout-line at the hole.

"JP! You OK?" My voice crackled at the strain.

There was a very faint, muffled reply.

"I'm OK." He sounded a mile away.

"He's OK, Jamie!" I hollered. "How are you doing?"

"My harness is really digging into me. But I'm OK."

I now needed directions on how to get to the other side of the crevasse—and to get JP's weight off of Jamie. I didn't dare get any closer to the hole. I slowly got up on my knees, which helped the voice trajectory.

"Are...you...facing...Jamie?"

There was no reply. He didn't get the question.

"Are you facing Jamie...OR...Terry?"

A pause...then, "Jamie." That was the pivotal point in the rescue: JP would anticipate the questions I would ask, and I the answers he would give.

"Can...you...touch...the...wall?"

"Yes." That was good; he wasn't spinning, and could stabilize himself.

A climber in a crevasse can only ascend the rope to where it cuts into the snow above him. How far it cuts in depends on how soft the snow is. Getting over the lip is the problem. I could sense JP knew I was going to have to cross to Jamie's side to help get him out. The question was, where?

"How...wide...is...the...cruh-vasse?"

There was a pause. JP had to wonder if I meant wide to his left and right or front to back. He had to know that I needed to know how much bridge—or ceiling—I needed to cross from front to back.

He told me what I wanted to know. "Eight...feet."

"Jesus!" If he could touch the far wall, then I was right at the edge—maybe over it. I backed up a little.

"Should...I...cross...right...or left...of...you?" JP's answer would be relative to JP facing Jamie's direction. We both had to assume we were oriented the same way.

"Go... right!" His reply was unambiguous. Only JP knew what the inside of the crevasse and the covering over the top were like. The most critical decision was his. "How...far?" How far did I need to go to get enough snow over the hidden chasm to, hopefully, allow my passage without collapsing it again? He was ready with the answer.

"Thir-dee...feet."

"Thirty feet...three...zero?"

"Y-yes!"

I backed up on my hands and knees, letting the rope back out. I continued until I had all 40 feet of rope out. It would be just enough—unless JP's estimate was short.

I crawled like a soldier under gunfire, making a wide arch with JP's hole as the pivot, pulling my pack along on the other tail of rope. I kept the slack out of the rope. I had to consider we might be in a maze of such crevasses. I crawled 80 feet to Jamie and got on my feet.

"Hurry," Jamie pleaded, "It's killing me. My legs are going numb." I could see the waist loop of his harness pulling down between his legs, digging into the top of his pelvis. Because the pull was downward, toward his feet, none of the forces were absorbed by his leg loops. He was clearly in pain.

"Hang on, Jamie; it won't take me long to get an anchor." I knew the quality of the snow was poor for holding an anchor. When we had leveled tent platforms and built wind barriers, the snow was sugary and did not pack well. Ice axe shafts and the plate-like "dead man" snow anchor would be ineffective or untrustworthy, and it was too far to dig down to the glacier ice to get in ice screws. There was no point in wasting time to confirm my suspicions, so I went with the one anchor I knew I could get.

I moved ten feet past Jamie, removed the avalanche shovel from my pack and excavated a three-foot-deep trench as fast as I could. I girth-hitched runners around my pack, placed it in the bottom of the trench and boot-packed the snow on top. It would have held a small truck.

I fastened a Prusik knot to the weighted rope just below Jamie and attached that to the pack anchor, stabbing my ice axe shafts into the system for good measure.

"OK, Jamie. Let JP onto the other rope." He inched backward, transferring the weight to the buried pack. His harness was trying to peel his pants off. Jamie had held JP's weight for about 40 minutes, with some bare skin in contact with the snow.

Jamie was able to sit up and take his own pack off.

I secured Jamie's pack sideways, near the hole, sliding a Prusik knot along the new anchored rope for my own security, and dropped the loose end down to JP over the top of Jamie's pack to keep the rope from also slicing into the snow. I could see JP's helmet ten feet below the hole. We made eye contact for the first time.

"JP, switch your ascenders to the slack rope. It's anchored and ready for you to climb out on."

In a few minutes, he was on the surface, unscathed.

Falling into a crevasse roped up is serious business. We had worked as effectively as anyone could expect. The whole operation took about 50 minutes. Falling in without a rope is often a farewell scene.

"How do you feel, JP?"

"Not too bad," he said. He was undaunted.

"You know, we can call it a day and go back to camp and start again tomorrow," I suggested.

"I'm okay—really. I say we keep going."

I looked at Jamie. He was a little haggard looking, but recovering. "My waist is a little sore, but I'm OK. I want to keep going if JP does."

The mist hugging the surface of the glacier had vanished, and we found a thick bridge over the bergschrund a ways further. Once above it, we untied from each other and climbed simultaneously about 700 feet up the lower couloir, to save time. When the terrain steepened and turned to ice, I twisted in a pair of ice-screw anchors and we tied in again with the full lengths of both ropes. We were excited to be front-pointing on crampons and swinging an ice axe in each hand.

Jamie led a crux pitch on blue ice and a mix of angular white granite. Above, the couloir opened wider and uniform; but we had a problem. Slabby snow with loose, grainy crystals separated the outer layer from the hard ice. Depth hoar. This was bad news.

Pockets the size of basketball courts could pull out and launch down the ice, right through us. I took charge of detouring to the edges and over rock tongues, which delayed us considerably and prevented any hope of summiting that day.

It became windy, and a light snow whirled through the air. The change in weather conditions brought with it a sense of urgency. We were still a long way from the ridge—just how far was hard to tell. The slope of the terrain was growing steeper, and the foreshortening effect more deceptive. We were on the lee side of the ridge, with cornices above us. This meant that if the precipitation became heavy, we would be in a bad place for avalanches.

We came up with a plan. We tied both of the climbing ropes together, which made for a 320-foot rope with a knot in the middle. Jamie and JP tied into one end, about 15 feet apart, and I went on the lead end. I gave a few items from my pack to the other guys to lighten me up, and I took off.

Crusted snow over the ice made for easier footing for a while. I front-pointed and double-tooled as fast as I could, running out the ropes several times. I couldn't place ice screws for protection because of the knot halfway between me and JP; so I used them at the belay stations. Jamie and JP climbed simultaneously. I exited onto the ridge with burning calves. The wind was harsher on the ridge, and the snow was packed hard.

We were tired, dehydrated and needed a rest after sprinting to the ridge. I set my pack down behind a gendarme of rock encrusted with snow and ice, getting out of the wind. We were in the clouds. That night, it would get dark.

"I think we better plan on bivouacking here," I suggested. "Finding our way down in this visibility and worsening weather is not a good thing to do, especially being tired."

"I think we better start looking for a place to dig a snow cave," Jamie said.

"I hope we can dig one in this hard snow. Why don't you guys see what you can come up with and I'll get the stove going? Hopefully, we won't have to spend the night in the open." I could feel the exasperated looks beaming at me from behind their glacier glasses.

"That would suck," Jamie replied.

We each carried a short, insulated pad. If we did not get a snow cave dug, the wisdom of climbing an Alaskan peak without sleeping bags to save weight was going to be unambiguously tested.

The ridge had steep flanks on both sides, but it was wide enough in the notch for us not to be anchored if we were careful. I pumped the MSR stove and started melting blocks of snow.

"Over here," JP shouted. "I think we can dig a cave."

"Holy crap, I'm not sure we can get one big enough for three guys in that drift," I complained.

"I think it's about our only choice," JP said.

"OK. Then, let's do it."

We went to work with both shovels while the stove sputtered in the wind gusts nearby. We excavated a cave big enough to sit side-by-side in, with a place for the stove at our feet. Packs were jammed into the crawlway below our feet, and a hole poked through the ceiling with an ice axe shaft to ventilate the stove fumes and exhaled air. I prayed the wind would not scour the walls away and leave us naked to the elements.

We were like three kids sitting under a dining room table with blankets covering the sides. Snug as bugs in a rug. One at a time, each of us was able to remove the shells of his double boots and rotate his socks, drying them against his chest.

The most important concern in any bivouac is staying warm. We remained comfortable without sleeping bags. Tolerating boredom is also an important issue—unless you can sleep through the whole thing. For just such an occasion, we were prepared.

We each carried a single filterless cigarette. We broke our "ciggies" in half and took a smoke break every two hours, passing a half around as if it was a joint to get a tobacco-buzz that helped us to doze off.

Yeah, yeah, I know...the nicotine, or whatever it is in cigarettes, is a vasodilator and studies show this diminishes core temperature and increases the risk of hypothermia; but our accumulated body temperature output warmed the small volume of space, and the cigarettes were a source of relaxation and entertainment. Keeping morale high trumped the minimal loss of core temperatures. Why do you think so many soldiers in every war have smoked cigarettes? We exhaled toward the ventilation hole in the ceiling, and none of us ended the expedition with a smoking habit.

We spent about eight hours in our little cave grotto. As soon as it was fully light outside, we emerged. The skies were clearing, but it remained windy. A few inches of snow had accumulated and drifted.

We had a decision to make. Should we continue for the summit, or return to our base camp?

A steep step above the notch prevented a view of the rest of the ridge. The map indicated the ridge laid back, closer to the summit. The most important thing was to keep our water supply replenished. We had enough fuel to reach the summit and descend to base camp, and just enough food to pull off the climb, and a shelter to come back to if we had to spend another night. Fuel for a second night might be tight. We were completely out of cigarettes.

What weighed most heavily on my mind were the snow conditions. A few inches were probably manageable. Wind can build dangerous soft wind slabs after it transports snow off other slopes. The south ridge fanned out into a wide slope below us. The wind could have transported snow from other slopes and built slabs feet thick.

The Mount Cleveland Five may have been fooled by such a circumstance.

"Think of it this way," I said, still optimistic about going for the main southeast face later, "we will spend less energy, need less recovery time and be more fit to go do the big route in a few days if we don't burn ourselves too hard trying to do the lesser objective. I think what we've done so far has been an excellent shakedown, and we are working very well together".

"I'm good with that," Jamie replied. I looked at JP.

"I'm with you guys."

So we went down.

Jamie, JP and I descended the south ridge, triggering several four-to six-inch slabs that ran harmlessly away from us.

Near the base of the ridge, I made a route-finding mistake. Instead of following the fall line to the East Fork of the Kahiltna Glacier, which would have entailed a few crevasses we could see from above, I talked Jamie and JP into taking a more direct route back to camp. Before we knew it, we were mired down in a maze of crevasses. I got hollow plunges with my ice axe shaft to the right and the left, but solid ones just ahead. I crawled on my hands and knees, as if probing through sheetrock to stay over a wandering hidden beam with multiple elevator shafts on either side. When

I ran out of rope I belayed JP to within 30 feet from me, and JP belayed Jamie to about 30 feet from him. We didn't dare be in the same place, in case we collapsed a weak bridge over an undetected crevasse. Progress was slower than leading pitches up steep ice. It took us hours to go about two city blocks. We emerged from the maze and back to the safe zone of our campsite without incident.

We lounged around camp for the next two days, as the weather became more stable. I felt we had performed well together through several challenging circumstances and was comfortable climbing with my two young partners on the big mountains of the Alaska Range.

The three of us absorbed the awe of being in a magnificent corner of the planet from within our 40-foot-by-40-foot, probed safe zone. We read, told stories and drank tea. I came to the conclusion that an attempt up the broader face and steep ice couloir of my proposed route, with sketchy snow conditions, was more than we ought to risk. I would have another opportunity the following year (1993), with excellent conditions, and climb the southeast face of East Kahiltna Peak with Pat Callis.

On the second day of rest, Jamie, JP and I roped up and ski-toured further up the glacier. We could see the face better further from the base and took photos from different angles for future reference. We needed an alternative plan.

"O.K., consider this..." I submitted after studying the mountain and scheming. We stood together and I pointed out what I thought would be the easiest route to the summit, taking advantage of our snow cave on the ridge. I proposed we start on a moderate slope with a few short ice cliffs and crevasses further down glacier, between the S-couloir and the crevasse maze. This lower-angled slope reached high onto the mountain and narrowed into a couloir not as steep as the S-couloir.

The upper couloir meandered through granite towers and led to the south ridge not far below our snow cave. Because the climbing would be easier and we would need less hardware, we could afford to carry sleeping bags, more fuel and food. With an early start, we could cache the provisions in the cave and continue light for the summit. We had the snow cave as a resource. If we forfeited the face, at least we could have a shot at the summit of a seldom-climbed peak.

In 2003, I visited Jean Kanzler at her home in Bozeman to show her the old climbing chock I had found eight years earlier, in the Humbug Spires.

She handled the long-lost item with less reverence than I had anticipated. We took a stroll through her extensive flower gardens and returned through the pantry to her back door. Hanging on the wall were four vintage ring-angle pitons and one long, soft iron blade with a couple of carabiners on a shoulder-length sling.

I reached up and lifted the sling off of the coat hook.

"Don't look," Jean said.

"Huh?"

"I didn't want you to look," she explained. "I didn't want you to be disappointed that the color markings were different than the markings on the nut you thought might have been Jerry's."

It was too late. I held the gear sling in one hand and examined the pitons with the other. Rodents had gnawed much of the length of the one-inch tubular webbing along the edges. The nylon felt weathered. Obviously the gear had been left unattended outside for a period of time.

"These pitons were found with the boys on Mount Cleveland," Jean said. I stood, transfixed. Thirty some years later, I held in my hand hardware that had gone down the avalanche with the Five.

"Was this all of them?" I asked. There were so few.

"Yes, I think so."

"Were there any left back in base camp?"

"Not that I know of."

The carabiners were marked in double bands of light blue tape, the sling in bands of green and dark blue. What that meant was Jim, Jerry, Clare and Ray were marking their gear with double colors, which included the old nut. The rusty pitons had been hammered in and out of cracks, probably on previous climbs, and were not marked. There was also a chain link, which was common to use as a descending ring, through which a rope could be passed and retrieved after a rappel.

If the Mount Cleveland Five only took five pitons into the mountain, then they had already made the decision not to attempt the north face on that trip. And if that were the case, Bob Frauson had been successful in discouraging a winter attempt on the north face; but Frauson did not know it. With the base camp discovered where it was, Frauson had to assume the Mount Cleveland Five went for the north face. The decision was probably made during the hour or so it took to drive between St. Mary in Glacier to the boat dock in Waterton.

It would have been simpler to place the base camp below the west face if the first winter ascent of Mount Cleveland, by any route, was the main goal. Reconnoitering the north face probably remained at least as important. A base camp under the north face would allow both. No doubt a north face attempt would have occurred the following summer. It looked to me like the Five had taken a few pins to rappel from if time and difficulty became problematic between the north and west faces.

Jean was right. The color markings on the recovered gear were different than those on the nut. In Jean's mind, either the pitons or the sling were a relic of Jerry's and had become a shrine to her. When I first saw the old pins, I immediately had a feeling they were from Mount Cleveland and quickly searched for color markings. There they were—blue, and blue and green. My assumption was these were Clare and Ray's color markings. I didn't say anything because I had always thought the blue and red tape markings of the climbing nut was probably Jerry's and I didn't want to push my suspicion further and disappoint Jean. It was probably best to go ahead and believe we each had a tangible relic of Jerry's. It didn't really matter at that point.

Jamie and JP thought my plan to regain the south ridge of East Kahiltna Peak was a clever idea, and we packed up with renewed excitement. We loafed around camp like a pride of lions waiting for the sun to traverse the sky. We would begin when the sun was not on the face—when, hopefully, the snow would be the strongest.

As the sun dropped behind Mount Foraker and the temperature dropped, we tied in, shouldered our packs and skied roped up to the base of the newly proposed route. The skis dispersed body weight as we picked our way through some crevasses. I remained skeptical that conditions had improved in a few days' time, and felt uneasy as we cached our skis and changed into crampons.

Jamie was on the point. This time I "led" from the middle. It was easier for Jamie and I to communicate about route finding through the crevasses. This put Jamie in line for a 30-foot step of exposed, steep ice leading to open crevasses above. JP and I crouched at the base.

A hundred feet of rope paid out after Jamie disappeared over the bulge. Then came a startled shout.

"What'd he say, JP?"

"I dunno—I couldn't understand him."

"Maybe he fell." JP braked the rope.

"I don't think so." After a few moments the rope continued out to its full length and JP and I heard the cadence: "Off-be-lay-ay."

Above the bulge, I could see what had happened. There was an open crevasse about ten feet wide. Jamie had crossed it on a thick bridge to the right. A short distance above the crevasse, a 30x20-foot slab of snow 18 inches deep released below his feet like a piece from a jigsaw puzzle. The slab had accelerated toward JP and I. Jamie had yelled "avalanche" to warn us to take cover but the mass of snow was gobbled up by the crevasse and none of it reached JP or me. Jamie continued to the next exposed ice and belayed JP and me to his position, where we held counsel.

"I don't think things are looking very good, you guys," I said. I was concerned on one hand and disappointed on the other. "I think we've just seen the writing on the wall."

"It scared the crap out of me when it went," Jamie admitted.

"It doesn't look like things have changed since we did the couloir, " I continued. "I'm worried about what's above. The big one might be waiting for us up there."

"It sure doesn't look very difficult," Jamie said. "We could probably move together."

"Probably."

JP was silent, leaving the discussion to Jamie and me. Locks of his long hair emerged from under his helmet and flowed over his open hood. He had the eye of the tiger. He was ready to push on—I just had to say the word.

"I'll go out and have a closer look, " I said, swapping positions on the rope with JP. "I'll take a belay, just in case things goes to hell."

I knew my younger partners were looking to me to make the decision as I kicked steps to the left below the roll of ice. Maybe Bob Frauson had been right. Maybe there needed to be a leader on Mount Cleveland: "... someone to make hard and fast decisions, should demanding situations arise." Maybe all the other adults, even those that did not know climbing, were right. Maybe there should have been an older, more experienced climber on the Mount Cleveland expedition.

On the other hand, experience can mean nothing. Experienced climbers get killed all over the world. Maybe being experienced is less important than just having patience— patience for listening to one's self, based on what you see and feel. Listening to one's self is trusting there will come another day—a day better than this one.

I traversed a rope length to a break in the roll that formed an hourglass passage in the broad slope above. My ears began to ring with tinnitus and my body grew vaguely numb. I wiggled my fingers and toes. They were plenty warm. Silence enclosed me, as if I was inside an invisible bubble.

I no longer felt the breeze of colder air sinking to lower elevations after sunset.

I looked back at Jim Kanzler's son and his buddy. We were now too far away for casual communication. Their eyes were trained on me like owls, intent on what I would do next.

I stood pondering the mountain above. The next 1,500 feet were as flat as a pool table leading to passages through the granite towers below the ridge. It would be about as difficult as walking across an inclined parking lot.

Still, I was nervous. It simply looked too easy, too inviting. I could see the scene on Mount Cleveland during the last days of the 1960s. There were the Mount Cleveland Five, traversing under a long cliff band onto the west face after gaining the northwest shoulder of the mountain from their camp, beneath the north face. They were warriors and psyched to be making what would have been the first winter ascent of Glacier Park's highest mountain. There was not much snow at the base for later December, perhaps mid-shin deep on the level, bare where the wind had scoured the snow off in places; but many feet deep where wind had deposited snow transported by wind.

High in the northern bowl of the west face above them, the snow may have looked minimal, leading to a series of low, rime-plastered cliff bands 3,000 feet above. Beyond there, the summit was waiting. They worked diagonally through breaks in the lower cliffs. They could not see much of the bowl until they were in it. Things had to be looking good...or so they thought.

"OK, Kennedy," a part of me said. "This is a gift."

"A gift?

"Indeed."

I began digging what is called a "hasty pit" through the snow with the adze of one ice axe, steadying myself with the other. I chopped down to the blue-gray ice and scooped out my excavation with my arms until I had a vertical gouge from the top of the snow to the ice, deeper than I was tall.

"Oh, my, God! Look at this!" The cross section was very simple. Three feet of sugary snow on top of the ice flowed out of the bottom of the cross section like hollow popcorn seeds spilled onto a countertop. Above this was another three-foot layer that broke apart like a cookie as I chopped through it. Bells began ringing; red flags were waving.

"These are the same circumstances as they were in," I whispered to myself.

"This is the gift."

"The gift?"

"A chance to choose again."

"A chance to choose again?"

"Sure. You see what is sloughing into your lap. You recognize that creepy feeling. You can spin the cylinder on the revolver and give it a go or you can bow out gracefully. Isn't the freedom of the hills great! The freedom to choose. Such a gift!"

I could see the Mount Cleveland Five continue upward. By then, time must have been of the essence. December 29th was one of the shortest days of the year and The Five had to keep pressing for the summit. Darkness would come quickly. Bob Frauson recalled periodic cloud caps on the mountains in Glacier in the days after their departure. The weather was unsettled—no doubt there was wind.

I drew a deep breath. I was standing in a terrain break at the bottom of a big slope. Gravity kept the whole slope creeping downward—the ice over the rock, the snowpack over the ice. The ice was more like plastic; the top layer of snow more like glass and in between was snow that packed like white sugar. Of course, it was wind-loaded. Was it packed hard? Or was it a fragile soft slab?

A snowpack is constantly coaxed downhill by gravity. Somewhere on the slope, the slab compresses and is prone to buckling. Should that happen, somewhere on the upper slope the snowpack will split apart. The whole slope above us could have been resting on those same sugary ball bearings of depth hoar I had just uncovered. There was no way to be sure the whole slope was like that. It would depend upon how thick the snow over the ice was.

Could I see a compression zone on East Kahiltna Peak? No. There was nothing to see. I just understood it would be there; probably at a roll in the terrain and there was one just above us, where the exposed ice I had traversed under rolled back into the snowpack, and it was a little less steep. I was standing at a break in that roll, at the hourglass, where it would be easiest to continue upward. As I dug my hasty pit, I was in effect cutting a slice out of the compression zone.

I glanced back at the other two. Neither had moved a muscle since I left the belay. They were waiting for me to give the thumbs-up sign and we would start making our way up the easy slope. I suppose we could have made the ridge before the sun came up. The weather looked as though it would hold.

Recovered items from the Mount Cleveland scene were strewn over 3,000 vertical feet. They were caught somewhere above the tracks "leading into a fresh avalanche," Bud Anderson had seen from the air. The Mount Cleveland Five likely marched through the fragile compression zone without knowing and it buckled suddenly, fracturing the slope simultaneously hundreds of feet above them in a jagged arch known as the crown fracture. This is what Peter Lev first saw while he, Pat Callis and Jim Kanzler searched the west face of Mount Cleveland. The wind slab would have collapsed onto the weaker depth hoar and, instead of compacting and bonding; the weight of the slab pressed the air out of it, sounding like thunder from a distance.

Whoomph! The northern bowl of the west face went in motion all at once and accelerated downward with five young warriors. Jamie was just a year old when his uncle Jerry and the others were swept away.

Bob Frauson entered my mind. All he wanted was to prevent anything like the Mount Cleveland tragedy from happening. Frauson had carried the dead and dying off of the battlefield. He had recovered the bodies of young men his age who had been sent to war to do the bidding for those who vied for a stake in the world.

A part of Bob must have died with those soldiers. Most of them were his age—the same ages of the Mount Cleveland Five. I wondered if Bob Frauson might have gone on to be a figure in American mountaineering had he not suffered the experience of war. Maybe his mission in life after the war was to see that other people did not put their lives on the line or their families at the risk of spending the rest of their own lives grieving and wondering what might have been. Bob Frauson and Hal Kanzler had been through all of that.

I would have liked nothing more than to have climbed a new route on a peak in Alaska with Jamie Kanzler and JP. We had climbed a nice line to the south ridge, but didn't make the summit.

It may well have been Jamie, JP and I would have ascended the easy slope above and reached the summit and returned and not a thing would have happened. Or, we just might have taken ten more steps and history would have repeated itself. Experience would have meant nothing.

Twenty-two years had gone by since the Mount Cleveland tragedy—long enough to grow up all over again in Columbia Falls along the Flathead River, below the mountains of Glacier and the Bob Marshal Wilderness. I smiled to myself. It was a gift and I had chosen.

I just shook my head. Not with Jim and Lindalee's son. Not for all the shattered lives, the severed relationships, the blame and bitterness, the loneliness and survivor guilt that still continued. Not for all the men who did not come home from Okinawa or Riva Ridge. Not for the lives that might have been.

That was freedom. "Not on this day. Not on this mountain. Not on my watch." That was my gift from the past. A great weight slid off of my shoulders, into no-thing-ness.

"Jamie!" I shouted, and the bubble burst. The subzero air licked against my face. I could hear the turbulence in the ventilation holes of my helmet when I turned my head just right. "Jamie! Take in the rope, I'm coming back!"

I retraced my steps in the twilight of the middle of the night, just below the Arctic Circle in May. As I reached Jamie and JP, I said, "Let's get the hell out of here!"

I did not have to convince my young partners. They got it. Jamie cutting the slab on the slope below us was hairball. We were just lucky to get a warning shot. The Mount Cleveland Five may not have gotten one.

Eighteen years later, after Jamie, JP and I had been on East Kahiltna Peak in Alaska, and 17 years since Pat Callis and I had returned from a successful first ascent of the southeast face of East Kahiltna Peak, Pat and I were cragging near Bozeman. Pat was in his early 70s and I in my mid-50s. We had been steady climbing partners for decades. I asked Pat, "What do you think Jamie and JP would have done if I had not been there?"

He stared for a moment at the first foothold in the limestone of the route we were about to climb, pondering my question. Then he smiled as he looked over at me. "You *know* what they would have done."

"That's what I thought."

I belayed Jamie and JP down simultaneously to speed up the process of retreat. As the rope paid out, I looked back at my tracks. I had followed the Mount Cleveland Five all these years, and they ended a short distance beyond...at a hole in the snow.

At 3 a.m. we reached our ski cache and started back to camp. JP stopped abruptly and exclaimed, "Wow! Look at that!"

We halted and gawked up into a shimmering curtain of green and blue streaks tinged with violet.

"It's Northern Lights—the Aurora!" Kanzler exclaimed, craning his head back.

"It looks like it's right above us!" JP added.

"If I didn't know better, I would say we were in it," I whispered. I don't think they heard me. We skied back to camp with a part of me left behind on the slope above the crevasses—nothing more than a smile.

Left to right: JP Gambetese, Jamie Kanzler and the author at
Kahiltna Base camp, May 1992. Kennedy collection.

JP Gambetese exits the crevasse. Surface hoar crystals are evident on the under surface of the collapsed bridge and side walls, May 1992. Photo by the author.

Jamie Kanzler is followed by JP Gambetese third-classing in the S Couloir, East Kahiltna Peak, May 1992. Photo by the author.

The southeast face of East Kahiltna Peak, May 1993. "Betazoid"—
the Kennedy-Callis route—follows the narrow ribbon of ice just to
the right of the lower central pillar to the summit, just left of center.
The S Couloir is out of view to the left. Photo by the author.

Epilog

R. Glenn Kennedy and **Betty Terry Kennedy** lived a quiet lifestyle in the family home until Glenn passed away on November 14, 2009, at the Montana Veteran's Home in Columbia Falls. He had a bachelor's degree from Montana State College (later named Montana State University), and taught school for several years elsewhere in Montana before retiring from the aluminum plant after 30 years of service. Betty played clarinet in a community band and brought good cheer to everyone she met including the day she passed away on September 17, 2014, in Bozeman.

Merry Kay Kennedy received a master's degree in Counseling Education from the University of Montana in 1997 and is a retired junior high school counselor in Fallon, NV. She raised three daughters and is an avid one-acre farmer.

Dan Kennedy has been a CPA since 1979 and has owned his own firm. He received an MBA from Alaska Pacific Alaska in 1995 and is involved with civic organizations. He and his wife, Janet, were married in 1985 and raised three children.

Anaconda Aluminum Company (AAC)'s plant in Columbia Falls began production in 1955 and remained one of the largest employers in northwest Montana for four decades. It was purchased by Atlantic Richfield company in 1977, then sold to local investors in 1985 and became known as CFAC. Glencore Mining Company bought the plant in 1999 as aluminum production declined in the US. The plant produced its last aluminum in 2009 and is now an EPA superfund site, and is being demolished.

Roger Newman earned his DDS degree at the University of Minnesota Dental School and has practiced in Columbia Falls since 1981. He and his wife, Peggy, were married in 1978 and continue to pursue many outdoor activities.

Eddie Woster designed and built a house in a stand of ponderosa pine on land he inherited near Columbia Falls in 2009, after retiring from a building supply company in Santa Barbara, California. He is an artisan, creating one-of-a-kind pieces from wood, metal and clay.

Jim Kanzler was Big Sky Resort's first ski patrol director, serving from 1972 to 1978 after beginning his career at Bridger Bowl outside Bozeman. He joined the Jackson Hole ski patrol 1978, becoming the lead avalanche hazard forecaster for Bridger-Teton National Forest and the Jackson Hole Ski Resort from 1986- 1999. Jim was an Exum Mountain Guide in the Tetons during the summer for 22 years. He worked at the resort with information technology until he passed away on April 18, 2011, in Wilson, Wyoming, near Jackson Hole.

Jean Kanzler lived in the Bozeman area after the Mount Cleveland tragedy. She never remarried. Her home was surrounded with carefully tended gardens. For many years she made a journey to the Flathead Valley in May to lay lilacs on Hal's and Jerry's graves. She passed away on February 11, 2014.

Bob Frauson retired from the National Park Service in 1982 to a rural home south of Columbia Falls with his wife, Ann. They were married for 50 years and raised two daughters who went on to work for the Grand Teton National Park Service. He passed away on June 20, 2008.

Pat Callis, PhD, at age 78, continues his capacity as tenured Professor of Chemistry and Biochemistry at Montana State University. He teaches advanced quantum chemistry and spearheads original research. He and his wife, Gayle, raised a son and a daughter and have grandchildren. Pat is the holder of an age-group record in the rugged 20-mile Bridger Ridge Run, and continues to climb ice and rock at a high level.

Jim Emerson lives in Helena, Montana, where he is retired as a city employee and continues his craft as a potter. Jim and his wife, Barb Belt, are wilderness and wildlife conservationists, volunteering to care for injured raptors and predators. They climb, ski, skate frozen lakes and travel the continent.

Douglas "Dougal" McCarty went on to earn a master's at the University of Montana and a PhD at Dartmouth. He is a mineralogist for Chevron in Houston, Texas, and oversees an internationally renowned clay mineral laboratory. Dougal worked with Jim Kanzler on the Big Sky Resort professional ski patrol for two years. He still climbs and he and his wife, Bridget, downhill ski.

Brian "Breo" Leo received a bachelor's degree in still photography from Montana Sate University in 1976. He has been a cable television contractor for 23 years and owner of Sigma Technologies in Kent, Washington. He was a Big Sky Resort professional ski patrolman with Jim Kanzler for three seasons. He skis and climbs infrequently, but can still take the "sharp end" of the rope.

Steve Jackson is the Curator of Art and Photography at the Museum of the Rockies and an Adjunct Professor at Montana State University in Bozeman, teaching courses in the history of photography. He remodeled a house in an older section of Bozeman and built a cabin on family land near Rogers Pass. He still skis and stays in good physical condition cycling, hiking and running.

Barry Frost served in the U.S. Army intelligence and the Montana National Guard. He worked in Bozeman outdoor retail stores before retiring from Big Sky Carvers after 22 years of service. He and his wife, Toni, raised one daughter. He hunted, fished and skied, throughout his life, but climbing was always his first passion. Barry passed away on the Fourth of July 2015.

Lindalee (Kanzler) Cleveland climbed for a few years after her divorce from Jim Kanzler. She was the first full-time female professional ski patrolman at Whitefish Mountain Resort (Big Mountain) near Whitefish, Montana in the late 1970s, where she built her own house and raised Jamie. She remarried and lives in the Flathead Valley, where she skis and is an avid fisherwoman.

Chad Chadwick earned an Associate Degree in Mechanical Engineering from Northern Montana College in 1970 where he was a competitive swimmer. He and Jim Kanzler operated Mountaincraft in Red Lodge from 1972-74. Chad has competed in dozens of triathlons, raced sailboats and is now retired from the oil refining industry. He still climbs rock and ice climbs and skis.

Craig "Dr. Z" Zaspel received his PhD from Montana State University in 1975 and teaches physics and astrophysics and does research at the University of Montana Western in Dillon. He and his wife, Karen, were married in 1979 and had two daughters. Craig still climbs rock and skis the backcountry.

Jamie Kanzler has worked in the ski industry since 1987. In 1996, he became an on- site construction manager for Doppelmayr, building aerial ski lifts in 13 states. He and his wife, Jennifer, have two children: James Dylan (born 2003) is an age- group national-caliber slope-style skier; Jacqueline (born 2008) is the only female Kanzler born in at least five generations. The whole Kanzler family skis.

JP Gambetese drove snow cats and grooming equipment with Jamie Kanzler from 1990-1996 at Brighton Ski Resort in Utah. In 1998, JP became a structural ironworker and has worked in that capacity since, spending much of his career high above the ground on steel beams. He is still an avid climber.

The Mount Cleveland Five traverse onto the west face of Mount Cleveland, December 29, 1969. From right to left: Jerry Kanzler (leading), Ray Martin, Mark Levitan, Clare Pogreba. Their fate awaits them just around the corner. Note the water stains and light leaks on the photo. The camera was buried on Mount Cleveland for seven months. Photo by Jim Anderson, courtesy of Don Anderson.

Jim Kanzler, 1977. Photo by the author.

Glossary of Terms

aid climbing: (or **direct aid**) placing weight on anchor to rest on or move upward from. Often ranked from A1-A5.

arete: a narrow rib or ridge of rock usually a part of a larger feature.

belay: (noun) a station where one climber handles the rope; (verb) to keep the other climber from falling completely off the mountain or rock using the rope.

bong: pitons for cracks from two to six inches wide. When driven, they sound like "bong" rather than "ping".

bolts: permanently fixed anchors that are hand or power-drilled into the rock.

cams or active cams: complicated anchors that fit into rock cracks that spring outward and adapt to the crack dimensions.

carabiner: oval or D-shaped metal link with a gate into which the rope or other gear can be clipped.

chalk: gymnast's chalk to dry sweat and give better grip.

chicken head: a smaller protrusion in the rock where a loop of webbing can be slung to provide an anchor or to provide a hand or foot hold.

chockstone: a rock that is stuck between the walls of a crack or chimney. Gear that does the same thing and used as an anchor. A chock or a nut.

Chouinard Alpine Hammer: a shorter hand held tool with a hammer head on one side for driving pitons; and a pick that could be used for ice on the other.

Chouinard-Frost Piolet: the first ice axe to be designed with a curve in the pick, which allowed secure purchase in most conditions on steep ice.

cirque: the end of a valley that ends in surrounding higher mountainous terrain.

class or difficulty ratings: 5.4 is easy...5.8 is difficult if wearing boots and a pack. The higher the number after the "5", the more difficult the rating.

cleaning: The removal of anchors by the second climber placed by the lead climber.

corn snow: snow crystals that have melted and refrozen enough times to be the consistency of corn.

crack climbing: using cracks in the rock to jam fingers, hands or arms and feet into to gain purchase.

crampons: steel spikes that fasten to boots used in snow and ice; some pre 1970s crampons had just ten vertical points used on easier snow climbs (snow slogging); most crampons have 12 points, including two front points to allow climbing on steep ice.

crown or fracture line: the vertical surface of snow that remains after a slab of snow fractures and releases, becoming an avalanche.

debris: the material deposited at the bottom by an avalanche or rock slide.

depth hoar: snow that deforms into sugar-like crystals that do not bond to each other.

dish: the shape of some holds.

Dulfersitz: an old method of wrapping the rope around the body to descend.

EBs: The premiere smooth-soled, high-topped climbing shoes of the 1960s and 70s that preceded the "sticky rubber" era.

edging: placing the climbing boot on angular holds.

face climbing: using holds on the rock (as opposed to cracks) to advance upward.

flash: to climb on the first try without falling or resting on anchors.

free climbing: (or free ascent or to go free) climbing without the climber placing his or her weight directly on the anchors for an assist or rest.

free soloing: climbing without the protection of a rope. A fall would be typically fatal.

Friends: the first widely used active camming devices invented by Ray Jardine.

gear protection: anchors such as pitons, chocks (nuts) or cams.

girth hitch: an adjustable knot used to tie the climber to a anchor.

Goldline rope: an archaic nylon rope type that was very stretchy; and stiff to handle.

hand drill: the holder for a drill bit (noun); to drill by hand (verb).

hanger: a metal loop that attaches to a bolt allowing the rope to be attached with a carabiner.

horn: an outcrop of rock that allows a sling to be attached for an anchor.

ice axe: a tool used in the hands, either singly or in pairs on steeper climbs. Ice axes pre 1970s had straight picks that made purchase on steep ice nearly impossible until the pick became designed with a curve.

ice screws: metal tubes 3-12 inches long with threads that can be augured into ice to serve as an anchor.

Jumar: (noun) a ratchet device that can slide one way on a rope. (verb) the act or ascending a fixed rope with Jumars or similar devices.

klettershoe: the German word for climbing shoe.

knifeblade: a piton with a blade that is very thin and short.

nut: climbing anchor: (see chock or chockstone) having various size and shape modifications.

Perlon rope: or cord; rope of various diameters for climbing.

pick: the long pointed appendage of the ice axe. Prior to the early 1970s ice axes had straight picks and were replaced by curved or drooped picks that held better in ice.

pin: short for piton.

piton: a wedge-shaped anchor driven into a crack with a hammer to which the rope can be anchored using a carabiner.

pumped: fatigued; especially in the forearms when the muscles feel tight and the grip becomes weak.

rack: the collection of equipment organized on a sling carried around the shoulders.

Raichle: a Swiss mountain boot manufacturer.

rappel: descending on a rope. A breaking devise is most often used.

reversed droop: an ice axe pick where the concaved aspect of the picks arc the faces up and forward.

runner: a length of webbing or rope attached to an anchor often used to let the climbing rope run more freely.

Salewa: a German mountaineering gear manufacturer known in the 1970s for their early designs of ice screws.

sealskins or "skins": fabric that can be attached to the bottom of skis with the "hair" oriented in one direction, allowing one to ski uphill (like a ratchet). Originally made from sealskin and hair.

self arrest: stopping one's self during a slide on snow with an ice axe or other implement.

spot: (verb) to guard a climber as they leave the ground to reduce the risk of injury.

sling: a loop of webbing or rope with a variety of uses.

smear: a way of placing the toe of a climbing shoe onto small, rounded holds.

spin drift: loose snow sifting down a slope or face; smaller than an avalanche.

Stitch Plate: an early design of rope braking device use for belaying.

sticky rubber soles: the smooth soles of climbing shoes that are soft and grippy.

SVEA stove: a small white gas stove carried by climbers or backpackers common up to the mid 1970s.

swami belt: webbing looped around the waist, and used like a harness prior to the early 1970s before commercial harnesses were common.

talus: larger rock fragments from cell phone size to car size.

temperature gradient snow: crystals or facets; snow flakes that have been deformed by differences in surrounding temperatures. (see depth hoar.)

third class climbing: climbing without the safety of a belay.

trad (or traditional) climbing: the climber places all the protective gear into cracks and another member of the party removes the gear to be used again above.

webbing: flat nylon strapping for various uses.

wind slab: a layer of snow deposited by wind onto a slope. The bonds within can be very weak and subject to avalanching with little or no provocation.

About the Author

Photo by Laurel Graf.

Terry G. Kennedy was born in 1954 in Fort Benton, Montana. He lives with his wife and life-partner, Diane, on an acre of land with a small stream running through it. His daughter, Lindsay, is an artist in Portland, Oregon. Diane has three adult sons: Keith, Adam and Carl.

Terry earned his Master of Physical Therapy degree at the University of Puget Sound in Tacoma, Washington in 1991 and is now a physical therapist in private practice in Bozeman, Montana.

He was a seasonal National Park Ranger and a professional mountain guide in the 1980s. He has climbed in the Alaska Range, the Yukon, the Canadian Rockies, the contiguous United States and Ama Dablam near Mount Everest in Nepal.

He still climbs and runs, hunts and gathers. Other writing projects are in the works.

Index

137, 148, 312–13; Humbugs 1970s, 66–71, 73, 86, 101, 215–17; Humbugs after 1970s, 299; ice climbing, 60–66, 86, 117, 138; Little Chief Mountain (east face), 220–29; mountain guide (Exum Mountain Guide) xxiii, 191, 193, 201, 232, 239, 248; Mount Cleveland (north face), 10, 14–15, 19, 81, 122, 136–137, 149–150, 153, 157, 160, 162–84; Mount St. Nicholas, 7–8; Mount Siyeh (north face): first attempt 185–92; second attempt, 193–200; third attempt, 201–204; fourth attempt, 247–69, 317; ski patrol/ avalanche forecaster, xxii–xxiii, 10, 63, 66, 99, 137, 169, 199, 296

Kanzler, Lindalee (Lindalee Cleveland) xi, xxiv–xxv, 55, 64–65, 69, 72–73, 77–80, 83, 90–91, 137, 173, 232–33, 240, 301, 318, 325

Kennedy, Betty xi, 2–4, 23, 25–31, 34, 36–37, 99, 125, 155–58, 209, 215, 241, 248, 296, 302, 323

Kennedy, Dan xi, xxi, 2, 14, 17, 21, 32–34, 36, 42, 50, 154, 160, 209, 247, 266, 296, 323

Kennedy, Lindsay xi, 38, 269–270, 283, 296, 302, 333

Kennedy, Merry Kay xi, 3, 51, 79, 242, 323

Kennedy, R. Glenn xi, xxi, 2–3, 5, 13–16, 20–23, 25, 30, 32, 34, 37, 46, 50, 63, 84–85, 99, 125, 153–58, 181, 189, 215, 220, 241, 248, 323

Kletterwerks 248

Kroger, Chuck 175

Kruger, Jim 27, 30, 275–77, 282-95

L

Leo, Brian "Breo" xix, 66–70, 82–83, 99, 117, 137–39, 150, 161, 237, 243, 246–47, 325; Dirty Sox Club, 67–69, 85; Gallatin Canyon, 216, 247; Granite Peak in winter, xix, 61, 67, 85, 137; Humbugs, 69–70, 73, 137, 247; ice climbing, 117, 138; Silver Pillar (Beartooth Mountains) 137–47; ski patrol 137

Leritz, Ed xi, 42-43, 51, 72

Lev, Peter xiv, xviii, xx, 9–12, 86–92, 104, 117, 138, 150, 152–53, 175–77, 206, 317

Levitan, Mark xi, xiv, xviii, xxiv, 5, 11, 26, 29, 86, 88, 117, 153, 178, 327

Little Chief Mountain 189, 222, 224, 229

Liver Eatin' Johnson (Jeremiah Johnson) 92, 232

Livingston, Montana 63, 132, 138, 208

Logan Pass 26–29, 31, 36, 155, 215, 220, 270, 272, 275, 283

Logan, Jim 239

Lone Mountain xiv, xxiii, 88, 104

Lowe, Alex xx, 106, 180, 299-300

Lowe, George xiv, 85, 89, 104, 195, 203

Lowe, Jeff 187, 195, 209

M

Mad Wolf (see also Mount Siyeh) 185, 199, 202, 206, 230–31, 239, 250, 259, 265, 298; Blackfeet Warrior 185; Jim Kanzler nickname 199, 239, 259

May 31st Couloir 237

Many Glacier 181, 205, 209–10, 212, 248

Martin, Ray xi, xiv, xviii, xxv, 49–50, 56, 77, 101, 153–54, 203, 258;